British Pro-Consuls in 1914–1929

This book discusses the deeds of four British rulers of Egypt who, during the years 1914–1929, were removed by the Foreign Office ostensibly on account of their inadequate responses to the challenges of Egyptian nationalism.

With the First World War and Egypt's colourful politics as background, C. W. R. Long tells the story of McMahon, Wingate, Allenby and Lloyd and their principal opponent, Sa'ad Zaghlul. The great events of the time are discussed – the rise of the Wafd Party, the uprising of 1919, the murder of Sir Lee Stack and the Allenby ultimatum. The author sheds new light on the strife of members of the Cairo British High Commission among themselves and with the Foreign Office, on the struggle between Egypt and Britain for ownership of the Sudan, on Egypt's fight for independence and on the failure of democracy to take root in the country.

British Pro-Consuls in Egypt, 1914–1929 will be essential reading for all those interested in the history and political history of Egypt.

Richard Long is a full-time writer on Arab world topics. After Lancaster Royal Grammar School and National Service he studied Arabic and Persian at St Catharine's College, Cambridge, and Turkish at McGill University, Montreal. He spent of the next 27 years as a civil servant in seven Middle East countries (six Arab, not including Egypt, and Turkey). In the 1990s he directed Islamic Studies at Newcastle University, taught at Durham University and travelled regularly to the Middle East. He is the author of *Tawfiq al Hakim, Playwright of Egypt* (1979), *Bygone Heat: Travels of an Idealist in the Middle East* (2001) and numerous contributions to Arabic and Islamic journals.

RoutledgeCurzon studies in Middle Eastern history

British Pro-Consuls in Egypt, 1914–1929

The challenge of nationalism

C. W. R. Long

RoutledgeCurzon
Taylor & Francis Group

LONDON AND NEW YORK

Transferred to digital printing 2010

First published 2005
by RoutledgeCurzon
2 Park Square, Milton Park, Abingdon, Oxon OX14 4RN

Simultaneously published in the USA and Canada by
RoutledgeCurzon
270 Madison Ave, New York, NY 10016

RoutledgeCurzon is an imprint of the Taylor & Francis Group

© 2005 C. W. R. Long

Typeset in Baskerville by Wearset Ltd, Boldon. Tyne and Wear

British Library Cataloguing in Publication Data
A catalogue record for this book is available from the British Library

Library of Congress Cataloging in Publication Data
A catalog record for this book has been requested

ISBN 978–0–415–35033–0 (hbk)
ISBN 978–0–415–59501–8 (pbk)

there should be a fairly good understanding between the Khedive and a few of the highest Egyptian officials on the one hand, and the British Consul-General and a few of the highest British officials on the other hand.

(The Earl of Cromer, *Abbas II* (London: Macmillan, 1915), p. 8)

To Jan (who loves Egypt),
Andrew, Swithin and Edward

Contents

Abbreviations

ADC	Aide de Camp
AMS	Assistant Military Secretary
APO	Assistant Political Officer
AUS	(Foreign Office) Assistant Under-Secretary
BA	Gertrude Bell Archive
BEF	British Expeditionary Force
C-in-C/C in C	Commander-in-Chief
CIGS	Chief of the Imperial General Staff
CO	Commanding Officer
CS	Civil Secretary
DMI	Director of Military Intelligence
DNB	*Dictionary of National Biography*
DSO	Distinguished Service Order
FA	Financial Adviser
FM	Field Marshal
FO	Foreign Office
GLLD	Lord Lloyd Papers
GOC	General Officer Commanding
GSO	General Staff Officer
HC	High Commissioner
HE	His Excellency
HMG/HM's Govt.	His Majesty's Government
HP	Hardinge Papers
ICS	Indian Civil Service
NOPCE	Wingate's *NOTES ON THE POLITICAL CRISIS IN EGYPT, 1918–20*
PPS	Parliamentary Private Secretary
PUS	(Foreign Office) Permanent Under-Secretary
RAFVR	Royal Air Force Volunteer Reserve
SAD	Clayton and Wingate Papers in the Sudan Archive
YLship	Your Lordship
ZW	Sa'ad Zaghlul website

Preface

This book had its genesis in the Gertrude Bell exhibition, which my wife played the major part in creating in 1995 and which, in a touring schedule that is not yet complete, has been on display in the House of Commons and in Egypt, Jordan, East Jerusalem and Syria. It drew my attention to the neglect of Sir Arnold Wilson, the Acting High Commissioner in Iraq (1918–20) with whom Bell had a bitter and unforgiving quarrel, and I at first proposed to write his life. When, however, I discovered that John Marlowe had already done a thorough job on him, I abandoned the idea in favour of a topic I had come across during my research – the unceremonious removal from their posts by the Foreign Secretaries of the day or officials acting for them of four in succession of his roughly contemporary counterparts in Egypt, who enjoyed no further diplomatic employment after their removal from Cairo. One of the four, Lord Lloyd, himself noted:

> It is a fact well worthy of remark that the last three of my predecessors in Egypt had vacated their offices as a result of serious differences of opinion with Whitehall. Sir Reginald Wingate had been superseded in his post, and so had Sir Henry Macmahon [*sic*], while in Lord Allenby's case the differences which had led to his departure had been far more grave than any differences that I had had.[1]

It seemed to me that this remarkable catalogue of repetitive victimisation and its Egyptian political backdrop should be better known.

The resultant book is about the deeds in Egypt (and the Sudan) of these four British rulers of the country during the years 1914–29. (The involvement of three of them with Palestine must await the third part of the trilogy of which this is the first). The amount of space I have devoted to Wingate is much greater than to the other three. He kept enormous amounts of personal and official memorabilia and his life is vastly better documented than those of the others – with Lloyd's coming a poor second, Allenby's third and McMahon's (although his name as such will live the longest) nowhere, since he left no worthwhile records. Although, in political terms, most of this period in Egypt's history was dominated by Sa'ad Zaghlul, it is not one of my aims to analyse his somewhat neglected career. The appendix devoted to him is therefore short, but it is supplemented by the references to him that occur *passim*.

I should like to thank Mrs W. G. Street, Wingate's granddaughter, and Professor John Charmley, Professor of Modern History at the University of East Anglia, for permission to quote respectively from the Wingate Papers held in the Durham University Palace Green Library Sudan Archive and the Lloyd Papers at Churchill College, Cambridge. I am grateful for facilities accorded me at both venues, and in addition at the British Library (Arnold Wilson papers), Cambridge University Library (Hardinge papers) and the Public Record Office at Kew. (It seems to me regrettable that Britain possesses no central archive. The peripatetic research necessitated by scattered locations bears hard on the time and pocket of an unsubsidised author.)

I am greatly indebted to my friend Professor Hisham el Kadi for computer assistance and advice over the transliteration of names I have not myself seen in Arabic. I will not make the routine statement about the task of writing Arabic in the Latin script but merely note that here the letter 'ayn is indicated by ', hamza by ', and, since transliteration styles differ from person to person, names originally in Arabic often appear in more than one form, e.g. Zaghlool, Zaghloul, Zaghlul, Zaglool. The versions I consider most desirable, as well as the variants used in quotations, are all, however, included in the Index, and it is hoped, therefore, that recognition will not present readers with difficulty. (I apologise on behalf of those I quote who have used the terms England, English and Anglo- when the correct forms were Britain, British and British-.)

My wife has to the utmost supported my work on this book (and on its predecessor and volumes in progress) and never once complained about the amount of time I have devoted to it over the last five years.

Richard Long,
Bromsberrow Heath.

Introduction

Our position in Egypt was so unusual and so ill-defined that the Foreign
Office never had any very fixed ideas on the subject ... the High Commissioners were very much in the position of navigators trying to steer an ill-
found ship through seas beset with shoals and reefs with no course set nor
charts available.[1]

(C. S. Jarvis)

In the aftermath of the 'Uraby Revolt, which began on 1 February 1881,
Britain bombarded Alexandria in July 1882 and in the following
month occupied Egypt, a cornerstone of the Ottoman Empire since 1517.
The decisive battle, on 13 September, was Tall al Kabir, between Zagazig
and Isma'iliyyah, and lasted no more than 40 minutes.[2] The first British
Agent and Consul-General, known familiarly as the Resident, was Sir
Edward Malet, who quickly made way for Sir Evelyn Baring on 11 September 1883. Baring – known as 'Overbaring' on account of his 'brusque
manner and want of more courtier-like ways'[3] – became Lord Cromer in
1892 and thereafter was generally referred to as 'The Lord'. Characteristic
of his style was his January 1893 instruction to the Ottoman Viceroy, who
held the title of Khedive: to conclude the crisis brought about by the illness
of the Prime Minister, he forced 'Abbas Hilmy to appoint Riaz Pasha as successor to Mustafa Fahmy and required him to 'adopt the advice of Her
Majesty's Government on all questions of importance in the future'.

Cromer departed in May 1907, a year when numerous political parties
were founded, and was succeeded by Sir Eldon Gorst. The new Resident –
in 'a sudden change from tutelage to almost complete independence'
through which 'Egyptian autonomy, far from gaining, rather lost ground'
– allowed Egyptian ministers and, particularly, the Khedive a much freer
political hand than they had enjoyed until then[4] but 'was destroyed at
home' by 'a country which treated him badly and got over it at once'.[5] He
was replaced in 1911 by Lord Kitchener,[6] who maintained 'a stringent
control over the proceedings of the Khedive'. In his time, '[t]he best fea-
tures of genuine but heretofore relatively voiceless Egyptian Nationalism

survived' but 'the occupation of the … Nationalist demagogue … was gone'.[7] After Kitchener came the four representatives who are the subjects of this study. (It was the heyday of the Old Diplomacy, when ambassadors were much more important and had far greater freedom of action in the short term than now that vastly improved communications have given presidents and prime ministers the whiphand over them.) They failed to relate to Egyptian aspirations or to handle Egyptian nationalism (whether fronted by the Khedive or the politicians) in a manner of which Whitehall approved.

The conditions imposed by the First World War denied Sir Henry McMahon contact with the politicians for whom nationalist activity had been the *raison d'être* before 1914. So much of his time was spent in trying to control his staff that British supremacy was eroded. Even though Sir Reginald Wingate and Sultan Husayn Kamil claimed a long-standing intimacy, the relations between them suffered. Turmoil, which had been endemic since Cromer, continued among the leading British figures and made it necessary for Wingate to devote disproportionate concentration to combating it. With the ending of the war, the politicians – now unleashed and anxious to make visible progress towards the independence they believed with some justification had been held out to them as a perhaps distant postwar prospect – were no longer debarred from attempting to resume contact with British officials. In the upshot, Wingate, Lord Allenby and Lord Lloyd (also referred to as 'The Lord' and in Cromer's class as an autocrat) were all unable to meet the challenge. They fell short through their inadequate handling (in the Whitehall view) of the claims of Egypt, which martial law and its role as a military jumping-off point for the Allies had temporarily stifled and careless wartime British pronouncements and President Wilson had encouraged.

The official titles of Agent and Consul-General gave way in 1914 to that of High Commissioner, an appellation now used of British ambassadors in Commonwealth countries. McMahon, the first to hold it, lasted 23 months in office, Wingate 25 months, Allenby six and a quarter years and Lloyd four years. McMahon and Wingate were backwoodsmen whose postings to Cairo were serious misjudgements. The erratic Allenby – a soldier who had had no diplomatic training before being catapulted into his Cairo post and came close to losing his new job within a fortnight of taking it up – was 'completely at sea in the stormy ocean of Egyptian politics'.[8] Despite the forthrightness of his opinions about his predecessors, the term in office of Lloyd, the diplomatist jack of all trades, was a fiasco even greater than theirs. The spectacle of him – an ambassador completely distrusted by his own government, which had its fingers crossed about him from the start and quickly became anxious to get rid of him – is astonishing.

The first two of the four were removed summarily, McMahon's shortcomings being made clear to him while Wingate was left in the dark. Allenby and Lloyd – both, unlike them, larger than life – departed as the culmination of years of strife with Whitehall. All were treated badly at the end, Lloyd – who had most earned the displeasure of the Establishment – worst of all. By the time of his departure, Egypt's democracy had collapsed, nationalism had been cowed and the country had returned politically to square one. All remained to do.

Part I

McMahon, January 1915–23 December 1916
Col. Sir Henry McMahon (1862–1949) GCMG, GCVO, KCIE, CSI

Colonel Sir Henry McMahon came late – after the First World War had begun – to an Egypt swamped by martial law arrangements and with top priority awarded to the needs of the army. Activity in the General Assembly, Egypt's only political institution, had ceased before his arrival, leaving only the pro-British Sultan for him to cultivate in his task of maintaining and developing Britain's relations with its new protectorate. His lack of knowledge of the Arabs and Egypt and infighting among his staff led him to neglect his contacts with Husayn Kamil and caused his premature recall by the Foreign Office.

1   Let everything slide

Surprise appointment

> Throughout the British Empire there is no place in which the occupant enjoys greater freedom of action than that of British agent and consul-general in Egypt.[1]
>
> (Gorst)

Before McMahon reached Cairo, in reaction to the Ottoman Empire entering the First World War on the side of Germany, General 'Conky' Maxwell, Commander-in-Chief of British forces in Egypt, had proclaimed martial law on 3 November 1914, outlawing nationalist activities and suppressing the nationalist papers, *Al Liwa'* and *Al Garidah*. Britain declared war on the Porte on 5 November. The following day, Maxwell announced that no assistance from Egypt would be called for in the conduct of the war. On 18 December, after much hesitation over the advisability or otherwise of annexing the country and, Cromer claimed, 'deferring to local opinion', which argued against it,[2] Britain declared Egypt a Protectorate – known for want of a more technically appropriate name as the Velvet Protectorate – which was no longer to be under even the titular suzerainty of Istanbul. 'The tie with Turkey', Cromer generalised, had 'never been of the smallest benefit to Egypt or to the Egyptians.'[3]

Among the consequences of Britain's concomitant restriction of the political rights of Egyptians 'at a time when the exercise of those rights was just reaching full expression'[4] was the vetoing by the Acting Resident, Milne Cheetham[5] (supported by Foreign Secretary Sir Edward Grey), of Sa'ad Zaghlul's appointment as a wartime minister.[6] This was on account of the anti-British stance he had adopted immediately before the war. More visibly, the nominal ruler, 'Abbas Hilmy, who 'had many aptitudes but was trickier than a Stuart king',[7] was now replaced. His uncle and successor, Husayn Kamil, 'a winning personality' with 'a heart-felt concern for the welfare of the fellahin'[8] who Cromer believed possessed 'all the qualifications necessary to fill the high office to which he has been called with advantage to the people over whom he will rule',[9] was given the title of Sultan, the same as that of Egypt's erstwhile Ottoman master. Sir Valentine

Chirol,[10] the leading journalist, said of these developments that 'we forcibly modified the status of Egypt and gave her a new ruler without vouchsafing any explanation to her people or taking into our confidence the representative bodies with which we had ourselves endowed her'.[11] One bright spot was that Britain undertook 'to consider the future status of Egypt regarding self-government'.[12]

One of the country's representative bodies put out of action was the General Assembly (Al Gam'iyyah al Umumiyyah), consultative in status and called by Cromer 'useless and cumbersome'.[13] Husayn Kamil had been its President before the war. It was originally created, as a dual legislature with the Legislative Council, by the Organic Law of May 1883, which was based on the report written by Lord Dufferin – British Ambassador in Istanbul and future Viceroy – after his Special Mission to Egypt, from November 1882 to May 1883, which sought to get reform of the country off on the right foot. The Assembly had 82 members (46 elected, with the rest appointed from the Council and the Cabinet) and the Council 30 (14 appointed, the remainder elected). Neither body functioning efficiently or independently, both were dissolved in March 1907 before being reconvened in February 1909 and – under the 1913 Organic Law promulgated by Kitchener – then replaced by a single legislature. This was the Legislative Assembly (Al Gam'iyyah al Tashri'iyyah), composed of 91 members, 66 elected and (to represent minorities) 17 nominated plus the Cabinet. Muhammad Mazlum Pasha,[14] a minister in Cromer's time, and 'Adly Yakan Pasha were appointed to be its President and Vice-President. Sa'ad Zaghlul, who stood on a platform of greater Egyptianisation, judicial and educational reform and priority for agriculture and was now strongly supported by the anti-Kitchener Khedive, was chosen as second Vice-President and Deputy Speaker. In these capacities, newly an opponent of the occupiers of his country, he 'discovered his real talent for rousing the national feelings of the Egyptians against the ministers who were co-operating with Britain'.[15] He had 'hypnotic control over the deputies'[16] and as a debater was 'more than a match for any of the ministers, none of whom could stand up to him'.[17] 'Abd al 'Aziz Bey Fahmy, whose 'interminable and closely reasoned speeches' gave him much prominence in 1913, seconded him in opposition.[18] The Assembly did not survive for long. It met from January to June 1914 before Husayn Rushdy Pasha, Prime Minister throughout the War, first, on 18 October 1914, adjourned it until the following 1 January and then, on 27 October, re-adjourned it 'until arrival of a normal situation'.[19] (The 'adroit'[20] Rushdy was described by Cromer as 'a master of petty intrigue and ... so wedded to tortuous courses that he was incapable of steadfastly pursuing for long any really loyal and straightforward course of action'.)[21]

On 18 June 1914, Kitchener had left Cairo on summer leave, only to find himself named Minister of War in the Asquith Government. He took up the position on 3 August. He still, however, 'kept his lien on his post in

Egypt'[22] and was able – by the force of his personality and thanks to remarkably casual systems – to continue to remain in charge in Cairo in a way which would be impossible now, giving his disembodied orders through Cheetham, 'a competent if colourless subordinate',[23] for a period of some six months. (For that long at least, true to form, he contrived to draw a proportion of the salary and allowances of the post.) Such an arrangement could not go on indefinitely, and Kitchener realised that the war would last too long for extended ventriloquisation to remain feasible. He therefore recommended, to general surprise,[24] that McMahon, whom he had known in India, succeed him on a caretaker basis.[25] Having had his home leave cut short, McMahon arrived in Cairo in early January 1915, too late to take part in the decision-making that had resulted in the declaration of the Protectorate and the imposition of martial law. Zaghlul was criticised for being among the party welcoming him at the station.[26]

Sir Henry McMahon (1862–1949) is known for the McMahon Line, which he drew in the Second Simla Convention of 3 July 1914 in an attempt to regularise the frontiers of British India, China and Tibet, and for his part in the fateful Husayn–McMahon Correspondence.[27] The latter – by failing to define the place of Palestine in the post-Ottoman British scheme of things – paved the way to the special status accorded it in the Sykes–Picot Agreement, to the Balfour Declaration and to the creation of Israel on Arab land.

Like his best friend Allenby, with whom he had been at Haileybury and then at a crammer, Wren's in London, which declined to take Wingate on to its books, he failed the ICS and entered Sandhurst on 10 February 1881, the fifth of 110 successful candidates. He took the sword of honour in the following year and was posted to the King's (Liverpool) Regiment in India. He spent almost no time as a soldier, transferring from the 1st Sikhs of the Punjab Frontier Force to the Punjab Commission in 1887. He joined the Indian Political Department in 1890 and remained in it for the 24 years before his assignment to Cairo; from 1905 to 1911, he was Agent to the Governor-General of Baluchistan. He was a specialist demarcator of other frontiers than those affected by the McMahon Line. He was political officer to the mission that, by agreement between Sir Mortimer Durand[28] and the Amir of Afghanistan, established the Durand Line on the Hindu Kush as the boundary between Afghanistan and India in 1893. (It is now the Afghan–Pakistan frontier.) In 1894–96, he settled the Baluch–Afghan border and in 1903–05, less successfully, the Persia–Afghan frontier in Sistan. He was a regular recipient of honours, being awarded the CIE in 1894, the CSI in 1897, the KCIE in 1906 and the GCVO in 1911, in which year he became Foreign Secretary to Lord Hardinge, the Viceroy, responsible for both the Foreign and Political Departments of the Government of India; in his new post, 'his friendly contacts with every branch of the service were of the greatest value in helping to co-ordinate policy'.[29] It was with a distinguished Indian Political Service record, and an understanding of Sino–British relations second to none, that this 'rather pedestrian

Indian Civil Servant'[30] received the incongruous posting of Agent and Consul-General in Cairo in December 1914. It has been unconvincingly claimed that his appointment 'came as no surprise to those who knew his qualifications'[31] and it should certainly have been to his advantage, if it is true, that he belonged with Lawrence, Sykes and Curzon in the 'West Arabian School'[32] which championed Sharif Husayn rather than Ibn Sa'ud for principal Arab ally against the Ottomans.

There has been considerable controversy about the terms of McMahon's appointment. Kitchener expected eventually, when the war ended, to return to reoccupy the post he had unwillingly vacated, and this was generally understood;[33] Wingate told Sir William Robertson, CIGS from 1915 until February 1918 and the leading military exponent of the belief that the war would be decided on the Western Front, 'When Lord Kitchener went to the War Office in 1914, I am under the impression that he had every intention of returning to Egypt when the War was over.'[34] McMahon himself claimed later that no one had told him but, if he took as little concentrated interest in personal administration as Wingate, he may not have appreciated the significance of facts of which he can hardly have been unaware and on account of which, for example, his emoluments suffered. In internal Foreign Office minuting, John Tilley, the Chief Clerk, indicated that:

> the reason why Sir H. McMahon is drawing only £6460 instead of £7600 is that Lord Kitchener on becoming S of S for War made it clear that this was only a temporary arrangement and that he remained *de jure* Agent & Consul General and would draw the same salary as if he were on leave.[35]

On the other hand, after his removal – indeed just as his successor was being prepared to share his fate – it was claimed in an adjournment debate in the House of Commons[36] that when McMahon was recalled, 'He was informed for the first time that the appointment which he held was a temporary one.' Cecil Harmsworth,[37] Under-Secretary of State for Foreign Affairs, responded by saying what was no doubt true, but wide of the point, that McMahon knew that, in relation to Kitchener, his appointment was temporary. This may be all he did know, having no inkling that, failing Kitchener, he would still be treated as an unestablished occupant of his position.

Unlike his predecessors who presided over what was interchangeably termed the Agency or Consulate-General, McMahon headed a High Commission and was styled Resident or High Commissioner, a title considered appropriate for the ruler of a Protectorate. He was also Egypt's Minister of Foreign Affairs and housed that Ministry in his Residency compound, deputing Cheetham to take charge of it. McMahon had been selected to stand in for Kitchener ahead, among others, of two candidates who were prominent civil servants in Egypt. The leading contender had been Ronald Graham, seconded as Adviser to the Ministry of the Interior in 1911, who at 44 was felt to be too young; he was popular and reliable and had been in Egypt since 1907, acting as Agent and Consul-General several times. (Robert Vansittart, in the Residency from 1909 to 1911, described him as 'a mild and competent man much favoured by Hardinge and marked for success ...', the embodiment of our profession' and the personification of the 'old ... school of diplomacy'.)[38] The other aspirant was James Haines,[39] the Under-Secretary of the Ministry of Agriculture, whose candidature Graham success-fully opposed because he was the nominee of Lord Edward Cecil, the Financial Adviser and leader of the opposition to successive Residents.

Many considered that McMahon was a poor choice and the majority view is that he failed in Cairo. He would have faced a difficult enough time under normal circumstances, but his arrival after hostilities had begun, together with the complications of the war as it affected Egypt, made his task an almost impossible one and limited the powers that his position presupposed him to possess. (The civil authority was crushingly outweighed by the military, a quarter of a million strong, which boasted of at least 100 officers of Brigadier-General rank and above, rising later to about 150, and staff officers a full-size battalion in strength by 1915.) There were many sub-factors in his disappointing performance. They included rumours of friction between him and the Sultan; Husayn Kamil's irritation at, he complained, being left in ignorance of Britain's develop-ing views on policy; the changed relationship of Egyptians and Britons consequent upon the imposition of the Protectorate and martial law; the open secret that McMahon was only a stopgap; jealousy among those – especially Graham – who had wanted his job and thought they could have done it better; and unclear civilian and military chains of command, as exemplified by those in which Colonel Bertie Clayton repeatedly featured.

After moving from Khartum to Cairo in autumn 1913 to succeed Sir Lee Stack,[40] by the following year Clayton had come to occupy three offices at the same time and often had little or no executive assistance in carrying out his various tasks as Sudan Agent,[41] Egyptian Army Director of Intelligence and British Army DMI. As a consequence he had regrettable differences with his principal line manager, Wingate, the Governor-General of the Sudan. Even such a stickler as Wingate himself was confused. In March 1916 he wrote to Clayton, 'I am rather puzzled as to the position which you now occupy with regard to Sir Archibald Murray.'[42]

McMahon's alleged inadequacies as an administrator also played their part in his lacklustre showing, notably his habit of not delegating anything important to Cheetham and his other diplomatic staff and an apparently cavalier approach to the work. Graham told Hardinge, 'Mac means well but the job here is altogether beyond him and the native name for him "Ma ma kaan" "Let everything slide" is certainly appropriate.'[43] Stack told

Wingate, 'the High Commr does nothing, Cheetham is in despair and Storrs rules everything'.[44]

British troops were in Egypt to maintain the peace, keep the Suez Canal open, defeat the Ottoman armies in Palestine and Syria and carry out the agreed policy towards the Arab Revolt, which began in June 1916. The Commander-in-Chief, Sir Archibald Murray, had been a major failure on the Western Front. He regarded McMahon (whose military rank was three rungs below his) as unqualified to contribute to the debate over policy towards the Revolt for which the High Commissioner was responsible, and he was able to make 'the spectacle of the High Commission running a private war sufficiently ridiculous'.[45] He broke up established working arrangements with impunity. In the early summer of 1916, he sent Clayton – responsible for the despatch of munitions, money and supplies to the Revolt – to London, with chaotic consequences. Hogarth,[46] Director of the Arab Bureau under Clayton, told Wingate:

> The departure of Clayton at a very inopportune moment, and certain difficulties between authorities here which became more strident as soon as he was gone, has [sic] caused delay . . . The C in C seems never to have realised Clayton's position in regard to you and . . . temporarily threw out of gear the whole machinery of our communication with you.[47]

McMahon's relations with Murray were delicate, since the latter's 'tortoise army'[48] considered civilian issues of little moment compared with the need to expel the Ottomans from the Levant. The establishment of the Arab Bureau[49] by Clayton in February 1916 damaged them because McMahon allowed it to appear to be a rival to Murray's own intelligence section at Isma'iliyyah. In October 1916, after the High Commissioner had changed his mind backwards and forwards for four months, McMahon – 'who continued to direct its politics'[50] – yielded place to Wingate as General Officer Commanding in the Hijaz, responsible for British military co-ordination with the Revolt. This move soured relations between Wingate and Murray. McMahon seems to have dealt with Murray to some extent through third parties. Clayton – whose 'imperturbable genius' was hard put to it to keep civilian–military contacts cordial[51] – told Wingate, for example, of an attack by McMahon on Cyril Wilson,[52] military adviser and political head of the British mission to Sharif Husayn, in September 1916. Conducted in an 'ill-considered and unmilitary way . . . very unjustifiable and most unfair', the High Commissioner appeared to be making proxy accusations against Murray, with whom he was in fundamental disagreement over policy towards the Revolt. This seems characteristic: McMahon usually communicated with Husayn through Wilson despite the fact that his line manager was Wingate.

The High Commissioner not only lacked the power to knock heads together but also seems not to have possessed the expertise to do so. A vital ingredient in this was the impossibility of him overcoming in wartime his lack of knowledge of Egypt, the Egyptians and Egyptian economic conditions, which gave his political subordinates, most of whom had had long experience in Cairo, the whiphand over him. Strife among the British was not new. There had been a long history of difficulties between his predecessors and their staff. Gorst, adopting a policy which 'amounted to the government of Egypt through the Khedive',[53] faced serious opposition from British officials who objected to him promoting Egyptian members of the administration. Kitchener, impregnably connected at home, had been able to avoid open conflict with his British staff, but they had become disaffected and restive under him and, during the interregnum, Cheetham had been unable to keep them under control.

McMahon, to whom both his own Residency staff and those Britons who worked for Egyptian ministries were answerable, seems to have failed to assert himself over them all, allowing them to treat him and his authority with some contempt; the Arab Bureau, for example, routinely corresponded over his head with the Admiralty and the War Office. The chief alternative foci of power, apart from the generals, were Cecil, Graham, Cheetham and Sir William Brunyate,[54] the Judicial Adviser, 'a man born to provoke Egyptian hatred to an extraordinary degree'.[55] Graham and Brunyate had (with Cheetham and Ronald Storrs, the Oriental Secretary) made up the quartet which framed the arrangements for the Protectorate, and their positions were firmly entrenched. Of Cecil's acolytes, McMahon seems to have given particularly full rein to Brunyate who – the kind of inflexible British official Egyptians hated, 'a "tank" of a man without social finesse'[56] – combined 'exceptional intellectual ability and practical efficiency'[57] with a sarcastic and dismissive manner to which even his friends objected. But the chief spanner in the works was Cecil, on whom McMahon came to rely to an extent which further threatened his own authority.

McMahon had initially looked for advice to Maxwell, commanding the Suez Canal and Western Fronts until he was replaced in the former theatre by Murray in January 1916. The process bringing this about, threatening shambles on the ground, was described by Col. Repington, the military journalist:

> Grey, McMahon, and K. [Kitchener] all insist on Maxwell remaining in command in Egypt, though Murray has gone out to command. An absurd line of demarcation has been drawn along the canal. R. [Robertson] strongly opposed this and wanted one commander, and the poor PM was in a quandary to decide between R and K. Finally he supported K . . . But the PM will make Murray full General, and then in case of need he can order Maxwell about.[58]

Colonel E. S. Herbert,[59] Commandant, Cairo District, and Wingate's regular correspondent, told him:

> As far as one can gather all is confusion here; 90 generals in Egypt at present & a good deal of friction among them; I suppose now that Sir A. Murray has arrived things will be cleared up again. "Conky" rather sore, I'm told, about his status.[60]

Clayton volunteered to Wingate that 'to have made a comparatively junior man, who is really only a Major General, a temporary full General over his head is rather hard I think, and somewhat unnecessary'.[61] Nonetheless, Maxwell accepted the loss of the Canal command 'in what everyone thinks a most public-spirited manner'.[62] There was widespread commiseration for this 'sympathetic and effective commanding officer' who, with Cheetham, was a strong opponent of British annexation of the country.[63] Although the object of the change was to reduce his workload, he continued to be responsible for countering the Sanusiyyah[64] in Libya and remained martial law supremo, attached to the Residency as Military Administrator. He was finally brought home, and Murray was made C-in-C, Egypt, in March 1916, to the distress of the Sultan. (Herbert told Wingate, 'The departure of Maxwell has been the one topic of conversation, HH is I hear frightfully depressed about it, and wanted to wire home. His eyes filled with tears when he was talking about it the other day.')[65] The removal of 'the one who had more experience of that part of the world, and who knew the situation better than the rest'[66] was also to the concern – in addition no doubt of McMahon – of Wingate, who cattily told Clayton that, since Maxwell's knowledge of Egypt was far greater than the High Commissioner's, his withdrawal was likely to turn out to be a blunder.[67] Herbert remarked to Wingate before Maxwell's departure became final:

> I trust Maxwell won't go in the end, it wd. be a calamity for Egypt, being the one man who knows the way it's run; it wd. be then thrown back again as it was in August 1914, on Cecil, Cheetham & Graham, who wd. of course be delighted, & do all in their power to belittle Maxwell & his work: I really don't know what Egypt wd. have done both from Civil and Military point of view without Maxwell.[68]

In substitution for Maxwell, McMahon turned for advice and support, not to Murray, whom he distrusted, but to Cecil.

Born in 1867, Lord Edward Cecil was the fourth of the five sons of the 3rd Marquess of Salisbury and much the shortest-lived. The black sheep of the family, he failed Sandhurst before joining the Grenadier Guards in April 1887, and failed the Staff College afterwards. He was ADC to Kitchener in the first phase of the reconquest of the Sudan, the 1896 Dongola Campaign, being mentioned in despatches, and became Baden-Powell's chief staff officer at Mafeking; he shone in the role and seems to have given his commander the idea of scouting. He joined the Egyptian Army in 1901. Thereafter, in the autumn of 1903 Cromer appointed him Sudan Agent and Egyptian Army Director of Intelligence in Cairo, where he attracted the nickname of Bunty, and then successively Under-Secretary of the Egyptian Ministries of War (1904) and Finance (1905). That he should be responsible for huge sums of public money caused mirth at Hatfield House; his father had regularly to pay off his debts as a luckless gambler and the family considered him hopeless at managing his own finances. Having frequently said, 'If Gorst succeeds Lord Cromer, I leave Egypt by the first boat',[69] he failed in the event to do so; he devoted one of his less mature literary passages to quoting Gorst as alleging '(though not to me) that I am ignorant of the country, that my Arabic is very bad and that I am anti-native and generally inefficient'.[70] He was 'a deposed court favourite' under him but remained 'a heavyweight, and that noble head, looking like its own marble sculpture, always impressed'.[71] Since he would faithfully do as he was instructed, Kitchener promoted him to Financial Adviser in November 1912 in succession to Sir Paul Harvey,[72] obtained a KCMG for him and regarded him as his Prime Minister.[73] In his first year in his new job he allowed a secretary to relieve him of a substantial slice of his private funds.

Cecil was well placed to be the most powerful man in Egypt. Since the extravagance of Khedive Isma'il (1863–79) had first led to foreign involvement in the country's finances, his post, which controlled the purse-strings, had become the dominant one in the governmental structure. Not having competed for the top job, although having it in his sights,[74] Cecil clearly considered it more satisfactory to remain the senior Adviser, especially while he could continue to control the High Commissioner. Although he had no vote there, 'the wittiest of Anglo-Egyptians'[75] and 'one of the wittiest men in the Empire',[76] he was the only Adviser to sit, looking like Tommy Cooper in his fez, with the Egyptian Council of Ministers.[77] (The Judicial Adviser had the right to attend cabinet meetings when judicial affairs were under discussion.) During the post-Kitchener interregnum, he threw his weight around, encouraging officials to report to him, instead of to Cheetham, and peremptorily inviting his fellow Advisers to take a cut of a third in their salaries, to be repaid without interest, 'as a gesture of patriotism'.[78] There was no let-up under McMahon, who seems to have subordinated his Residency staff to the Advisers, even getting them to draft for him: 'the British Advisers had become the *de facto* Cabinet of Egypt; and the Financial Adviser ... had become virtually Prime Minister'[79] once more.

Graham, the most bitter of the disappointed candidates for the High Commissioner's job, was knighted in 1915 and, to significant Egyptian regret, transferred to the Foreign Office in London as Assistant Under-Secretary, responsible *inter alia* for Egyptian affairs and working closely with Hardinge as he had in Tehran and St Petersburg. In his NOTES ON THE MAIN POINTS WHICH HAVE GIVEN RISE TO THE PRESENT SITUATION (October 1919), Wingate – after his removal – declared that Graham would be 'content for the moment with the new arrangements because they upset his rival's plans and he himself could wait and watch – he had many friends in E of whom his principal ones, and who kept him in close touch with Egyptian affairs, were MH (head of Chancery), BS (Int. & Fin) and BC' [Egypt, Mervyn Herbert, Burnett Stuart and Clayton]. Many candidates sought to replace Graham at the summit of a ministry which, Clayton told Wingate, 'is deplorably weak and dilatory to my mind'.[80] Cecil's power was further displayed when Col. Herbert wrote to Wingate in September 1916, correctly forecasting that Haines would get the job: 'There are 3 favourites; I place them in the order of merit; Haynes [*sic*], Morice, Clayton: 1st named is FA's candidate, the last is R. Graham's, but as "Bunty" (FA) [Cecil, Financial Adviser] pulls all strings, Haynes will walk in.' He said that, if he did:

> then Bunty will have all the Advisers, save Brunyate, dining with him nightly at 'The Turf';[81] and as Brunyate licks his boots, he has the pack complete; now he must pull H. Commr. out of the Residency and swing himself in: meanwhile H. Commr. and he are the greatest pals!!! ... Of course Cecil delegates Graham off; but sorry he is not going further than the FO as there he may 'spoke the wheel'.[82]

Graham, who was expert at blocking candidatures, had himself had the key role in ruling Cheetham out as his successor because, as befitted a diplomat who was to spend the rest of his career in Europe and Latin America, he 'does not know a word of Arabic, very little of the country and practically nothing of the people or officials and though accurate and painstaking is terribly slow'.[83] This left the way open for Haines, despite his lack of directly relevant experience and crosscultural insight. ('He was even reported to have interviewed Muslim notables with his dog sitting on his shoulder!')[84] In the event, he failed in the job.

In April 1916, Hardinge, the departing Viceroy, stopped off in Cairo on his way home to begin his second spell as Foreign Office PUS. He made no secret of his unhappiness at Cecil's dominating position.[85] Wingate – who had already deplored to Clayton the misfortune that 'a Sultan whose interests and sentiments are so entirely Anglophile ... is not being more judiciously dealt with'[86] – said that Husayn Kamil complained to Hardinge about McMahon's exclusion of him from discussion of Egypt's future.[87] If McMahon was indeed not in contact with the Sultan, as he was of course not able to be with the nationalist politicians, his political activity must indeed have been scanty. Clayton had remarked, 'There is little doubt too, from what I hear, that the Sultan has not been made the most of and is "fed up" to a certain extent. A grievous pity!'[88] (One irritation had been when his nomination of Sa'ad Zaghlul as a Cabinet replacement for Isma'il Sidqy, who had had to resign after a scandal, had been rejected the year before.)[89] Hardinge, who as Viceroy had apparently 'had little hesitation in selecting McMahon to be his foreign secretary',[90] told Wingate later, 'I never understood why McMahon was ever appointed to Cairo ... I always regarded him as rather a stupid man, of second-rate ability ... He was appointed without my being consulted at all.' With regard to Cecil, he said:

> I could see, when in Cairo, how things were moving and I even told McMahon that the system would not work and that things were going wrong ... I knew that it would not be long before he would fall into the hands of a man stronger than himself, and being of a reactionary tendency he very naturally fell into the hands of Edward Cecil.[91]

This quickly came to pass. In the September Graham told Hardinge that the High Commissioner now lay completely in Cecil's pocket.[92] On 1 October, thanking him for his good wishes on his departure, he warned Wingate:

> We all feel that Sir H. McM. [*sic*] ... however conversant he may be with frontier tribes, at the present moment ... is not up to the complicated job here and never will be and at the present moment he is far too much in the hands of Cecil, whose influence I believe to be dangerous.

McMahon had congratulated Cecil on 'the respect and confidence of the Sultan that you enjoy',[93] but Herbert had told Wingate that 'The man who loathes "Bunty" is HH.'[94] Graham continued:

> At any rate even if Cecil's theories are right, which I doubt, he is regarded by the Sultan and all the natives with so much dislike and suspicion that it shakes my whole position for it to be imagined that he is directing policy and – unfortunately – the natives have no confidence in Storrs. Cheetham ... is kept entirely out of current affairs – Sir H's avowed idea being that the Councillor should no longer take charge in his absence, but should be supplanted by the chief Egyptian official present at the time, i.e. the FA. I consider this idea pernicious and do not believe that the FO will tolerate it for a moment. I have been standing up to Cecil with some measure of success and was most anxious to be succeeded by someone who would follow the same policy of independence. But I fear this cannot be expected of Haines.[95]

Though the system was for the High Commissioner to issue instructions to Advisers after consultation with the Egyptian Prime Minister, after

McMahon's removal Wingate told Hardinge that his predecessor had **'turned over a great part of his powers to Cecil'**. Though he must have known how things had been under Cromer, to whom – of Cecil's predecessors – Corbett,[96] and before him Gorst, were 'in effect Prime Minister',[97] he added, 'McMahon's "idiosyncracies" went further than I think you are probably aware. It was not so much that he kept everything in his own hands but that he **turned over a great part of his powers to Cecil**' and 'apparently used Cecil as a kind of Prime Minister with far too wide discretionary powers'.[98]

2 Treated in a disgusting way
Surprise dismissal

> I knew that it would not be long before he would fall into the hands of a man stronger than himself.
>
> (Hardinge)

To Clayton, to whom he was unlikely to have been insincere, Wingate had initially welcomed the appointment of McMahon, 'From all accounts . . . a good and capable administrator[1] . . . I am sure', he said,

> that Sir A. McMahon's vast Indian experience – especially in dealing with Persian Gulf and Arabian questions – will be invaluable, and his appointment would seem to presage an attempt at co-ordinating British policy in regard to Moslems in India, Arabia and the Near East . . . his selection as the High Commissioner seems to me a particularly happy one.[2]

He came rapidly to abandon this conviction. More crucially, to his own eventual detriment, he became keen to avoid face-to-face contact with McMahon, actuated perhaps by resentment at being subordinate, at least in theory, to a soldier far junior to himself, a full general, and with no experience of dealing with Arabs. Although he told Clayton on 7 January 1915 that 'everything is going on quietly here',[3] in his first letter to McMahon, the day before, he said:

> May I offer you my hearty congratulations on your new appointment . . . You will of course have your hands very full for some time to come – mine also are too full to admit of my coming to Egypt for the present, but you will find Colonel Herbert fully posted in all Egyptian Army concerns, as is Lt Colonel Clayton in Intelligence and Sudan Government affairs.[4]

Three months later he doubted whether – though he would be able to 'run up now and then for a change to Erkowit or Sinkat when the weather gets hot' – he would be able to 'get out of the Sudan till the war is over . . . and it is just as well that any of those who think that this is possible should disabuse themselves of the idea'.[5] They had included Graham, as well as Clayton, soon both urging him to come to Cairo to help steady the ship, particularly in relation to troubles among the civil servants. They did so vainly, Wingate declining on the pretext of pressing business in the Sudan[6] but no doubt in reality because he did not want to have to defer to McMahon and his staff.[7] There was a dash of stubbornness, one of Wingate's prominent characteristics, in his stance.

By August he was criticising McMahon to Clayton:

> I very much regret to see that in the copy you sent me of the High Commissioner's telegram to the Foreign Office about the Senussi and peace negotiations he talks of the *Egyptian* Sudan: I hope that when you next have a chance of calling his attention to this slip you will do so – It is statements of this sort coming from those in high authority that do the harm in the Foreign Office.[8]

Soon he was inviting Clayton to share his wider disillusionment: 'I think we quite understand each other in regard to our view on the Government of Egypt and I do not think things will ever get right until important political changes take place.'[9] Lawrence correctly observed of Wingate that, 'as criticism slowly beat up against McMahon he disassociated himself from him'.[10] Kitchener died on 5 June 1916. The Arab Revolt, supported at first from a base in Wingate's own territory, at Port Sudan, began the same day. After these events, his attitude to McMahon came to verge on indirect (though often fairly directed) insubordination.

The relationship of the High Commissioner in Cairo and the Governor-General of the Sudan in Khartum was not clearly delineated. Like the Sirdar,[11] the head of the Egyptian Army, the Governor-General was appointed by the Khedive on the recommendation of the British Government.[12] (When Wingate held both posts, out of deference to his military rank he was as often as not referred to by the former title.) The Governor-General had no direct exterior dealings but it was not his constitutional duty to subordinate himself to the Resident in Cairo.[13] Much depended on the comparative strengths of character of the two men involved at any given time, as Wingate's waverings show. Cromer's relations with Kitchener had been uncomfortable and approaching breaking-point by the time the hero of Omdurman departed. For more than seven years Wingate worked in tandem with Cromer. He made his own definition of their relationship by telling the Lord, 'I hope that I never forget that my position is . . . that of Lt Gov. under you as Viceroy'[14] and, for his part, Cromer, who had an 'almost paternal affection' for him,[15] considered Wingate, unlike Kitchener, to be biddable, treated him as his deputy[16] and kept a tight grip on the Sudan. (As Lawrence Grafftey-Smith observed,

'The British Agent and Consul-General ruled Egypt and, in effect, the Sudan.')[17] On the departure of Cromer and his replacement by Gorst, Wingate modified his stance and sought to rid the Sudan of what he saw as 'excessive Cairo control'.[18] With Kitchener as Resident, on the other hand, he became more amenable to direction from Cairo. From the beginning of the First World War, and especially after the accession of Husayn Kamil, however, he made no bones about his resurrected wish that the Sudan should be entirely free of control by Egypt. McMahon remained relaxed on the subject despite promptings from Cecil. After one, McMahon noted, 'I have discussed this with Lord Edward. Agreed to let it stand over till I see the Sirdar. It should be put up to me when he comes here' – which of course he never did. Two months later, Clayton told Wingate, 'As regards the Sudan, his attitude seems to be to leave it entirely to you and not to interfere. He told me that things had been so well run there that he was perfectly content to leave it alone and to devote himself to grasping the immediate problems facing him in Egypt.'[19]

Even though McMahon showed little disposition to upset the Khartum apple cart, Wingate expected his lengthy experience of the area to be brought into discussions on regional policy. Governor-General of the Sudan for fifteen years before the appearance of his new superior in Cairo, he soon began to jib at the High Commissioner ignoring his advice, which was, admittedly, often proffered without being asked for. For long periods, his attempts to contribute to the debate on Hijaz strategy – no doubt both unwelcome and unpalatable to the struggling McMahon, responsible for policy – received no acknowledgement from Cairo. ('Suffice it to say that Sir Henry did not bother to answer Wingate once.')[20] Within three months of McMahon's arrival, Wingate began to complain about not being consulted. In response to one expression of the neglect he was feeling, Clayton wrote:

> I think you know my views as to the manner in which you have been treated and the way in which your unique experience of this country and its problems has been made no use of ... I think many mistakes might have been avoided had your advice been freely asked. You made it very clear that all your knowledge and experience was at disposal and yet it was not used![21]

In August, Wingate told Clayton:

> There can be no doubt that the Home authorities do not realise the facts and almost certainly conclude that Memoranda sent home through the High Commissioner represent my views as well as his ... Of course you know that in the peculiar circumstances this is not the case, and I do not urge that it should be so ... If ... the High Commissioner or the Foreign Office think it unnecessary to consult me, and at

the same time if the views sent from Egypt are those with which I am supposed to be in accord, then you will understand that misconceptions are possible . . . I appreciate more than I can say the way in which you have kept me going in matters under consideration on which of course in my position I should have been officially consulted.[22]

He believed that McMahon's neglect of him was comprehensive. Cromer shared his concern and, when Wingate told him in September that 'I seldom hear direct from McMahon and a considerable number of my letters to him remain unanswered',[23] said in reply, 'I have been constantly pressing the point that McMahon should be in frequent communication with you.'[24]

Wingate sent to Col. A. C. Parker, Kitchener's nephew and the Arab Bureau's first Executive Director, famous for his disconcerting stare,[25] copies ('for your eyes only') of letters he had written to Hogarth and Murray and of telegrams he had exchanged with McMahon – as 'of course I do not know exactly how far he will inform you of what has passed between us'.[26] They were on a theme of which he did not let go:

When one thinks of the old days with Lord Cromer ['my old friend and Chief'] and Lord Kitchener in the Agency chair, and how they would have dealt with such a matter, you can perhaps appreciate my feelings and what I have had to submit to practically ever since the war began. I do not so much blame Sir H. McMahon, as he could not have appreciated the relations between his predecessors and myself in matters of this sort . . . I do not wish you to let either the High Commissioner or the C. in C. know that you are aware of what has passed.[27]

July 1916 was Wingate's most rebellious month. On the 5th, he complained to Hogarth that he was in 'the present somewhat nebulous condition'[28] because McMahon had not sent him definite replies to telegrams about their respective roles in which he had demanded 'a free hand in political as well as military questions, in so far as the Sherif and local policy is concerned'.[29] On 9 July, three days after a crucial appearance by Mark Sykes before the War Cabinet, he wrote to Robertson, as he had frequently done to Kitchener after McMahon's coming,[30] to make his position clear:

the enclosed telegrams – which I send you for your *private* perusal (as they may not have been referred home) – will show you my attitude in the matter . . .[31] very opposite views are held by some authorities and I fear that is the source of trouble at the present moment.[32]

After despatching Cyril Wilson on reconnaisance to Jiddah to assess its suitability as a base for British liaison with the Sharif, he told Major H. D.

Pearson, RE, his temporary representative there, 'I sent several telegrams to the High Commissioner and followed them up by forwarding Wilson's report with a pretty stiff covering letter from myself.'[33] He complained to Robertson soon afterwards about non-political aspects of his relationship with McMahon: 'That it should be necessary for me to refer on a purely military matter through the High Commissioner in Egypt, seems on the face of it to be unsound.'[34]

Wingate became more agitated in the autumn about things in Cairo generally. In September, on the subject of the Sultan, he told Herbert:

> it is very unfortunate, to my mind, that he is obliged to admit that he knows nothing of the policy of the British Government in regard to Arab affairs – I venture to think that had he been taken into confidence from the first, a great many of our present difficulties would not have arisen – but will our Government ever learn?[35]

Stack fed his discontent by writing to him in the same month from Cairo, 'Things seem at sixes and sevens here and no love is lost between any of the heads ... a deplorable state of affairs. In some quarters, the war has accentuated the scramble for self instead of diminishing it.'[36] Also in the September, Wingate declined to attend a conference in the Residency on the Hijaz command and allied matters. This was despite a plea from Clayton, who after his move to Cairo had of course remained in regular contact with him, often behind McMahon's back.[37] In a disconnected PS to a long letter of 24 August about the Hijaz, he had said, 'I do know how distasteful it would be to you personally but you could do such an immense amount of good here.'[38] Again, on 13 October, Wingate point-blank refused to travel to Cairo to confer with McMahon.

Towards the end of the High Commissioner's short term, sensing that he was doomed, Wingate became obstructive and insolent towards him. Having just said that six holes of the Gazirah Club golf course were unplayable on account of mosquitoes, Colonel Milo Talbot – a long-retired old friend whom Wingate had made successful use of in pacifying the Sanusis[39] – pleaded with Wingate, 'Is there any chance of you coming down here? It would rejoice the Sultan's heart to see you. I don't think you would find McMahon difficult to deal with, and it might make things easier with Murray.'[40] But Wingate could not even bring himself to say 'goodbye' to his predecessor. Four days after the announcement of his own appointment to Cairo, he wrote to the Military Attaché in the Residency, Colonel J. K. Watson – formerly senior ADC to Kitchener and 'Abbas Hilmy and 'a natural diplomat who not only knew Egypt and everybody in it but ... could talk the most obstinate and digruntled Egyptian into a sweet and sunny mood in a few moments'[41] – and asked him to explain to McMahon:

how very sorry I am to have been unable to fall in with his proposal to meet at Halfa – I should have greatly liked to have got to know him but it is absolutely impossible for me to leave Khartoum at the present juncture – I am hard at work morning, noon and night and the number of telegrams pouring in from all sides, coupled with Darfur operations . . . and the state of affairs in Abyssinia, makes any idea of leaving Khartoum out of the question. Besides with my impending move to Cairo towards the end of the year . . .[42]

The Grand Qadhi of the Sudan, an Egyptian whom Wingate regarded as 'very reasonable and undoubtedly loyal to the British régime', corroborated claims about the malaise at the heart of the body politic by telling him that 'the utter lack of sympathy between the English [*sic*] administrators in Egypt (without exception) and the natives was, in his opinion, the principal cause of the present estrangement'.[43] Herbert reported to Wingate that it operated at the highest level. The Sultan, he said, 'could not understand the policy of HM's Govt., nobody kept him informed'[44] and Graham gave further detail, informing Hardinge that 'Mac will not keep in touch with him and tell him what is going on . . . The Residency also does silly things like asking him to dinner by telephone – which hurt him badly and are taken by him as a direct attempt to destroy his prestige.'[45] As Wingate travelled up the Nile to replace McMahon in Cairo, Husayn Kamil claimed that, in McMahon's time, he had for over a year had no contact with the Residency, which had been completely overshadowed by a Cecil-led 'Comorra' of British advisers (the Sultan had to explain the meaning of the term to Wingate) which high-handedly dictated to him and his ministers and saw no need for discussion or consultation[46] – and which Graham told Hardinge he considered badly needed 'shaking and routing out'.[47] Under these demeaning circumstances, the Sultan could be of no assistance to Britain.

After seeking the advice of Murray, Kitchener and Grey, McMahon rejected three or four applications from Cecil to rejoin his regiment,[48] which does not look like the action of a weakling but was perhaps dictated by fear of losing his principal aide. It seems undeniable, however, that he was unable to escape from the clutches of him and his Comorra. Cecil himself said of him, 'He is quite charming and I could never want a nicer chief. He is strong and confident with a great knowledge of administration and a very highly developed sense of humour.'[49] Of others who were, as he put it, 'privileged to work' with McMahon, Storrs was 'struck with admiration for his faculty of making up his mind on great matters, of courageously taking decisions and of no less tenaciously maintaining them . . . that he never once obtruded Indian repercussions or other irrelevancies into major Near-Eastern issues'.[50] Lawrence praised his 'experience and acumen'[51] and, referring to ideas which led to the formation of the Arab Bureau, said that 'his shrewd insight and tried, experienced mind understood our design at once and judged it good';[52] the feuding generals were not worthy to clean his boots.[53] Lloyd had no doubt that he had high ability. A 'great conversationalist', his friendliness was the subject of frequent comment. On her brief attachment to the Arab Bureau, Bell found him and his wife 'far the nicest people whom I have met ... They are both charming, so pleasant and agreeable'.[54] On a Nile journey, they were 'so friendly and such pleasant travelling companions'[55] and they gave her a standing dinner invitation. In the *Dictionary of National Biography*, Henry Holland underlines McMahon's 'unusual capacity to win the trust and affection of the leading personalities on both sides', of frontiers at least, and speaks of his 'gift of friendliness'.[56]

Disapproval of McMahon seems to have been slow to gather, and in his first year Whitehall appears to have thought well of him. He sent his Military Attaché, Col. Bigham, home with a memorandum and MS covering letter of 18/23 November to Grey, in which he made out the case (he calls it 'the sordid facts') for his salary to be raised to £8,000 tax-free. In a minute of 15 November, Tilley had said he was 'not in the least impressed by Sir H McMahon's appeal for greater dignities and for means to support the added lustre of a High Commissionership' and remarked, 'I may say also that Capt. Bigham is to ask the Office of Works to build palaces for the High Commissioner in Cairo and Ramleh & supply magnificent furniture and plate, &c.'; a comment on the minute said, 'I entirely agree with Mr. Tilley. Such demands now are both improper and absurd.'[57] Nonetheless, Grey authorised for him a £2,000 special payment for out-of-pocket expenses, plus a renewable six-month grant of £1,000.[58]

Sykes, the disastrous effects of whose unchecked amateur inclinations on Middle Eastern affairs were to culminate in the monstrous Sykes–Picot Agreement of April/May 1916, went in June 1915 on a special War Office mission to investigate the military and political situation in the Near East and India and to assess the reactions of British officials in the East to the De Bunsen Cabinet Committee report. (The report, two months earlier, made the recommendation, which was not accepted by the British government, that after the war the former Ottoman Asian territories should be divided into Anatolia, Armenia, Jazirah/Iraq, Palestine and Syria, whereas Sykes and Georges-Picot[59] sought to share the Arab sections of the expiring Empire out between Britain and France.) He called in at least twice to Cairo – Zaghlul told him that Egypt should be represented at the eventual peace conference – and saw McMahon in action. He was not impressed. Others have shared his view. McMahon, often referred to as 'hapless' and as 'Poor McMahon',[60] is charged with having been weak, unimaginative, dilatory and indolent. Though Storrs states that, except when on home leave, the High Commissioner only took one week's holiday – and that dominated by a visit by the Prince of Wales – commentators accuse him of having 'whiled away his time sailing on the Nile'[61] and of running an administration which was, 'at the best of times, fitful and indecisive'.[62] Christopher Sykes, perhaps influenced by his father's critical stance, claims that McMahon 'was of feeble personality and without any remarkable gift of imagination or mental drive' and 'very much the wrong man for the place and time'.[63] An enigmatic sidelight on these opinions is shed by McMahon's claim to have offered to knock the teenage Kipling down the first time they met.[64]

It is hard to reconcile the strictures on McMahon with his career attainments. It seems inappropriate for him to be spoken of as 'inexperienced'[65] and for Chirol to describe the ex-Foreign Secretary of India as 'new to diplomacy'. The journalist, however, perhaps came close to the truth when he averred that the administration had broken down before McMahon even arrived in Cairo, that – since it was wartime – the generals inevitably overshadowed him and that he never 'seems to have enjoyed the real confidence of the Foreign Office'.[66]

When Kitchener was drowned, the question of replacing him in Cairo, whether substantively by McMahon or by someone else, became acute. Dismissing McMahon took some time to implement and perhaps was not straightforward. Sykes contributed to the adverse picture by telling the War Committee that in Cairo there had been 'a steady effort to carry on the administration as though very little was afoot, with the result that people have gone in for junketing, entertainment, and have drifted into a tendency to let things slide'.[67] He said that McMahon 'was not up to the tasks confronting him'[68] and advocated his removal because he 'had not filled Kitchener's boots'.[69] Simultaneously, Wingate intensified his opposition, weakening support for McMahon by habitually writing over his head to London despite the High Commissioner's protests.[70]

The task of dismissing McMahon fell to Graham, who had so much wanted his job and now held the rank of Minister in the Foreign Office. Cecil was unable to parry the stroke. McMahon had only just returned from a home leave, during which he and Graham had no doubt met and nothing was said to him even though Graham had known what was in the wind for several months. (Before his transfer from Cairo, he told Hardinge, 'I thought my going was to coincide or follow Mac's, but there must have been some hitch about this . . . I must say I should have liked to see Wingate securely installed before I left.')[71] Now, in a piece of 'rare bureaucratic torture indeed',[72] McMahon learned from a 'decipher yourself' telegram from Grey that he was to be immediately superseded.[73] 'The telegram cordially thanked Sir Henry for all that he had done, but stated that His Majesty desired a man who was better acquainted with Egyptian affairs to settle matters in that country after the War.' It promised him an honour. Wingate believed that the government also gave him a grant of £5,000,[74] which, no doubt correctly, compares ill with Allenby's £50,000 and Haig's £100,000. A Reuter telegram[75] announced that the Governor-General of the Sudan had been appointed 'to the post of High Commissioner in Egypt provisionally occupied by Sir H McMahon'. Rendering McMahon a non-person, Wingate himself told King George V's secretary,

Lord Stamfordham, that he was going to Cairo 'to succeed the late Lord Kitchener'.[76]

Despite the upheaval in Cairo, a planned visit by Storrs to Sharif Husayn during what turned out to be McMahon's last week went ahead. (Herbert reported to Wingate that the Sultan was 'furious at Storrs going to Jeddah, could not make it out; he hates Storrs, who as far as I can see is for ever dropping in there casually, the excuse being that he comes with messages from H. Commissioner'.[77] Storrs said, 'I hate leaving the McMahons during their last week. HE said: "It's infernally inconvenient but the larger issue must prevail". Characteristic of Sir Henry McMahon.'[78] Commenting on the dismissal, he said, in his affected way, '*il modo ancor m'offende*',[79] a view shared by Hogarth, who maintained that McMahon 'has never had a fair chance'. Clayton told Wingate:

> It has of course been a severe blow to Sir Henry but I think he quite realises the priority of your claims to the substantive appointment now that poor Lord K. has gone. He is taking it very well indeed, though, and is very dignified in his attitude. I fear it will be a severe blow financially as . . . I fancy [he] has no private means.[80]

Wilson opined to Clayton, 'I do think from all I've heard that McMahon has been treated in a disgusting way for which I am more than sorry as he is a Sahib and was awfully kind to me at my "strafing" time at Ismailia.' In the suppressed original edition of *Seven Pillars of Wisdom*, Lawrence characterised McMahon's dismissal as the mark of 'our insincerity'.[81] Bell told her father, 'I personally regret the McMahons – she's such a dear. But he is not good enough, not decisive enough for times like these.'[82] She commented that the McMahons 'have been very badly used I think – very discourteously anyhow'.[83] On the debit side, Harry Boyle[84] considered that McMahon 'did nothing to consolidate British influence' in Egypt,[85] where Grafftey-Smith's judgement was that 'his passage had hardly raised a ripple'.[86] Christopher Sykes, postdating the occurrence some nine months, declares that McMahon was 'abruptly dismissed by an irritated government (as usually happens to men in his position)'.[87] In a letter to Wingate five months later, Graham said that McMahon was wrongly regarded by many as 'a much ill-used man if not a martyr, who was the victim of intrigues on the part of his subordinates and especially his own staff'. Such a conclusion, he protested, stemmed from 'the lack of a proper appreciation of what has happened and one-sided accounts which have been steadily propagated'.[88] At least Graham did not stand in the way of the conferral of the promised further honour upon McMahon who, although not, like his successor, even minimally ennobled, was raised to GCMG for his work in Egypt.

McMahon not unnaturally resented his summary removal and complained to Hardinge that he had been put unfairly in a position in which the Egyptians 'cannot but suspect that I have been intentionally misleading them'.[89] He voiced doubts about the choice of Wingate as his successor,[90] though he wrote politely to him in the course of handing over:

> I need hardly say that I am very sorry to leave Egypt, especially just when, after two very trying years we seem to be entering upon pleasanter times, and when the moment is arriving to put into effect the numerous projects of progress and improvement that I have been studying and working at ... I feel very sore at the way in which HMG have treated me, in never letting me know that my appointment here was only a temporary one and in giving me no warning of their intention to displace me ... I heartily welcome you as my successor and there is no one to whom I would rather hand over charge.[91]

Having done so unavoidably at arm's length, he left Egypt on 23 December.

In an adjournment debate in the House of Commons on 4 March 1919, over two years later, Major Earl Winterton[92] said that McMahon had:

> been treated with very scant consideration ... a very considerable measure of credit must be given to Sir Henry McMahon for his conduct of affairs. I make myself responsible for the statement that during these two years no official exception was taken to Sir Henry's conduct of affairs in any despatch or communication sent to him by the Foreign Office ... notification of his successor appeared in the *Gazette* before he had time to communicate with the Foreign Office by despatch in the usual way.

He went on to ask:

> If it was necessary to have a man who was acquainted with Egyptian affairs, why was not Sir Reginald Wingate appointed immediately after Lord Kitchener was recalled? ... No doubt Sir Henry's reputation suffered great damage from the very hasty and inconsiderate nature of the recall ... He ... gets no pension in respect of his services in Egypt ... many people are curious to know who is the adviser of the Foreign Office on Egyptian matters, because some very remarkable acts of policy have been done during the last three years.

Responding, but not to the last point, Harmsworth said that the telegram from Grey:

> explained that in the very difficult circumstances of Egypt ..., in his judgement it was necessary to have someone in that position who had special experience and knowledge of the country and of the people

and the complicated problems connected with them, and he pointed out that the then Sirdar's knowledge of Egypt was of such a kind as to make him peculiarly qualified to fill the position of High Commissioner.

He did not convince. Lieutenant-Colonel Sir Samuel Hoare, the future Foreign Secretary, said that the GCMG 'seems to me to be no recompense whatever for a public servant, who has given most distinguished service to the State in India and in Egypt during a most critical time'. He added, 'he should suffer in no way financially from having his Indian career cut short'. Sir H. Craik[93] observed that, if his appointment was temporary, his Indian job should have been kept open for him. Mr MacVeagh (Nationalist, South Down) asked, 'Has no use been made of his services and, if not, why not? There is something at the back of it which the House has not been told.' Major Hills, Conservative and Unionist MP for Durham City Division, and Mr. Devlin (Nationalist, Falls Division of Belfast), also supported McMahon, none speaking against him.

Part II

Wingate, December 1916– January 1919

Gen. Sir Francis Reginald Wingate, Bt. (1861–1953) GCB, GCVO, GBE, KCMG, DSO

The need to keep order among his British staff and to protect his own position prevented Wingate from taking advantage of his long-established good relations with the Sultan in order to enable British–Egyptian relations to register progress. His efforts were not aided by the Foreign Office's failure to decide what postwar British policy towards Egypt was to be. When Husayn Kamil died after less than three years in office, his thrusting successor, Sultan Fu'ad, who claimed that Wingate did not understand him, formed an alliance with the resurgent nationalists of the Ummah Party which Whitehall considered that Wingate should have thwarted. His relationship with the new Sultan seems to have been entirely devoid of positive content, allowing Fu'ad, acting as a catalyst, to give his nationalist protégés free rein and the Foreign Office the excuse to summon Wingate home.

3 All this rush of war work

Wingate of the Sudan

> I fear the HC has tough job in front of him in Egypt and unless he changes considerably his methods are not the ones likely to succeed in getting it straightened out.[1]

(Stack)

Lowly born, after leaving the Royal Military Academy, Woolwich, Wingate served with the Royal Artillery in India and Aden. He spent his remaining 34 employed years in Egypt and the Sudan, the latter being the venue for all but the first and the last two of them. His 35 almost unbroken years in the Egyptian Army brought him more rapid and further promotion than he would perhaps have enjoyed if his career had been played out in less remote and more important theatres than the Sudan.

On 6 June 1883, as an officer of the 4th Infantry Battalion at 'Abbasiyyah and a Lieutenant in British terms, though a *bimbashi* (senior major) in Egyptian, he was received in audience by the Khedive Tawfiq. He earned regular distinction. In 1884 he became ADC and AMS to the first Sirdar, Major-General Sir Evelyn Wood, VC (1882–86). With Sir Francis Grenfell,[2] who succeeded Wood and whom Wingate called 'my much respected and beloved old chief',[3] he took part in the 1884/85 expedition which failed to relieve General Gordon, first Governor-General of the Sudan. Briefly ADC to Wood in Colchester in 1886, he became the Sirdar's AMS once more, then Assistant Adjutant-General for Recruiting and – embarking on his long career in military intelligence – Egyptian Army Director of Intelligence from 1887. He relinquished his involvement in recruiting on being appointed Director of Military Intelligence at the beginning of 1889 and – equally important for his future – becoming responsible to the Adjutant-General for the civil administration of the Egypt–Sudan Frontier District. Having already recorded two mentions in despatches, in September 1889 he was awarded the DSO after the Battle of Tushky. (In it, 'Abd ar Rahman an Nujumy, the Khalid b. al Walid[4] of the Mahdiyyah,[5] led an expeditionary force well into Egypt on behalf of the Khalifah, the Mahdy's successor, and met overwhelming defeat at the hands of Grenfell.) Wingate earned another mention in despatches at the Battle of Tokar, in East Sudan, in 1891. In 1894, he was temporarily Governor of the Red Sea Littoral and Commandant at Suwakin. In the 1895 Birthday Honours he was made a Companion in the civil division of the Order of the Bath, in part in recognition for his success in freeing Slatin[6] from more than eleven years of captivity by the Khalifah. In 1896 he participated in the Dongola Campaign, in 1897 in a mission to King Menelik II of Abyssinia which aimed to divert that potentate from the idea of allying with the Khalifah or with France. (Wingate understudied Rennell Rodd,[7] Cromer's deputy, and acted as treasurer to the expedition, with a 'vast hoard of Maria Theresa dollars' in his charge.)[8] In 1898 he was at the Battle of Omdurman and involved in the Fashoda affair, the Franco–British confrontation on the Sudanese White Nile at which Marchand was worsted by Kitchener; Wingate kept Kitchener – Gordon's successor as Governor-General and Grenfell's as Sirdar – on his toes and won the day over the French by persuading him to hoist the Egyptian flag, not the British, there.[9] He was rewarded with the title of Pasha, the post of Adjutant-General of the Egyptian Army and a KCMG. On 24 November 1899, having cornered the Khalifah, as commander of a flying column he won the final battle of the Mahdiyyah at Umm Diwaykarat, just above Aba Island where the Mahdy had first announced himself.

On 22 December, at the age of 38, he succeeded Kitchener in his two posts, combining the duties of Governor-General of the British–Egyptian Sudan, the Condominium established by the Conventions of 19 January 1899, and Sirdar. According to Boyle, Rodd's successor, he was just in the nick of time:

> A more hopeless muddle than that gallant General left in the Sudan was never seen ... The truth is that Kitchener only just left, and made way, for the more open and wise policy of his successor (Sir Reginald Wingate) – just in time to avert a terrific catastrophe.[10]

From April to June 1909, Wingate led a Sudan Government team consisting of Slatin, Clayton and Armbruster,[11] to fail to meet the Mad Mullah of Somalia in Berbera.[12] In 1911 he might well have succeeded Gorst in Cairo if the priority need at the time had not been to find Kitchener a job.[13] He was promoted Lieutenant-General in 1912 and General the following year. On 4 October 1916, although still based in Khartum, he became, in addition to his other posts, General Officer Commanding in the Hijaz.

Wingate, whose staff referred to him 'familiarly (and affectionately)'[14] as Master, remained Governor-General and Sirdar for 17 years and was responsible for building Port Sudan (opened in 1909), for the annexation of Darfur province in March 1916, and for irrigating the Gazirah, the vast cotton-producing area to the south-east of the capital. Kitchener claimed that during Wingate's rule a 'great increase . . . has taken place in the indi-vidual prosperity of its inhabitants . . ., which is the result of careful admin-istration . . . it is not too much to say there is now hardly a poor man in the Sudan'.[15]

The statistics of Wingate's service in the sapping climate of Khartum, where there were no electric fans, refrigerators or wheeled vehicles,[16] are impressive. Throughout his time there, however, except from the out-break of war until his posting to Cairo, he was away for four and a half months each year. His practice was to spend six weeks in Cairo, take the cure in Karlsbad or Marienbad and remain three months in Britain. He was always received by the monarch, the Prime Minister and the Foreign Secretary and regularly stayed at Windsor and, with Slatin, Balmoral; Queen Victoria asked to be godmother to the Wingates' daughter, who was accordingly named after her. (In the other direction, British and foreign royalty came to Khartum in such numbers – ostensibly to enable Wingate to raise British influence in the Sudan but no doubt also to boost his personal glory – that Cromer had to call a halt: 'We have had quite enough royalties at Khartoum. They cause no end of trouble and expense. They interfere with the work, and their visits certainly do no good and may do harm.')[17]

Long before McMahon learned that the axe had fallen, Grey offered Wingate the job of High Commissioner to Egypt:

> In my opinion there is no one so well fitted as yourself, by your special knowledge, experience and personal qualities, to fill the post . . . the absence of trouble in the Sudan is attributed to your personal influ-ence and policy . . . the situation would be safe with someone at Khar-toum in whom you have confidence and with whom you could be in close touch, and yourself in Cairo . . . I consider it would be desirable in the public interest that you should go to Cairo.[18]

Wingate resigned as Governor-General 'with some reluctance' and accepted the offer, as he told Curzon later, 'as it was represented to me . . . that such a course would be in the interests of His Majesty's Government'.[19] In the same month as he arrived in Cairo to take up the post, the Asquith government was replaced by that led by Lloyd George. Wingate scarcely knew the new Prime Minister, although he had had a successful negotiat-ing hour with him at Balmoral in 1912[20] and the occasional round of golf at North Berwick with Balfour, the new Foreign Secretary. George Lloyd said that Wingate brought with him to his new job 'administrative ability, . . . a thorough knowledge of Egypt and her ways, and a sound judge-ment'.[21] He had good Arabic and knew everyone who mattered in Cairo. What he lacked was the experience necessary to work a complex bureau-cracy (such as hardly existed in Khartum), to make a success of handling his British colleagues in Cairo and London and to react as Whitehall wished to an Egyptian nationalism released from its wartime fetters and impatient to make the progress it believed it had been promised.

Wingate's nomination won general acclaim, much of it soon to be regretted. He and the Sultan – intimate friends for over thirty years[22] – had had a voluminous correspondence, and the 'universally respected'[23] Husayn Kamil, 'unique in Egypt in being without an enemy',[24] was reported as having said, 'the day the Sirdar occupies the Residency, I shall consider myself in Paradise'.[25] That day had arrived, and the time had come for McMahon's omissions *vis-à-vis* the Sultan to be repaired. Storrs declared that 'the Egyptians and even the English [*sic*] are almost demonstrative in their satisfaction'.[26] Clayton told Wingate, 'The appointment will be very warmly welcomed on all sides in Egypt and I hear delight expressed already on all sides ... I am so glad you are coming.' He believed that the new dispensation 'will do away with a thousand difficulties and inaugurate a very different state of affairs'.[27] Herbert, one of the first to hear the news, said, 'Now I expect we will get a little bit of discipline in the Egypt. Govt., and more important, among the young gents of the Residency.'[28] Bell, who had not met Wingate and was still very junior, told her father that she was glad about the change: 'the Sirdar with his energy and his unexampled grasp of Arab politics, is the very man for the job. He will take a strong line, I know ... I look forward to it with satisfaction.'[29]

Although it had not had far to look, the Foreign Office rejoiced at finding such a well-qualified successor to McMahon. Hardinge spoke optimistically of the prospects, telling Wingate

> with what confidence we look forward here to your régime. It was everything to us at this juncture to be able to fill the post with someone possessing your long and intimate experience of Egyptian affairs, and the esteem in which your name is held throughout the Middle East.[30]

Graham said, 'The presence of Sir R. Wingate at the Residency is a guarantee that the Sultan will be treated with that punctilious regard which is due, and which is of much importance if we are to obtain the best results from his co-operation.'[31] Sykes was enthusiastic. A keen if, in the final analysis, ineffectual name-dropper, Wingate – Cromer's 'old pupil'[32] – was gratified that 'our dear old Chief Lord Cromer' was delighted at his appointment, writing to say, 'I think you are much the best man for the place.'[33] Grenfell confided:

> I am sure you know that Cromer was most anxious that you should take his old place, and was very happy when it was finally arranged. He told me of the progress of his interviews with Gray [*sic*], and I was delighted, as indeed were all your old friends, at the success of the denuement [*sic*].[34]

Even Wilson praised the step. To Wingate, he said:

> I cannot tell you how delighted I am that HMG has appointed you High commissioner in Egypt and may I say that a better appointment for Egypt and for this Arab Movement could not have been made. My only regret is that when I have finished this job and return to the Sudan you will not be there which cannot at all be the same thing.[35]

To Clayton, Wilson commented, 'I am of course delighted at the Sirdar getting the HCship ... Master will I think do the job A1.'[36] No doubt without conscious irony, Lord Midleton wrote to say, 'I am glad that you will have at the Foreign Office a sympathetic helper, ... my son-in-law Graham.'[37]

When Wingate was transferred to Egypt, it was to a country whose conditions – because he had latterly kept away from it so much – were 'almost as unfamiliar to him as they had been to Sir Henry MacMahon [*sic*]'. This was the shrewd view of Chirol, in enlightening contrast to those of Lloyd and Hardinge, the latter quoted above.[38] Perhaps it was also Wingate's own. At any rate he was, foolishly, to tell Graham, 'you know Cairo ways far better than I do'.[39] He had been in the Sudan too long to be able to adapt himself to them.

En route from Khartum by rail and water to take up his new post, Wingate was summoned to a lengthy interview on the Sultan's yacht at Aswan on 21 December. Six days later, four after McMahon's departure, he was installed. He never looked back to the Sudan. A fortnight after his transfer, Stack, about to become Acting Governor-General there, complained to Clayton that 'the Sirdar has done nothing in the way of either commanding the Army or governing the country ... his only instructions to me are to carry on and keep him informed of anything which I consider he should be told'.[40] Three months later, he confirmed Wingate's preoccupation with pastures new, where – thanks mainly to the Sultan's trust in him – he was immediately 'able, by tact and firmness, to restore some confidence and goodwill to official relations'.[41] Stack lamented, 'Not much do I get from the Residency, it is a case of "out of sight out of mind" as far as the poor old Sudan is concerned.'[42]

George V banned alcohol at his wartime receptions and Wingate followed suit, greatly increasing the numbers he could afford to entertain. The British in Cairo are unlikely to have relished the prohibition but found the new High Commissioner's devotion to the task a welcome change after the easygoing McMahon. Demonstrating how much latitude was allowed to Britain's representatives overseas then, Wingate on the other hand forfeited a great deal of goodwill and caused resentment and insecurity among the Residency officials in Cairo (and in addition left Stack very short-handed in the Sudan) by bringing four of his staff – including his Private Secretary, Symes,[43] and Keown-Boyd,[44] his Private

Secretary-designate – with him from Khartum. Reuter announced on 10 November:

> Some members of the personal Staff of His Excellency the Governor General and Sirdar will accompany His Excellency to Cairo to maintain close and constant inter-communication between Sir Reginald Wingate in Cairo and the Acting Governor General and Acting Sirdar at Khartoum.[45]

Wingate's version was that 'I am taking two or three of my personal staff with me as I shall continue to do a good deal of Sudan work, at any rate until the end of the war'.[46] Hogarth rightly anticipated trouble among the Cairo colleagues: 'knowing what they are like', he said, 'I expect a battle royal'.[47] Clayton – who had so wanted Wingate to come – anticipated that he himself would be shut out by the High Commissioner and lose his Arab Bureau position. In the event, Storrs was made almost redundant by Symes and Keown-Boyd. On reflection, Stack thought that Wingate was thus getting rid of the Oriental Secretary. No stylist, he told Clayton:

> The appointment of Storrs as APO causes me to think especially when Master writes to me to say he has written to Lord Hardinge about the shortness of the Residency staff. Does he want to get rid of Ronald and get Symes and KB permanently on to his staff.[48]

Storrs himself, however, claimed to feel, 'though a trifle *désorienté*, no sort of surprise or grudge at the immediate diminution of my own duties and position'[49] and went off to Mesopotamia on secondment to the short-lived non-job of Political Officer representing the Egyptian Expeditionary Force. It says something for Wingate's power over his subordinates that he asked Baker Paterson, his stenographer, to rejoin him not in Khartum but in Cairo ('I am taking with me . . . Major Symes, Mr Keown Boyd, Captain Alexander [his aide-de-camp] and yourself') and to hurry back unless 'Dr Acland is against it' with 'some clothes, hats etc.' he had ordered from three shops in London.[50] (Paterson travelled home on his leave and errand journey in the P & O ship *Arabia* which was torpedoed and sunk by a German submarine off Cape Matapan on 6 November 1916. Only two (crew) of the 723 on board were lost.)[51]

Wingate's task in Egypt looked superhuman, especially as, unlike in the Sudan, he had to make do without Slatin, who until the outbreak of war had been 'his eyes and ears' in Khartum[52] and whom he consulted on almost every important question. He retained overall charge of the Sudan and – *pace* Stack – was more interventionist in its affairs than most of his predecessors as High Commissioner – and than, as Governor-General, he had latterly allowed Cairo to be. He had proposed to Grey an announcement in Khartum of his continuing close involvement with the country which concluded, 'In the circumstances demonstrations and farewell ceremonies will be unnecessary.'[53] Grey approved his suggestion. Wingate told Wilson that 'the natives of the Sudan ... as long as they feel that I am still looking after their interests from Cairo, ... will not worry, and Stack makes a very popular "wakil" [deputy]'.[54] He assured Cromer that 'The new arrangement which enables me to retain practically control over the Sudan for the period of the war has contributed largely to the general acceptance by the Sudanese people of my departure from Khartoum.'[55] To Grey he boasted that 'The new arrangement whereby I continue to generally direct Sudan affairs from Cairo has given unmixed satisfaction on all sides.'[56] He said that he and his wife 'hope often to return to the Sudan',[57] but they never went back.

Wingate had already – 'in its darkest moment, at real risk in reputation'[58] – acquired overall responsibility for British involvement in the Arab Revolt, as well as for the associated Arab Bureau. Now the execution of policy – besides Egypt – towards Aden, the Yemen, Abyssinia, Somaliland and 'other bordering foreign possessions'[59] including Libya fell to him. The Foreign Office rejected his characteristic suggestion that he be in addition C-in-C of British forces, as his successor was to be. Clayton suggested the idea, which would have done a good deal to strengthen Wingate's position *vis-à-vis* the generals in Cairo if he had been able to take advantage of it. In a letter to Wingate, Clayton said:

> What I hope is that they will make you C in C as well. It ... would do away with all chance of misunderstandings (which have not been few) between Military, Civil & Diplomatic. No one knows as well as you how to coordinate Military and Civil interests and make the two pull together for the public good ... It appears to me so obvious a course, now that they have in you the man who possesses all the necessary qualifications ... I *know* you could do it.[60]

The idea was rejected by Balfour the following month, but not before it had irritated Murray, concerned at the apparent attempt of a non-fighting general to take the administration of martial law (which Maxwell had bequeathed him) over from him. As early as 5 November 1915, Wingate had telegraphed Grey to pass on his opinion that:

> the only source of possible friction between the civil and military authorities in Egypt is in relation to the administration of Martial Law ... *in the event of friction occurring* [emphasis added], I conceive that it might be a relief to Sir A. Murray and advantageous to HMG if the exercise of the powers conferred under Martial Law was vested in me. So long as I remain a General on the active list there would be no difficulty in effecting this change of administration, if found to be desirable and in the general interest.[61]

As late as 23 November, with the sort of persistence which was soon to destroy him, he was still trying to convince the Foreign Secretary of the desirability of a change which would certainly have made his life at least hierarchically easier in Cairo:

> any organization involving duality of responsibility in connection with this [winning the war], seems to me to detract from efficiency. Although I have not been in Egypt for more than two years, I gather from various sources that all is not quite as it should be in this respect. In view of the 'Protectorate' status of Egypt, it might suit HM's Govt. to add to the HC's status that of nominal C. in C, thus placing the administration of Martial Law under his general direction and making the GOC of the Troops subordinate to the High Commissioner, merely in a general and non technical sense ... in order to avoid the duality which I believe has been only too apparent since the war began.

He concluded by saying, typically, 'I beg YLship will not hesitate to at once put the suggestion aside, if you consider it undesirable in any way.'[62]

Wingate thought that he had been appointed to Cairo as a consequence of the Sultan's complaints to Hardinge about McMahon,[63] whom he was at pains to discredit. Writing about Husayn Kamil to Graham in his first month as High Commissioner, he said:

> I cannot but think that had my predecessor taken more trouble about him, the situation might have been very different – I think he felt himself ?fussed and he could not stand being dealt with by some of the subordinate staff of the Residency.[64]

Ten days later he warned Hardinge, 'I propose to write to you at greater length on the extent to which my predecessor seems to have lost grasp of the machinery of government.'[65]

He had not expected to be impressed by the state of things in Egypt. 'Just imagine', he had told Clayton, 'if I worked the Sudan on the watertight compartment system of Egypt – our administration would collapse in a week.'[66] Now, having recently passed up so many opportunities to witness the actual situation on the ground, he told Stack:

> I often wish that you were here so that I could express to you my feelings and thoughts in regard to the chaotic condition of things in this country, and the more I compare it with the Sudan, the more do I feel that we are to be congratulated on having evolved a sound system there of which I do not see in any way the counterpart in Egypt – nor do I see how we are to reach it under present political conditions.[67]

To Sir William Garstin,[68] he spoke of 'my perplexities in regard to the government of this country and the many changes which are necessary to make it efficient'.[69] Raising the subject of the long-term administration of Egypt, he stressed to Graham his conviction that 'the whole question requires very careful consideration' but complained that 'concentration on these all important questions is by no means easy'.[70]

The war had, in a felicitous sentence, 'made the glittering vice-regency of Cromer a bureaucratic nightmare, a proconsular graveyard'.[71] The civil administration remained in the doldrums, line management had not been sorted out and – as a result of the unceremonious dropping of McMahon – the strife among British officials was certain not to abate. Above all, there was the Sultan. Now that he had the chance to mollify Husayn Kamil, take advantage of his support to keep Egypt in line and enlist his endorsement for British policies, Wingate found his scope for action severely restricted. To Graham he bemoaned 'all this rush of war work'[72] as, like McMahon, he had to bow to the demands of the Army, which had failed under Murray to dislodge the Ottomans from Palestine but was now preparing a further attack under Allenby. Although the Foreign Office was worried about Egypt's resentment at the forced labour corvée, which at its height impressed some 117,000 of the country's sons, it too had to yield to the Army's needs. Even when the war ended and Wingate asked for the release of the Egyptian workers, Allenby considered that he had several months of essential further tasks for them and Wingate had to back down. Lloyd deemed Wingate's position 'indeed unenviable', with his administration 'half suppressed by the existence of martial law, wholly overshadowed by the swollen HQ and Base organisations of a large Expeditionary Force, and . . . incapable by reason of the drain of war duties of undertaking all its responsibilities'.[73] Wingate's own authority was to be inexorably downgraded by the military who, as the war dragged on, took things more and more into their own hands. He was to be frequently attacked by the Army for what it saw as the inadequacy of the Egyptian contribution to the war effort which it had been excused from making. This must have been particularly galling to a general, overshadowed as a soldier first by Murray and then by Allenby and playing an armchair role. His inability to do much to make up for the inadequacies of McMahon's dealings with the Sultan must have been a severe disappointment to both of them.

In personal terms, Wingate was on a hiding to nothing. Beside the soldiers who expected to rule the roost, the overmighty Col. the Lord Edward Cecil was still *in situ* and intending to remain the real ruler of Egypt. The change of administration in London had greatly strengthened his position. To crown his other advantages, he was the nephew of the new Foreign Secretary and a younger brother of Lord Robert Cecil, Balfour's Parliamentary Under-Secretary, as he had been Grey's. Even had he not acquired a reputation as a ruthless eliminator of competitors[74] – unprepared to tolerate rivals – Wingate could not but have confronted him, risking an unavoidable clash with leading politicians at home while prevented by *force majeure* from devoting his energies to developing Britain's political relations with its Protectorate and enlisting the Sultan's willing assistance in the process. Cecil's family connections were major contributors to Wingate's downfall, not in themselves but in the clumsy way he – who had been able to manage both Cromer and Kitchener – handled them. His preoccupation with them was to allow the accusation to be made that he had failed to monitor the development of the nationalist approach which heralded his downfall.

4   Fullest confidence in you
The Comorra

All through history the Cecils, when any friend or colleague has been in real trouble, have stabbed him in the back – attributing the crime to qualms of conscience.[1]

(Harold Macmillan)

Wingate had been hearing about rivalries among the British in the administration in Cairo for years, not least from Graham, who from closer at hand had long been familiar with the Cecil problem. Late in the day, he remarked to Wingate, 'Between ourselves, I fear that you may have more trouble with the British side of the Administration than you are likely to have with the Native.'[2] Wingate, for whom dealing with his co-nationals had not been a strength in the Sudan, wanted any dissension to be brought to an end immediately and accordingly did not hesitate to plunge his hand into the Cairo hornets' nest. In the description of it he wrote after his departure, entitled NOTES ON THE MAIN POINTS . . ., he said:

During the McM. period, it was only natural that McM. should delegate his powers largely to EC (with whom was closely associated WB) – gradually all real power disappeared from the Residency – MC became much disgruntled – and the Committee of 4. (i.e. EC, WB, RG, and MC) resolved into their component parts – EC & WB worked together, and both were opposed to RG and had little opinion of MC but remained friendly with him. MC disliked EC but liked WB. RG disliked all three and they reciprocated his feelings – they knew he aspired to HC (EG had promised RG he should succeed him if he did not return) and this interfered with their own plans . . . The sudden appearance from the rival Sudan of RW as HC upset all plans . . . [The abbreviations respectively represent McMahon, Cecil, Brunyate, Cheetham, Graham, High Commissioner, Gorst and Wingate].[3]

Wingate and Cecil had known each other for a long time. They were together on the Dongola Campaign. On the 1897 mission to Abyssinia,

Cecil – sent out from the War Office – commanded a 'small protective force'.[4] The following year they were colleagues at Fashoda.[5] Cecil then joined Wingate in the Egyptian Army from 1901 to 1903. In 1903 he became Sudan Agent and Director of Intelligence in Cairo and in 1905 Under-Secretary of State in the Egyptian Ministry of Finance. In 1901, the Egyptian Council of Ministers had delegated control of the Sudan's finances to the Financial Adviser and so, when Cecil attained that post in 1912, he had oversight of Wingate's, both official and private.

There is disagreement about the Wingate–Cecil relationship. On Cecil's secondment to the Egyptian Army, the former, it is claimed, was glad to be reunited with someone with whom he described his connexion as one of 'friendship'; when Wingate was posted to Cairo, their friendship is stated to have already lasted for 20 years.[6] Sir Ronald Wingate maintains that Cecil and his father 'were old friends, of the Sudan campaigns, Abyssinia, Fashoda and the Sudan Agency, and no personal difference ever clouded their relationship'.[7] On the other hand, the assertion[8] that, by the time Wingate became High Commissioner, Cecil 'had long since fallen out' with him seems far closer to the truth of the matter and is supported by a letter from Stack to Clayton.[9] Accordingly, Cecil, showing a different face from the one about which Bell had gushed in letters[10] to her mother from the Nile, clearly showed, in Wingate's first year in Cairo, that he despised him:

> If I had to do with an abler man, or as I was very nearly saying, a less foolish one, I have no doubt I could find a *modus vivendi*. But he has always, as a matter of policy, got rid of any strong man who was near him. This was shown in the Sudan again and again.[11] Further, his vanity . . . has to be known to be believed. He will stop at practically nothing to get rid of anyone whom [*sic*] he fears may be a competitor . . . as you know, my ambition has always been to be at the head of Egyptian affairs, as I should have been if Lord Kitchener had lived.[12]

Later he said, 'He is really pitiable. He is afraid of his own shadow . . . what can you do with a weak frightened man of inferior intellect?'[13]

Wingate consulted Graham about Cecil even before arriving in Cairo. The new High Commissioner can hardly have settled into his seat when Graham – without paragraphs, in a dreadful hand and perhaps encouraging Wingate to set about Cecil's dismissal[14] – wrote to say that he had received almost identical letters of complaint from the Sultan and from Rushdy Pasha:

> All the natives dislike and fear Cecil and think that Brunyate, Hayter,[15] Haynes [*sic*] &c are strictly controlled by him . . . The position of FA is altogether too strong and your predecessor was completely in Cecil's hands. The Sultan and natives hope that you will do something to curtail his power and to put things on a proper footing.[16]

A fortnight later, Wingate confirmed that, for Husayn Kamil, 'of course the head of the "Comorra" was his main source of irritation'. He quickly also became his own, as Wingate found himself under criticism for having 'let the Englishman [*sic*] in this country down' by not immediately taking strong action following complaints by British advisory staff that the normally pro-British Sultan had received them discourteously at Asyut on 4 January. (Haines thought that this atypical behaviour was possibly attributable to the Sultan's resentment at Sharif Husayn becoming *King* of the Hijaz.) Wingate blamed Cecil for the criticism. 'I daresay', he insinuated to Graham, 'you would have no great difficulty in tracing the source of these rumours.'[17]

Prepared to act largely on the basis of hearsay, Wingate needed no prompting to do something about Cecil. His chance came when, in a letter of 16 January, within days of him taking up his post, the Financial Adviser asked him – as he had in vain asked McMahon – to uphold his standing application to rejoin his regiment for the duration of the war.[18] It was a strange request for the uncrowned King of Egypt to make, unless he could not get away fast enough in order to do Wingate down at home. It is odd, too, that instead of merely recommending that Cecil's application be accepted, Wingate should go to great lengths, and masochistically offer hostages to fortune, in making out a case where none appears to have been needed. In communications to Hardinge on 31 January, he supported Cecil's application. The first was a telegram seeking Foreign Office concurrence in his agreement to Cecil's request. Then, in a Personal and Secret letter, Wingate said, 'I have come to the conclusion that Edward Cecil's temporary withdrawal from Egypt would be an advantage.' Vertiginously developing an argument he had seen no need to take time to consider, he continued:

> I see more and more that he has been allowed during the last two years to exercise much of the influence which previously belonged to HM's Representative. I find that the Residency has lost prestige ... he has occupied a position which appears incompatible with the use of proper authority on my part in the way of administrative decisions, appointments and so forth. You will probably agree with me that the resulting situation cannot possibly continue and I think it would be best for Cecil to be absent for a time. I should be glad therefore to have your consent to his own proposition to go away which he has strongly urged on me.[19]

Noting that 'McMahon apparently used Cecil as a kind of "Prime Minister" with far too wide discretionary powers', in a follow-up letter to Hardinge the same day, he wrote:

> I am simply astonished at the extent to which Cecil has not only established a sort of ascendancy over the other advisers but used his

position at the head of the finances to make the rank and file of officials, British and Egyptians, look to him for promotion and rewards.
The natural consequence of this is an exaggeration of his personality
and actual power which in my belief is not entirely for the good of
Egypt. I am convinced that the strings must be drawn together again
into the hands of the High Commissioner if I am to be able to carry
out the policy you may indicate.

Most important of all, 'his relations with the Sultan and Ministers notably
are not in my opinion satisfactory and I think I ought not to be hampered
by this fact in dealing with the Egyptian Ministers in circumstances, sure to
occur sooner or later, where our views are not quite in accordance with
their ideals'.[20]

In a telegram on 6 February, Hardinge reported that Balfour had
agreed. Graham, not in step but in this matter an ally, told Wingate in a
private letter the next day that his telegrams about Cecil had 'created a
considerable flutter in high quarters – in fact Mr. B. [Balfour] and Robert
C. [Cecil] who is very powerful with him – have been sitting with their
heads together ever since and Hardinge is unable to extract an answer
from them'.[21] On 14 February, Hardinge – in an act which seems unkind –
said that he had shown Wingate's 31 January letter to Balfour 'and on the
whole I think it will have a very good effect'.[22] Stack commented to
Clayton:

The news about Cecil going did not actually surprise me but this short
time in which the decision has occurred since his [Wingate's] occu-
pancy of the HC's chair has. From the standpoint Master has always
taken up towards the finance in Egypt in general and to the individual
in particular a climax was bound to have arisen sooner or later unless
he had modified his opinions on reaching Cairo and seeing the situation for himself . . . Symes mentions the matter in a few discreet lines,
putting it on the score of leave and adds 'His absence from Egypt for a
few months may simplify the question of increasing control from
here. His departure (I think) may jolt the administrative machine at
first.' To me who knows as much about the relations of the 2 men and
considerably more of the Egypt machine than he does this is puerile
diplomacy . . . It looks as if, like the Sudan, the elimination of his outstanding personages around him was [*sic*] beginning.[23]

Cecil indeed departed. While he was at home and the likelihood of him
coming back or otherwise remained uncertain, Wingate made the case for
him not to return at all – a dangerous game, given the positions of power
occupied by Cecil's relatives. On 24 March he told Hardinge, 'the effect,
on the Sultan's still disturbed mind of the late régime and of the part
played in it by E. Cecil, makes me doubt if his return to this country is

really in its best interests'. Heroically, and as though conscious of the fact that he was chancing his arm, he continued:

> as I have had the pleasure of knowing Mr. Balfour for many years and of admiring his great breadth of view – I am ... sure he will never allow personal considerations to influence his judgement – if, therefore it is thought best, in all-round interests, that E. Cecil should eventually return to his post here, then I should have to stipulate that he would loyally identify himself with the policy of HM's Govt. as indicated through the High Commissioner.[24]

In the same letter, penned within three months of becoming Resident, and revealing that he was unsighted about his government's policy towards his country of posting, Wingate offered his resignation to Hardinge on the ostensible grounds that the British government which had appointed him was no longer in office. He was extremely prone to make this sort of fatalistic gesture. In 1915, a Works Battalion of the Egyptian Army, of which he was of course then head, mutinied after assurances that it would not be away from home for more than three months, or go on active service to Gallipoli, had proved empty. When it lost nine killed and seven wounded as a result of a British commanding officer handing out summary punishment, Wingate remarked to Clayton, 'It will be for the British authorities, should my position as Sirdar become difficult, to decide whether it is best in all round interests to let me go to the wall.'[25] Now he said:

> unless HM's Govt. is prepared to fully trust me in the matter of carrying out whatever policy it may eventually decide to adopt in regard to Egypt, it would be better that I should make room for someone else. As I think you know, I accepted my new position because, I thought, that HM's Govt. wanted me to take up the post in the public interest; but should the change of Govt. have brought about a change of view in this respect, I am quite prepared to return to the Sudan.

He added, repeating a point made before:

> but in that case, I should stipulate that as Governor General I should have direct access to HM's Govt. and should be in no way under the High Commr. of Egypt ... I therefore place myself unreservedly in the hands of HM's Govt. to do what they consider best ... I am quite prepared to accept any decision they may make as it will be based on what is best in the public interest.[26]

In his reply on 19 April, Hardinge said, 'I have spoken to Mr. Balfour on the subject and he has authorised me to give you assurances of his fullest confidence in you. I may add that there was never any doubt on this point.'[27] (Wingate made a second application to resign, this time on health grounds, in the summer of the same year. Concluding the question in a letter of 7 September, Hardinge indicated that the doctors had said that there was no reason for him to resign. 'Mr Balfour ... is delighted that you will be able to continue to hold your post in Egypt. It is the firm wish of all those who have the best interests of Egypt at heart.')[28]

On 16 May, Wingate reverted to the subject of Cecil, telling Hardinge that he was 'inclined to advise that E. Cecil's leave be indefinitely prolonged'.[29] Now, however, Balfour ended the phase by writing to Wingate on 18 July, to inform him that he had decided his nephew should return to Cairo. Beginning by saying that 'Reports have reached me from various sources, which I cannot ignore, that certain difficulties have arisen between you and Edward Cecil', he continued: 'It is not right, nor in the public interest, that the Financial Adviser should be too long absent from his post, and I am therefore writing to Edward Cecil to ask him to return to Egypt not later than the end of September.' He concluded:

> I feel sure that there can be no question of personal friction between you, and, if there is a real divergence in official matters as to the scope of the Financial Adviser's authority, I would suggest that the question should be officially referred home for my decision.[30]

By agreeing to Cecil's request for leave, therefore, while neither taking full advantage of his absence in order to wrest control of the administrative machine back from him nor succeeding in preventing him resuming his post, Wingate had merely given the Financial Adviser the opportunity – one he was in the event unable to seize – to buttress his position.

In a *Private* letter about Cecil to Wingate which perhaps said more about its author than its subject, Graham described a leave visit from him:

> He called on me here in a smart new uniform – though his turn out was a little impaired by his wearing a very old belt which he must have had as a slim young guardsman – it met with great difficulty at the last hole, so much so that the end of the strap could not be tucked in![31]

During his leave, Cecil wrote several times to Wingate, making it mostly seem that all was well between them. It is a mystery why he bothered to write so often and at such length. One of his letters, on 16 May,[32] was ten manuscript sides long. Polite in tone, it did not sound like the work of someone who was seriously trying to change the course of his career:

> I am told I am to have a very interesting job in France ... Chalmers told me that there were persistent rumours of my resignation ... I hear the

Sultan writes long letters to Graham ... which I hope you see before they go out as such correspondence might be undesirable ... PS I hear my job has to do with Press and Intelligence but nothing certain.

Another, the same day but typed and 'official', was businesslike and, at times, threatening. With doubtful justification, it warned Wingate – of whose financial acumen Cecil had no great opinion – to keep his nose out of Egypt's finances. Ronald Lindsay, who was acting for him, had told him, he said, that Wingate was:

> suggesting a new method of dealing with the Budget. As I understand him you are in favour of appointing a committee to apportion the amount to be allowed for expenditure to each Department and doing away with our veto in such matters. I think ... that you would agree that this is a very radical change and one to which certain grave objections exist ... No one, I venture to think, who has not actually worked in the Department has any idea how difficult it is to keep our finance on a sound basis.

This, he continued, was not the time for such a change: 'the expert financial opinion in Egypt' was not in favour of it and nothing should be done without the approval of the British government, to which 'the finance ... are themselves responsible through the financial Adviser'.[33]

The Sultan had anticipated skulduggery during Cecil's absence. Writing conspiratorially to Graham on 27 March, he said: 'Vous savez que Lord Cecil est à Londres. Je me demande ce qu'il prépare encore pour nous.'[34] And in fact, Hardinge had already written to tell Wingate that the Cecil brothers were plotting against Foreign Office control of Egypt.[35] As early as 21 February, Graham included in a manuscript letter to Wingate a section marked 'Very confl.' which told him that Robert Cecil[36] had 'put forward a proposal that Egypt should now be handed over to the Colonial Office! no doubt inspired by Nigs [Edward Cecil]. It is rather too bad, but we shall Scotch it all right.'[37] In one view, Cecil's suggested reform – which should, of course, have been raised through Wingate – would thus, 'he hoped ... restore British policy in Egypt to a Cromerian robustness'.[38] Certainly, Graham being no friend of Cecil and having charge of Egypt at the Foreign Office, the *démarche* did indeed have him – as well, no doubt, as Wingate – in its sights. Wingate himself noted in para. 7 of his MAIN POINTS that the Cecil plan 'principally aimed at his rival <u>RG</u> who had now got the full support of <u>Ld H</u>' [Hardinge].[39]

The proposal took the form of a memorandum entitled 'Future Egyptian Administration'. Despite the fact that his brother's arguments were unconvincing and seemed riskily *ad hominem*,[40] Robert Cecil submitting it to the Cabinet, strongly recommended that it should be looked at by an *ad hoc* committee. In a letter to Wingate on 5 May, Graham said that the idea was to form a Near Eastern Department to run Egypt, Mesopotamia and possibly other areas. He hoped that 'you in Egypt will not suffer by this and I do not think that either Lord Cromer or Lord K. would have relished the idea of exchanging a free hand and support from home for more definite home control!'[41]

Hardinge complained to Wingate about the difficulty of dealing with the Cecils:

> You will, I am sure, understand what a difficult position one is in here in connection with your Financial Adviser and his two official relations in this Office ... Between you and me, there is undoubtedly a great deal of underground intrigue going on, in which your Financial Adviser seems to be a past master.

He savaged the memorandum, which advocated that oversight of Egypt be 'taken away from the Foreign Office and vested in some outside department recruited from Heaven knows where. Ronald Graham and I', he said, 'have written very strong memoranda against the scheme.' He had urged that it should receive no serious consideration until Wingate had commented on it. (He did not do so officially, and was not asked for his views, which cannot have raised Curzon's later opinion of him.) Hardinge concluded, 'If people would only try to concentrate upon doing their duty and winning the war instead of starting these hare-brain schemes.'[42] Graham maintained that 'the motives for bringing the matter up were mainly personal'[43] and in a piece of tit-for-tat, Robert Cecil claimed that Graham's opposition, too, was personal and motivated by his desire to be High Commissioner.[44]

On 9 November, Hardinge told Wingate that he proposed in the New Year to set up the nucleus of a Foreign Office Egypt and Mesopotamia Department.[45] At the end of the month, he envisaged a sub-section of the Foreign Office War Department 'whose main object will be to deal with Egyptian questions through Ronald Graham and myself ... There will hardly be enough work for them [its staff] to fill up their time.' It would be 'the skeleton of a department which may develop considerably when we have in addition the control of affairs in Mesopotamia. For this purpose we are proposing to utilise Storrs.'[46]

In the short term, though not in the long, the Cecils lost the argument. The Cabinet (Egypt Administrative) Committee was composed of Balfour (president), Curzon and Milner,[47] none of whom presumably had anything better to do at that stage of the war, and Storrs acted as Secretary. It sat first late in September 1917 and in several sessions interviewed Edward Cecil, McMahon, Cheetham (also on leave), Hardinge and Graham. Cecil was supported only by McMahon and possibly Milner. (Graham believed that the latter had 'said that ... he could not have imagined it possible that so feeble a case could have been made as was presented by EC and Sir

HM.')[48] Storrs had felt that 'a transfer to the Colonial Office would be disastrous, if only for its effect on Egyptian opinion, where it must be interpreted as a veiled or incipient Annexation'.[49] Wingate agreed with the final report submitted by Curzon in February 1918. Its recommendations were that, until the war was over, responsibility for Egypt should not be taken away from the Foreign Office, and a Department of Egyptian Affairs under Graham should be strengthened. When the war ended and Edward Cecil was no longer around to revive the subject, however, Hardinge was unable to bring his plans to fruition. Egypt rapidly came under the Colonial Office after all, as a result of a Cabinet decision of 31 December 1920 to set up a Middle Eastern Department. Churchill succeeded Milner as Colonial Secretary a week later.[50]

The whole business of Cecil himself, in general a rather pitiful character (his only son was killed in the first year of the war), petered out in bathetic fashion. All his talk of other jobs, and a later claimed acceptance (before he changed his mind, perhaps when Balfour ordered him back to Egypt)[51] of the new post of assistant military adviser to the Ministry of Munitions in London, came to nothing.

On 20 October, having told Hardinge that he was shocked at Cecil's appearance when he saw him again after a gap of eight months, Wingate took the opportunity to pour scorn on the intrigues of the Financial Adviser, who had made a habit of publicly baiting him and his wife.[52] He mocked the intention Cecil had attributed to him to change the financial system in Egypt: it had caused alarm 'both in the Treasury and in the City ... which he evidently either fostered or took no steps to combat', 'the wise and experienced Financial Adviser' had had to race back to retrieve the situation, etc, etc. He noted that he had had 'a very long experience of my raconteur's [sic] somewhat erratic ways'. These were Cecil's methods 'and we have to make the best of them, and now that they have got their trusted financial expert back I hope the inmates of the Treasury and the City Houses will have no more restless nights!'[53]

Though Cecil had already fallen seriously ill with what was belatedly diagnosed as tuberculosis, as late as 14 November Brunyate was defending him to Wingate. (This was in connection with a proposed commission on the Capitulations and constitutional reform, when Rushdy 'feared that the Financial Adviser, whose name had been suggested by Minister of Education 'Adly, rather lacked the conciliatory spirit so useful for such discussions'.[54] On 15 November, however, Wingate sent a Private and Personal Decypher Yourself telegram to Robert Cecil, announcing that 'Tubercle bacilli have been found in the sputum of Lord Edward and there is evidence of disease at a comparatively early stage in the left lung.'[55] Cecil complained in a note to him, 'I am rather sorry it was thought necessary to wire home.'[56] Wingate was quick to write him off: 'Lord Edward Cecil is ill and doctors report that he will not be fit to resume work for some considerable time.'

Now that Cecil was no longer in a position to act as protector of his troublesome deputy, Lindsay, Wingate seized his chance to kill a second bird with the one, fortuitous stone:

> Mr. Lindsay would naturally act for him, as he has done most of this year, but he is in real need of leave and I think it very desirable that his leave should not be further deferred. In these circumstances, I recommend that Mr. Lindsay should start at the end of this month and that as a temporary arrangement Sir W. Brunyate should be appointed to act as Financial Adviser.[57]

On 7 December, Graham unchivalrously reacted to the likelihood that Cecil would have to leave Egypt again by saying, 'I confess between ourselves that I prefer him in Egypt rather than in England [*sic*], as he is a past-master in "spreading an atmosphere!".'[58] In fact, Cecil departed again later in the month. A year afterwards, on 13 December 1918, he died of influenza in a sanatorium at Leysin in Switzerland.

His widow, Violet, had married him in 1894 but had not accompanied him to Egypt after being with him in South Africa earlier. There she established a service supplementing the official rations of hospitalised British troops and was regularly unfaithful with Milner, the High Commissioner; she was depressed when Mafeking was relieved, liberating her husband.[59] Hayter wrote about Cecil to her, in surprising terms, on 26 December: 'He treated the Ministers like human beings, not like figure-heads, and they repaid him with very real affection and confidence.'[60] She married Milner in 1921 and herself published her first husband's book.

In a letter to Hardinge, Wingate had noted that Cecil had a number of friends who strongly supported him, 'notably Sir W. Brunyate',[61] whose 'dictatorial inclinations' Lloyd thought had probably been exacerbated by McMahon's strong reliance on him; Rodd said of him that his bad points were 'conspicuously incommensurate with his ambition'.[62] The Judicial Adviser, Lloyd believed, had become 'dangerously out of touch with the currents of thought which were now flowing strongly'.[63] Wingate reported[64] that Rushdy had hinted that ministers might resign if Brunyate became chairman of the Capitulations and constitutional reform commission, which was finally set up in December. After he had been so appointed, Rushdy in the following year – during which Wingate incongruously told Hardinge that the Judicial Adviser 'gets on well with the native ministers'[65] – leaked a November 1918 Brunyate Note on Constitutional Reform, drawn up at the request of Egyptian ministers, which caused great offence. Making recommendations which might once have been to the point but were no longer appropriate, and harshly critical of the performance of those Egyptians who had been active in politics, it 'entirely ignored the existence of the national sentiment which the war . . .

had stimulated in Egypt'.[66] It angered most educated Egyptians and nationalists by recommending the replacement of the Egyptian legal code by one of Indo-British type and the establishment of a Senate with a large number of foreign officials to shadow an entirely Egyptian consultative Chamber of Deputies.[67] To Rushdy's claim that, since 'Egypt would in effect be governed by a five per cent minority of non-Egyptians', the proposals would cause an explosion in the country, Brunyate is alleged to have responded by saying, 'Je l'éteindrai avec un crachat.'[68]

Like McMahon, Wingate seems to have been able to exert little control over Brunyate, of whose legal capacity he said he had a high opinion.[69] Despite Egyptian reservations about him (and despite Lloyd seeking to be Cecil's successor if he did not return),[70] after Lindsay's departure the appointments Wingate had recommended were approved, to the disappointment of Graham who, however, saw no alternative.[71] Brunyate, now the 'arrogant financial adviser',[72] thus gained entrée to the Egyptian Cabinet, which the other members would have found uncomfortable or worse. After Wingate's fall, Brunyate continued in his old ways. A British solicitor in Cairo, J. P. Forbes, told the ex-High Commissioner that, before the appearance of Allenby as Special Commissioner, Cheetham was completely under the thumb of Brunyate, who did not seem to realise 'that he is a British official in a British Protectorate'.[73]

Another leading member of the Comorra, Haines, now Adviser to the Ministry of the Interior, was deficient in his allotted role of Wingate's main source of information on the opinions and activities of Egyptians. He was unable to relate to the people of the country and had a haughty manner.[74] In Lloyd's view, he was not 'equal to his duties'; he rejected all criticism and advice and most exemplified the 'state of blissful ignorance' displayed by British officials during the war, having become completely out of touch with Europeans, the Egyptian upper classes[75] and current events. His inadequate intelligence-gathering helped fatally to weaken Wingate who, partly in consequence, was insufficiently armed to withstand Graham when his personal crisis came. After it, Haines was to dismiss the possibility of civil strife on the eve of the March 1919 uprising.[76]

Wingate's second most important intelligence resource had been housed in the Residency. After bringing several of his Khartum staff with him to Cairo, however, he neglected it, depriving himself of vital insight by allowing Storrs to feel underemployed and to depart. The High Commission member with the best contacts and the soundest knowledge, Storrs – though still based there – was in effect lost to Wingate, being often away in London, the Hijaz, Iraq and Najd.

Despite Cheetham's alleged ignorance of Egypt and his outposting under McMahon, the British government had knighted him – as well as Graham – in 1915. Wingate in Khartum had told Clayton, 'I am delighted to hear that Cheetham and Graham have got KCMGs – they have had a very trying and difficult time and are thoroughly deserving of the honour.'[77] Cheetham received many responsible postings after Cairo. He should have been capable of usefully supporting Wingate who, within a month of becoming High Commissioner, had (fulsome as so often) told Hardinge:

> You say with the greatest truth, that I will find an excellent co-adjutor in Cheetham. It would be impossible to find anyone more loyal and hardworking, or more ready to extend to me the fullest help and assistance in picking up the threads of this somewhat complex situation. He has worked indefatigably and I should greatly value some official expression of the appreciation of the Foreign Office for all his good work in very trying and difficult situations. I am very hopeful that the changes here and Cheetham's reinstatement in the position from which my predecessor moved him and to which he has now returned, will lead to a great improvement in many directions.[78]

In the upshot, Wingate significantly failed to inspire confidence in Cheetham,[79] as in Brunyate, and the High Commissioner's early euphoria about him in the end changed to painful disillusionment.

5 Not perhaps a very clever man
The misfit

He is a queer devil.
  (Cyril Wilson)

Before transferring to Cairo, Wingate had for 17 years been the uncrowned King of the Sudan, exercising personal rule in a backwater. When he and Graham were under consideration for High Commissioner, the latter commented to Hardinge that in Khartum his rival was 'disliked by the British officials whom he fusses and worries to death'.[1] He could get away with it in a small set-up a thousand miles south of Cairo. Not having had charge of a sizeable bureacratic machine was, however, inappropriate training for the top job in Egypt and made him therefore not the best choice to tangle with Cecil and others. Nor did the fact, demonstrated in Khartum, that he was much better at handling relations with the people of the country than with his own co-nationals.[2] That said, he maintained his own coterie of colleagues on whom he depended and, like a caring pater-familias, treated them well whatever their rank and praised them unre-servedly; Clayton is the supreme example of this. On the other hand, he sometimes deluded himself about the mutual regard which he believed characterised these relationships. For example, when he remarked to Clayton, 'we are all three such old and tried friends',[3] he was voicing a sen-timent to which Stack, the third of the trio, would have been unlikely to subscribe with equal fervour. As Governor-General of the Sudan, Wingate misled himself about Wilson's view of him when, at the end of 1916, Murray appointed Clayton (now Brigadier-General) to direct the cam-paign in the Hijaz, for which he was ideally suited, while overall military responsibility remained with Wingate. Wingate told Robertson that Wilson was prepared to be the British representative in Jiddah, liaising with Sharif Husayn, 'if he can look to me as his chief; but otherwise he declines to attempt such a delicate and difficult task, under the present nebulous organization'.[4] The truth was that Wilson preferred to work directly with Clayton: 'I am so glad you are running the show in Cairo', he told him. 'I was desperately afraid Master and Symes were going to do it all.'[5] Two months later he remained of the same mind: 'ever since you took the job earlier this year, things have been infinitely better ... for me'.[6]

Perhaps as another consequence of his one-man rule in the Sudan, Wingate – dapper, short and stocky[7] ('a portly person in a tall fez, with a regimental bandmaster's white waxed moustache')[8] and 'a man of strict propriety and many missions' whom Vansittart rated neither very remarkable nor much fun[9] – seems to have thought himself indispensable. After appointing him High Commissioner, Grey asked him to consider 'in the public interest ... whether, without a holiday after these trying years, you can take up a new post in Egypt without risk to your health'.[10] Wingate, who made such a show of putting the public interest first and of being a disciple of Cromer, now broke his own habit and his hero's rule that 'a big official should take leave every year if possible as much for the sake of HMG as for his own sake'[11] by declining the offer, to his ultimate loss. Over a year later, Hardinge hinted strongly that he should go on leave when Cheetham returned from his,[12] but Wingate again resisted: 'with so much going on here, and the time being somewhat critical, I feel that I ought not to take advantage of your permission unless my state of health makes a change absolutely necessary'.[13] Indeed, he had no break at all until his final departure. He was not averse to his subordinates going on vacation and allowed Cheetham – as he had Cecil – to precede him in making personal contact in London. On this, Graham commented barbedly, 'I am glad to hear that Cheetham is coming home ... it will be very welcome to me to have someone here who is well-informed as to the true state of affairs both past and present in Egypt.'[14]

With Balfour and Robert Cecil to deal with, Wingate's immovability is unlikely to have had an adverse effect on his attempt to overthrow Edward Cecil, but his self-defeating stubbornness on the question must have given the impression that he felt he had nothing to learn. This must have been a disappointment to those who had expressed such high hopes of him for Cairo. It certainly denied him the chances of face-to-face briefing in London and of introducing himself to the Lloyd George government. The opportunity to get himself known by those at home who had only his performance on paper by which to assess him did not recur. Brief contact with birds of passage was no substitute, such as that with the Colonial Secretary, Edwin Montagu,[15] who reported to the War Cabinet after a visit to Egypt from 26 to 30 October 1917:

> Let me say that I formed a good opinion of Reginald Wingate ... He is not perhaps a very clever man. His great knowledge of this part of the world and his character and manner have given him, so far as I can judge, a striking hold over the respect and affections ... of the Egyptians.[16]

Symes found Wingate sympathetic and kindly[17] and Humphrey Bowman[18] spoke of his 'never-failing courtesy', saying that 'No Chief could be more considerate than Wingate to those who worked for him. He had the knack of doing and saying the right thing at the appropriate moment.'[19] Others were irritated by some of his character traits but those who appointed him to Egypt had had long experience of them and should have been prepared to discount them. As befitted the holder of the sobriquet Abu Hibr [the Father of Ink],[20] he was almost invariably prolix. In February 1900 he wrote at least 113 letters and telegrams to Cromer.[21] He would frequently follow a long telegram with one lengthy letter amplifying it and another in recapitulation. (We have seen an example of this.) Graham, whom Vansittart had had to urge 'to pitch his Notes shorter',[22] had confided to Hardinge that Wingate would 'give you lively times at the FO with his 10 page telegrams'.[23] After he had returned to the Foreign Office from Egypt, Graham tried to stem the flow: 'Speaking generally', he advised Wingate, 'I should say that the higher authorities are so buried under masses of correspondence that they are relieved [?] to hear as little as possible from abroad except on matters of real importance'; with regard to minor details, he recommended that, 'as a general rule, you should settle them yourself trusting to FO concurrence'.[24]

Wingate was extremely fussy and pedantic. Wilson told Clayton, just before Wingate left for Cairo, 'He is a queer devil and just now is doing his best in a way to mess things up by having started a War committee in Ktm you know the sort of thing.'[25] Stack felt that he had to write to apologise for not letting him know in advance about his presentation of prizes at the Military School in Khartum, at which in a previous letter he had said: 'I made a little speech rather of the colloquial type of Arabic and was glad to hear afterwards that it was generally understood.'[26] Although Wingate was able to find time for 'nine or eleven holes of golf' most afternoons,[27] this characteristic was no doubt the cause of his complaint, or boast, to his brother-in-law, General Sir Leslie Rundle,[28] that 'I have literally not had a day off since I set foot in this country in August 1914 [*sic*]'.[29]

Wingate was often tactless. He had claimed that, 'in spite of a general absence of a weekly holiday', the Residency's coverage of Egyptian affairs (as distinct from 'Arab affairs for which Clayton and Symes ... are available') became difficult if Cheetham or Mervyn Herbert (First Secretary) were away. In a letter to Hardinge,[30] in the midst of war, he took the PUS to task for letting slip in his 30 November that the staff of his planned 'sub-Department in the Foreign Office to deal specially with Egyptian affairs' would have time on their hands. When he realised that he had been thoughtless, he tried to limit the damage: 'I am afraid, from the tone of your letter, that you think I am opening my mouth very wide and that I am not sufficiently mindful of the great strain and stress which the war puts on us all.'[31] The successful conclusion of the war registered no let-up in his badgering of Hardinge, when, for example, he agitated for major decisions to be taken on the basis of a hint by the Sultan that:

there could not be a more favourable time than the present to settle once and for all the future of Egypt – and I think he is right ... The general spirit of self-determination to which the war has given birth, has taken a firm hold in Egypt and I think it is only just that the Sultan, his Ministers and the Egyptians generally should be told how they stand.[32]

He often indulged in irritating understatement, frequently 'venturing to say' and using 'not entirely' or 'not quite' instead of 'certainly not'. At its worst, this attained a breathtaking diffidence. Letters to Grey about his wish to be C-in-C as well as High Commissioner and later to Hardinge on the desirability of inviting Zaghlul to London, were the most ill-judged of all. He ended the former, as we have seen, by saying, 'I beg Your Lordship will not hesitate to at once put the suggestion aside, if you consider it undesirable in any way.'[33] The latter concluded with the remark that he 'would make no further reference to the contents of this letter in a public despatch – nor will it be recorded in this office files. I feel that these ideas may not perhaps be palatable to HMG and in that case they can be treated as if they had not been written.'[34] How tentative could a British representative be? In the penultimate month of his High Commissionership, Wingate demonstrated to the full the extraordinary *naïveté* of which he was capable in communications to the Foreign Office, of 6 and 25 November 1918, which handed it the ammunition with which to do him down and of which details will be given later. In his reply to the latter, Balfour took full advantage of the opening Wingate had gone out of his way to offer him.

Like many of his contemporaries, Wingate had a long pedigree as an attempted obfuscator of the line between official and personal communicating though he was a more persistent violater of it than most and his habit of writing over the heads of his superiors or to the staffs of his equals caused problems throughout his career. In February 1890, Baring and the GOC, Egypt, Lieutenant-General James Dormer, accused him of underhandedness for establishing close relations with the War Office Intelligence Department through non-official channels. As DMI, he marked 'perfectly private' views he sent to London which differed from those of Kitchener. During a period acting as the 'pompously titled'[35] Governor of the Red Sea Littoral and Commandant at Suwakin from May to September 1894, he wrote 'privately' to the subordinates of his successor as DMI. Later in the year, he made trouble for himself by showing Cromer a 'private' letter from the War Office about a possible railway from Suwakin to Berber.[36] He was still up to his old tricks in his last year in the Sudan. He frequently wrote unsealed letters – sent, as he put it, 'under flying seal' – to McMahon for Clayton to read *en route*. He would advise him that 'it is better you should not appear to have seen it'.[37] When the system broke down, he asked him to agree 'some prearranged sign – say Solomon's seal' when their letters were not to be shown to others,[38] and they proceeded in all seriousness – at least on Wingate's side – to mark such correspondence with a crude Star of David inside a circle. An example was when, with regard to the situation in the Sudan, he told Clayton:

> I have summarised my observations in a private letter to Lord Kitch-ener and cannot do better than send you a copy, but please remem-ber it is for your eyes only and I do not wish anyone to know that I have written directly to him . . . PS Of course you can use the informa-tion contained in my letter to Lord Kitchener should you be dis-cussing matters with the High Commissioner, but I do not wish you on any account to let him know that I have written to the former.[39]

The following month, in connection with his attempt to cut Cecil down to size and in reference to 'copies of the correspondence between him and Sir Henry McMahon, in which their respective points of view are fully exposed', he tried to make up for clumsy paper-management by saying to Graham:

> In dealing with him [Cecil] at the FO I trust that these and my open telegram will be the only documents referred to – the *secret and per-sonal* wire was merely for the secret and personal information of Lord Hardinge and those whom he thought it necessary to consult – if Mr. AJB or RC tell EC [Balfour, Robert Cecil, Edward Cecil] about it, the situation between us would necessarily become very difficult and strained.[40]

Like Churchill, who covered the Boer War for the *Daily Telegraph* while fighting in it, for financial reasons Wingate twice attempted to combine his military duties with working as a Reuter correspondent. In August 1889, during the Tushky campaign, he caused Dormer some embarrassment thereby.[41] In March 1896, as DMI and Press Censor in the Dongola Cam-paign, he forged a monopoly relationship with David Rees, Reuter's representative in Cairo and a close friend of Boyle, who, uniquely, had the run of the Chancery (the political heart of the Residency), was often helped out over his 'financial scrapes'[42] and 'to the disgust of other correspondents was often given news before they were'.[43] Although armed with Cromer's permission, for his pains he raised doubts about his judgement and got himself and his co-conspirator, Slatin, into hot water with *The Times*.

During his successful career in the Sudan, doubts had from time to time been voiced about certain aspects of Wingate's administrative and financial performance. In 1900, Gorst accused him of 'administrative incompetence'.[44] In 1907, Cromer, who on the other hand considered him a sound administrator, said:

> Wingate has done very well in the Soudan . . . But I cannot conceal from myself the fact that he is very local, and has not got any firm grip

of the main principles on which the Government of the Soudan, or indeed of any other country, has to be conducted. Also, he is ignorant as a child of everything connected with financial affairs.[45]

Harvey, then Financial Adviser, frequently crossed swords with Wingate in 1907/8. In the latter year, unimpressed by his draft Sudan budget for 1909, Gorst recommended to Harvey that 'it would be as well to bring home to the Sirdar what the financial situation of the Sudan really is'.[46] After becoming his heir in Khartum, Stack was uncomfortable with Wingate's administrative legacy. The fact was not new to him that the 'whole administration has been trained to report the most minor matter', but he complained about the 'masses of trivial detail that is daily poured into the Palace'[47] when 'I am working ... with practically one of everything in place of two or three as the case may be under the old regime'. He informally drew to Clayton's attention an administrative lapse when Wingate failed to consult the Foreign Office before being 'impetuous' in taking 'precipitate action' over the coronation of the new Queen of Abyssinia at which Major Pearson should have represented him. The result was an exercise which 'seems to have been botched ... A case of being too clever ... net result is their [Eritrea and French Somaliland] representatives went and ours didn't. Common sense is as useful in diplomatic matters as in most other.'[48]

Stack also thought that Wingate was presiding over lapses in communication. When he was not told that Cyril Wilson was visiting Cairo, he remarked to Clayton, 'The matter of information does want looking into for the old system has been rather upset and nothing put in its place.'[49] He was left in the dark about the movements of Sykes and Georges-Picot during their 1917 Middle Eastern tour and thanked Clayton for background on their mission which 'gave me the insight I think I ought to have in order to understand the trend of events. Not much do I get from the Residency.'[50]

Wingate was always financially stretched and careless about money. Before moving to Cairo, he short-sightedly did not ask about pension arrangements or, through boycotting Egypt during McMahon's High Commissionership, realise the strain on his pocket the job would exert. He complained to Graham that it was 'manifestly unfair' that he should have to fund 'all the medical work required in the Residency which consists ... of thorough examinations of this building and its annexes as well as the two buildings in Alexandria, besides weekly inspections of all natives attached to the staff'. He was incredulous that he should be expected to foot the bill for the whole scheme.[51] As with his reporting, he found the distinction between the private and official sides of his finances difficult to maintain. It had been much simpler in Khartum, where he made liberal interpretations of pension regulations[52] and frequently paid Sharif Husayn more than the approved subsidy figure of £125,000 per month, sending it up to a peak of £375,000 in November 1916. In Cairo, he early bewailed to Stack, 'They look on things in a very narrow way in this part of the world, especially financially, but I hope in due time to get them to enlarge their ideas.'[53] The line of demarcation became clearer but his practice – encouraged by the novelty of his powerful position – was to spend more than his departmental heads thought sensible.[54] London objected to his action over the increased rent of Villa Zervudachi, his Alexandria summer residence: 'I am to express Mr. Balfour's regret that Sir R. Wingate should have closed with Mr. Zervudachi's offer before learning that the proposal was acceptable' to the Lords Commissioners of the Treasury.[55]

The first open revolt against Wingate was over finance. It came from Ronald Lindsay, Cecil's close friend. Seconded from the Foreign Office like Graham, his first post had been St Petersburg, where he served with both him and Hardinge. In July 1917, with Cecil away in Britain, he handed in his resignation and Wingate accepted it. He reported, 'I think he is very tired and his wife has been ailing for a long time.'[56] Cecil, however – perhaps demonstrating his superior authority over Wingate in his own area of work – asked Lindsay to remain in post until his own return. Lindsay, to whom the DNB attributes 'sympathetic understanding of opinions that were not his own', thereupon detailed the reasons for his proffered resignation to Wingate. He told the High Commissioner that his wish to resign had nothing to do, as Wingate had let it appear, with:

> private and personal reasons, especially to my wife's health . . . this resignation was due purely to the fact that in the course of the last six months I have become convinced that your views and mine on the principles of finance and on the manner of carrying them out are entirely irreconcilable. I am therefore unwilling to remain a day longer than absolutely necessary in a position of responsibility where I have to do things which I cannot regard as justifiable.[57]

When Cecil proceeded on his terminal sick leave in December, Wingate was able to despatch Lindsay as well. He maintained his version of events to Hardinge – justified retrospectively by the fact that Lindsay's first wife, Martha, died in 1918 – by saying, 'I am glad it has been possible to let him have this little change of which he stands in much need, and he was of course very anxious about his wife's state of health.'[58]

Actions, and inaction, of Wingate *vis-à-vis* London contributed to the establishment of the case which was to be made against him. We have noted the accusation which followed the Sultan's allegedly discourteous behaviour at the very start of his High Commissionership. In July 1917, when he minuted the War Office with a weak case for T. E. Lawrence to receive the 'immediate award of the Victoria Cross', the rejection of his strong recommendation led Lawrence to refuse the DSO which had been approved.[59] Just before Allenby took Jerusalem on 9 December 1917,

Wingate visited him at the front and, suspected by Hardinge of seeking to enter the city with the troops, found himself harried back to Cairo before he could do any damage;[60] he was able to complete a visit in July 1918.[61] In the summer of that year and in the context of the Arab Revolt, over the question of the transfer to Aqabah of regular units then with 'Aly and 'Abd Allah,[62] Lawrence found him over-polite in an approach to Sharif Husayn and had to ask Allenby to take over the task.[63]

Although Gorst thought him 'by nature an alarmist',[64] there are many other examples of Wingate failing to put his case across. Lloyd said, 'Wingate never succeeded in inducing the Foreign Office to give his views the weight which, as events conclusively proved, was due to them . . . his advice in regard to Egyptian politics [was] persistently disregarded in Whitehall.'[65] He added, however, that it 'was scarcely given with the force or insistence which might have ensured it a hearing, and, most unfortunate of all, was never accompanied by an adequate description of the dangers to be feared'.[66] Chirol agreed, feeling that 'his wiser counsels were not listened to, perhaps because they were not urged with sufficient insistence'.[67] To Wingate's indignation, the Milner Report was to make the same criticism. Like McMahon, in Chirol's opinion Wingate never 'seems to have . . . enjoyed the real confidence of the Foreign Office' or to have tendered advice which caught the attention of Whitehall.[68] (There his two chief correspondents, Hardinge and especially Graham, were in any case, as Wingate knew,[69] no friends of his.) When he was recalled, he was to fare no better orally than he had in writing.

An underlying cause of the antipathy of Graham, Hardinge and others was perhaps that Wingate, with his *petit bourgeois* origins,[70] was not of the class of the PUSs, respectively present, future and acting, with whom he found himself dealing: Hardinge, Lindsay and Graham were all of, or connected with, the aristocracy. Another was that he was not sophisticated. The Sudan had not required sophistication of him. He had been hardly a month in Cairo, however, when Storrs – himself the acme of urbanity – decided, echoing Gomer, that Wingate 'knew a great deal about local issues, but lacked the sophistication and comprehension needed to deal with politics in London'.[71]

Having reached the height of High Commissioner, Wingate seems to have thought that there was no limit to how much further he could rise – and to how naïve he would be permitted to be. In August 1917, he recommended that the High Commissionership 'should be held by someone highly placed in the social world – e.g. a member of the Royal Family or a wealthy Peer', assisted by an expert deputy High Commissioner. If the implication was that he himself should be ennobled, the Foreign Office gave no sign of detecting it, as it was to be unable to avoid doing so in the case of the more aggressive approach to the question by his second successor.

For Wingate to irritate Graham and Hardinge was one thing. Irritating

Balfour, even though they knew each other at home, was quite another. Wingate contrived to do this when, five days before his world began to collapse in the face of the assault of Egyptian nationalism, the Foreign Secretary sent Sharif Husayn a telegram, in the name of Lawrence, via Wingate and over the heads of him and Allenby.[72] Understandably, Wingate thought that this was a strange procedure and held up the telegram in order to check with the Foreign Office.[73] One can appreciate Wingate's annoyance that an invitation to Faysal was not to come through him. He, after all, was in total charge of Hijaz policy. It would have been more sensible for him, however, to express tactful surprise than mount an exercise in pedantry which looked like obstructionism. In the event, he was shocked to receive a severe rebuke from Balfour, blaming him for holding his telegram up:

> The fact that Colonel Lawrence's message was sent to you in official telegram should have made it clear that it was in accordance with considered views of His Majesty's Government. It is most regrettable that valuable time has been lost by your holding it back. It should go forward at once.[74]

Wingate sent the invitation on to the Sharif, as coming from Lawrence, without further delay. At the same time he telegraphed Hardinge, complaining about 'the rather sharp rebuff in the Foreign Office Telegram',[75] and wrote to Balfour, 'apologising and explaining'.[76]

6 There seems some faulty staff work here

The nationalists

I feel sure that had you been previously warned as to the nature of their visit and the absurd proposals they meant to put forward you would have been chary of receiving them as a deputation.

(Graham)

Egyptian nationalism delayed no further than the spring of 1917 in adding to Wingate's discomfiture. On 24 March, referring to Sultan Husayn Kamil – who had perhaps launched a straw into the wind with the offence British staff perceived him to have offered them on his fourth day in his post – he told Hardinge, 'I have no sort of doubt in my own mind that he and his Ministers hope the Egyptians may be given more freedom in the *Interior* government of their country than exists at present.'[1] In April, the Sultan asked the Foreign Office to open more senior positions to his countrymen;[2] on 5 May, Graham told Wingate that he had sent a non-committal reply to this which suggested that 'the moment for raising questions with regard to the future administration of Egypt will be when His Highness visits England [*sic*] as we hope he will at the end of the war'.[3] Rushdy, also in May, repeated the Sultan's question, complaining about the British takeover of the Ministry of Foreign Affairs on the declaration of the Protectorate and seeking clarification of Britain's overall position in Egypt;[4] he received the same reply, this time from Wingate.[5]

Husayn Kamil died on 8 October at the age of 64, and the hope of a smooth path to the independence Egypt believed that it had been promised, and Wingate had not ruled out, was lost. Two days later, his half-brother, the non-Arabic-speaking, 'financially dishonest and by nature authoritarian'[6] Prince Ahmad Fu'ad, a product of the Italian military academy in Turin, who had once been in the running for the throne of Albania,[7] succeeded as Sultan Fu'ad; he was awarded the GCB on his accession. Boyle was to record that – with 'His ludicrous blunders when talking Arabic, his affairs with Italian mistresses' and the general belief that 'his sole object is to maintain himself in his present comfortable post' – Fu'ad 'has not a friend or a sincere well-wisher in Egypt. He is not respected like Sultan Hussein Kamil, nor dreaded like Abbas Hilmi.'[8] Chirol reported him to be 'universally *dis*respected'.[9] Wingate – although there was no other candidate for the post – had opposed his nomination, believing that – known for his 'implacable hostility to parliamentary government'[10] – he would be unco-operative. His fears must have been reinforced when, less than a month into his reign, Fu'ad received Montagu during a stopover in Egypt after visiting the Viceroy. Montagu, now Indian Secretary, was under the impression that Egypt already had considerable autonomy. When he voiced this view, Wingate reported, 'the Sultan turned to Ruchdi ... and said: "Listen to this, Ruchdi, Mr Montagu thinks we have autonomy in Egypt", and followed his remarks with a hearty laugh.' Wingate commented that 'our Egyptian friends are all out for as complete autonomy as they can get – it appears that the Sultan said to Montagu that he hoped that Egypt would be granted full autonomy in due course'.[11] Montagu noted that 'Fu'ad was easily led and vulnerable to nationalist intrigues.'[12]

Wingate reported to Hardinge on 29 November that Fu'ad, inspired by Rushdy,[13] had told him, when Husayn Kamil was on his deathbed, that he wanted alterations to the Cabinet. Ushering in a phase of collaboration between Sultan and politicians, he had reverted to the subject 'a couple of days ago', nominating Sa'ad Zaghlul and 'Abd al 'Aziz Fahmy to replace the inadequate but pro-British Ahmad Hilmy Pasha – 'he could not possibly shake hands with him' – and Sir Ibrahim Fathy Pasha, the Ministers of Agriculture and Awqaf respectively, to whom he referred 'in terms of great contempt'; in one British diplomatic view, they 'had no moral right ... at all' to be in the Cabinet.[14] McMahon had more than once raised the claims of Zaghlul, observing that, since holding his two Cabinet posts in the period 1906 to 1912, he had been twice denied ministerial appointments, and warning that it would be unwise to keep him out indefinitely. Now Wingate said of him, 'I know Saad Pasha Zaghlul well and although he has a reputation for Nationalism, he has undoubtedly great influence with the people as an orator and is a power in the land.' Maintaining his balanced tone, in sharp contrast to that adopted by Graham, he continued:

Abd el Aziz Bey is also a Nationalist Lawyer who has the reputation of being honest and incorruptible ... the retiring Ministers ..., although I believe they ... might be counted upon as strong British supporters, are, nevertheless, hardly desirable to retain in view of the popular resentment against them.

Fathy Pasha, he added:

has unfortunately the reputation for unnatural vices and I fear the evidence against him in this respect is only too convincing – It is also thought that he is easily corruptible ... In any case, when the Sultan and his Ministers want to get rid of a colleague on these moral grounds it hardly behoves the protecting Power to interfere.

With regard to Hilmy, he 'suffers from general incapacity and want of knowledge ... I do not think we have any strong grounds for supporting his retention'.

Wingate recommended a part-change. 'That the inclusion of Zaghlul and Fahmy will give the reconstituted Ministry a somewhat nationalistic tendency is undoubted', he conceded, 'but on the other hand I am not altogether averse to this.' With particular regard to Zaghlul, he said, 'I am not at all sure that we would not be wise to secure his support on the side of the Government rather than have him in opposition' – which, in relation to the claims of Yasin al Hashimy, a little later, to be Iraqi Prime Minister, Bell found 'not a very reassuring reason'.[15] With regard to Fahmy, however, 'There are rumours that Fahmy Bey's wife is Ruchdi's mistress, and if this is really so it would certainly be a strong reason for rejecting his candidature.'[16]

In December, however, when Rushdy, too, called for the substitutions to be made, Wingate now deemed nationalism to be looking threatening and changed his mind. He reminded the Foreign Office that nationalist pressure could be expected after the war. He said that Brunyate had reported Rushdy as describing the intervention of the British Government in the choice of Ministers as 'abusive'. The Prime Minister had gone further, adumbrating a programme which involved 'a complete break with the past'. Asserting that 'The basis of our control of Egypt is the "advice" of His Majesty's Government' and that Rushdy 'proposes to free the Egyptian Government from this control except in certain limited respects', he linked his fear that 'The whole system of our Protectorate would ... be endangered by any such change' with his conviction that 'we cannot accept either of his nominees for Ministerial rank without a grave warning that we are not prepared to grant the measure of wholesale autonomy which he has enunciated'.

Responding on 12 December, Graham agreed with him in rejecting the idea of two 'avowed nationalists' replacing the pro-British ministers.[17] In a minute, he concurred in Gorst's view of Wingate:

> I think Sir R Wingate ... is inclined to take Rushdi Pasha too seriously. I was his Adviser at the Interior for several years. He is exuberant and volatile, and scarcely a week passed without his starting some hare or other – occasionally useful but generally wild. I never found any difficulty in squashing the latter ... He often used to me the language he has now used to Sir W. Brunyate, but I never gave him any encouragement nor allowed the matter to go any further.[18]

Since Hardinge, pointing out that Zaghlul was said to be 'anti-British',[19] was of the same mind about the substitutions, Wingate was sent on 15 December the main lines of a reply to deliver to the Prime Minister.[20] This said that 'His Majesty's Government are not convinced by the reasons given for the retirement in present circumstances of the two Ministers whom it is proposed to dismiss and they do not think the new Ministers wholly satisfactory.' Of the proposed new Minister of Agriculture, ignoring Cromer's assessment, it continued:

> There are serious objections to Saad Zaglool who has always been troublesome and a *mauvais coucheur*. His conduct in attacking the policy of the Ministry as he did should really exclude him from any further participation in the Government ... the Prime Minister is undertaking large personal responsibility in putting forward a politician with a record such as Saad Zaglool. This responsibility must be shared by the Sultan who has strongly endorsed the recommendation of the Prime Minister.

In a letter to Wingate on 20 December which in part duplicated his minute and harked back over three years, Graham spoke of Zaghlul and Fahmy – whom Chirol considered to have played 'the part of legitimate opposition'[21] – as 'a couple of Nationalists who, although moderate, had distinguished themselves by their violent attacks on Lord Kitchener and his policy in the last months of the [Legislative] Assembly'. Now upholding a Cromer rule,[22] he declared that the Prime Minister's claim that the Sultan could dismiss ministers 'without consulting us is ludicrous'.[23]

Typical of the indecisiveness of its originators under Balfour, a Foreign Office telegram of the same date, composed at 2350 hrs, backed down, too late. It read, 'I have no objection to Saad Pasha Zaghlul as a Minister if you recommend him nor to Aziz Bey Fahmy becoming Under Secretary of State as a step towards Ministerial rank in future',[24] provided that the Sultan undertook not to make changes without British agreement. This volte-face did not lead to action. Although Fathy, whom the Sultan disliked the more, was eventually replaced, although not by Fahmy. Fu'ad, in response to his reverse, which left him 'bitterly angry',[25] for six months ignored Rushdy and his cabinet. He instead took his counsel from an 'officine nocturne' consisting, among others, of his two rejected nominees, Zaghlul, who was a gambling companion of his,[26] and Fahmy.

Wingate alerted Hardinge on 24 December to his belief that 'we must expect a very frank *exposé* of National aspirations when the war is over and the settlement has to be made on several pending questions'.[27] On the same day, he told Balfour that a nationalist aim which was gaining ground was to 're-open the Legislative Assembly on the return of peace'.[28] The Sultan continued to express his dissatisfaction with the Protectorate, which he complained prevented him from learning of Cabinet decisions until the British had approved them. On 25 August 1918, Wingate warned Graham that he expected 'the Sultan and his Ministers to open their mouths wide when the War is over'.[29] On 31 August, he forecast to the Foreign Office that, postwar, Fu'ad might find courting the nationalists an attractive way of bolstering his image and position;[30] Graham pooh-poohed the idea, declaring in an absurd comment, which should have come back to haunt him, that 'the calm sea of Egyptian politics is scarcely ruffled by puffs of breeze which may be variable but do not presage any kind of storm'.[31] On 19 October, anticipating 'a somewhat troublesome winter', Wingate reported to Hardinge that 'President Wilson's "self-determination" ideas have taken a strong hold on Sultan Fuad, who is all for "Home Rule"' and warned that the British government 'must expect a movement in this direction on the part of certain sections of this country after the war'. Indeed, 'a deputation of Egyptians on conclusion of Peace means to apply to President Wilson to support Home Rule for Egypt'.[32]

The Foreign Office had given him – 'the one man who ... would be most concerned in the effects of such a declaration'[33] – no prior warning of the publication of the Anglo-French [*sic*] Declaration on 7 November. Commenting on it next day less forcefully than Arnold Wilson in Baghdad, he told the Foreign Office:

> I think it is not unlikely that the self-determination policy ... may have its repercussions amongst Egyptian Nationalists who will no doubt desire similar treatment for Egypt. I have no definite indication that active agitation in this sense is at present probable, but there are rumours which I cannot altogether ignore that influential natives wish to sound the American Representative here with a view to their aspirations being made known to President Wilson.[34]

To Graham, he said:

> I think we must expect a repercussion of this statement in Native circles here who will argue that as self-government is to be allowed to all territories liberated during the war, why should the same principle not be followed as regards Egypt, which was also liberated but placed under British protection *after* the war began?[35] ... I have no doubt that HMG has a ready answer for all such criticisms, but it would help me greatly to know, as soon as possible, the line I should adopt when they come, as they undoubtedly will.[36]

His son claims that, to his request for:

> something he knew did not exist, ... As usual, he received no reply ... For two years, a deaf ear had been turned by London to Wingate's reiterated requests for a definition of the Protectorate, to allay the

fears of Sultan, Ministers, Nationalists, Moderates, and public opinion. Suggestions for an authoritative commission to come to Egypt had been refused.[37]

Wingate reiterated to Graham that 'There can be no possible doubt that the ideas of self-determination ... are affecting him [the Sultan] and the Egyptian Nationalist Party', Hizb al Ummah. Playing into his hands with staggering artlessness, he continued, 'Meanwhile there is undoubtedly a growing unrest on the part of the British Officials who, as you know, have never yet failed to freely criticise Kasr-el Doubara' – the square in central Cairo on which stood the Residency,[38] here personifying the High Commissioner himself. He believed that they were blaming him 'for encouraging Native nationalist aspirations'.[39]

On 12 November, the Sultan telegraphed President Wilson to congratulate him on his Fourteen Points and inform him of 'l'expansion irrésistible des principes de liberté et de droit qui grâce à votre action s'imposent désormais dans le règlement des affaires des nations'.[40]

A month after arriving in Cairo, Wingate had set out for Hardinge, who did not demur, his policy on dealing with the people of the country:

> I have been overwhelmed with work ever since my return to Cairo and the visits from natives and others have taken up much valuable time – but I am convinced that it is very desirable for the foreign and native element to be allowed to keep in touch with the Residency and though one grudges the time spent in this way, it is helpful in the long run.[41]

His stance was put conclusively to the test at the end of the war. On 5 November, after a period of more than four years during which political dialogue at sub-Sultan level had been largely driven underground, Zaghlul called on him to request that the Legislative Assembly be allowed to resume its sittings.[42] Wingate's response that Allah was with the patient[43] earned him an accusation from the Foreign Office that such interviews gave a boost to nationalism.[44] On 13 November, two days after Compiègne, as 'with the Armistice the kettle of Egyptian local politics boiled ominously',[45] he called on Wingate again, this time with a two-man delegation and – according to Ronald Wingate – 'with the tacit approval of the Sultan'.[46] The *démarche* had been at least two months in the preparation and had involved a circle which included the Prime Minister,[47] through whom, and Cheetham, the request for the interview was routed. The call converted the Hizb al Ummah, with which the three and Rushdy had all been associated before the war, into the Hizb al Wafd: 'Thus was born the Egyptian *wafd* ... And thus began the end of Wingate's career.'[48]

Wingate reported to London by telegram the following day:

In the course of the last 48 hours I have had three interviews of some importance. [The third was with the American Diplomatic Agent, Mr. Gary.] Reviewing these now, in the light of the last, I have little doubt that they were all intentionally meant to lead up to the one end, viz: – the representation at the Peace discussions of prominent Egyptians anxious to state their own case for either a much larger share in the Government of this country than they now have, or even complete autonomy ... Yesterday I received a visit from three very prominent Egyptians.

After giving some account of Zaghlul – to whom 'Abd an Nasir accords the lapsed title of Vice-President (or Deputy) of the Legislative Assembly,[49] – Fahmy and 'Aly Pasha Sha'rawy,[50] he continued:

There took place a somewhat stormy, but entirely friendly, discussion ... [marked by] extreme frankness on both sides ... at times the discussion became distinctly heated.[51] They and the party they represent (which is not inconsiderable or negligible) will demand complete autonomy for Egypt ... they entirely dissociate themselves with [*sic*] the methods employed by the late Mustafa Kamil, Mohammed Bey Farid and their followers, though they do not disagree with the bases of the Nationalistic movement they initiated ... they consider themselves far more capable of conducting a well-ordered government than the Arabs, Syrians and Mesopotamians to whom the Anglo-French [*sic*] Governments [*sic*] have granted self-determination as expressed in the recently published official statement. (You will remember that in my private telegram to the Foreign Office of November 8th, ... I pointed out that this statement would almost certainly lead to the raising of questions in regard to the future government of Egypt) ... Egypt had shown a spirit of great loyalty during the War, ... they had helped forward its prosecution by men and money, and ... now all danger from Turkish aggression was over, they expected their reward, viz: independence.

They concluded:

We look on England [*sic*] as our closest friend and ally by whose strong right arm we have been set free; we shall ever be loyal and faithful to her and we should make an alliance with her of perpetual peace and friendship; we should be prepared to sacrifice our men and money should she require them in future wars, and we should range ourselves with her, by treaty ... In return for this we should expect to be given complete autonomy, though we should probably accept a measure of financial supervision on the part of His Majesty's Government, such as existed ... prior to 1882. We should also guarantee special facilities for British ships traversing the Suez Canal.

Much later, Wingate received from an Egyptian friend a transcript of the Wafd's account of the meeting. A very fair document, it concluded by reporting:

> The High Commissioner answered that he heard what they said and that he considered the conversation to be of a purely friendly nature and not official, adding that he had no conception of the plans and ideas of the British Government in regard to this question.[52]

Chirol supports his last remark, claiming that the British government had never had an Egypt policy and continued for some time to be 'too busy with other matters to conceive one'.[53]

Commenting on his visitors' presentation and casting doubt on their motives, Wingate added, 'to anyone less conversant than I am with Egyptian methods, their contentions would appear to have been dictated by pure patriotism'. Yet again, he repeated that 'The theories enunciated by President Wilson, and so largely subscribed to by the allied Powers, are bound to have a repercussive effect in a country constituted as this is.' He concluded by indicating the reason why his interlocutors were in future to be called the Wafd (delegation):

> They finally announced that they had every intention of proceeding to London when transport was available, in order to place their views before the Authorities and the British people, and to this I replied that – with liberty-loving people like the British – no serious opposition was likely to be raised and in any case they were free agents.

As they left, Wingate 'quoted an Arabic verse from the Koran which is the counterpart of the saying "*tout vient à qui sait attendre*"'. This remark sounds very like the one with which he had bidden Zaghlul God-speed the previous week and was in any case likely to have been seen in London as ill-chosen.[54]

He went on to describe the next 'interview'. He had perhaps paved the way to it by offering a hostage to fortune before the Protectorate, when on a visit to Cairo, by giving Rushdy his view – one endorsed by Storrs, as also by the Protectorate declaration – that the question of independence for Egypt would be considered after the war.[55] (Maxwell had apparently strayed into the political arena and gone further by promising that with the coming of peace Egypt would have self-government.)[56] He reported:

> A few hours after these gentlemen had left me I had a visit from Ruchdi Pasha, the Prime Minister. He told me that the three gentlemen had called upon him after leaving the Residency and I had a strong impression, from what followed, that they were acting with the knowledge (though not necessarily the approval) of the Sultan and

his Ministers; for, Ruchdi Pasha pulled out of his pocket the copy of a letter he had written to the Sultan, proposing that he and 'Adly Pasha should proceed at once to London to take part in the Peace discussion ... In presenting this, he remarked that, in his opinion, it would be very advisable for his three visitors to proceed to London and put up their case 'as in the event of their request being refused, the charge of inadequate representation of the Egyptian question could not be brought against us responsible Egyptian Ministers, as might be the case if we alone were delegated to proceed to London'.[57]

With 'the idea of meeting Egyptian nationalism halfway',[58] Wingate was, according to an interesting insight, thus pressing for the Wafd – who he believed to be intending to achieve their aims if necessary by revolutionary activity – to be received in London in order to pre-empt less manageable nationalist demands and methods.[59]

The day after he wrote his telegram to Hardinge, Wingate received one in reply to his of 6 November. It appeared to be from Graham,[60] who is in any case unlikely not to have read it, but may have emanated from Curzon. (It recalled an exchange the year before, when Graham remarked that 'Lord R. Cecil has been complaining lately that we do not get enough current information from you'[61] and Wingate replied by asking if he really wanted more reports on the internal situation.) It said in part, 'We have had up to now no indication of such Native aspirations nor of form they are likely to take ... You should keep me fully informed of any developments on lines you mention.'[62] In response to the implication that Wingate had not done so here to fore, his son says with some justice that he had 'faithfully reported to the British Government ... the many clear indications' of these for almost two years[63] but adds that Curzon probably did not know this. The only comment by Wingate himself, pencilled on the telegram later, was, 'I have most scrupulously carried out the instruction contained in the last paragraph of the above telegram.'[64]

On 20 November, in a letter to Hardinge, Wingate summarised the interviews again at some length. He noted that they 'were evidently part of a pre-arranged plan of campaign, of which the Sultan was – at any rate to some extent – cognizant'.[65] On the 24th, in another letter to the PUS, he reported that Zaghlul and 13 associates, the Committee of Fourteen, had now asked for permission under martial law to go to London. Taking an unconscious risk, and bearing out Symes's claim that 'My chief was in favour of lifting the lid to allow an escape of steam',[66] he added:

> there is going to be a very determined all-round attempt to raise the Egyptian question and, if possible, get it settled once and for all. And I repeat my own conviction that the present appears to me a favourable time to grasp the nettle and have it seriously tackled.

He mentioned that 'the absence of any reply from the Foreign Office to our telegrams is somewhat disquieting' and said that, 'Pending some such expressions of views, I am not replying to the applications of the Extremists to go.'

A general, though perhaps not a specific, reason for the slowness of the Foreign Office to reply was well summarised by Russell Pasha, the legendary Commandant of the Cairo Police from 1918 to 1946:[67] 'the culmination of the Nationalist movement ... was being treated somewhat unsympathetically by a Britain torn with her own post-war worries, making her unreceptive to something that seemed of much less urgency'.[68]

In a telegram to the Foreign Office the next day, Wingate reported 'indications of a campaign directed against the Protectorate', said that he had banned public meetings and demonstrations and – carelessly provoking the telegram which was to arrive from Balfour on 2 December – noted that Zaghlul and Fahmy had been 'taking advantage of the fact that they were received at the Residency to represent their movement as a lawful one'. Zaghlul had formed his Committee to:

> seek through peaceful and lawful means, wherever opportunities offer, to obtain the absolute independence of Egypt, in conformity with the principles of liberty and justice, whose cause Great Britain and her Allies have espoused and by which they seek to liberate the weak peoples.

The Committee was now organising a highly effective, nationwide petition – the Tawkilat campaign – for Zaghlul to be allowed to travel.[69] While stating that he could not regard him and the Committee as 'in any way representative of the sounder elements of Egyptian opinion',[70] Wingate repeated, 'I still think it advisable that as soon as restrictions on travel are removed a hearing should be given in London to any Egyptian politicians who wish to address themselves directly to the Foreign Office.'

While a minute of 25 November by Graham, who on every reckoning was junior to Wingate, charged that 'the residency and the palace are not working in as close harmony and contact as they ought to be' and regretted that Wingate 'did not turn down these Nationalists in much firmer language than he seems to have used',[71] it was not until the 27th that Wingate at last received a reply to his post-13 November communications in the shape of a telegram from Balfour, no less. The Foreign Secretary said: 'HMG desire to act on a principle which they have always followed of giving Egyptians ever increasing share in the Government of the country and rate of Egyptian progress towards self-government must depend on Egyptians themselves.' Coming into focus, he continued:

> As you are well aware stage has not been reached at which self-government is possible. HMG have not the intention of abandoning

their responsibilities for (?order) and good government in Egypt and for protecting rights and interest of both native and of (*sic:* and other?) (?population)s of the country.

In conclusion, while 'No useful purpose would be served by allowing Nationalist leaders to come to London and advance immoderate demands which can [*sic*] be entertained', the government 'would always be ready to listen ?with sympathy to any reasonable proposals on the part of Ministers or other Egyptians[72] and would welcome a visit from Rushdi Pasha and Adly Pasha to express their views'. A visit would not be opportune at the moment, however. When they did come, 'your presence here will be essential'.[73]

Duff Cooper declares that Balfour 'ought to have known better' than to put Rushdy and 'Adly off: 'It was worse than inept, it was discourteous.'[74] Chirol claims that the uncompromising rebuff was relayed to Zaghlul 'with less than Sir Reginald's usual tact ... in a somewhat curt note from his private secretary', which means of transmission the leader of the Wafd resented;[75] when he asked the reason for the rejection of his application, he received no direct reply.[76] One could certainly understand it if the suddenly altered character of the Foreign Office's responses to his reporting had unnerved Wingate and caused him to conduct himself atypically. He must have regretted that he had changed his mind, so short a time before, about recommending the inclusion of Zaghlul and Fahmy in the Cabinet, which would have ruled out any prohibition on their travelling to London. It is interesting to speculate that, if Rushdi Pasha alone had called on him and had asked for Zaghlul to accompany him to London, matters might have turned out very differently.

Allenby was to characterise the rejection of the nationalist application to visit Britain as 'our unfortunate refusal'[77] and Wavell, his biographer, as a 'great blunder'.[78] The Milner Report was to regret the postponement:

> it would appear that, in spite of the insistence with which the High Commissioner appealed for their reception, the real urgency of dealing with the Egyptian problem at that critical moment had not been realised ... it is obvious, after the event, that Egyptian Ministers should have come to London when they proposed to do so, and Sir Reginald Wingate, whose advice on this subject was fully justified by the sequel, would have done well, in our opinion, to urge his view with even greater insistency.

On 29 November, in contrast, Graham in further minuting criticised 'the half-hearted attitude adopted by the residency' towards the Egyptian situation. 'The extremist leaders', he said, 'ought never to have been received by Sir R. Wingate except for the purpose of being told not to make fools of themselves.'[79] Three days later, a second telegram arrived from Balfour which made matters worse. Ignoring Wingate's comment that the party Zaghlul, Fahmy and Sha'rawy represented was 'not inconsiderable or negligible', the Foreign Secretary said, 'I note that Extremist Leaders are exploiting fact of your having received them at Residency, which was unfortunate . . . I understand leaders of movement do not carry much weight.'[80] (Wingate noted later that 'the words "which was unfortunate" to which I had objected, had been inserted in the original draft of the telegram by higher authority',[81] a term which on this occasion hid the identity of Sir Eyre Crowe,[82] who had already accused Wingate of being 'deplorably weak'.)[83]

The furore aroused by Brunyate's Note on Constitutional Reform had given some immediacy to Rushdy's request for him and 'Adly to enter direct discussions with the British government. Now, when Wingate told the Prime Minister of Balfour's decision that no useful purpose would be served by a visit from Zaghlul, his note raised in Rushdy's mind the spectre of annexation. The note and Brunyate's blueprint proved the principal spurs in the decision of him and 'Adly to hand in their resignations, which were not to be accepted until 1 March. With hindsight, Balfour correctly surmised that 'unreasonable attitude of Ministers may be due in part at least by [*sic*] alarm lest proposed Constitutional Reforms submitted by Sir William Brunyate might be approved by HMG without their being given an opportunity of expressing their opinion'; he pledged that no steps would be taken without full consultation with them.[84]

On this strange matter of Rushdy's resignation following the rebuff to the nationalist leader, Lloyd commented that London's reply:

> left the field open for Zaghlul . . . Zaghlul had gained the ear of Egypt: if he himself [Rushdy] went to London, while Zaghlul remained at home, whatever he brought back would be repudiated with scorn and his influence would be entirely destroyed. He now, therefore, hardened his demands and insisted that he would not go to London unless Zaghlul went too and shared responsibility with him.[85]

On 7 December, on which day Graham was criticising him in a minute for not being able to handle Fu'ad and claiming that this was 'the root of the whole trouble',[86] Wingate wrote to Hardinge, offering his resignation for the third time:

> If it is really the view of HMG that I should not see representatives of all shades of opinion at the Residency, I feel that I ought not to be here, for my conception of how best to serve my Country in my present position, is to act as I have done hitherto – and I would like to make it quite clear that should HMG feel that I have not handled matters in a suitable manner – and in consonance with their policy and wishes – I hope that no personal consideration will interfere with

their ideas that a change of High Commissioner may be desirable ... I
beg you will understand the personal equation as regards myself is
non-existent ... I am entirely at your disposal should it be thought
that a change is desirable in the interests of our Country.[87]

On 12 December, a Foreign Office telegram announced that the
government would receive Rushdy and 'Adly in about March, and the
following day Graham repeated Balfour's point that Wingate should come
to London at the same time. Wingate said that this amounted to being
'summoned by you'.[88]

If in his undoubted anguish at the way things were going, and at the
sudden prospect of losing a job he prized, Wingate did not see this as his
death-sentence, his psychological condition cannot have been helped by
the next exchange with London. On 18 December, he reported that the
Sultan had endorsed the resignation of his ministers and had declined to
tell the nationalist leaders – as suggested in a Foreign Office telegram of
the 11th – that 'by their present agitation, they are rendering a real dis-
service to Egypt'. (Since Balfour thought them lightweight, it is not clear
why he considered that the Sultan should reprimand them, unless the
intention was that Wingate should thereby vicariously caution himself.)
Proposing action which was suicidal in someone who was being positioned
for removal and was now considered weak, Wingate warned that the
Sultan's failure to comply 'may involve sacrifice of his own position'. On
the Foreign Office reply, of 23 December, which declared that 'the time
has probably passed at which "denunciation of Extremist movement by
the Sultan would have served a useful purpose"', he commented later to
Balfour, 'one whom I regarded as my Chief and friend':[89]

> my consternation ... may be imagined when, on pointing out to His
> Majesty's Government that the Sultan had refused to acquiesce in
> denouncing the Nationalists, and that it might end in my having to
> insist on his abdication, I received instructions that it was unnecessary
> to press the Sultan further. There can be no doubt that this weaken-
> ing on the part of the Government was at once realised by the Extrem-
> ists as well as by the Sultan, and both were not slow to take advantage
> of it.[90]

On an extract of the reply, in his *Notes on the Political Crisis in Egypt*, he
made a note in pencil: 'Letting me down in this way was fatal. R. W.'[91]
Conscientiously deepening his own grave and in one view seeking 'to co-
opt the Wafdist leadership',[92] in a response to it by return he 'urged FO to
permit the two Ministers to go to London *at once* and a few of the Extremists as well when *the whole trouble* might still be averted'.[93] Despite this,
Lloyd comments, 'It was never made plain to Whitehall that a situation
was developing so critical that only the utmost caution and forethought

could prevent disaster. Indeed, it is clear that neither the civil nor the military authorities in Egypt realised this themselves.'[94]

On 28 December, Wingate wrote Hardinge his extraordinary private letter, offering advice which, if the PUS found it distasteful, he was to pretend that he had not received. Though certainly beginning to realise that his was a lost cause, he now suggested that Rushdy and 'Adly be invited to London to discuss topics related to the collapse of the Ottoman Empire rather than 'internal reforms in Egypt'. He urged that 'more good than harm' would follow an invitation to the 'Extremists' to visit London for a 'straight talk'. Did he really expect Hardinge to strike the letter from the record rather than use it in evidence if necessary?

On 1 January 1919, in a remarkable softening of his position, Balfour told Wingate by telegram:

> if you consider mere presence here of Egyptian Ministers would have a pacifying effect in Egypt and ease the situation and if after considering danger of appearing to yield to pressure you are prepared to recommend that they should be allowed to come before March I have no objection to their arriving during the course of February ... In no case can they be permitted to go to Paris during the sessions of Peace Conference.[95]

Meanwhile, Robert Cecil told the Foreign Secretary on 4 January that he had suggested to Lloyd George that, if Wingate were to be recalled, Allenby would be a suitable successor:

> This he warmly approved ... But the Prime Minister wanted nothing done which would preclude Wingate's return to Egypt if that were decided on ... But I ought to add that everyone to whom I have spoken about W. is confident that he is not up to the job.[96]

On 16 January, Wingate informed the Foreign Office of a bargain he had struck which reflected his belief that by now 'the atmosphere was too highly charged for Rushdy to accept a invitation without being accompanied by Zaghlul'.[97] He reported that the Sultan had agreed in Cabinet to the resumption of their duties by Rushdy and 'Adly and that the two were prepared to travel to London after him on condition that Zaghlul and some of his colleagues – though not members of the official delegation – were permitted passports. On his arrival there, Wingate would make the case – as if he had not already made it *ad nauseam* and irreparably harmed himself in the process – for the Wafd to come to London too, on or about 10 February. Overlooking the fact that he was supposed to be accompanying the resigned Prime Minister and Minister of Education and that, if they did not travel, his own journey would in theory be without purpose, he added that no decision was necessary on this before his own arrival in

London.[98] In a telegram of the same date, he told the Foreign Office that the position of the ministers 'would be hopeless unless Saad Zagloul were shown to be incapable of redeeming his promises'. Expressing a view which some have felt unjustified, 'To attain this end it was', he continued, 'in their opinion essential for him and his associates to leave Egypt and return empty-handed.'[99]

Graham was now acting for Hardinge, who had gone off to his unhappy assignment at the Peace Conference which was inaugurated on 18 January 1919. Wingate's hindsight reading of the resultant situation, in his NOTES ON THE MAIN POINTS, was that:

> his supporter Ld H. had gone to Paris with A.J.B. – R.G. was in a position of great power in Ld H's place and Ld C. had naturally to defer to R.G.'s local knowledge of Egypt. His 'head of the chancery M.H. was R.G.'s great friend – so was B.S. – R.W.'s Councillor M.C. was difficile, there had been differences between them with regard to W.B. and the Sultan' – 'R.G. opened his campaign against R.W. by getting first B.S. to London and later M.H. He also enlisted on his side T.L. ...'[100] [Hardinge, Balfour, Graham, Robert Cecil, Mervyn Herbert, Burnett Stuart, Wingate, Cheetham, Brunyate and T. Loyd].

It is interesting to note Wingate's inclusion of Hardinge among those he believed to be his supporters and his resentment that others had got to London ahead of him.

Graham opened his account on 19 January by at last responding to Wingate's resignation letter, six weeks after he had written it, in one which was marked by staggering hypocrisy and must have taken some time to reach its addressee:

> I think it must have been the phrase 'which was unfortunate' to which you refer. This was added by the higher authorities to my draft, but I am sure it did not imply any intention of curtailing your freedom of action in receiving all and sundry of the natives who seek interviews with you. I entirely agree with you that it is essential for the High Commissioner to give audiences and to keep the Residency doors wide open. I think that what struck the authorities here as somewhat unaccountable was the fact that Saad Zaghloul and his friends should have (at least so it appears) concerted their action with the Sultan and probably Ruchdi Pasha if not others of the Ministers and then have come to see you as a Deputation without your having any previous knowledge of the objects and aims of their visit. There seems some faulty staff work here. We also gather that the agitators made great capital out of having been received by you and obtained signature to their petition in the Provinces on the ground that their movement had the approval of the Residency. I feel sure that had you been

previously warned as to the nature of their visit and the absurd proposals they meant to put forward you would have been chary of receiving them as a deputation.

A more sensible and balanced view of Zaghlul and his Wafd was
expressed later by Clayton, who in Bell's account said:

> It would be impossible to maintain that they were not representative
> of the country. Sa'ad Zaghlul was Vice President of the Legislative
> Assembly which is chosen by an elected body, several others were
> members of the Assembly, and all had held high official posts of one
> kind or another.[101]

Graham ended by assuring Wingate that the government 'continue to
have every confidence in your skill and judgement and we are all looking
forward greatly to seeing you over here and discussing all the Egyptian
problems with you'.[102]

7 I can do no more than thank you
The fall

poor Wingate has been a failure – he did well in the past. Egypt was evidently too much for him . . . Le roi est mort, Vive le Roi Allenby.[1]

(Wingate)

On 21 January 1919, Wingate, his wife, Symes and Graham's ally Mervyn Herbert left Egypt from Port Sa'id. Although in that month Osmond Walrond[2] told Milner, whose private secretary he had been in South Africa, that there were 'so many cooks circling round a very weak and tired man',[3] Hardinge was misleading his readers when, in his memoirs, he claimed that Wingate 'had been suffering from ill health' and was going on sick leave.[4] While he was on the high seas, Graham continued to work against him, on 22 January telling Hardinge that he considered Wingate's 'private interviews with the nationalists' to have been extremely 'irregular'.[5] Hardinge passed this criticism on to Balfour and told him that he endorsed it himself.[6]

From 29 January to 2 February, Wingate stopped in Paris, where the Peace Conference was in full swing. He saw Robert Cecil, Hardinge and Crowe and had lunch with both Lloyd George and Balfour, bringing away from the latter the self-deluding impression that the Foreign Secretary was 'in general agreement' with his policy. Balfour told him to go into the details with Curzon, Lord Privy Seal and Acting Foreign Secretary, in London, where he arrived on 3 February. (Bell noted Clayton's comment that 'his going was looked upon by all Egypt as a sure sign that independence was near',[7] but when Zaghlul learned that he was not appropriately met on reaching Britain – perhaps partly because so many people of note were in Paris – he drew the conclusion that this was another demonstration of the British government's lack of interest in his country.)[8] On the same day, Cheetham, Acting High Commissioner once more, reported that Rushdy and 'Adly had – on the strength of the Wingate bargain of 16 January and without retracting their resignations – resumed their duties.

On 4 February Curzon declined to see Wingate, who had to make do with frequent meetings with Graham, Acting PUS, and other officials for almost a fortnight. Graham stressed that Zaghlul would not be welcome in

London[9] and committed to paper the ludicrous remark that 'American Military Authority imagine Egypt is "seething" when in reality she is only "teething".'[10] On 6 February, a Cheetham telegram noted the anxiety of Rushdy and 'Adly to depart. Next day, Zaghlul – speaking for a party the second article of whose constitution declared that it aimed 'to seek the complete independence of Egypt by all legal and peaceful means, that is by negotiation with Britain'[11] – gatecrashed a public lecture to call for the abolition of the Protectorate. On 10 February, Wingate noted that Rushdy and 'Adly ought to have started out;[12] the continuing silence from London about them suggested in Cairo that his plans were not finding support in the Foreign Office.[13]

He was finally received by Curzon on 17 February. He admitted that, in an unpleasant interview,[14] 'it was . . . clear to me from the outset that I had failed to carry conviction'.[15] He tried to persuade Curzon to send Cheetham a telegram he had drafted, which read:

> I shall be glad to see Rushdi and Adly Pasha in London and to hear their views on Egyptian questions as soon as it is convenient for them to come to England [*sic*]. Sir R. Wingate has explained their anxiety that members of the Extremist Party would not now be prevented from leaving Egypt. The extravagant opinions apparently held by this party preclude any possibility of its members being received here officially or being regarded as an Egyptian delegation but I have no objection to your exercising discretion in granting permits to leave Egypt to such Egyptian politicians as may apply as private individuals for same.

Wingate argued that his text would at once enable Rushdy and 'Adly to withdraw their resignations, appease the nationalists and please the Sultan. He said that Curzon's contrary view – shared by Graham – was that it would allow the nationalists to 'hold a pistol to our head'. Although Balfour had in theory delegated responsibility for dealing with Wingate to him, Curzon felt that he should send the draft to the Foreign Secretary, while making it clear that he disagreed with its contents. On 24 February, Balfour too rejected it, which he could hardly have failed to do in view of Curzon's opposition.

On the same day, Wingate commented in his *Notes on the Political Crisis in Egypt* on a telegram which Curzon had received from Cairo:

> Sir Milne Cheetham telegraphed to the FO minimising the agitation. He described how the two Ministers had lost popularity, how the delay in reply from London had diminished their prestige, how Zaghlul Pasha and his friends had lost influence. In short, 'this agitation which they have organised is dying out or is at any rate quiescent in the country at large'.

At this point, in a bitter pencil note, he remarked:

> Clearly Sir RW's *diplomatic* staff were only too glad to have achieved his withdrawal from Egypt. The agitation had been 'quiescent' in Cairo because Sultan, Ministers and Nationalists reposed confidence in Sir RW's influence with His Majesty's Government. Few men in temporary charge would have accepted responsibility for telegram to the FO so absolutely at variance with the considered reports of his chief. Was the Acting High Commissioner persuaded that such a telegram was sure of welcome? . . . It looks as though both Sir Milne Cheetham and the FO regarded the absence of Sir RW as a quieting factor.[16]

On 26 February, Curzon sent Cheetham a telegram in substitution for Wingate's draft of the 17th. It said that the nationalists:

> with the possible exception of Abdel Aziz Bey Fahmy, appear to be men of doubtful standing and antecedents . . . to facilitate their journey to England [*sic*] by relaxing the existing restrictions on travelling, or to go further by receiving them at the For. Office if they came, would imply a measure of countenance and recognition to which they are certainly not entitled, and of which, if conceded, they would be likely to make the same illegitimate use that they did of their original reception at the Residency.

It renewed the invitation to Rushdy and 'Adly, 'or to any Minister or Ministers deputed by His Highness and the Council of Ministers', and promised 'full and sympathetic consideration . . . to any representations or proposals they may desire to submit, in regard to the future relations between Egypt and the protecting Power'.[17]

Cromer had adopted a favourable opinion of Zaghlul, McMahon had championed him and the Foreign Office had withdrawn its objections to him on 20 December. It is surprising therefore that Curzon should have again been so insistent that he was 'of doubtful standing and antecedents'. It is interesting to note the implication that it was the mileage the nationalists allegedly got out of their appointment with Wingate, not his receiving them, which had offended.

Cheetham delivered the telegram to Rushdy on 1 March and, as a result – one which Wingate's original would have been unlikely to bring about – the whole of his administration joined him and 'Adly in vacating their offices the same day, with the complete approval of the Sultan. The Acting High Commissioner, who in Hardinge's opinion 'could not be described as a strong man',[18] was to be all at sea as events unfolded.[19] (Frank Balfour[20] reported about him that 'Billy C. and Co were quite useless which I confess I am not astonished to hear as he was never exactly a man of iron.')[21] He was severely handicapped, in trying to form a new government, by the non-co-operation of Zaghlul and his allies, who dared the Sultan to supersede them: 'How can it have escaped Your Highness's counsellors that the terms of Rushdi Pasha's resignation do not allow any honourable and patriotic Egyptian to take his place?'[22] When, on 6 March, they ignored a warning from the GOC, General Watson, Cheetham telegraphed to recommend their deportation. Provoking the fair comment about the Residency from Lloyd that 'It was perhaps inevitable that they should seek in this way to console themselves for their ignorance of conditions precedent'[23] and about Cheetham that he 'had correctly read the prevailing mood there [in the FO], if not in Egypt', where he 'did not have the slightest suspicion of impending trouble',[24] the Acting High Commissioner said that the movement 'has Bolshevik tendency', that the feeling behind it 'must have been growing during several years, and that an explosion at some time was inevitable'. It is remarkable that he should admit to having seen no sign of the resurgence of nationalism.

Igniting 'the spark needed for revolution',[25] Cheetham was authorised to deport Zaghlul, two future Prime Ministers (Sidqy and Muhammad Mahmud) and Hamid Pasha al Basil,[26] a prominent tribal member of the Legislative Assembly who, 'Very picturesque . . ., always wore the flowing robes and soft long-tasselled fez of his class.'[27] Martial law was proclaimed. On 8 March, as Stamfordham was hoping that Wingate would 'get an opportunity of breathing some Dunbar air before your return to Egypt',[28] they were arrested before being deported to Malta next day.[29] Zaghlul was to remain in exile for two years.

On his copy of the note in which he commented on these events,[30] Wingate wrote in pencil:

> I am convinced that the FO contention 'that revolution had long been contemplated and prepared for' is rubbish – it is true the fellahin were upset by the labour corps recruiting and the exactions necessitated by the War – but the revolution was the direct outcome of the mistaken policy of HMG – in which they were aided and abetted by the ignorant Diplomatic Staff in the Residence

whom he had had two years to lick into shape.

The uprising had been provoked by such factors as the declaration of the Protectorate, the deposition of 'Abbas Hilmy, a fall in coffee prices,[31] the supersession of Maxwell, the non-inclusion of Egypt among the countries earmarked to benefit from President Wilson's Fourteen Points[32] and perhaps by Allenby's removal of his headquarters from Cairo to Khan Yunis with the object of coming to closer grips with the Ottomans.[33] Grafftey-Smith considered that the root cause was the one singled out by Wingate – the corvée, otherwise known as 'compulsory volunteering', which at its height – under British pressure – produced 125,000 men for the labour corps: 'As thousands of breadwinners disappeared, leaving their families unprotected; as man after man returned from Palestine or Iraq maimed, or not at all; the British became an object of cursing in every village.' He believed that it also fostered 'the nationalist, anti-British sentiment . . . among the fellahin who were to be its indispensable instrument of violence'.[34]

In the reported words of Clayton:

> At the outbreak of war the old link with Turkey was broken without any consultation with Egyptian feeling . . . Egypt found herself obliged to provision our armies and provided labour corps both inside and outside the country. The Egyptian government had (without any pressure) spontaneously contributed £4000000 to war expenses. The trade of the country had suffered and prices had risen.[35]

Wingate himself contributed to the outbreak by allowing his wife to become patron of an appeal for the British Red Cross which squeezed even further villagers[36] who were already forced to supply 'cereals, forage and beasts of burden' for the war.[37]

Proving that Zaghlul, now 'father of the people and enemy of the sultan',[38] *did* represent it, within days Egypt burst into flames with the slogan 'Religion for God and the Homeland for All'[39] as 'the ground was prepared for Zaghlul to succeed where Arabi failed'[40] 37 years before. Serious disturbances – involving all sorts and conditions of men and women, meeting together in mosques, churches and synagogues[41] – began on 10 March. Demonstrations turned into rioting and looting; schoolchildren, the turbulent students of Al Azhar and civil servants joined in; government offices and law courts in particular were attacked (the offices of Faris Nimr's pro-British *Al Muqattam* newspaper were ransacked); and a general strike gripped Cairo. Telegraph wires were cut,[42] 200 stretches of railway line were wrecked and more than sixty stations were damaged or destroyed.[43] The countryside rose, and Lower Egypt came to a standstill as disorder swept through. There were riots in many places, including Damanhur, Zagazig, Mansurah and Tantah. In the last, 'the most fanatical town in Egypt',[44] government property was destroyed, railway lines were pulled up and 14 rioters were shot and killed and 50 wounded. In Zagazig and Minyah, 'provisional governments' were set up, and Soviets arose in some villages. In mid-March, as Cheetham 'completely lost his nerve',[45] the uprising reached Upper Egypt, where a British civilian, and seven soldiers and a prison inspector travelling by train, were killed by a mob three days later.[46] Hatred for the British led to ugly atrocities, such as the mutilation and other physical abuse of dead bodies, not least by women who temporarily broke out of their veils and rose to support the revolt of their male colleagues. The security forces no doubt gave a good account of themselves. Clayton told Bell that 'Nothing like it had been seen in Egypt, no Englishman [*sic*] was safe in the streets.'[47]

Meanwhile, on 9 March, Wingate had suggested in a note to Curzon that 'an early announcement of the despatch of a Commission to enquire into the whole situation might rally Anglo–phil[*sic*] natives to our side'.[48] The following day, he pathetically told Hardinge, 'As soon as the Cairo situation clears up (I hope this may be in the course of a few days) I am going to ask the FO if I may go to Scotland for a short rest – this should set one up for the summer. Presumably the conversations in London with the Egyptian Ministers will not now take place.'[49]

On 15 March, with the situation completely out of control, Cheetham – in a humiliating turnround – asked for the Wafd to be allowed into Britain. The following day, from their headquarters in St Mark's Cathedral,[50] the leaders of the women's movement in Egypt, Zaghlul's wife Safiyyah,[51] Sha'rawy's wife, Huda and Muna Fahmy Wissa, unveiled, led an unprecedented demonstration in Cairo, demanding independence. At the same time, at a meeting with Watson and Clayton, a nationalist group (Fahmy, Lutfi as Sayyid and Muhammad 'Aly 'Ulwy Bey) was pressured into trying to exert a restraining influence and agreed to issue an appeal for the strikes to cease.[52]

As Curzon was telling Balfour that the Acting High Commissioner was not in control of events,[53] and as news of his deputy's move into the Residency reached Wingate,[54] a telegram from Curzon on 17 March ordered Cheetham to give no ground to the Wafd and bring the rioting to an end. It was followed the next day by another 'quite inexplicable'[55] lurch when Balfour in Paris sent a telegram to 'FO Sub-committee' which, in response to the violence, belatedly gave Wingate what he had asked for at the very start:

> The restoration of order and formation of a competent Government must be immediately and unconditionally carried through. But in the meantime there need be no concealment of our readiness, after this has been satisfactorily accomplished, to discuss in London (?alleged) grievances with Egyptian Ministers. If they think their task would be better performed if they were accompanied or immediately followed by persons qualified to represent the Nationalist case even in its extreme form, I can see no objection.

Included among Wingate's *Notes*[56] is a 'paraphrase' of this document, which betrayed the influence of his draft telegram which Curzon and Balfour had rejected on 17 February. By its reversal of Curzon's policy, it showed that the initiative had passed to Zaghlul.[57] Wingate has written on it in pencil, 'This telegram was not seen by me till *some months* after it had been received', but in fact he was not left in the dark, despite the claim of his son to the contrary, for long.[58] In a letter from Paris the following day, Hardinge told him that he and Balfour had agreed that, once Egypt was back to normal, ministers should visit Britain to discuss the situation: 'and if those Ministers consider it desirable that others from Egypt, whether extremists or otherwise, should be summoned to the Council in London, His Majesty's Government would consider the propriety of doing so'. In a disclosure which need not have disturbed Wingate, he added that Allenby, the military supremo of the area which included Egypt, 'should arrive here to-day or tomorrow, and I feel sure that Mr. Balfour will consult him upon the situation'.[59]

On 18 March, Graham called Wingate urgently to London from Dunbar, where he had gone to his home six days before. Late on the 19th, Balfour – adopting the coyness which characterised his dealings with his old golfing partner whenever he was within physical reach – sent him a telegram, which will have crystallised any suspicions Hardinge had aroused, to tell him that Allenby was going to Cairo:

> Prime Minister and I think in addition to his military rank he ought to be given complete civil authority and he will be therefore appointed Special High Commissioner with supreme Civil and Military control. This makes no technical change in your position.[60]

Wingate had, of course, in vain asked for the two roles to be combined in himself and was to claim to Curzon that 'my qualifications to administer in this dual capacity are certainly equal to those of Sir Edmund, now Lord Allenby'.[61] It must have been galling to him, also a general, that Allenby's untried political and administrative skills should have been considered superior to his own.

On the 20th he was immediately received by Curzon. In the light of the continuing turmoil in Egypt, Wingate retracted his view that the nationalists should be received in Britain. He repeated his recommendation of 4 September 1917 and 9 March that a royal commission be sent out to Egypt and argued that he should return at once to Cairo. Curzon, however, claimed that the pace of events made the continuing availability of his advice in London essential.

Wingate must have begun by now to realise that his days were numbered: a letter of 12 March from Symes told him that Cairo gossip had it that he was to be replaced.[62] Nonetheless, Balfour told Curzon on 20 March that Allenby's posting 'would not of itself displace Wingate who would for the present retain the post of high commissioner. It is probable that he will not return, though an immediate decision on this point is not necessary.'[63]

On 21 March, in *Rough Notes by Sir R. Wingate on the Situation in Egypt* which he wrote for the Foreign Office to confirm what he had said to Curzon the previous day, Wingate – perhaps reverting to his true, intelligence *métier* – described what was happening in Egypt as:

> little short of a revolution and must be suppressed with a strong hand at once. (a) 10,000 Troops should be sent to Egypt from Palestine and

Syria. (b) As much of the Mediterranean Fleet as possible should be sent to Alexandria at once and Blue-jackets and Marines landed in relief of such troops as can be spared for despatch to the most disturbed centres in the Provinces. (c) Shipping should be detailed to bring the 26th Division from the Dobrudja ... (Allenby's) demands for whatever Military, Naval or Aerial assistance he may require should be met at once.

He again advocated his own return, which:

might have a tranquillising effect, though the situation is so much out of hand that I may be exaggerating whatever personal influence I might have. In any case the situation now calls for immediate repressive measures and I much doubt the efficacy of giving way to the extremists by allowing them to come to England [*sic*] at present: the psychological moment when such permission might have been efficacious has passed. They should be told that 'until law and order has been restored it is useless for them to appeal for a hearing'.[64]

In a manuscript letter of 26 March, following up his telegram, Balfour told Wingate that though Allenby's 'appointment as Special High Commissioner leaves the position of the existing High Commissioner untouched', there was no doubt that:

two great officials cannot exercise their functions simultaneously; they cannot both govern Egypt at the same time.[65] So long therefore as General Allenby is dealing with the existing crisis your services will hardly be required ... How long this exceptional period will continue, and what shape the future Government of Egypt will take neither I nor any other man can say with confidence.

He concluded, ominously if anachronistically:

In the meantime I can do no more than thank you for the great services which you have performed in the Soudan and Egypt, and for the administrative skill which has done so much for the well-being of their inhabitants.[66]

The '1919 Revolution'[67] was extinguished by the end of March, except in Upper Egypt, where it continued until the second half of April. Around a thousand Egyptians, 36 British and Indian soldiers and four British civilians died; 47 Egyptians were executed,[68] 34 for the Upper Egypt train attack.[69]

On 31 March, ignoring advice offered him by Wingate in a letter of 23 March,[70] Allenby informed the British government that he proposed to give 'all respectable Egyptians, whatever their views, the freedom to travel'.[71] At about the same time he told Wingate, 'I wish this had been done when you first advocated it, we are some month too late … I wish your advice had been taken.'[72] In contrast, also on 31 March, Wingate contacted Curzon urgently and told him – 'very forcibly' – that 'It would be a very grave mistake to give in to the Extremists *after* they had been guilty of the grossest acts of lawlessness and bloodshed.' Curzon informed Balfour in Paris that, like him, Wingate did not look with favour on the initiative Allenby had recommended.[73]

On 3 April, Wingate wrote in despair to Hardinge about his successor's attitude to the nationalists. 'It means', he said, 'immediate calm and the eventual loss of Egypt … I do not believe that Allenby, splendid soldier and administrator as he is, knows anything of Egyptian politics.'[74] The same day, Curzon, Wingate and Graham called on Bonar Law to argue their case. It is uncertain precisely what occurred,[75] but the Acting Prime Minister told Lloyd George that he had formed a 'poor impression' of Wingate: 'I would have no faith whatever in his judgement. On the face of it I should be inclined to agree with Allenby.'[76] Wingate claimed that Curzon had 'supported my policy up to the point of *threatening* to resign but withdrew on BL representing the Cabinet aspect',[77] their host's insistence on which caused the colour to drain from Curzon's cheeks.[78] Since Curzon and Wingate were of a mind on the point at issue, the implication must be that Bonar Law was unimpressed by Curzon's advocacy also.

After the meeting, Curzon wrote to Balfour, asking him to reconsider and enclosing a memorandum summarising Wingate's views:

> To give way *immediately*, as is now suggested, would be fraught with the gravest dangers. Our real power and authority will have practically gone, and we shall be at the mercy of agitators any time they care to repeat the methods by which they will say they have obtained their ends in the present crisis.[79]

He added that Wingate was 'probably not the right man to return as High Commissioner to Egypt'. For his part, Wingate noted that Allenby's 31 March recommendation 'tallied with Sir RW's original advice, much had happened since HMG had rejected it … but HMG considered that, having specially despatched General Allenby to restore order, it was essential that he should be trusted and his advice accepted'. He added, bitterly, 'Had that principle been observed towards Sir RW Egypt would have been piloted through without bloodshed.'[80]

On 13 April, Curzon told Wingate in a private letter that he did not agree with Balfour:

> I am personally *entirely* opposed to receiving the Nationalist Deputation from Egypt. I regard them as responsible for the troubles occur-

ring the past three weeks and would have no truck with them. What Mr Balfour may wish to do, I have no idea. He, and not I, is responsible for bringing them over, and if he desires to see them the responsibility will be his.[81]

On 2 June, Wingate had a meeting with Graham. The time of both was running out, since the following month Robert Cecil posted the AUS overseas.[82] Next day, Wingate wrote to Curzon: 'I gathered ... that there are certain criticisms of my conduct of affairs in Egypt of which hitherto I have not been fully informed by the responsible authorities, but which have clearly influenced the judgement of His Majesty's government.' He said that, 'in my position as High Commissioner, I have every right to be informed immediately of such criticisms in detail and given every opportunity of either refuting them, or admitting their justice'. He asked to be told who had said what and added:

> should any reflection be cast on my personal character or official reputation, I shall have the right to demand a full and complete judicial enquiry into the whole conduct of my administration ... I have no intention whatever of resigning from this position without such judicial enquiry.[83]

In response, on 14 July, six weeks later:

> I then had a verbal *apologia* from Lord Curzon, who informed me that it was necessary that General Allenby should remain as Special High Commissioner for the Present [*sic*], and that he was authorised to offer me the Governorship of the Straits Settlements,[84]

which he declined. An important post, it was not appropriate for the occupant of one second only to the Viceroyalty of India.[85] Wingate said, 'however generous and honourable a recognition of past service, ... in the circumstances, the transfer from Egypt will appear to the public as at best a <u>solatium</u> to a worthy officer who had been a failure in Egypt.'[86]

Curzon, who had become Foreign Secretary in October, then attempted to secure for him a government directorship on the Suez Canal Board, but the seat went to one of Lloyd George's private secretaries. Another disappointment followed. On 23 July, 'It was not thought advisable to grant my request for a judicial enquiry, but I was given an assurance that I should be protected from public criticism if my personal reputation was questioned.'[87]

Wingate's fate had become a matter of lively speculation and the possibility of his removal was deplored. Frank Balfour wrote to Capt. Ulrich Alexander, Wingate's ADC:

What about the little man? Is there any chance of his coming back. The on dit in Cairo was that he had been offered to return in September and to be given a proper official send off to crown his work of thirty years and that he had refused it. I don't know how its [*sic*] regarded at home and whether he is blamed for it all. If he is I think it is damned unfair and I suppose due to the hostility of the FO. Anyway the little man did foresee what was coming and I believe if they had followed his advice the whole thing might have been averted. When Bert [Clayton] had an interview with the Sultan not long ago HH said to him, 'Ah Sir Reginald was right from the beginning', meaning of course about letting Zaghloul and Co go to the conference . . . I think it is damned unfair to blame the little man for the crass incompetence of the Egyptian official and incidentally the FO.[88]

Alan Dawnay, who had been prominent in the Arab Revolt, wrote to Wingate, 'It must be truly *heart-breaking* to see the whole of your three years' [*sic*] work undone by the perverse imbecility of the clay gods at the Foreign Office.'[89] Herbert (now Brigadier-General) said, 'I kept on expecting you back any day, I wonder when you *really* are.' He concluded, 'You were right, the Turf Club (as always) wrong, Zaghlool & Co shd. have been allowed to go originally, if they had, there wd. in all likelihood have been none of this trouble.'[90] On 14 August, Sir Alexander Baird wondered 'whether the Authorities at home have apologised to you for not having followed your advice about the country? They must feel that they made a mistake which it costs much to put right'; six months later, he said, 'we are in the mess because your advice was not taken'.[91] In two letters in September, Maxwell wrote, 'You appear to have been treated as badly as your predecessor MacMahon [*sic*] was . . . Our great officials certainly have treated you with scant courtesy but this seems their way.'[92] Stamfordham commiserated from Balmoral:

> no impartial opinion can deny that you have been very badly treated. Possibly some explanation or partial justification may be found in the sort of dual government at the Foreign Office. But the fact of Curzon's never seeing you for a fortnight after your arrival in London will be hard to explain if you publish your story: as to the utter volte-face about allowing the Ministers and nationalists to come to Europe, I really don't see how the Govt. will excuse themselves.[93]

From within Wingate's former official circle, Hayter wrote, 'No one ever had a better or kinder chief than you have been to me, both in the Sudan and in Egypt.'[94] Garstin declared:

> I think you have been disgracefully treated and with the grossest ingratitude both by the Government and the nation. To replace you

in an appointment that you never sought and which you so ably filled, without a word of thanks, seems to me to be the limit even for these days of scurvy treatment of Public Servants. No one has done more for England [*sic*][95] . . . It makes me *sick* . . . you have been treated with the greatest ingratitude. You know that all your friends are very angry about this matter . . . your friends are all very indignant.[96]

Sadly, there is no letter of outrage or condolence from Clayton, who gave Wingate faithful support and encouragement over nearly two decades but whom at the end the ousted High Commissioner included in the list of those who had contributed to his downfall.

Balfour tried to lay the blame on Curzon for what was being done to Wingate.[97] He had admitted to the Lord Privy Seal:

> It is not an easy situation to handle. Wingate is a good fellow, and has been a very valuable and distinguished public servant. He gave specific advice on a difficult problem, warning us that if his advice was not followed trouble would ensue. Thereupon we practically tell him that he is not the man most competent to deal with the situation thus created, and that somebody else must be put in his place! This, I take it, is the skeleton of the story, and it is not one very easy to clothe in attractive flesh and blood.[98]

Replying on 30 September to a letter from the Foreign Secretary of the 22nd,[99] Wingate said:

> I note what you say as regards your having had nothing to do with the Administration of the Foreign Office – as distinct from the work of the Peace Conference – since the beginning of the present year . . . I was, however, informed by Lord Curzon that the decision was made in Paris when my advice [of 17 February] as to dealing with the Egyptian situation was turned down. Furthermore, in view of the telegram which I received from you on the 21st March, of which I enclose a copy [it announced Allenby's posting to Cairo] I think I had reason for concluding that Foreign Office affairs were still – to some extent – in your hands. I also enclose copies of letters, dated 11th and 13th April, which passed between Lord Curzon and myself, dealing with the visit of the Nationalists to Europe, which go to show that many of the decisions were taken in Paris and not in London.

He claimed that Allenby's new policy was in fact his own original one – one he now of course opposed because the nationalists would attribute its reinstatement to the success of their policy of violence – and that the government had adopted it, without diluting their determination to dispense with his services even before Allenby reached Paris on 19 March:

when it is shewn that if my original advice had been taken probably
no disturbance would have occurred . . . to insinuate that Government
was placed in a difficult position at the outset by my original reception
of the nationalists at the Residency, and by my not turning them down
more strongly, is altogether unjust . . . should His Majesty's Government decide to remove me from the post of High Commissioner for
Egypt, I shall respectfully ask to be furnished with an official statement of the reasons, and if these reasons are in my opinion insufficient, I shall . . . feel it incumbent on me to appeal for a public verdict,
by asking for the complete documentary evidence to be laid before
parliament, so that the truth may be known and my action be judged
accordingly.[100]

It was not until 2 October that Curzon broke the news to Wingate, who
must have been expecting it for a long time, that he was to be perman-
ently replaced on the 15th. His Majesty's Government, he said:

are confident, from your well known loyal and patriotic character,
that you will appreciate to the full the motives which have induced
them to arrive at this decision, which, it is needless to add, involves no
reflection whatever upon yourself or your services in the past.

He also suggested that Wingate had no more than the goverment seen the
crisis in Egypt approaching.[101] Lloyd considered that thus was Wingate 'so
unjustly and discourteously superseded';[102] Bowman voiced the widespread view that 'His . . . recall reflected not upon him but upon the
Government that ordered it. It was an act unjustified by the circumstances
and unworthy of the Cabinet of the day.'[103] Wingate replied twice to
Curzon. Unofficially, on 9 October, he told him that he did not consider
that 'the reasons given in your official letter for my treatment are, in any
sense, a justification for the manner in which I . . . have been removed
from my post. I intend therefore to press for a public verdict.'[104] Ten days
later, responding officially, he objected to the slur in Curzon's letter on
his alleged lack of foreknowledge of the imminence of the revolution. He
pointed to the fact that he had repeatedly warned the government of 'the
recrudescence of nationalism in Egypt and the probability of a determined effort by the nationalist Party to obtain their demands on the cessation of hostilities' and of the effect the Anglo-French [*sic*] declaration
would have on 'Egyptians holding nationalist sentiments'. He pointed out
that he had 'received no public recognition from HMG throughout the
War' except the award of a GBE, 'this decoration being considerably lower
in rank to others I already possessed'.[105]

Wingate, like Wilson in Iraq, showed particular resentment about
Foreign Office treatment of him – 'His language about this conscientious
and hard-working branch of Her Majesty's Civil Service was unprintable'[106]

– and about Allenby. Writing in bleak bitterness to Milner, he called his successor 'the great conqueror and administrator on whom we pin our faith to regenerate and give us back the Egypt which Wingate all but lost for us'.[107] He told Grenfell that Allenby, with whom he had always enjoyed cordial relations, 'was guided by me in the whole of his Palestine and Syria policy ... [H]e saw the chance ... of stepping into my shoes and then ruthlessly kicked down the ladder by which he had climbed to eminence'.[108]

On 18 November, Wingate completed his *Notes on the Political Crisis in Egypt*, consisting of 'The Removal of Sir Reginald Wingate from Egypt' and six appendices. On 6 July 1920, he was made a Baronet. He had been encouraged to seek 'a distinguished mark of Honour' by, among others, Craik,[109] and according to one authority Lloyd George had upheld a Curzon recommendation of a Peerage for him, conditional on him not broaching the subject of his treatment in the House of Lords.[110] He told his cousin, Sir Andrew 'Dan' Wingate, an Indian civil servant for 35 years, how the recommendation of a Peerage had been countermanded by Curzon who 'with his own hand crossed out Peerage & substituted a Baronetcy. I have this on the best authority.' He attributed the downgrading 'to the fact that from the moment he made his decision at the memorable interview he and I had with Bonar Law ... he had no other alternative than to scapegoat me'. The revision, which ensured that '[h]is services to the British Empire ... have never been adequately recognised',[111] of course effectively ruled out any possibility of Wingate speaking out in the Lords.[112]

For a long time he was undecided what, if anything, to do in an attempt to vindicate himself and hit back at those who had brought his career to its sudden end without giving him any convincing justification for doing so. Hardinge's only contribution to his decision, contrasting with the action he himself had taken when criticised by the Mesopotamia Commission, was a cool letter in which he said, 'I do not think that you will gain anything by making public your side of the question.'[113] Milner, too, advised him not to make a public outcry because, if he did not, further government employment might come his way. None did and, when Milner married Violet Cecil, Wingate was encouraged in the belief that it had been the 'close Cecil connections' of 'my old friend Sir Frederick Milner'[114] which had led him to give him misleading counsel.[115] On 31 March 1921 he saw a draft copy of the Milner Report, which included mild adverse references to him. He protested to Curzon, who did not reply until 4 July. When Wingate wrote again on 12 July, requesting him to ask Milner to explain why his Report he said that he had not put forward his views on nationalism with sufficient insistence, Curzon did not answer.[116] It was sad that Wingate did not feel able to tackle Milner directly. He heard later that the critical comments on him in the Report had been inserted at the suggestion of the mission leader himself in order to give the government 'some excuse for their action'.[117]

8 Unequipped personally
The verdict

it is clear from the sympathetic letters I receive from innumerable friends and well-wishers, that they (like myself) are at a complete loss to understand the reasons for my treatment.[1]

(Wingate)

Wingate's downfall, like McMahon's, was occasioned by a combination of factors. There were both genuine and invented reasons for his failure. The former were not brought out into the open but had a cumulative effect, leading to the invocation of the latter as the excuses for his removal. Wingate himself, in voluminous efforts to justify himself and reclaim his job which flouted the maxim 'never complain, never explain', overlooked the fact that – whatever the rights and wrongs and whatever your defence – if they want to get rid of you, they will. He had not the slightest suspicion that the real reasons were those which made his disapproved dealings with Egyptian nationalism the excuse for his ouster, almost as though he had been promoted to be High Commissioner in Egypt purely with that purpose in mind. When the moment came, he found that the royal connections he had cultivated from remarkably early in his career and the contacts he had nurtured in high places – and which led him to think himself impregnable – were of absolutely no practical use to him, except perhaps over the question of his shocking pension situation.[2] No one spoke up for him openly.

Wingate was given little in the way of reasons for his dismissal and had to engage in guesswork – guesswork into which he put remarkably little focused effort and which left him short of the mark and believing that the ostensible reasons were the only ones. In his *Notes on the Political Crisis in Egypt, 1918–19–20*,[3] he says merely:

The justification of the removal of Sir R. Wingate from Egypt appears to rest on the following charges:

a   That Sir R. Wingate did not warn the Foreign Office of the coming agitation and that he himself was taken by surprise.

b   That his reception of the Nationalists in November 1918 was 'unfortunate' and stimulated the agitation.

c   That consequently he is so far responsible for what happened as to warrant his removal.

It is certainly worth examining these charges, and allied ones, in order to see what kind of case the Foreign Office, and Graham in particular, made out against Wingate and to consider whether or not the Foreign Office, Balfour and Curzon were right to dismiss him on the pretext of allowing Sa'ad Zaghlul, 'Abd al 'Aziz Fahmy and 'Ali Pasha Sha'rawy to call at the Residency on 13 November 1918 – for there can be no doubt that, had that call not taken place, Wingate might well have been able to see out his term. As it was, many chickens seized the opportunity to come home to roost in order to reinforce the case against him.

The overt accusations against him were eight in number. The first, that he did not warn the Foreign Office about the nationalist threat, is easily disposed of. Numerous examples of his repeated attempts to express his fears have been given above. He seems eminently justified in his claim to Balfour that:

> there was ample evidence in the Foreign Office that, from the moment I first assumed office as High Commissioner (1.1.17.) up to the Ministerial crisis in November 1918, I had persistently warned the Foreign Office Authorities of the recrudescence of Nationalists ... That, in the face of such evidence [he gives details], ... the Foreign Office Authorities should assert that they had not been warned, and infer that had they been warned they would have taken such action as would have averted the crisis, are contentions which cannot justly be maintained.[4]

Most commentators agree, having no doubt that Wingate sounded the alarm more than adequately but that the government nonetheless did not take his warnings seriously or perhaps did not collate them adequately. The prime examples of this were Graham's December 1917 minute, scorning Wingate's fears about Rushdy's 'programme', and his response to Wingate's 31 August 1918 despatch, which pointed up their contrasting 1914 and 1919 modes of thinking.[5]

Second, in a minute on 25 November 1918 which was not copied to Wingate, Graham charged him with neglecting his relations with the Sultan. While the demands of unexpected, competing preoccupations rendered their results disappointing to both him and Husayn Kamil, Wingate undoubtedly found Fu'ad more difficult to work with. It is strange that, when the latter received Montagu, Wingate does not appear to have been present throughout their discussion.

Third, in the same minute, Graham charged him with being 'weak' on

13 November. Wingate did not know that this epithet had been used of him and thus did not challenge its validity. Lloyd, however, was right to criticise him for accepting the claim of the delegation to speak for Egypt – 'an impossible demand' which pulled the rug from under Rushdy and his government[6] – and in general for a feeble performance:

> he made no reference to the constitutional position, did not point out that the Council of Ministers was the accredited representatives of Egypt and that questions of Egypt's foreign relations could only be discussed with them. He appears, in fact, hardly to have realised the full implications of this visit.[7]

Further, Wingate told Zaghlul and his party – in response to their declared intention to communicate their views direct to the British authorities at home – that 'in any case they were free agents'. They were, of course, nothing of the sort and were unable to come and go as they pleased. Fu'ad could deal without intermediary with the Foreign Office and plan to visit Britain to confer at the highest level without fear of obstruction; at a meeting on 12 October, he 'remarked that as Wingate did not understand him, he was looking forward to going to London after the war in order to discuss Egyptian problems directly with the officials in the Foreign Office'.[8] The same was not the case with Zaghlul and his colleagues. Wingate himself noted later that 'no one could leave without a permit'.[9] It was not Zaghlul whom Hardinge in London had had in mind when, on the subject of annexation, he told Wingate, 'At the end of the war it is probable that leading Egyptian Ministers and other notables will visit this country and there will then be an opportunity of finding out what their real feelings are on this and kindred subjects.'[10]

Balfour did not unveil the opinion Wingate believed he held that in receiving the nationalists his High Commissioner was reverting to obsolete Gorst policies.[11] In his 2 December telegram, fourth, he characterised Wingate's interview of Zaghlul and his colleagues as 'unfortunate'[12] – a charge which Graham nullified in his 19 January letter.[13] Ronald Wingate was right to stress his father's perfectly correct anxiety 'to know the view of Zaghlul and his party'.[14] Wingate's pressure on the Foreign Office for the veteran nationalist to be received in London was, however, certainly a mistake, since it is the basic job of an ambassador to field as many of the developments in his territory as he can, not pass them on routinely to his political masters at home. Graham did not indicate what 'which was unfortunate' *did* imply. For his part, Wingate complained to Balfour, too late, that 'to insinuate that Government was placed in a difficult position at the outset by my original reception of the nationalists at the Residency, and by my not running them down more strongly, is altogether unjust'.[15]

Fifth, Graham said, also on 19 January, that:

what struck the authorities here as somewhat unaccountable was the fact that Saad Zaghloul and his friends should have (at least so it appears) concerted their action with the Sultan and probably Ruchdi Pasha if not others of the Ministers ... without your having any previous knowledge of the objects and aims of their visit.

Elie Kedourie dismisses the first part of this accusation as a complaint with 'little substance' which 'reflects ... the prejudice which ... ministers and high officials in London entertained against Wingate'.[16] Wingate himself had preempted it when he indicated to Hardinge on 14 November that he had 'little doubt' that the interviews:

> were all intentionally meant to lead up to the one end, viz. – the representation at the Peace discussions of prominent Egyptians anxious to state their own case for either a much larger share in the Government of this country than they now have, or even complete autonomy ... I had a strong impression ... that they [Zaghlul, Fahmy and Sha'rawy] were acting with the knowledge (though not necessarily the approval) of the Sultan and his Ministers.[17]

To Hardinge six days later, before any reaction to the episode had arrived from London, he said that the call was 'evidently part of a pre-arranged plan of campaign, of which the Sultan was – at any rate to some extent – cognizant'.[18] The lack of certainty which Wingate evinced in his first letter is indeed, in an official with a background in intelligence as long as his has been, perhaps surprising on the face of it. But as High Commissioner, charged with the responsibility for far more tasks than one man could possibly oversee and swamped by the immediate consequences of the Anglo-French [*sic*] Declaration and the armistice, he was dependent on his staff for this kind of information and, on account of their in-fighting and to a lesser extent of the reshuffling which followed his irruption from Khartum, their concentration on the trends in Egyptian society and politics was not all that it should have been. Nonetheless, if anyone should have seen the crisis coming, Wingate should have. (Cheetham showed in the interregnum between him and Allenby, and especially in his telegram of 6 March, that he had been anything but an informed observer of the scene.)

Sixth, on 19 January Graham expressed his confidence that 'had you been previously warned as to the nature of their visit and the absurd proposals they meant to put forward you would have been chary of receiving them as a deputation'. In fact, Wingate's regular reporting of the hopes of the nationalists – raised to some extent by loose British talk about a new, postwar status for Egypt – indicates that there can be no doubt that he knew very well the likely nature of the 'absurd proposals' his visitors would wish to put before him on 13 November. As to receiving them 'as a deputation', is the applicability of the title was determined by views or numbers? In other words, did Rushdy and 'Adly constitute 'a deputation', but one of which Graham approved?

Seventh, in a minute on 22 January, Graham accused Wingate to Hardinge of 'irregular' conduct in holding 'private interviews with the nationalists',[19] a point which had been already dealt with when Wingate told Hardinge, in his 31 January 1917, letter, 'I am convinced that it is very desirable for the foreign and native element to be allowed to keep in touch with the Residency', a policy to which the PUS had not objected.[20] Though it was perhaps excessive of Wingate so to encourage Zaghlul that, after their 8 November meeting, he should return five days later with a 'delegation', if the Residency doors are to be kept 'wide open', how can a call on a High Commissioner be accounted 'irregular', let alone 'private'?

The eighth and last charge is the most important. It is the one most frequently levelled at Wingate, the one most uniformly voiced by his detractors and the only one of those he was aware of to which he did not respond. In his 2 December telegram, Balfour claimed that 'Extremist Leaders are exploiting fact of your having received them at Residency.'[21] In his 19 January letter, which constitutes most of the case against Wingate, Graham had said, 'We gather that the agitators made great capital out of having been received by you ... on the grounds that their movement had the approval of the Residency'; and in his 26 February telegram, Curzon described this as the Wafd making 'illegitimate use ... of their ... reception at the Residency'.[22] Since it is a central role of a British representative overseas to be in touch with all shades of local opinion, it was not only proper, but also consistent, for Wingate to be in contact with Zaghlul, who had, after all, been a constructive minister under Cromer and Gorst. (It could perhaps be argued that – following his emergence as a nationalist under Kitchener – contact with him should have been made and maintained more discreetly and at a lower level than that of High Commissioner, perhaps by Cheetham, of whom the British government approved.) The principle applied equally to a delegation. Kedourie is right to say:

> he could hardly have refused ... to receive three men as prominent in Egyptian society as Zaghlul and his two friends; it was, further, Cromer's policy, and a tradition which he bequeathed to his successors of whom Wingate was one of the worthiest, that the British representative in Egypt was accessible to all classes of men.[23]

He was certainly correct to give them audience – at least as correct as Balfour was to receive Edward Cecil officially. The exoneration is not diluted by the nationalists' exploitation of their reception, which was an uncontrollable consequence of Wingate's unexceptionable action in giving them an audience.

It remains a grave charge against Wingate – one which is never mentioned – that, despite his consistent and conscientious reporting of the likely ambitions of the nationalists, he at no point indicated that, if thwarted, violence would be the path they would choose in order to bring their demands to the attention of the British government. Nor did he suggest that the political state of the country and the influence the nationalists had on it meant that it needed but one event (the transportation of Zaghlul) for the lid of the kettle to blow off in the 1919 Revolution and prove that Wingate 'had better grasped the situation than the Foreign Office had'.[24]

Wingate's supporters maintain that events following his departure from Egypt, under both Cheetham and Allenby, vindicated his policy towards the assaults of Egyptian nationalism and demonstrated that he should not have been removed and 'allowed to bear the blame for the Government's failure to take his advice until forced to do so by bloodshed and disaster'.[25] While he has been deemed responsible for the Revolution to the extent that he did not take firmer stands against the methods used by the Army to recruit Egyptians and commandeer their goods for the war effort,[26] it could indeed on the one hand be argued that the riots would not have occurred if the Foreign Office had endorsed his recommendation for Zaghlul to be received in London – though the consequences of a failed mission would have been likely to be major. It may, on the other, be suggested that Wingate's reception of Zaghlul at the Residency led to them. It is, of course, impossible to be sure. The armistice and the Anglo-French [*sic*] Declaration, promising self-determination to Arabs who had been freed from Ottoman rule, marked the beginning of a phase free of some prewar (and wartime) restraints. Egyptian nationalism, abetted by an impatient new Sultan in Fu'ad, would therefore, whatever Wingate had done, have seen, and sought to take advantage of, emerging novel opportunities.

After his supersession, Wingate justified himself in a letter to Balfour:

> What would have happened, I ask in all respect, had I refused to see these Nationalists. I am confident the answer is that their agitation would have taken immediate practical shape, and the deliberations of the Peace Conference would have been disturbed at the outset by an explosion which my personal influence succeeded in preventing, and which broke out four months later.[27]

His claim in his *Notes* that a refusal to receive 'these men ... would certainly have precipitated the outbreak'[28] is convincing.

In his NOTES ON THE MAIN POINTS, he maintained that 'the FO. was divided into AJB & RC versus Ld H. & RG'. He also admitted that it:

> was having very varied and probably widely divergent reports on Egyptian affairs. RW followed the correct course of keeping Ld H. &

> RG in close touch with the situation ... whilst RG was also kept in touch with certain elements which were hostile to RW by MH, BS [Balfour, Robert Cecil, Hardinge, Graham, Wingate, Mervyn Herbert and Burnett Stuart].[29]

He wondered if, in the reverse direction, his lack of precise information from the Foreign Office was behind some of the Egyptian requests, like the Sultan's, to go direct to London. When he had gathered that Aden was to be added to his area of responsibility, he had had to write to Graham to say, 'I suppose in due course official instructions regarding the change will reach me ... I gather that Aden is still under India as before.'[30] An extraordinary item in the balance-sheet is certainly his vain pleas to be told the British government's policy towards Egypt. In a letter of 21 March 1917, Graham admitted, 'The higher authorities here did not take up your suggestion to adopt the opportunity of formulating changes of policy required owing to the establishment of a Protectorate. Indeed, no one here has any very clear ideas on the subject.'[31] Three days later, Wingate demonstrated that he was in the dark when he referred, in a letter to Hardinge, to the government and 'whatever policy it may eventually decide to adopt in regard to Egypt'.[32] On 25 May, he asked Graham 'to be made acquainted with the policy of Government in regard to the future of Egypt'.[33] In a telegram on 8 December, he besought the Foreign Office to let him have 'some indication from you as to our future policy of a more definite nature than I have yet received'.[34] On 28 May 1918, he wrote a letter to Graham which, *inter alia*, was:

> seeking some light as to the policy which His Majesty's Government intend to pursue after the War ... when it comes to the Sultan questioning me as to his ideas on the future administration of the country it is vitally important to me to know how far I can indicate to him what is in the mind of His Majesty's Government in this respect ... in the absence of instructions I shall of course be very careful not to commit His Majesty's Government to any definite line of action either as regards the future administration or the succession.[35]

On 25 July, Hardinge told him, 'I cannot at present enter into the large question of what our future policy in Egypt may be.'[36] On 19 October, Wingate reported to him that Fu'ad had asked 'what the policy of the Home Government towards Egypt will be'; he added, 'I am sure that when it is possible to give any sort of indication of "how the cat is going to jump", you will help me if you can, so as to enable me to shape my course.'[37] As late as 8 November, he reverted to his question of 18 months before and sought from the Foreign Office 'some indication of the views of His Majesty's Government ... regarding the future of Egypt'.[38] On 14

November, he told Hardinge 'that he had no conception of the plans and ideas of the British Government'.[39]

It could be argued that Wingate's failure to go home for briefing before replacing McMahon was in some small part responsible for his state of ignorance but the government could have insisted that he come and, if it had wished and had had a policy – which Chirol among others doubted – could very easily have kept him in the picture.

Wingate's defence of himself against the accusations by Balfour, Curzon and Graham, the overt case against him, is feeble because it was both belated and misconceived. His decision not to speak out publicly is difficult to understand. (Cyril Wilson quoted Baird to him as saying, 'If Wingate only chose to speak he has them all by the short hairs.')[40] But the charges against him are not sufficient to justify his removal as an immediate consequence of 13 November. The reasons assumed for his withdrawal are far from convincing and are not much better than excuses to mask the truth, which was that the real reasons underlay those discussed above and had a cumulative effect which was decisive. It is necessary to look to the factor which had brought him to the point where one addition to the charge-sheet would automatically result in his fall. This was that the intention of the Cecil interest, and perhaps Graham, was to unseat him by one means or another when they could. This, as Kedourie agrees,[41] was the basic cause of his downfall. The way to it was paved by antagonisms Wingate had created in the Sudan, particularly with Elward Cecil. They were exacerbated by the inadequacy of the 'extraordinary political flair', which Symes so admired,[42] to keep him out of trouble when he took Balfour on over Cecil and challenged the Foreign Office with his persistent and masochistic promotion of the demands of Zaghlul. It is a misinterpretation to claim, as Wingate's son variously does, that 'Wingate was dismissed because he could not make the politicians see the obvious'[43] and that 'it was his advocacy of the case for the Egyptian that caused his downfall'.[44]

If the reasons assumed for his removal were the wrong ones, his performance in Egypt did nothing to protect his position. Cairo seems to have seen a decline in his powers. The fresh, short-sentence writing style of his youth had gone and indecisiveness and hesitancy had crept into his work, as Stack noticed. Commenting to Clayton on a note on the future Political Status of Egypt Wingate had composed, he said:

> It is odd that with someone having 30 years experience of the country and holding the post of HMG's High Commissioner should ask anyone to write a despatch on a matter of such vital importance, indeed the biggest issue in the history of Egypt since its occupation. Anyhow the course you took was the right one, they will have your views plainly. What are Master's own views? Has he any?[45]

Another example, of many that could be adduced, was his response when Brunyate vetoed price control proposals made in 1918 by James Craig, Head of the Supplies Control Board, who forecast the following year that without them there would be an insurrection within twelve months and resigned when his warnings went unheeded. Wingate contented himself with complacently remarking that he hoped the Minister of the Interior would be ready to deal with any unrest caused by shortages.[46]

In his own summary of his achievements in Egypt, Wingate said, 'I assisted to consolidate the Protectorate, supplied the constantly growing needs of the Army in the field, recruited the various Labour Corps, and yet maintained absolute internal quiet among a population, of which the influential element was pro-Turk.'[47] His performance in the job – good enough to enable him to bring Britain in Egypt out of the war unscathed – was, indeed, not such as, by itself, to justify his dismissal. Nonetheless, the view that on balance he was 'unequipped personally' for his Cairo post[48] seems a fair one. It was cruel that his valuable achievements in other spheres, notably his masterminding of the Arab Revolt, should in the end have counted for nothing. It was crueller still that his removal should have been handled in such an underhand and disrespectful manner and that he should never have known the true cause of his fall.

Part III

Allenby, 25 March 1919–14 June 1925

Field Marshal Edmund Henry Hynman, Viscount Allenby of Megiddo (1861–1936) GCB, GCMG, GCVO, KCB, KCMG, CB

Allenby sought not to dominate his Egyptian colleagues but to engage in teamwork with them. He quickly released Zaghlul – who returned from the exile he had suffered in the Wingate–Allenby interregnum less co-operative than he had been prepared to be before it – but split the nationalist movement by bringing to Cairo the Milner Mission Wingate had proposed. He banished Zaghlul again for refusing to give up political activity hostile to the settlement he sought.

Allenby successfully pressured Lloyd George to end the Protectorate and give Egypt a sham independence, announced in the 1922 Declaration. As a consequence of it, Sultan Fu'ad received the title of King. Zaghlul, released once more, became Prime Minister and sailed close to the wind until his resignation following the assassination of Stack and an unauthorised, seven-point Allenby ultimatum. When its enforcement brought the Wafd victory in elections, Allenby required Ziwar Pasha, the new Prime Minister, to take anti-democratic steps to keep the party from power. Fu'ad, who had obtained enhanced legislative authority from the Allenby-inspired Constitutional Commission, suspended the constitution and set about ruling absolutely as Allenby's various misdemeanours culminated in his recall.

9   A man of no principles

The release and rearrest of Zaghlul

this was the actual beginning of the loss of British prestige in Egypt, and the end of a situation which had been carefully built up during Lord Cromer's wise regime ... The mischief that can be done to a country through ignorance, even with the best intentions, is incalculable.

(Hardinge)

The termination of Allenby's services – inevitable after the writing had been readily visible on the wall for many months – was contrived in a different way from that of which McMahon and Wingate were the victims. In his case, a Diplomatic Service spy with the 'cover' of being a member of his staff was set upon him without notice; he may have been preceded by a visitor whose purpose was also domestic espionage.

At Arras, in the same month as Second Gazah, Allenby was considered to have failed with his 3rd Army, but in the Levant, where he took command of the Egyptian Expeditionary Force on 29 June of the same year, 1917, he was 'massive and masterly ...', a new Samson – much too good for the Turks'.[1] Storrs, who called him 'that loyal, great-hearted chief ...', the last of the Paladins',[2] was only one of innumerable admirers. Allenby as diplomat was a different story, the Bull certainly living up to the name he had won on the battlefield. The justification for Foreign Office suspicion was rather greater in his case than in those of his successor and predecessors. He had had no training for his post and he was a ditherer. As a consequence, from his very first initiative – when he decided to release Zaghlul and his companions from the exile which Cheetham had organised for them – to his last, when he attempted to take unbalanced vengeance on Egypt for the murder of Stack, he was out of step with Whitehall. His end was inglorious. Having broken Zaghlul before working to suspend democracy in Egypt and deny him and the Wafd the opportunity of returning to power, he, in his turn, was broken by Austen Chamberlain. The matter of his replacement was, as normal, impolitely handled, and Allenby only heard that he was to have a successor when Reuter's announced his name.

Allenby travelled to Paris on 18 March 1919 in order to inform the allies about Syrian developments. On the 20th, Balfour – perhaps having rejected Hardinge's championing of Graham's claims[3] – announced the General's posting to Egypt as Special High Commissioner with full civil and military powers.[4] He set off immediately for Cairo. He had no experience as a civil administrator, a role for which, in Lloyd's view, Wingate's qualifications 'were better than those of anyone who could be suggested to succeed him'.[5]

When Allenby reached Cairo on 25 March, order had – in three days, according to Nimr,[6] despite silence from London – been largely restored in Lower Egypt. This, through action which Clayton called 'a poor advertisement of 40 years British rule in Egypt',[7] was the result of 'vigorous use of British military force by General Bulfin'.[8] This 'energetic and powerful personality', who had been 'a tower of strength' at the Marne and been seriously wounded at Ypres,[9] had deputised for Allenby when he went to the Peace Conference[10] and had hurried across from Syria; he had only taken over from Generals Watson and Morris, commanding the Cairo Brigade, on 17 March. Though Middle and Upper Egypt were still in disorder and the railway connection with the south was to remain unusable for months, on balance 'Great Britain had easily maintained effective military control over Egypt – except for a few days . . ., when the provinces as well as Cairo were out of hand.'[11].

Allenby's first move was to call a meeting of leading citizens at which he demanded a return to law and order. He promised 'to make careful inquiry into all matters which have caused discontent in the country' and said:

> I cannot believe that any of you will not assist me in every way, and I am prepared to rely on you to set to work at once with a view to calming the passions now set loose. After quiet has been restored, I feel confident that you will trust me to inquire impartially into all grievances.[12]

While the martial law authorities announced that non-peaceful demonstrations would be severely punished, a diverse group of '*ulama*' and ex-ministers (including Rushdy), as well as some nationalist leaders (Fahmy, As Sayyid and Hafiz 'Afify), responded by calling for them to cease altogether.[13]

While Allenby's naïve words had a calming effect in Egypt, in Britain they caused apprehension because they seemed out of character. They also appeared to be in conflict with policy, as the *Manchester Guardian* noted: 'General Allenby's speech the other day sketched a programme which implies a very different temper from the temper in which Mr Balfour received the studiously moderate and proper requests of the Egyptian Ministers.'[14]

The change of tack was not Allenby's unaided idea. Both earlier and now, Clayton and Bulfin – unlike Patterson[15] – had advocated concessions to Egyptian opinion;[16] Wingate had noted that Bulfin had warned that 'unless a few representatives of Egyptian notables (presumably "extremists") are allowed to proceed to London to state their case, severe repressive measures will be needed and a large garrison will be required to remain in Egypt'.[17] On the Egyptian side there was even greater pressure. The country had no government and the need to form one was a priority. The ex-ministers were willing to resume office and to work with the not quite extinct Hizb al Ummah for renewed co-operation, on condition that the exiles returned[18] and travel restrictions were lifted. Convinced of their sincerity, Allenby on 31 March issued a proclamation which announced that in his view 'the time has come when responsible Egyptians with the interest of their country at heart should submit ... a statement showing what steps they considered necessary to restore tranquillity and content'.[19] Maintaining his boiling kettle image, Symes said that Allenby 'not only refused to clamp the lid back but, some thought deliberately, threw it away as useless'.[20] The same day, he recommended by telegram the immediate release of Zaghlul from Malta and said that he proposed 'to issue passports to any respectable Egyptians who may wish to visit Europe, without reference to colour of their requirements, as is done in Palestine and Syria'. This would bring Egypt into line 'with other nations as regards liberty of movement'. He also reported to the Foreign Office that – shades of Wingate! – he had received a long memorandum from an Extremist Deputation and that, since 'I have shown I can repress agitation', he proposed to see its members.[21]

Allenby's telegram was received at the Foreign Office with alarm and astonishment. Sent to call Egypt to order, it made him appear more 'soft' than Wingate. But having armed him with extraordinary powers, the government could hardly ignore his advice or withdraw him within a fortnight of the start of his assignment. Curzon had initially put forward a plan, which appears to have had its origins in Wingate's attempt to cut Cecil's Financial Adviser post down to size, for a commission of enquiry under Milner, the Colonial Secretary, as an alternative to releasing Zaghlul. Despite Curzon's strong disapproval,[22] Allenby had insisted on maintaining his chosen course.[23] 'It was not the first nor the last time', Cooper observed, 'that politicians have been disappointed in their belief that soldiers are stupid creatures who understand nothing but the use of force.'[24] The Cabinet reluctantly accepted its Special High Commissioner's proposals,[25] which suggested that governing Egypt with military might was in the long term impracticable,[26] and Lloyd George cabled Allenby his complete support.

Allenby's announcement on 7 April that Zaghlul and his colleagues were to be released followed rioting four days earlier in which nine people were killed and 60 wounded.[27] Much influential opinion considered the step, on 'the razor-edge between wise conciliation and ill-advised surrender', justified.[28] Nimr made no criticism of it,[29] Baird was convinced that there was no alternative to bringing the exiles home 'at once'[30] and Clayton defended it to Bell as 'a necessary measure as the deportations had been a mistake and it was better to cut our loss than persist in the error'.[31] Many of the expatriate British, however, loudly dissented, considering that Zaghlul and violence had won and accusing Allenby of a lack of resolution.[32] A leading resident described the new policy as calamitous for British prestige and security and as forcing formerly co-operative Egyptians into the nationalist camp.[33] 'Bloodshed and violence', Grafftey-Smith remarks, 'had done what poor Wingate's arguments failed to do.'[34] At home, Lloyd said that the freeing of Zaghlul was a 'surrender to the forces of disorder . . . so sudden and so complete that it appalled all experienced observers'.[35] Later, Hardinge spoke contemptuously of Allenby:

> it was imagined by Lloyd George that in him he had found a strong man who would impose the view of the British Government upon the Sultan and would defeat the Nationalists. No greater mistake was ever made . . . Lloyd George thought that through Allenby he would be able to administer a severe lesson to the Egyptians. Allenby . . . received . . . full power to carry out a firm and strong policy in Cairo, which he promised to carry out immediately on his arrival . . . but when he reached Cairo he proved himself quite unfit to cope with the Egyptians, and, to Lloyd George's intense dismay, he absolutely climbed down and granted the extremists everything they had asked for. It was indeed a miserable affair and Lloyd George and Balfour felt deeply the humiliation of the situation . . . this was the actual beginning of the loss of British prestige in Egypt, and the end of a situation which had been carefully built up during Lord Cromer's wise régime . . . The mischief that can be done to a country through ignorance, even with the best intentions, is incalculable.[36]

In a comment on this diatribe, Vansittart suggests that Lloyd George misinterpreted Allenby's action as he 'displayed such good china-shop manners that the Prime Minister mistook them for weakness'.[37]

Bimbashi Joseph McPherson,[38] whose account of Egypt's civil troubles during this period is perhaps the most detailed and graphic, accused Allenby of ignoring his advisers and making up his own policy.[39] Lloyd claimed that Allenby had no confidence in his staff, who were 'entirely ignorant in regard to the situation with which they had to deal' and furnished him with 'scanty and inaccurate' information.[40] In due course he replaced Haines, Brunyate and Douglas Dunlop on an Acting basis at Interior, Justice and Education by, respectively, Clayton, Amos[41] and Patterson. Lloyd considered that he should have made these changes immediately on his arrival.[42] The nationalists thought so too. On 6 April, the Intelligence

Department of the War Office produced a list of 'the demands of the present nationalist movement', drawn up by 'Ulwy Bey. They included '3. The "Brunyate law" should be abolished "root and branch", 10. that Sir W. Brunyate should leave the country (otherwise his life is in danger). 11. Mr Haines to be replaced. 12. Mr Dunlop to be replaced.'[43]

On 9 April, Rushdy resumed office as Prime Minister, leading a pro-British cabinet, and two days later those members of Zaghlul's Committee of Fourteen who had not been deported – including Fahmy, Sha'rawy, As Sayyid, 'Abd al Latif Bey Makabaty,[44] Mustafa an Nahhas and 'Afify – left for France. They collected their liberated colleagues at Malta en route and arrived in Paris on the 18th. Zaghlul and his key team members were to remain there, vainly lobbying the Peace Conference for some fourteen months; the British treated them as private individuals and not as a delegation.[45] From Paris, Zaghlul conducted a secret correspondence with 'Abd ar Rahman Fahmy, Executive Secretary of the Wafd's Central Committee, in Egypt. It was carried on in invisible onion water ink in the margins of magazines and concerned the Wafd information programme and the activities of those working against the interests of the party, the chief of whom Fahmy believed to be the wartime Prime Minister Muhammad Sa'id Pasha, who was 'out to wreck Zaghlul and the Wafd at any price'.[46] The fact of the interchange was not divulged to the rest of the Committee.[47] Meanwhile Sidqy, notorious for his incessant womanising at the conference,[48] found the time for 'activities in the night-life of Paris', Grafftey-Smith said, which 'were reported as establishing various records, some of which may still stand'.[49]

If Whitehall's hunch was correct that Allenby's main reason for freeing the deportees was to divert their attention away from Egypt to Paris,[50] it must have been reinforced when – convinced that the strength of the nationalist movement was much greater than Cheetham had been reporting[51] – he urged that the Milner Mission appear as a matter of urgency.[52] Its arrival while Zaghlul and his colleagues, as it appeared, remained in no position to organise their threatened nationwide boycott of it would clearly have been advantageous. In fact, however, the release of Zaghlul, Sidqy, Mahmud and Al Basil earned the Residency a respite of less than a week before strikes, intimidation and attacks on the troops resumed as nationalist euphoria erupted. Nineteen British soldiers were wounded and eight, and seven Armenians, were killed during the period 9 to 11 April.[53] The ex-ministers who had pledged themselves to co-operate strove to help bring matters under control, but in vain, so that on 21 April Rushdy resigned again. Allenby continued to bombard Curzon with demands for the Mission to be despatched by the middle of May and for him to be allowed to announce its imminent advent. He had to order civil servants to return to work from their strike in which 'Aly Mahir was prominent[54] and schools to reopen or be shut down.

There were strong divergences of view about Allenby's early period.

McPherson summarised it as the 'days of shame' and 'interregnum of impotence' of 'that master jackass Allenby'; Britain in Egypt should either govern or 'clear out', he thundered: 'At present we are doing neither.' Allenby, 'a bitter disappointment and a failure from the first, undoing much good work which Bulfin was achieving, had', he maintained:

> the inspiration of a madman, and in opposition to his own advisors at the Residency, who were weak enough to agree with him in most things, and in violation of the basic laws of government, and of common sanity, decided as a sop to Cerberus to pay the blackmail demanded and set up Zaghlul and their other false Gods on a pedestal, in opposition to solemn declarations of our statesmen and his own proclamations; so on 7.4.18 [*sic*], the proclamations re these heroes were annulled and an announcement posted up that Zaghlul and Co. were to be released and allowed to proceed to Paris ... there was not an Egyptian who attributed this concession to kindness or magnanimity on the part of the British: in it they saw nothing but fear on the English [*sic*] side and strength on their own ... My first act was to put up a mourning card in my office: In Memory of British Prestige in Egypt, Died April 7 1919 (Octave of All Fools).[55]

In contrast, another British observer, Humphrey Beaman, an intelligence officer in Egypt during and after the war, gave Allenby all the praise that Macpherson withheld. He summed his opening phase up in glowing terms: Allenby, he declared:

> had come in a few months to perceive more than Cromer or Kitchener had ever been able to foresee, namely, that it would be necessary to give up, some day, the too strict and galling repression of all attempts on the part of Egyptians to have an appreciable share in their own Government.[56]

With Lloyd George's administration 'now implicitly convinced that Wingate had been right and Curzon wrong',[57] on 15 May, Allenby's deadline for its arrival, Curzon himself in the House of Lords announced the formation of the Milner Mission. It was to:

> inquire into the causes of the late disorders in Egypt and to report on the existing situation in the country and the form of constitution which, under the Protectorate, will be best calculated to promote its peace and prosperity [and] the progressive development of self-governing institutions.

It was now, however, Allenby's turn to backpedal. When Muhammad Sa'id agreed, a week later, to form a government, contravening Zaghlul's directive that 'no Egyptian should accept the governance of the country as long as the Protectorate was maintained',[58] to divert criticism he declared to a hostile public that his programme would be administrative, not political. He made it a condition of taking office that the arrival of Milner should be postponed until he had got into his stride, and in the event the Mission was delayed. First its leader was concerned about the likely effect on his health of an Egyptian summer and the wisdom of exhibiting urgency in the matter[59] and then in the autumn Allenby insisted on time to make a vain attempt to bolster the Muhammad Sa'id ministry to withstand the anticipated violence.

By July, over 800 Egyptians had been killed since Zaghlul's release.[60] Despite the widespread unpopularity at home of his first measures, that month Allenby was promoted to Field Marshal and in October Lloyd George made him a Viscount with a grant of £50,000. Wingate's chagrin must have been extreme. Following strikes in August in Cairo and Alexandria and an upsurge in anti-British propaganda, Allenby went on leave in September to collect his honours. Cheetham, whom Bell considered 'a typical FO man of the bloodless type',[61] stayed behind as Acting Resident yet again. On 16 September Allenby received a vote of thanks from both Houses of Parliament. He was awarded honorary degrees by four British universities and Yale. He visited Balmoral and became a Freeman of the City of London. On the official level, he called several times at 10 Downing Street – once accompanied by Faysal and Lawrence – without learning how the government saw its policy for Egypt in the short term. There was no sign of Milner emerging from his various duties in order to prepare for Egypt, and Curzon was always too busy to see his High Commissioner.

Four days after he returned to Cairo on 10 November, Allenby made a 'declaration of British policy' which he had with difficulty extracted from his government. This stated that Britain's policy for Egypt was to:

> preserve [its] autonomy under British Protection, ... develop the system of Self Government under an Egyptian Ruler ..., defend Egypt against all external danger and the interference of any Foreign Power ... establish a constitutional system in which ... the Sultan, his Ministers, and the elected representatives of the people may, ... in an increasing degree, co-operate in the management of Egyptian affairs.

It announced that the Milner Mission was finally in the offing. Its task was 'to work out the details of a Constitution ... and in consultation with the Sultan, his Ministers and representative Egyptians, to undertake the preliminary work which is required before the future form of Government can be settled'. It would not 'impose a Constitution' but 'propose ... a scheme of Government which can consequently be put into force'.[62]

In response to the announcement, Muhammad Sa'id resigned on

17 November, as he had said he would if his advice that Milner should not come were ignored.[63] Four days later, Yusuf Wahbah Pasha, a Copt who had been a wartime Minister of Finance, replaced him. In the face of the bombings of the period,[64] he showed 'a rare courage in agreeing to take office'[65] and was 'not to know a minute of peace and tranquillity throughout his term in government'.[66] On 20 November, extremist political agitation had broken out again and a campaign of violence began which brought death and injury to British nationals and the arrest of Wafd members.[67] Bell told her father, 'It's a deadlock in Egypt, and entirely our own fault. When they asked to be allowed to put their views before the British Govt [*sic*] in London the FO replied that HMG hadn't time to hear them!' She forecast that 'They will have to spend much more time now in putting things straight.'[68]

Milner and his team arrived on 7 December, causing Joseph McPherson to begin using a new name – King Log – for Allenby.[69] It consisted of Rodd; Maxwell; Sir Cecil Hurst, the principal Foreign Office legal adviser who was later President of the International Court of Justice at the Hague and of whom Chamberlain said that at Locarno 'I *believe* that Hurst spoke the decisive word in the German–Polish negotiations';[70] Brigadier-General Sir Owen Thomas, a Labour MP and expert on agriculture in Africa; the prominent Liberal J. A. Spender, former editor of the *Westminster Gazette*; and, as Secretary, Mr. T. Loyd, who had been in the Egyptian service, winning golden opinions all round, and at the Foreign Office,[71] where he had attracted Wingate's suspicion. Milner himself – 'aged beyond his years and exhausted by his work in the War Cabinet'[72] – had no reputation as a leader of missions, having returned empty-handed from one to Russia at the end of the war.[73] The Wafd could not be shaken from the conviction that his purpose was to 'weaken the national movement from within'[74] and Rushdy Pasha believed that his team 'would be unable to find three cats with which to converse'.[75]

Since Allenby's declaration had indicated that the Protectorate was in any case to continue – to the disgust of Lloyd, who considered that by 'the surrender of April' Britain had forfeited any right to call its régime by that name[76] – Egyptian politicians subjected the Mission from the outset to a complete and general Wafd-organised boycott masterminded by 'Abd ar Rahman Fahmy. (The claim has been made[77] that Allenby himself boycotted it, which would perhaps have been true to form.)[78] The Sultan and ministers, vainly trying to escape the criticism that they had failed to block its arrival, refused to give evidence. Nimr believed that Muslim hatred of being ruled by Christians and the resentment of their leaders at being passed over for office were at the root of nationalist sentiment in general and of the boycott in particular. He pointed to the examples of Zaghlul and Muhammad Mahmud, 'who held office in the provinces, was turned out by Haines and threw in his lot with the nationalists'.[79] Looking ahead, Clayton had suggested an even more convincing reason for the boycott of the Mission than these: 'the Egyptians refuse to have anything to do with it on the ground that they have sent their representatives to Paris and entrusted them with their views, which they will give to no others'.[80]

Except when it was able by cloak-and-dagger means to contrive interviews with 'representative Egyptians', the Mission found itself marooned in the Semiramis Hotel, having to make do with evidence from non-Egyptian sources and the Residency's files. If a member of the team appeared in public, or was expected to, demonstrations by nationalists, riots by students and attacks on suspected Egyptian collaborators followed. After one incident, Al Azhar was stormed by British troops and closed. Egypt, Bell told her mother, had 'turned into a second Ireland largely by our own stupidity'.[81]

Frustrated by his Mission's impotence, Milner issued a Declaration of his own on 29 December. His statement that he was of open mind caused Lloyd to consider that thereby the Mission 'tore up its own terms of reference and committed the British Parliament to the abandonment of the Protectorate'.[82] The Declaration had some of the desired effect, emboldening moderate politicians and civil servants, and even leading members of the Wafd (persuaded by 'Adly), to meet Mission members privately, but its leader quickly found that little in the way of useful facts resulted.

The Mission left Egypt in February 1920 to write its report.[83] Its recommendations were with Curzon on 17 May. They were that there should be a British–Egyptian treaty granting Egypt full internal self-government and the right to conclude international treaties; the Legislative Assembly should be revived as soon as feasible; the number of advisers should be reduced to two; Britain should have the right to retain modified Capitulations, to keep military bases and to prevent foreign interference in Egypt; and she should declare her intention, while being alive to Egyptian interests and guaranteeing Egypt a fair share of the waters of the Nile, to retain control of the Sudan.[84]

'Adly, the only leading politician able both to keep his independence and (for the time being) enjoy cordial relations with Zaghlul[85] as well as with the Mission, used his good offices to bring pressure on the boycotter-in-chief; Walrond acted as an intermediary between him and Milner. As a result, Hurst visited Zaghlul in Paris in late May and invited him to meet the Mission in London.[86] Following the frustration of his hopes at the Peace Conference, Zaghlul accepted and, with seven other members of the Wafd – and just as he might have done in Wingate's time – made his way to Britain, arriving on 7 June. There had been a sea change in London, too. Only 18 months after Graham, Hardinge, Curzon and Balfour had disdained the nationalists and used them as the excuse to bring Wingate down, Sir John Tilley in the Foreign Office telegraphed Graham in Paris on 2 June:

Saad Pasha Zaghloul and following members of his party Ahmed Loutfy el Said, Mohamed Ali, Hamed al Basel, Sinot Hanna, Abdel

> Latif el Mukabaty will prob apply for visas to come to London almost imm pse arrange for all facilities to be afforded them.[87]

Discussions between Milner and 'a set of self-appointed politicians who had no formal authority to negotiate on behalf of Egypt'[88] lasted until August with 'Adly present. In Lloyd's judgement, Zaghlul, proving an imaginative and stubborn negotiator, persuaded Milner to give ground even over British interests and 'altered the whole British position in Egypt'.[89] The result was a Milner–Zaghlul Agreement,[90] otherwise known as 'The Memorandum of August 18, 1920', which envisaged the conclusion of a treaty under which Britain on an unspecified date would 'recognise the independence of Egypt as a constitutional monarchy with representative institutions' and sponsor its entry into the League of Nations. It allowed Britain to retain her military foothold, the Financial and Judicial Advisers and the Capitulations and to protect her strategic interests and the Empire's communications but made no mention of the Sudan.[91] Lloyd considered that it committed Britain 'to large concessions while (Zaghlul) himself remained committed to nothing'.[92] The Mission, however, was ready to throw its weight behind it and recommend it to the British government, provided that 'Zaghloul Pasha and the Delegation are likewise prepared to advocate it, and will use all their influence to obtain the assent of an Egyptian national assembly to the conclusion of such a Treaty as is contemplated'.[93]

Zaghlul, in no kind of official position to be able to impose the fruits of his negotiations, now sprang a surprise by asking for endorsement from home, in one view displaying 'his fatal lack of vision and the true qualities of leadership'.[94] He despatched to Egypt four of his colleagues (Mahmud, As Sayyid, Al Makabaty and 'Aly Mahir) who knew, as Milner quickly learned, that Zaghlul felt that even more could be obtained from the British.[95] They spent from 7 September until November making propaganda for the Agreement and obtaining reaction to it. Allenby was on leave – and rumoured during 1920 to be going to be replaced by Graham or Rodd. Storrs's successor Ernest Scott, now the Acting Resident, wrote to Curzon from Alexandria to say that, not surprisingly Muhammad Sa'id was the Memorandum's principal opponent.[96] In contrast, 47 of the prewar General Assembly's 49 members still in circulation approved of its terms.[97] Zaghlul's emissaries returned to London to report, however, that 'the Egyptian people were favourably disposed towards the proposals but ... that there were certain points of which further modification was desired'.[98] (Huda Sha'rawy's Wafdist Women's Central Committee had been left out of the consultation process but, obtaining a copy of the Agreement, also found its provisions unsatisfactory.)[99] Milner, like the British government and Allenby, had been hopeful so far. Now, although there were to be more vain negotiations with Zaghlul, Fahmy and 'Aly Mahir in the autumn of the following year, Milner lost patience. On the

Egyptian side, Zaghlul's criticism of 'Adly for the failure of Britain to offer better terms[100] led to a major split in the Wafd at the end of 1920.

The revolutionary proposals in the Milner–Zaghlul Agreement, like Allenby's first actions in Cairo, had provoked consternation in Whitehall. Bonar Law told Curzon that they 'came to me as a great shock'. The only thing to do, he said, 'is to send them out to Egypt making it perfectly plain that you are sending them as information from the Milner Mission and without any responsibility at all so far as the Government is concerned'.[101] Curzon was also taken aback by the Agreement,[102] whose clauses closely matched the hopes of 'Adly and Isma'il Pasha Sirry the former Minister of War.[103] He considered them a surrender to the nationalists and did as he was instructed, declaring himself not committed to them. Allenby, who gave priority to the Milner report proper, did not concur in them all, his thinking reflecting that of his senior colleagues. (Bell had recorded in her diary Clayton's view that, in her words, 'our object should now be to guard a. Imperial necessities in Egypt, b. international interests for which we had made ourselves responsible [Suez, Nile water, army and police] and let all the rest go'.)[104]

At the end of December, an Allenby letter said that 'A decision by His Majesty's Government, as to the future status of Egypt, is eagerly awaited here.' He complained, with some chronological exaggeration, that 'we can't expect anything definite just yet, as Milner does not seem, so far, to have presented his report – this, after a year's delay'.[105] The Report,[106] whose recommendations the British government had already discounted[107] and was in due course to reject, was not published until the spring of 1921, but early in January Allenby received an advance copy. It recommended that Britain should not impose a solution but open negotiations urgently for a treaty of alliance. Allenby supported the recommendation that the Protectorate, unilaterally imposed, be ended and replaced by a treaty reserving the most important British interests, the Canal and the Sudan. Curzon asked him to get a delegation together to go to London for negotiations and the High Commissioner wrote to Fu'ad on 26 February requesting him to select one to discuss the replacement of the Protectorate.

In March, Zaghlul published another manifesto, demanding a Wafd majority on the delegation and making conditions for participation in the discussions – 'Abolition radicale du Protectorat et acceptation des réserves, suppression de la censure et de l'état de siège avant tous pourparlers.'[108] But the British government's intention was to negotiate not with him but with moderate politicians,[109] of whom 'Adly was the chief. Although Fu'ad did not like him, on 17 March, under pressure from Lindsay, he appointed him Prime Minister[110] in 'a master-stroke of Egyptian Palace politics' which widened 'the irrevocable split in the nationalist movement that crippled it for the next three decades'.[111]

On 4 April, Zaghlul returned home. He had changed, during his exile becoming 'a truculent, overbearing man, difficult to work with'.[112] He made a huge triumphal entry into Cairo. In the eyes of the masses the 'shadow of God on earth',[113] he was convinced that he was 'the saviour of his country, appointed by God to carry out His will'. Popular adulation was pushing him towards megalomania.[114] Allenby said in a telegram on 16 April that the British concessions had caused amazement in Egypt,[115] but Zaghlul quickly signalled the reality of the situation[116] by bitterly denouncing 'Adly as a traitor and British puppet. In response, 'Adly's supporters, and politicians unhappy with Zaghlul's radicalism and tactics, in August founded a new political grouping – the Society of Independent Egypt, which was to become Hizb al Ahrar ad Dusturiyyin (The Free Constitutionalists' Party) – to back his ministry.[117] The new party caused haemorrhaging in the Wafd to which Zaghlul's 'intense egotism, ungovernable temper and domineering manner' contributed. Several months later, 'none of the originators of the [Wafd] movement remained with him. His immense popularity with the people nevertheless remained undiminished.'[118] On 29 April, Allenby – who could not reciprocate Zaghlul's liking of him[119] and was never able to work with him[120] – described him as 'a man devoured by self-conceit'.[121]

Harry Boyle, now retired, revisited Egypt from 14 April to 26 May,[122] apparently following his own suggestion to the Foreign Office, which welcomed the idea. Willie Tyrrell, Hardinge's successor as PUS, instructed him to take on 'the guise of an ordinary tourist' and observe 'the strictest secrecy regarding the whole matter'.[123] He was enjoined to treat it as 'extremely confidential and to mention it to no one'.[124] As to the purpose of his journey, although Lloyd disingenuously remarked that 'it happened that Mr Boyle … was revisiting Egypt … and has left a record of his impressions',[125] the suspicion is strong that it was to spy on Allenby. His 'cover' seems to have been to report on the situation and 'to reassure native opinion as to the genuine desire of His Majesty's government to achieve a solution of the present situation satisfactory both to Great Britain and Egypt'.[126]

In the shorter term, he was to attempt to reconcile Zaghlul and 'Adly on the delegation question. His efforts were in vain. ('Splendid scheme I had elaborated – two hours too late, as that pestilent Sultanic rescript as to the Delegation was published this afternoon. Not my fault. Saad ought to have come round sooner.')[127] After a meeting with Zaghlul on 30 April, he told his wife that the nationalist leader was 'quite, quite impossible. No sort of compromise, at least at present, to be looked for';[128] in retrospect on 27 May he added that Zaghlul was 'a fine old fellow and I love him, but quite hopeless'.[129] In the *Memorandum on Egypt* he wrote for the Foreign Office after his return, he said of him:

> Having a high respect for him as an essentially honest and well-intentioned man, I regretted to find him in a frame of mind which can only be described as utterly uncompromising and deaf to argument of any

kind . . . any degree of mild opposition, or even non-concurrence with his views, evokes an outbreak of irritation on his part. This is largely to be accounted for by the fact that he is of advanced age and in bad health; but . . . as an honest Egyptian, he is not of any high intellectual calibre . . . Zaghloul Pasha may be said to live in a fool's paradise. He is intoxicated with the atmosphere of excitement, adulation, and apparent enthusiasm in which he is kept by his immediate surroundings.[130]

More generally, Boyle found 'universal condemnation' of British rule and administration since Cromer:[131]

as matters now stand, we do not possess a sincere friend in the country, . . . one who would desire to see the continuance of British predominance in its present form[132] . . . At present the Egyptians are thoroughly dissatisfied, and a deep-seated feeling of unrest pervades the whole country.

Worse, 'British civil control . . . is regarded as having broken down, become wholly ineffective, conferring no benefits and exercising no authority.'[133] The Egyptians, he stated, had 'lost all confidence in British control as now exerted'.[134] His report said, however, that if it could be reformed, 'the immense majority of the Egyptian unofficial population' would be 'sincerely in favour' of its maintenance.[135] It called for the abolition of the Protectorate and martial law.[136]

Despite claims that Boyle's contact was 'almost exclusively with pro-British elements' and that he had no political judgement,[137] he had been a very popular figure during his long term of duty under Cromer and Gorst, and his pose as a tourist was predictably ineffective. His wife claimed that Zaghlul asked him to return to Egypt, quoting him as saying, 'If you, Boyle, will come back, and take over the Residency, I will go with England [*sic*] instead of against her – I will work for *you*.'[138] She attributed to her husband the statement that Allenby 'told him he would be mighty glad and relieved if my husband would come back and take over'[139] and maintained that all the party leaders 'expressed the ardent wish to see Harry Boyle in Lord Allenby's place'.[140] Boyle had no such ambitions, especially as he not only failed to uncover any ammunition which could be used against Allenby but indeed found him 'the best possible [fellow] for the present circumstances'.[141] He strongly approved of him as 'the one and only good point I can find in the whole horizon'[142] and 'the one valid asset of our present situation in Egypt, a status of quite inestimable value at the present troublous time'.[143] In short, 'He seems to me a very fine man. His Lordship makes on me the very best impression.'[144]

Boyle said that 'Adly was widely thought to be in the hands of Sidqy and 'Abd al Khaliq Sarwat,[145] the wartime Minister of Justice and unpopular largely because both were 'actively distrusted and disliked on the grounds of their personal character'.[146] During his stay, there were demonstrations for Zaghlul and against 'Adly in Tantah and serious rioting in Cairo and Alexandria. Wafd leaflets had reminded 'students ..., fellaheen ... and devotees that for the sake of your Fatherland, and for the consolidation of the throne of the nation and its faithful agent Saad Pasha Zaghlul ... heavenly laws and worldly laws allow killing and shedding of blood' and that the Prophet 'killed many in the way of spreading the Mohammedan call and exterminating the influence of backsliders'. In Alexandria on 23 May ('Red Monday'), 30 Egyptians and 14 Europeans were killed and 69 people injured[147] in events witnessed by Boyle. Allenby was criticised for not seizing control quickly enough.[148]

An Egyptian delegation was soon found. Including no Wafd member, it was finally made up of 'Adly (leader), Rushdy, Sidqy, Muhammad Shafiq (Minister of Agriculture, and another target of bomb-throwers), the judge Yusuf Sulayman[149] and Ahmad Tal'at, President of the Court of Appeal. Prepared to accept the Milner recommendations as a basis for negotiation over further concessions later, it left on 1 July, accompanied by Allenby.[150] Zaghlul was not included, though he gave it his support, because he had insisted that he, rather than the Prime Minister should lead it, which idea 'Adly naturally opposed.

The talks[151] lasted for more than three months, time which Allenby could hardly spare, especially as he was rarely asked for his advice.[152] ('October 21st. Allenby's return to Egypt which was fixed for tomorrow has, much to his rage, been put off.')[153] It was his firm opinion that Milner's proposals should be announced immediately and Egypt awarded independence at once, outstanding questions being dealt with later; were difficulties to arise, with the command of the relevant seas and the Canal base, Britain, he maintained, would have no difficulty in resuming authority if necessary. This approach was seen as naïve and weak by home politicians, especially Churchill, who inspired a press campaign against it.[154] With Curzon, Lindsay, Vansittart, Jack Murray,[155] head of the Foreign Office's Egyptian Department, and Duff Cooper making up the British team,[156] things began well, with differences removed over the Capitulations and the Advisers.

At home, Zaghlul was doing his best to block a treaty, making triumphal tours of the provinces and, in September, bringing out a group of four Labour MPs (they included future members of Ramsay MacDonald's 1924 Cabinet) and Major Harry Barnes, a Liberal representing Newcastle South, with whom to assail 'Adly. Lindsay described them as 'engine drivers or boiler-makers'.[157] Curzon echoed Bell's analysis of the situation when he told his wife on 21 October, 'I am sure we shall have an absolute rupture with another Ireland in Egypt.'[158]

On 17 October, Allenby was 'still hanging around waiting to be interviewed by the Cabinet. So far I have received no summons.'[159] In early November, Cooper, however, blamed him for the impasse: 'It is largely his fault for not having spoken up to the Cabinet in favour of concessions.' The guests at a dinner he attended, including Churchill and Montagu, 'agreed in their contempt for Allenby ... Winston said that if he had charge of Egypt the first thing he would do would be to get rid of Allenby and Zaghlul.'[160] On 17 November, while Allenby was still in London, Clayton, Amos, Patterson and Dowson, disregarding hierarchical considerations, sent him a supportive memorandum endorsing Milner's approach to the settlement and stating their belief that there would be serious trouble in Egypt unless the principle of its independence were conceded.[161] Two days later, the talks broke down over the questions of the retention of a British garrison, the control of Egypt's international relations and the Sudan.

On 3 December, Allenby, back in Cairo, had to forward a letter from Curzon to the Sultan which angrily placed on Egypt responsibility for the collapse of the negotiations.[162] 'Adly bore the brunt as the 'hectoring and ill-advised note ... swept him into resignation on a wave of national resentment'[163] on 8 December; Lloyd – cynical in such matters – claimed that he 'of course secured as much concession as he could, and then inevitably rejected the terms offered'.[164] His resignation was not accepted until 24 December and left Egypt, until March, once more without a government. On an Allenby proposal by telegram on 11 December that the Protectorate be unilaterally abandoned even though Britain could expect no concessions in return, Murray minuted, 'I do not think that HMG should be asked to provide Lord Allenby with a provisional pledge of this kind which he could then proceed to hawk round amongst potential Egyptian prime ministers.' Crowe, describing the High Commissioner's suggestion as 'his own complete *volte-face*', added, 'the line now recommended by Lord Allenby is incompatible with the course approved, if not advocated, by himself here'.[165]

On 19 December, Allenby banned a large meeting in Cairo planned by Zaghlul and, when he protested, ordered him to desist from political activity altogether. On his refusal, on 22 December he had him arrested by Russell Pasha. In transit to a second spell of exile, at Suez on Christmas Day Zaghlul is reputed to have relieved his British officer hosts of all their stakes at poker,[166] a game at which his superior skill contributed to dislike of him.[167] A week later he was deported to the Seychelles with Sinut Hannah,[168] Fath Allah Barakat (a landowner relative and confidant of Zaghlul who was to be Minister of Interior in his government), his brother 'Atif Barakat, Mustafa an Nahhas and Makram 'Ubayd. Their martyrdom boosted Wafd recruitment.

Richard Meinertzhagen[169] – not the most trustworthy of witnesses – reported that on Christmas Eve in London Churchill gave a Colonial Office lunch at which Lawrence was highly critical of Allenby; he was doing his best but did not understand the problems. Churchill predictably agreed and, when Lawrence referred to Allenby as 'a man of no principles' and, voicing a minority view, 'a hopelessly weak administrator',[170] went so far as to characterise him as a 'dud' general.[171]

10 Treated very scurvily

The fall of cat and mouse

> the Cairo Residency seems to me to be as variable as the British climate.
> (Tyrrell)

The rearrest of Zaghlul provoked violence throughout Egypt, especially in Cairo and on the Mediterranean coast. Allenby put a strong military presence onto the streets of the capital, limiting the death toll on the British side to a soldier and an official; anticipating Lloyd's methods, he had warships sent to Alexandria and the Canal. There was a ferment inside the Residency. On 12 January 1922, Allenby sent a Personal telegram to Curzon which incorporated a draft letter for which he demanded, 'without delay', authorisation to send 'without modification' to the Sultan. He said:

> The long delay has caused a rapid deterioration in the political situation ... What was possible last week may be impossible next week. I have dealt with Zaghlul and enemies of order, and now is the time to show confidence in and uphold those who are ready to work with us in the interests of Egypt.[1]

The draft resurrected his view of what British policy in Egypt should be. Lloyd calls it 'a clear-cut policy honestly and courageously adhered to', unique in the postwar period.[2] With the intention of bypassing the Wafd,[3] it proposed that Britain unilaterally abolish both the Protectorate and (as soon as an Act of Indemnity could be passed) martial law and, in anticipation of the conclusion of a treaty, recognise Egypt as an independent state,[4] while reserving to itself control of imperial communications and the Sudan, the protection of foreign residents in Egypt and the defence of the country.[5] The tone of his 'ultimatum' understandably annoyed the Foreign Office and Curzon, but the Foreign Secretary nonetheless promised to explain to his colleagues Allenby's concern about the serious situation in Egypt, without a government for more than a month, and to support him – like Wingate – 'up to the point of resignation'. He did not in fact do so, allowing strong criticism of him in the Cabinet and correctly suggesting that the draft was Egyptian handiwork, not by Allenby at all.[6] It had been composed by Sidqy[7] following 'exhaustive negotiations' with a large circle of contacts, most notably Sarwat and 'Adly, whose involvement in the matter perhaps explained Allenby's brusque tone with his principals.[8] In the upshot, he was informed that his proposals were not acceptable and – insultingly – instructed to send Amos and Clayton to London for consultations.[9] He had of course just returned from London himself and was required by the government's reply to provide – further shades of Wingate – 'fullest available information'.

On 15 January, Dowson and Amos produced for him the draft of a *Suggested Convention between Great Britain and Egypt* which advocated the ending of the Protectorate and recognition of Egypt as 'a sovereign State under a constitutional monarchy' backed by 'a perpetual treaty and bond of peace, amity and alliance'. The British High Commissioner would 'take precedence over the representatives of other countries', and Egypt – while free to forge diplomatic relations with whatever nations it chose – would not be able to conclude political agreements with any of them without consulting Britain.[10]

On 20 January, Allenby wrote a rejoinder to Curzon, in which – in language unexpected in an envoy – he threatened to resign[11] and said:

> Advice I have given to His Majesty's Government is my *final* considered opinion after full discussion with those most capable of advising me. I am certain that my proposals, if immediately accepted, will prove the basis of a lasting settlement in Egypt. If they are rejected, I foresee nothing but a rule of repression driving us to annexation of the country, which would greatly increase our difficulties ... any prolonged hesitation on the part of His Majesty's Government will seriously undermine my influence. Departure to England of two advisers could not fail to have same effect at once.

For the avoidance of understandable doubt, he added, 'Amos, Clayton, Patterson, and Dowson[12] have nothing to add to opinions they have already expressed. They are in complete accord with me.'[13]

On the other hand, he informed him that Walford Selby[14] was about to arrive in London on leave and suggested that the Cabinet should interview him; when he surfaced, the First Secretary said that he would resign if Allenby did and produced a telegram from the High Commissioner which claimed that all the advisers would too.[15]

On 24 January, the government asked Allenby not to resign[16] but declined to agree to his proposals without assurances from the Egyptians. He told Curzon next day that, in the absence of a government, he could not provide such assurances. In any case, the demand for them hazarded a great opportunity: 'now is the time to show confidence in and uphold those who are ready to work with us in the interests of Egypt'. If, he warned, the government 'will not take my advice now they throw away all chance of having a friendly Egypt in our time'. He hinted that he was 'committed to, and compromised with, Tharwat and his friends,[17] and added, 'Though I have divulged no secrets, my opinions are well-known here and if advice I have offered is rejected I cannot honourably remain. I therefore beg that my resignation may be tendered to His Majesty.'[18] Four of the Advisers, including Clayton and Amos, confirmed that they might do likewise.[19] In a further sign of restiveness among the staff, a slightly different quartet – Clayton, Dowson, Hayter and Patterson – composed a Memorandum during January in which they said that they:

> are unanimously of the . . . view that a decision which does not admit the principle of Egyptian independence and which maintains the Protectorate must entail serious risk of revolution throughout the country, and in any case result in complete administrative chaos rendering Government impossible. It must be realised that the whole structure of the Government is Egyptian . . . It is therefore impossible to exercise any British control without full Egyptian co-operation in all branches of the administration . . . Unless His Majesty's Government are prepared to give substantial satisfaction to the expectations which the Egyptians have legitimately formed . . . it will be impossible to form any Ministry . . . The Advisers have been carrying on for over two years in the belief that a policy of liberal concession would be adopted and have undoubtedly given this impression to the various Ministers and others with whom they have been in contact . . . if a contrary policy is adopted they cannot expect to retain the confidence of Egyptian Ministers or be able to render useful service in the future.[20]

Jack Murray attempted to pre-empt further disorder in the ranks during a further imminent absence by Allenby. In answer to a telegram of 26 January from Amos, he depatched one to him which, paraphrased in the Residency, began with a threat: 'It is undesirable that either you or your colleagues would take any action which will affect your own positions while Lord Allenby is absent from Cairo.' It concluded by appealing to their better judgement, telling them that 'the Secretary of State [Chamberlain] relies upon your loyalty to the interests of the Empire to avoid, at this juncture, adding to the embarrassments of the situation, already serious'.[21] The Foreign Office told Allenby that the government could not accept his resignation without hearing him in person.[22] He was again ordered to attempt to persuade the Egyptians to agree the British terms, after which the Protectorate would be ended. Pointing out that it was a futile task, the High Commissioner repeated that he would try. When he reported that 'Adly and his supporters had once more refused to consider the question unless the scrapping of the Protectorate were the first item on the agenda, the Cabinet sent him a 'very insulting'[23] telegram which accused him of consistently misinforming it and, against all the evidence, blocking its liberal intentions in Egypt. It called him home for consultations and to explain the 'violent metamorphosis' in his reporting and his two ultimata.[24] Cooper said at this point that Allenby 'has been ill-treated'[25] and, indeed, it looked like Wingate all over again. It took no specialist knowledge for Bell to say, 'I see Lord Allenby has been summoned home to "confer". It's usually the formula for dismissal – I wonder if that's what it means. Much as I like him I think we need in Egypt a better diplomat than he.'[26]

On 3 February, two months after he last returned from Britain, Allenby left Alexandria with the two officials, Amos and Clayton, whose presence in London had been so recently demanded. Cooper noted that the High Commissioner 'appears to have had a great send-off from all parties and nationalities'.[27] In contrast, when he arrived at Victoria on 10 February, it was an indication of the disapproval he had earned and of the likely outcome of his journey that there were no official car and no senior Foreign Office representative to meet him. Sir Philip Chetwode was, however, there and offered him a lift. Maintaining the comparison with Wingate, he delivered to the Foreign Office a 29-page despatch dated 2 February[28] – 'a shattering document' in the view of Henry Wilson, Robertson's successor as CIGS,[29] which rebutted the contents of its telegram seriatim and in unusually sharp language, some in Allenby's own Greek.[30] It concluded:

> The commission which I hold from His Majesty is to maintain His Majesty's Protectorate over Egypt. I have done so: but I do not think it has the elements of durability and I have now advised its being brought to an end, as it was established, by a unilateral declaration.

It included a well-worn protest: 'It appears to be suggested that I have not kept His Majesty's Government sufficiently advised of the steps by which the political situation has been transformed. This cannot be admitted.' There was impasse that evening: Curzon told him that the Cabinet could not possibly accept a despatch like his from one of its own representatives, and Allenby – insisting on it going through the normal channels – refused to retract his offer to resign. The Foreign Secretary – worsted by another soldier – was reported (not uniquely for him) to be in tears at the end of the meeting.[31]

After being made to wait for four days, on 14 February Allenby told Wilson that 'he was going to see LG tomorrow and was going to put very plainly before him that he must choose at once between his advice and his resignation'. He would refuse any longer to be kept 'hanging about being made a fool of'.[32] At last, with Amos and Clayton, he was received by Lloyd George and Curzon on 15 and 20 February.[33] At the climax of their discussions, in a famous exchange probably not quoted verbatim, Allenby said, 'Well, it is no good disputing any longer, I have told you what I think is necessary ... I have waited five weeks for a decision, and I can't wait any longer. I shall tell Lady Allenby to come home.' Knowing that, as 'a Liberal Prime Minister', he could not 'go down to the House of Commons and explain that he was less liberal-minded than the stern soldier whom he had sent out to govern Egypt', Lloyd George replied, 'You have waited five weeks, Lord Allenby, wait five more minutes.' Only a few small modifications – 'of a purely drafting character, designed doubtless to save the faces of those who had denounced the scheme as unacceptable'[34] – were then made to the High Commissioner's proposals. A likely reason for the climb-down was the Cabinet's fear that, if Allenby resigned, he would air his despatch in the House of Lords. His encounter with Lloyd George is either praised for bringing about 'the shift to a liberal [colonial] policy'[35] or reviled for initiating 'the long, painful, humiliating liquidation of the British position in Egypt'.[36] The government had the last word. Duff Cooper was astonished to hear Chamberlain assure the House of Commons a month later that 'it was Lord Allenby who had surrendered, and who when the Government's views had been explained to him "face to face" had gladly accepted them'.[37] Allenby did not forgive this claim.[38] Although Arnold Wilson was never called home, unless his final departure from Baghdad was a disguised removal from his post, in the resistance Allenby offered to British government policy for his country, and in his success in forcing his own convictions through, he much resembled the man who had until recently been his political counterpart in Iraq and stands in sharp contrast to Wingate, who suffered for his (unremarkable) persistence, while Wilson did not.

On 28 February, Allenby returned to a Cairo where, in his absence, there had been a series of assassinations and woundings of British troops and officials, to announce that the British government had agreed to his demands. He made yet another Declaration to Egypt, this one drawn up by Grigg (Lloyd George's Private Secretary), Jack Murray and Clayton.[39] On the one hand it unilaterally terminated the Protectorate, recognised Egypt as an independent, sovereign state and promised an early end to martial law; on the other, it 'absolutely' reserved '[t]he security of the communications of the British Empire in Egypt', the country's defence, the protection of foreign interests and minorities (this implied the retention of the capitulations[40] and of control of the Ministries of Justice and Interior)[41] and the Sudan 'to the discretion of His [Britannic] Majesty's Government until such time as it may be possible ... to conclude agreements in regard thereto'.[42] Toynbee justly comments that the Declaration's description of Egypt as an independent sovereign state was 'a diplomatic fiction', that the independence and sovereignty were 'imperfect, not only in fact, but in international law, since at that date the sovereignty over Egypt still belonged juridically to Turkey' and that 'In Egyptian eyes ... the British declaration had bestowed the name of sovereign independence upon Egypt with one hand and withheld the substance with the other.'[43] In fact, the Declaration bestowed limited independence and shelved the real problems of the Britain–Egypt relationship.[44]

Unsatisfactory as its provisions were in so many obvious ways, the Declaration did at least enable moderate politicians to resume co-operation in government. In March, Sarwat of Hizb al Ahrar, who when asked to lead an administration the previous December had been insistent that the Protectorate be ended first,[45] formed a government. The Sultan became King Fu'ad I, Egypt's independence was proclaimed and it took back control of the Ministry of Foreign Affairs. (On 18 September 1923, its first diplomatic representatives abroad were nominated by Fu'ad and 14 consulates were created on 6 November.)[46] There were, however, concurrent rioting and strikes by lawyers and schoolboys, and the lives of European officers again came under threat. A 32-member constitutional commission was appointed on 3 April, chaired by Rushdy and with Al Makabaty, 'Abd al 'Aziz Fahmy and 'Aly Mahir 'active and prominent' – the last taking, though fruitlessly, 'an extreme radical, populist and anti-monarchical line'.[47] It first met on the 11th and produced a report on general constitution and electoral law principles which was published on 21 May. Hizb al Ummah boycotted the commission, which Zaghlul, who would not allow the Wafd to have anything to do with it, called the Malefactors' Commission.[48] On 25 July, the seven Wafd members who had not been deported the previous December issued a manifesto inciting violence against the Sarwat Ministry and the British. Allenby ordered their arrest and they were sentenced by court martial to fines and imprisonment on 13 August. (They were freed on 14 May the following year.) On 1 September, Clayton, who had given in his notice on 6 May, resigned, 'The recent changes in the political and administrative situation having rendered inadvisable the retention of the post of Adviser to the Ministry of Interior.'[49] On 29 November, Sarwat – in conflict with Fu'ad over the drafting of the constitution, particularly its proposed reduction of the King's position to that of a constitutional monarch[50] – also resigned following trickery on the part of Nash'at Pasha,[51] the royal *chef de cabinet*.[52] He was replaced in December by Muhammad Tawfiq Nasim Pasha,[53] who had already served as Prime Minister from May 1920 to March 1921. He made some progress towards finalising a constitution before Allenby vetoed the award to Fu'ad – who was dissatisfied by the limited role the commission had given him – of the title King of Egypt and the Sudan, 'an integral part of the Egyptian Kingdom'. To Allenby's demand on 2 February 1923 that all reference to the Sudan be deleted within 24 hours, Nasim offered to agree on condition that the final decision be taken by the parliament. He resigned on the 5th, however, before the British responded.[54] Under strong pressure from Allenby, the King signed away his title to the throne of the Sudan a little later in the month.[55]

A wave of assassinations and bombings, a number of deaths resulting and British GHQ being hit, began in Cairo on 7 February following rumours that Allenby and 'Adly had discussed Zaghlul's release. On 5 March, more Wafdists were arrested for issuing a manifesto to mark the first anniversary of the 1922 Declaration. (Their trial was not proceeded with after the reported intervention of Lloyd George.)[56] The High Commissioner had to appoint a military governor of Cairo and put Zaghlul's home, Bayt al Ummah, which had become a focus for the trouble, out of bounds. The Foreign Office asked him to come home to discuss the violence, but on 9 March he declined on the grounds that his absence would suggest that the policy of the Declaration was under review.

In March, Lord Carnarvon, the half-brother of Aubrey and Mervyn Herbert, was in Egypt for the opening of the tomb of Tut Ankh Amun which he and his protégé, Howard Carter – who also found the tombs of Tuthmosis IV and Hatchepsut – had discovered four months before. He expressed alarm at the condition of Egypt:

> The whole business has been allowed to drift and the only thing to do is to get rid of Allenby. That is the first step and one that ought to be taken at once. He has been very weak, is badly advised, and I am sorry to say drinks ... I am not the only person who has seen him in that state. I am sorry for him, he is very straight, but slow and rather stupid. Nothing good will happen until King Fuad has been definitely told that he must behave or go and Allenby cannot do this.[57]

On 15 March, Yahya Ibrahim Pasha[58] of Hizb al Ahrar became Prime Minister, heading a Cabinet d'Affaires or neutral government. On the 31st, Zaghlul was unconditionally released from Gibraltar, whither he had been moved from the Seychelles after 50 women had petitioned Allenby to transfer him on account of his bronchitis. (His companions in exile were released on 1 June.)[59] Was his freeing, Lloyd wondered, 'yet another attempt on the part of the Residency to conjure away difficulties by concession?'[60]

The previous October, the constitutional commission had submitted a draft[61] to the government which led to the enactment of a new constitution on 19 April 1923 and its promulgation two days later.[62] Of Belgian inspiration, it provided for a 'two-degree system of election',[63] a bicameral legislature, a Senate with two-thirds of its members nominated by the King and one-third elected, and an elected Chamber of Deputies.[64] It was heavily biased towards the monarch, awarding him the lion's share of legislative power and the right to dissolve parliament.[65]

On 5 July, an Indemnities Bill gave European permanent officials (over a thousand of them British) the right either to retire on 1 April 1924 or to remain until 1 April 1927 in the first instance;[66] very many left in 1924, more in 1925. The bill brought martial law to an end and Zaghlul consequently returned on 17 September. He declared that he did not want a third period of exile and behaved circumspectly from the start.

In January 1924, the first democratic elections took place under the Constitution. Establishing a pattern which, until 1936, saw, first, the Wafd win the elections, then the King dissolve parliament or suspend the constitution and rule through puppets, and finally a popular outcry demand fresh elections,[67] the Wafd won 179 of the 211 seats. Yahya Ibrahim resigned after a term which Lloyd considered to have been 'prolific – an oasis in a barren desert of time';[68] Lawrence Grafftey-Smith, concurring,[69] rated the outgoing prime minister, however, 'a subservient tool' of the King.[70] Fu'ad asked Zaghlul to form a government, which he named the People's Ministry. Contrary to protocol, Allenby went to call on him.

At first, Zaghlul was at pains to dissuade parliament (in the opinion of C.S. Jarvis,[71] 'the most deliciously funny institution that has ever happened in Egypt or anywhere else')[72] from provoking the British lest negotiations on the reserved issues be jeopardised. It did not take long, however, for his nationalist character to come to the surface. His government made the Sudan its top priority and he said that it was an insult to independent Egypt for its army (some 65% of which was based in the Sudan) to have a British C-in-C. In early March – consistent with Allenby's maxim that it was 'a characteristic inherent in Egyptians not to be satisfied until their case has been presented personally to the highest authority'[73] – he asked to go to London to discuss a settlement of the matters still outstanding between the two countries, of which the Sudan and the Army were two of the most crucial. Now that he had attained respectability as Prime Minister, there was no question of renewed refusal. From the Wafd's point of view, the omens were good. Zaghlul and Ramsay MacDonald, who had become British Prime Minister and Foreign Secretary at the same time as Zaghlul had come to power in Egypt, 'had frequently expressed a mutual admiration'[74] and members of the Wafd had been received at 10 Downing Street during the peace conference. On 15 March, MacDonald sent Zaghlul a telegram 'couched in exceedingly friendly terms' which stated that the British government was ready for negotiations at any time.[75] Lloyd, for whom the 1922 Declaration was 'the sacred status quo'[76] considered that now began the

> steady but very considerable recession from the position which we had taken up in 1922. The points which were definitely reserved in that Declaration began almost immediately to be whittled down in the series of unsuccessful attempts which we had been making to secure a treaty which was in fact impossible to secure.[77]

On 31 March, *The Times* reported that Zaghlul had declared in Parliament that 'the Government adhered to the demand for the complete independence of Egypt and the Sudan' and 'was not bound by the Declaration'. Allenby confided in the Foreign Office his thought that 'if pressed to do so we might consider the abolition of the offices of Financial and Judicial Advisers'.[78] (In Declaration implementation discussions it was agreed that the Financial Adviser would cease to attend Cabinet meetings.) In a telegram to MacDonald, he said that Zaghlul, seen by Egyptians as 'a prophet sent to save his country', was 'at the height of his popularity old vain and in ill-health'.[79] On 10 April, MacDonald invited Zaghlul to come to Britain towards the end of June or at the beginning of July.[80] Allenby sought permission to offer discussions on aspects of the reserved questions in return for an offensive and defensive alliance committing Egypt to taking part in a war which involved Britain.[81] Although at the turn of the month he was sending MacDonald continual reassurance of Zaghlul's good intentions, he reported on 11 May that the previous day the Prime Minister had reaffirmed his non-recognition of the Declaration and stated that 'He would go to London in the hope of obtaining complete independence of Egypt and the Soudan by negotiation.'[82] (In the Foreign Office, Murray minuted on the telegram that 'If we were to take his repudiation of the Declaration ... at its face value, Egypt would automatically cease to be an independent State and would revert to its previous status of a British Protectorate.')[83] On 4 June, 'Izzat Pasha, Egypt's Minister in London, renewed the claim to the Sudan in a speech in Manchester.[84] On 19 June, Zaghlul said in the Chamber that the Sudan was an indivisible part of Egypt. Four days later, he declared that Egypt would not relinquish any of her rights in the Sudan and that he would open his impending conversations in London with a demand for the complete British evacuation of that country.[85] (In response, Lord Parmoor, Lord President of the Council, said in the Lords that 'his Majesty's Government is not going to abandon the Sudan in any sense whatever'.)[86]

There was a great deal of debate between Cairo and the Foreign Office, which was driven to distraction, as to whether or not London was indeed the right venue for the talks. Eyre Crowe's successor as PUS, Willie Tyrrell – whose sceptical minuting was exemplified by his remark, 'If ... our Cairo reports faithfully represent the state of affairs in Egypt'[87] – declared on 24 April that 'In this matter of the conduct of negotiations with Zaghlul, the Cairo Residency seems to me to be as variable as the British climate ... I do not think we need pay any more attention to Cairo suggestions which are subject to such frequent and violent changes.'[88] In the end, after Zaghlul had been slightly wounded in an attempt on his life on 12 July which had had the aim of aborting his journey,[89] the ill-omened 'conversations' took place in London on 25 and 29 September and 3 October.[90] Allenby – who must have spent half of his time as High Commissioner to Egypt out of the country – was present. They put to the test his belief that once Egypt was 'independent' the rest would follow. Zaghlul was 'utterly unyielding and intransigent'[91] and concentrated his demands on the reserved points and other irritations. Using an Allenby argument, he said that the British Army could guard the Canal from mandatory Palestine, but MacDonald – whom Zaghlul found, in power, changed from the man he had known before[92] – demanded guaranteed safeguards. The talks failed completely, allowing those who wished to to blame Allenby – without, in all probability, making allowance for the fact that his victory over Lloyd George had been obtained when there was no prospect of Zaghlul being his country's chief negotiator. In a despatch, MacDonald said that Zaghlul had again 'stated that the fact that a foreign officer was Commander-in-Chief of the Egyptian Army, and the retention in that army of British officers, were inconsistent with the dignity of independent Egypt'. With uncomfortable prescience, the Prime Minister added, 'The expression of such sentiments in an official pronouncement by the responsible head of the Egyptian Government has obviously placed not only Sir Lee Stack as Sirdar, but all British officers attached to the Egyptian Army, in a difficult position.'[93] He added:

> there can be no question of their [Britain] abandoning the Sudan until their work is done ... His Majesty's Government have never failed to recognise that Egypt has certain material interests in the Sudan which must be guaranteed and safeguarded these being chiefly concerned with her share of the Nile water and the satisfaction of any financial claims which she may have against the Sudan Govt. His Majesty's Government have always been prepared to secure these interests in a way satisfactory to Egypt.[94]

Zaghlul returned home on 20 October. On 18 November, he refused to renew the contract of Amos as Judicial Adviser and axed his post. The next day, the latest in a line of murdered British subjects, Stack, who 'symbolized the continuation of British power in the Nile Valley',[95] was shot and wounded in a Cairo street by seven gunmen as he returned home for lunch from his Ministry of War office. He was carried to the Residency, where Asquith was a house guest[96] and the Claytons were having lunch with the Allenbys. On hearing the news of the shooting, which was to lead to the disintegration of the Condominium which had ruled the Sudan since 1899, Zaghlul – perhaps exclaiming, 'We are lost'[97] – rushed round to the Residency to express his deep regret. He was met by Allenby, a longtime friend of Stack, who told him, 'This is your doing.'[98] He agreed immediately to offer a £E10,000 reward for information, as suggested by Russell, who described him as 'obviously much distressed',[99] and urged the doctors to save Stack and the police to catch his assailants. The last of the Sirdars died in hospital the next day.

In connection with the assassination, 36 people were arrested, including Makram 'Ubayd, 'Abd ar Rahman Fahmy – who had been convicted by British court martial in 1920 and released under amnesty – and Mahmud Fahmy an Nuqrashy Pasha.[100] (While the majority were freed on grounds of insufficient evidence, six were eventually committed for involvement and two for conspiracy in the commission of the murder. All eight were sentenced to death on 7 June, seven were executed on 23 August and one received penal servitude for life.)[101]

Allenby sent to London the draft of an ultimatum he wished to deliver to Zaghlul after Stack's funeral on 22 November. He intended it to be in the Prime Minister's hands before a sitting of the Egyptian Parliament, due to meet at 1700 hrs that day, at which it was thought that Zaghlul might resign. He asked for a reply by midday[102] to his proposals for action. These, Toynbee noted, 'under the Covenant of the League of Nations, could not legitimately be taken by a Member State against another State – Member or non-Member – which was sovereign and independent in the usual meaning of those words'.[103] Allenby insisted that at the funeral places should be reserved for Zaghlul and his ministers. The British in Egypt were outraged, and in particular Bishop Gwynne – Bishop of Egypt and the Sudan, who had not been known for his compassion on the Western Front – protested in the strongest terms during an outspoken meeting with Allenby. The High Commissioner, however, had his way and the Prime Minister and his Cabinet – Zaghlul then and thereafter concerned lest he himself be murdered, arrested or hanged – attended the service in the face of open hostility from the predominantly British congregation.

After the funeral, as Allenby left the Embassy, he knew that a response to his draft had come which was too long simply to be agreement to his text or to be quickly decoded. Pressing on regardless with his rehearsal for Sir Miles Lampson's performance in 1941, the High Commissioner – in civilian clothes (to the distress of George V)[104] and perhaps a 'slouch hat'[105] and escorted by the 16th/5th Lancers of which he had been CO – drove to the Prime Minister's office. Whether he suspected it or not, in setting out 'to demolish the basis of his lasting settlement',[106] he was hastening his career to its end. Zaghlul 'was roused by the clatter of a large force of cavalry outside, by the calls of a mass salute, and a fanfare of trumpets'.[107] Ignoring the fact that Egypt was supposed to be independent, Allenby burst into the Prime Minister's office, read out his list of demands in English, which Zaghlul did not understand (a written French translation was provided), and, giving him 24 hours to comply, marched out as 'the policy of concession was dropped with a vengeance'.[108]

Virtually the whole of Egypt's involvement in the administration of the Sudan was brusquely terminated[109] in the ultimatum, which included 'several points which might reasonably be regarded as irrelevant to the crime by which the ultimatum had been provoked'[110] and in one opinion was adjudged to constitute 'retribution so excessive that it looked like an intention to do Egypt permanent harm'.[111] It predictably earned him the plaudits of the British community. It began with a preamble which declared that the assassination 'holds up Egypt as at present governed to the contempt of civilized peoples'. Its seven clauses demanded a sincere apology, appropriate punishment for the murderers, the banning of all popular political demonstrations, a £500,000 fine, the issuing of an order within 24 hours withdrawing all Egyptian officers and purely Egyptian units of the Sudan Army from that country,[112] the derestriction of the share of Nile water for the Gazirah cotton scheme which Wingate had started south-east of Khartum ['His Majesty's Government therefore require that the Egyptian Government shall ... notify the competent department that the Sudan Government will increase the area to be irrigated in the Gezira from 300,000 feddans to an unlimited figure as need may arise'][113] and the immediate cessation of all opposition to Britain's claims to protect foreigners and minorities.[114]

The sixth point, by which Allenby 'brought British vengeance into every smallholding in Egypt'[115] and 'put his thumb on the country's jugular vein', infuriated the populace.[116] Bell quoted 'one Peterson who is the assistant foreign correspondent of the Times' whom she thought 'singularly level and unprejudiced' as saying that 'The Nile clause looks like a petty sort of revenge ... Everyone says that it is "punishment".'[117] Jarvis, taking the opposite view, considered it 'a diplomatic blunder of the first order – a purely commercial clause ... that obviously favoured the Sudan Plantations Syndicate'. He rated the ultimatum as a whole the opening of 'one of our sloppy periods during which we allowed the Egyptian Government to argue ... The lion's roar had died away to a feeble whimper and whining complaint.'[118]

A second communication, supplementary to the ultimatum proper, demanded the retention of the financial and judicial adviser posts[119] and contained the statement that 'Sudanese units of the Egyptian Army shall be converted into a Sudan defence force, owing allegiance to the Sudan Government alone and under the supreme command of the Governor-General.'[120]

The Foreign Office reply, for which Allenby had not waited, would have significantly diluted his demands[121] and cancelled the fine. 'The piling up on a dead man's body of a mass of material which the Residency had been unable to settle otherwise seemed improper and irrelevant to Whitehall.'[122] Much less harsh in tone, the London version added to the sixth clause an assurance that its implementation would not damage Egypt's interests.[123] The new Foreign Secretary, Chamberlain, on 24 November asked the Master of the *Fait Accompli* to 'explain more fully your reasons. I do not at present understand the extreme urgency under which you acted' and threatened to substitute the Foreign Office ultimatum for Allenby's own.[124] He likened Allenby's *démarche* to 'the action of the little boy who puts his thumb to his nose and extends his four fingers in a vulgar expression of defiance or contempt'.[125] Nonetheless, the British government upheld Allenby's action, as it would have been almost impossible for it not to. In a letter of 23 December, the High Commissioner told his sister, Nell, 'Stack's murder merely hurried a line of action, on our part, which had been inevitable. The attitude of Zaghlul would have necessitated my ultimatum anyhow.'[126]

Initially on 23 November, while accepting the first four demands, the Egyptian Chamber voted to reject the last three on the grounds that they were all 'contrary to existing agreements or understandings'. When, 90 minutes later, Allenby informed his host government that the two rejected Sudan-related items were being made the subjects of direct instructions to Khartum,[127] in what Lloyd called a 'childishly irresponsible reply',[128] Zaghlul made apology and accepted all but points six and seven.[129] This action caused Huda Sha'rawy to vacate her office as President of the Wafdist Women's Central Committee and, in a *Manifesto to the Men and Women of Egypt* in the newspaper *Al Akhbar* on 24 November, to demand the resignation of the Father of the Nation: 'Since you have failed while in public office to fulfil your mandate by positive action, I ask you not to be an obstacle in your country's struggle for liberation . . . I ask you to step down.'[130]

The £500,000 was paid at 1130 hrs on the same day. Half an hour later, Allenby told Zaghlul that in response to Egypt's rejection of the seventh demand, British troops would occupy the Alexandria tobacco customs' offices, which they did at 1600 hrs. He had ships sent to Alexandria and alarmed Whitehall by voicing the possibility of taking hostages there.[131] Ludicrously, and demonstrating how little training he had absorbed from his staff, he threatened to break off diplomatic relations.[132] On 24 November also, Zaghlul – in reaction to these dramatic events and not in the best of health – resigned. The Egyptian Senate and Chamber protested against the ultimatum to all the world's parliaments and to the League of Nations,[133] which in the upshot took no action because technically the matter was not an international one.[134]

Ahmad Ziwar Pasha, a pro-British moderate and the Senate's first President, succeeded Zaghlul on the day of his resignation. Under pressure from Allenby, on 29 November he agreed to fulfil the whole of the ultimatum, accepting Britain's demands with regard to all matters relating to foreign subjects, the terms of service, discipline and retirement of foreign officials[135] and the Financial and Judicial Adviser posts,[136] cancelling Zaghlul's abolition of the latter. A semi-official British résumé ungraciously declared that 'the settlement re-establishes the powers and privileges of the Financial and Judicial Advisers which were agreed upon when the British Declaration of February 28 1922 was issued, but of late, particularly under the Zaghlul Cabinet, were deliberately ignored'.[137] Toynbee comments:

> In forcing Ziwar Pasha and his colleagues to accept the terms of the ultimatum with little alleviation the British authorities were forcing them to commit political suicide, and were thus unintentionally paving the way for that return of the intransigent forces to power

which was accomplished in the renewed victory of the *Wafd* at the elections of 1926.[138]

Such independence and sovereignty as Britain had granted Egypt had been 'on the understanding that the vacuum created by the partial withdrawal of British control should be filled by an Egyptian parliamentary constitutional régime'.[139] Inconsistent with this was the task Allenby proceeded to give Ziwar of diluting Egypt's democracy[140] in order to crush the Wafd. As an opening move in this direction, on 24 December the Prime Minister obtained the dissolution of the Chamber,[141] where the Wafd's large majority had not been affected by his appointment.

British backtracking, in the attempt to limit the damage caused by Allenby's impetuosity, did not long delay. Egyptian units withdrew from the Sudan during the period 24 November to 4 December, to be replaced by the Sudan Defence Force. (On 27 November two platoons of the 11th Sudanese Infantry mutinied at Khartum and three British officers and four other ranks were killed. Of four Sudanese officers sentenced to death, three were executed.)[142] Honour was satisfied when the customs' building was vacated on 3 December.[143] On the 15th Chamberlain declared in the House of Commons that 'the intention ... to starve Egypt into submission by thirst ... never entered the mind of Lord Allenby nor the minds of His Majesty's Ministers at home' and apologised for the phrasing of the demand 'in quite unlimited terms'.[144] Allenby himself told Ziwar that the British government had 'no intention of trespassing upon the natural and historic rights of Egypt in the waters of the Nile'. It was prepared to tell the Sudan government not to implement point six on condition that a committee should meet not later than 15 February 'for the purpose of examining and proposing a basis on which irrigation can be carried out with full consideration for the interests of Egypt and without detriment to her natural and historical rights'.[145]

Nonetheless, Allenby had forced the hand of the Foreign Office once too often and now it had completely lost confidence in him. Chamberlain – influenced by Churchill (whose poor opinion of Allenby we have seen), the press and especially Lloyd, active in the background – had come to believe that the High Commissioner was out of his depth and, in the short term, like McMahon, in need of diplomatic guidance. Without prior consultation, and with his decision already published, Chamberlain informed Allenby of a long-planned decision to send his old friend Nevile Henderson to Cairo as Minister Plenipotentiary and Deputy High Commissioner. This development 'bitterly offended Allenby',[146] who naturally saw it as demonstrating a lack of confidence in him. He complained to Chamberlain, 'you have made a striking appointment to my staff in the midst of a crisis without consulting me, and published it without giving me an opportunity of expressing my opinion';[147] he would lose face and authority since the move would be clearly seen as his practical supersession. He asked in vain that Henderson should brief him for a week and then depart. Chamberlain reminded him that, although they had supported him, his ultimatum had not been approved by London, where influential people who had admired his firmness after the murder of Stack deplored his rashness[148] in the sequel.

On the day of Zaghlul's resignation, Joseph McPherson reached the pinnacle of his contempt for Allenby, 'the master jackass' who had been:

> at last kicked into the track, after fouling our pitch and the Gyppies' for years, trampling on our prestige and every sane basis of government, and committing every asininity ... I, for one, would rather shake hands with old Zaghlul. He has been treated like a mouse by a very cruel and silly cat: allowed again and again to run as he liked and then clawed back ... Allenby has let down his supporters, Egyptian and English [*sic*], and encouraged their enemies ... If he is showing firmness today, he will show weakness tomorrow, as ever, and undo any good that is done. There is no hope for us or the natives as long as that fool is here ... tell him if he wants to benefit England [*sic*] and Egypt, for God's sake to clear out.[149]

Henderson found himself in a touchy position but behaved tactfully throughout, Chamberlain seeming to be content for him to have nothing to do. He avoided office contact with Allenby as much as possible. The personal relations between the two men were warm, however. He wrote to a friend: 'I like Allenby ... I have done my best by inaction.' His arrival had, however, badly weakened Allenby's authority and, in any crisis, Henderson, by virtue of his 'plenipotentiary' title, would have taken charge. It was on account of his presence that, on 27 November 1924, the High Commissioner resigned.[150] Two days later, Chamberlain told him that he would be informed when he would be allowed to go.

Allenby sought at length, with some success, to justify the actions to which Whitehall had objected, provoking Chamberlain to shoulder some of the blame himself.[151] On 22 December, the Foreign Secretary – while complaining about the inadequacies of Allenby's reporting – congratulated him on his work in Egypt and appealed to him, 'when this crisis is passed', to:

> let me submit your request for permission to resign as the natural desire of a great servant of the Crown to take the opportunity offered by the end of one chapter of our relations with Egypt and the beginning of another as the proper moment to seek relief from the strain of such long and arduous service and the natural and most honourable close of your great career in the Near East, first as soldier and then as statesman.[152]

When Allenby declined to co-operate, the correspondence between the two became more outspoken[153] than during the earlier part of a connection always characterised by poor relations[154] and the High Commissioner appeared to throw caution to the winds. At the beginning of 1925, without authority from the Foreign Office (which had been keen enough to keep the grand old man of Egyptian nationalism out), he gave a definite and official assurance to British and Egyptian civil servants that 'the wicked old man', Zaghlul, would never be Prime Minister again.[155] On 12 February, he proposed that the C-in-C of the Egyptian Army should be an Egyptian, an idea ridiculed in the Foreign Office[156] and dismissed by Lloyd: 'It is hardly necessary to point out that such a proposal conflicted fundamentally with the 1922 Declaration.'[157]

At elections in March, despite the hostile efforts of Interior Minister Sidqy and the apparent reduction of its majority to vanishing point, the Wafd once again won the bulk of the seats.[158] But the opening session lasted less than a day before, following Zaghlul's election as President by 125 votes to 85,[159] the King refused Ziwar's offer to resign. Instead, when Allenby demanded the parliament's prorogation on 23 March, he granted an immediate dissolution. Seizing the opportunity offered by Allenby's hostility to the Wafd, and determined to obtain a revision of the electoral law in advance of the new elections which Ziwar promised for the autumn,[160] he went further by suspending the constitution, taking Egypt into an absolutist embrace. Climaxing his seizure of power, in August, with Allenby looking on with satisfaction, he prepared to rule, without parliament, through his own Hizb al Ittihad (Union Party), popularly known as Hizb al Malik (the King's Party), which had been created two months earlier.

On 11 April, the Residency denied reports in *Al Muqattam* on 3 April and in *Al Ahram* and *As Siyasah* on 10 April, both quoting the *Daily Telegraph* and the *Daily Mail*, that Allenby was retiring and being replaced by Sir George Lloyd.[161] Eventually, however, Grafftey-Smith had to take Allenby a Reuter announcement that Lloyd had been appointed to succeed him:

> He read this news item and rose to his feet, leaning his hands on his desk. He was rocking with emotion. In Spain, before the war, I had watched too many *corridas* not to recognise 'Death in the Afternoon'. He begged me to leave him.[162]

On 24 May, Bell passed the view on to her father that 'the FO have treated Lord Allenby very scurvily'.[163] He left the country on 14 June 1925, to the regret of many, including members of the Wafd.[164] Henderson remained as Acting Resident until Lloyd arrived, representing a British government which was as unsure as before the 1922 Declaration how best to tackle its outstanding Egypt problems.[165] As for Allenby himself, however, his fellow-soldier, Wavell, said that he had 'recognised the awakened spirit of a people'.[166] He may not have had 'the sublety and ... diplomacy to cope with the twists and turns of Egyptian political manoeuvring'[167] but, in one opinion, he 'had a better knowledge and instinctive understanding of the complex political problems of the Middle East than any member of the British Cabinet'[168] and 'His errors of judgement, which were undeniably many and serious, were outweighed by his unusually sympathetic understanding for Egyptian nationalism.'[169] Grafftey-Smith rated him a 'very great man'[170] and his Proconsulship as 'memorable for good'. Allenby had been able 'to extract Egyptian Independence from an unwilling British Government and then to extract a liberal Egyptian constitution from a reactionary autocrat. At the same time he managed to maintain essential British interests without forfeiting the respect, indeed the admiration, of Egyptians.'

It is clear that, although he repeatedly overruled their judgements, his staff were devoted to a man who – 'always courteous, always simple, always straightforward' and 'of surprising erudition'[171] – had everything, except a sympathetic approach, to learn from them.

Part IV

Lloyd, 21 October 1925– 23 July 1929
(Baron Lloyd of Dolobran (1879–1941) GCIE, GCSI, DSO)

Devoid of diplomatic instincts, little interested in making contact with Egyptians but determined to dictate his own policy to Whitehall, Lloyd was a spectacular failure as High Commissioner. He began well by persuading the King to end his absolutist rule and restore the constitution but, in opposition to Foreign Secretary Chamberlain's view, kept Zaghlul from power.

Lloyd's inability to see eye to eye with Chamberlain, the Foreign Office and Prime Minister Baldwin brought him down. He disagreed with his principals especially over 'independent' Egypt's desire to expand its army and to enact an Assemblies' Bill and a petrol tax, and was charged with speaking against government policy to foreigners.

He stood by complacently as Egypt returned to absolute rule by the King. He was blamed for the failure, which he had prophesied, of a British–Egyptian Treaty which had been negotiated behind his back. As his resignation was being required, further treaty talks were in train of which knowledge had been kept from him.

11 Arch-champion of British firmness

Apprenticeship

the most energetic man that I ever knew.
(Vansittart)

Resemblances between Arnold Wilson and Lawrence have been claimed.[1] A better-rounded pairing is Wilson and Lloyd, who both believed strongly in the Empire and Christianity (Lloyd was a Quaker), sympathised little with nationalism, devoted much effort to fighting Whitehall (Allenby did his share of this), maintained an inner circle of disciples (in Lloyd's case, his ADCs, who called him 'God' but were not always treated well), had a house in the Hitchin area and – in response to Hitler – took up military flying at an advanced age. Lloyd, though 'more sophisticated' than Wilson, possessing 'an incisive intelligence and an un-British logicality',[2] had 'much the same habits of physical and mental energy, much the same inclination to autocracy and intolerance, much the same views on imperialism, and much the same contempt for liberalism'. When they met, in 1907, Lloyd, Wilson said, made 'an indelible impression of firmness and energy on my mind'.[3] Wilson, however, was much the more human of the two and had no love affair with the Arabs, preferring Persians; Lloyd had early fallen under the spell of the East (at levels which were no threat to his self-importance) and shared Cromer's sympathy for the Egyptian *fallah*. Assessments of his Arabic attainments vary.[4]

As a convinced imperialist, Lloyd's watchword was that the legions should not be withdrawn. In the case of Egypt, he believed that he had already seen in the Milner–Zaghlul Agreement of 1920 a threatened first step in the process;[5] as High Commissioner in Cairo he was determined to stand by Allenby's 1922 Declaration. 'The arch-champion of British firmness whenever the reserved points were touched upon',[6] the impression he gives is of a British representative who, unlike Allenby, was a bully devoid of charm or flexibility. Whether or not the Foreign Office thought of him in this way, it objected more strongly to him, and perhaps consequently to his post being held by someone who was not a member of the Foreign Service, than it had in the cases of his three predecessors. This was perhaps partly because – brooking no refusal – he had forced an entry into the nobility. It also did not like the way in which, Vansittart said, 'the most energetic man that I ever knew' was in the habit of 'imposing progress'.[7] Further, 'George hated control . . ., was secretive and suspicious . . . His high sense of duty and dignity was . . . termed pompous by his staff, even more by the Foreign Office.'[8] It was characteristic of someone of whom the Prince of Wales was alleged to have said, when visiting him in Bombay in 1922, that he 'had not known what regal splendour was' before,[9] that he should reintroduce all the magnificence and privilege enjoyed by the great Consuls-General – a special train, use of the royal gates at Cairo railway station, precedence second only to the King, etc. – but which his most recent predecessor – unlike Wingate[10] – had been big enough to abandon.

Whitehall, which should have known after India, found that 'George was a difficult customer. He reported by letter rather than despatch, and often to SB [Baldwin] over Austen's [Chamberlain] head. The Foreign Office hated the first trait, Austen the second.'[11] He thus, Amery observed, 'contrived . . . to see to it that the general view of the Cabinet prevailed in his favour against the Foreign Secretary'.[12] There developed in his time in Cairo a sharp divergence between Cabinet and Foreign Office policy towards Egypt, the latter – and the Foreign Secretary – regarding as essential reserved points only the maintenance of imperial communications and the defence of the country itself. Officials wanted the 1922 Declaration to be leniently interpreted and Egypt's internal affairs to be interfered in as little as possible by Britain; the Cabinet, however, stood for firm adherence to the whole of the Declaration. Since Lloyd sided with the latter, no doubt regarding its members as his natural associates, Chamberlain and the Foreign Office saw him as using it as a shield with which to frustrate them.[13] Chamberlain's successor Arthur Henderson, too, quickly came to share the Foreign Office view of Lloyd, whom he accused, in relation to the Declaration, of exhibiting a 'marked determination to misinterpret or ungenerously to apply' it.[14]

It is not surprising, then, that Lloyd's High Commissionership was even more unsuccessful than Allenby's, if a little less chaotic. The Foreign Office/Cabinet disagreement over policy was not the only complication. Lloyd's term of office was also marked by his determination to do things his way and subordinate policy to his own interests. He had gunboats on the brain, saying, 'When I see those jacarandas [of the Gazirah Club golf course] in bloom, I know it's time to send for a battleship!'[15] He got off to almost as bad a start as Allenby when his use of H.M.S. *Resolute* to prevent Zaghlul from becoming Prime Minister was disapproved of by Nevile Henderson and another member of the diplomatic staff, the Assistant Oriental Secretary Laurence Grafftey-Smith,[16] who were secretly criticising his interventionism to the Foreign Office within nine months of his arrival in Cairo. Disagreement the following year with Baldwin, acting as his own

Foreign Secretary, led to Lloyd being out of step with the home government as a whole. In the upshot, the Foreign Office negotiated in London
and Paris (in both of which places he was available at the requisite
moments) a draft treaty with Egypt about which he was barely consulted;
when the Egyptian Parliament in due course rejected it, the Foreign
Office accused him of sabotage. Whereas it could not tell Wingate what
the government's policy was, it withheld knowledge of it, as it developed,
from Lloyd, whom it stripped of any shred of dignity.

For family reasons, Lloyd left Oxford without a degree.[17] Before arriving
in Cairo as High Commissioner in 1925, he had had – although only 46 –
an extraordinarily active and varied career, spent mainly in transitory jobs.
In November 1905, partly through the efforts of Bell,[18] he became an
unpaid honorary attaché at the British Legation in Istanbul, along with
Aubrey Herbert[19] and Sykes. From January to August 1907 he was a special
commissioner reporting on trading prospects in Muscat and southern
Iraq, where he met the great[20] Sir Percy Cox,[21] Political Resident in the
Gulf and Consul-General for Fars, Luristan and Khuzistan. In January
1910 he was elected as a Conservative to Parliament for West Stafford-
shire. He played a major part, remarkable in an opposition backbencher,
in stiffening the Asquith Government's resolve to enter the First World
War in support of France and Russia, earning the praise of Neville Chamberlain, who wrote to his step-brother, 'some day the country will be grateful to Amery, G. Lloyd, and you for having preserved her honour'.[22] With
the outbreak of hostilities, as a member of the Warwickshire Yeomanry, he
was assigned to a War Office outpost, the Intelligence Department in
Cairo, where he joined Herbert, Lawrence and the archaeologist Leonard
Woolley in the Arab Bureau in December 1914. In February 1915 he was
at the Ottoman attack on the Suez Canal and, in April, while still based in
Cairo, landed with the Anzacs at Gallipoli as a member of General Birdwood's staff. During the war he was mentioned in despatches six times. In
October and late November he was on a mission to try to persuade Russia
to do without Turkish coal imports. He saw in the New Year of 1916 in
Cairo with Bell, among others; 'wasn't it delightful?', she asked her
mother.[23] He then briefly joined Maxwell's Military Intelligence, identify-
ing traders with the enemy, before first returning as 2nd-in-command of a
Warwickshire Yeomanry squadron and then being offered to Cox by
Herbert. Bell wrote, 'George Lloyd is on his way here from Egypt – Sir
Percy [Cox] has asked for him. Won't it be delightful to have him.'[24] He
spent from May to late July as an emissary of the Arab Bureau, following
up his 1907 report in Basrah with Cox and Bell who, with Wilson, were
laying the political foundations for the British rule in Iraq which stemmed
from the Indo-British invasion of October 1914. In July 1916, two months
after Townshend's[25] army had surrendered at Kut and just before Maude[26]
resumed the drive against the Ottomans, Lloyd visited the Mesopotamian

front at 'Amarah and brought back harrowing accounts of soldiers suffering from a drastic lack of ice and a paucity of food. On his return to Cairo in October, Bell told her parents that he 'has done good work but even better than his work is the atmosphere of sanity he brings with him ... he is naturally so level headed'.[27] (Storrs speaks of his 'unique objectivity',[28] but this quality was not one which, when he became High Commissioner, was to be observed by his staff or his London correspondents.)

His return to Cairo was in order to work as one of Allenby's Chiefs of Military Intelligence. Bertie Clayton, a level-headed man if ever there was one, was Director of Intelligence; Lloyd was in charge of Advanced Intelligence, joining the Turcophile Wyndham Deedes (Political) and Meinertzhagen (Military), who claimed that Lloyd was his subordinate. In November 1916, as an emissary of Wingate, as Sirdar, he accompanied the French and Italian Arab Revolt liaison officers, Colonels Brémond and Barnabi,[29] to investigate the situation at Jiddah and Rabigh.[30] In February 1917, he went home to report to the Foreign and War Offices on his Hijaz findings.

In May he left London with Sykes – whom he thought 'essentially shallow',[31] 'slovenly, self-serving and *louche*'[32] – and Georges-Picot to enquire into politico-military matters likely to assume importance among the Palestinians and Syrians during Allenby's ongoing push against the Ottomans. Back in Cairo, he was involved in work on the Sykes–Picot Agreement – of which, in June 1916, he had approved[33] – and on concomitant consideration of the shape of the Levant after the assumed fall of the Ottoman Empire. He was with Allenby's army before Gazah. Then he went to 'Aqabah, which Lawrence – who he thought had 'rather an addiction to me'[34] – had just taken. He dined with Faysal and Zayd, Sharif Husayn's fourth son, and from 24 to 29 October rode with Lawrence from 'Aqabah to Al Jafr, east of Ma'an, to rendezvous with 'Audah Abu Tay', who had a castle there. He then went home to drum up support for Lawrence in his task of encouraging Faysal to ignore the Sykes–Picot Agreement, against which he himself had quickly turned.

In January 1918, Lloyd became Assistant to Austen Chamberlain on the British Delegation to the Inter-Allied War Financial Council. At the end of February he was asked to be Governor of British East Africa. In late May he was with Robert Cecil, who was in charge of the blockade of Germany. Awarded a KCIE, he was Governor of Bombay from December 1918 to December 1923; Chamberlain had advised Montagu to appoint him,[35] and the Secretary of State for India, in doing so, made clear his doubts in telling the Viceroy, 'it is not by any means a conventional appointment, and if I do not look upon it with confidence, I at any rate look upon it with hope'.[36] In the upshot, although in one opinion rated 'one of Bombay's greatest Governors' and 'perhaps in retrospect one of the greatest administrators this country has produced in the last generation or two',[37] Lloyd had an acrimonious difference of opinion with his second

Viceroy, Lord Reading, over policy towards Gandhi, whom he incarcerated. He left behind him, however, the Lloyd Barrage on the Indus to perpetuate his name. He asked Montagu for a peerage as a way of securing a 'public platform'; Montagu did not take the point, souring their relations.[38] In January 1923, he was made a Privy Counsellor and, in October 1924, became Conservative MP for Eastbourne. The Colonial Secretary, Leo Amery, offered him the post of Governor of Kenya in March 1925, and – with a vast amount of high-level achievement behind him – he became High Commissioner in Cairo in the October. Chamberlain objected to the way in which he had campaigned for the appointment.[39]

12 Rather severe language to your Secretary of State

Seeding the clouds

> it is a difficult job. I don't know anyone better for it than George if he
> won't try to be a little too much of a King Stork.[1]
>
> (Bell)

On 8 October 1925, Lloyd received a letter from the Private Secretary at
10 Downing Street. Crowning his second attempt to barge into the
peerage, which was strongly supported by Reading, it told him that the
King – somewhat reluctantly, considering the ennoblement premature[2] –
had been 'pleased to approve that the dignity of a Barony of the United
Kingdom be conferred upon you'.[3]

Although it was not until 10 October that Willie Tyrrell wrote formally,
on behalf of Chamberlain, to appoint their friend Lloyd High Commissioner for Egypt and the Sudan, in Cairo Nevile Henderson had known
for months of the posting, which was announced in the House of
Commons on 20 May. He was another friend of Lloyd's, from Eton days
and, left over from Allenby's time, had another year to serve in Egypt. 'It
will be an immense relief', he said, 'to be finished with the equivocal situation which has been existing here since I got out to Cairo in December
last.'[4] For his part, Lloyd flattered his stand-in, as Wingate had flattered
Cheetham: 'It is a real satisfaction to me', he said, 'that we are going to be
colleagues . . . and I know how fortunate I am in having you there to help
and guide me.'[5] Until his arrival, the two had a correspondence which
lasted the summer. The airs Lloyd gave himself in it was sufficient to disillusion Henderson before their first reunion.

He told Lloyd that the Egyptians 'are expecting an Indian tiger and
there is much talk of a return to the régime of Cromer and Kitchener'.[6]
He made very clear his hope – expressed to Prime Minister Ziwar and
perhaps contracted from Allenby – that the door would be kept firmly
shut against Zaghlul. He informed Lloyd:

> so long as I had any voice at the Residency, there would be no deal-
> ings of any kind with Saad Zaghloul . . . If any future elections again

gave Saad a majority, I would unhesitatingly advise the King once more to dissolve Parliament and to go on dissolving it till Saad was dead or the people had learnt wisdom ... He and Saadism in its anti-British form have got to be rooted out of Egypt ... Unless we want to clear out bag and baggage of Egypt we cannot afford to have anything to do with him again.[7]

In July he told Lloyd that a memorandum, the joint work of several members of the Egyptian Cabinet, had appealed for the Allenby ultimatum to be reconsidered 'on the ground of the restoration of friendly relations and presumably because Saad and not Egypt was responsible for what happened last year'.[8] He said in the same month, 'The tide is rising again now towards cooperation with the British'[9] and – music, no doubt, to Lloyd's ears – he warned in August that 'All our misfortunes here have been due to our own vacillations and the inconstancy of our purpose.'[10]

It was over the style of the welcome he expected that Lloyd most irritated Henderson. The Acting Resident had said on 19 June that 'when you arrive, say at Cairo, you should have guards of honour at the Railway station and at the Residency, but no cavalry escort and no guns'.[11] He reported that General Sir Richard Haking, GOC British troops, had asked whether or not there should be a Royal Salute. 'Lord Allenby had it', Henderson noted, 'though he probably was not entitled to it – at any rate after the abolition of the Protectorate.'[12] He warned that 'Fuad is highly susceptible and touchy and anything which might give the impression of a rival show or a prolongation of the Protectorate will undoubtedly be resented.'[13] The upshot was that, earning Henderson's disapproval, Lloyd ignored his advice, refusing to countenance a first appearance which differed in any way from that accorded his predecessor, guns and all. This was four-square with Lloyd's habit, once in post, of competing with the King, ruler of an allegedly independent country, by requiring royal treatment for himself.

He landed at Alexandria on 21 October and immediately faced a crisis. The constitution had been suspended since March and both the Wafd and the moderates were exercised about the fact that the administration had been placed 'on a purely Palace basis'[14] following the creation in January of Hizb al Ittihad. Ostensibly led by Yahya Ibrahim Pasha, acting as Prime Minister, in reality control of it lay with its founder, the 'very able'[15] Hasan Nash'at Pasha, 'young, arrogant and charming'.[16] Without ever having been elected, he had become the power behind the throne through his control particularly of the ministries (Awqaf, War and Foreign Affairs)[17] on which King Fu'ad aimed to base his projected absolutism. Henderson had advised Lloyd that 'The Zaghloulists cling to one last hope: Sir George Lloyd',[18] and many of them looked to the new High Commissioner in the first instance to persuade Fu'ad to restore parliamentary life by displacing Nash'at. Henderson, who had 'no great sympathy with democratic processes', had quickly fallen under the King's spell and 'the not unwelcome conviction that he was winning the confidence and goodwill of a king made him deaf to warnings that this might be a slippery slope'.

On 9 November, Ziwar returned from Europe, where he had been since July. His Hizb al Ahrar ad Dusturiyyin cabinet colleagues having been eased out by Nash'at in the early autumn,[19] he anticipated that he would not find adequate support for his rule in Parliament. Accordingly, he first blocked its reassembly and then, rather than turn the government over to the radical opposition, persuaded the King and Nash'at to dissolve it again after a sitting of a few hours. Thus he was able to retain his power, 'with the support of the Palace and the British, against practically the wish and opinion of the whole nation',[20] until the next elections.

Zaghlul, in contrast, had sought the continuance of parliamentary government. On 21 November, 190 ex-Deputies and Senators drawn from all the non-monarchist parties – Hizb al Watan, Hizb al Ahrar ad Dusturiyyin and the Wafd, with all but the last 'little more than the expression of the personalities who monopolized and manipulated them'[21] – met at the Continental Hotel after being prevented by troops and police from reaching the Parliament building. They declared themselves a legally constituted assembly, denounced the King's suspension of the constitution and called for fresh elections. Zaghlul was voted their President, with Muhammad Mahmud, now Hizb al Ahrar leader, and 'Abd al Hamid Sa'id, a member of Al Hizb al Watany, as Vice-Presidents.

Unlike Allenby, who had encouraged the abrogation of the constitution, Lloyd felt that the British could not remain for long associated with an unconstitutional state of affairs. It made them seem to be 'suppressors of the free Constitution which had only just been granted'[22] and the course Fu'ad and Nash'at were together following was not in the British interest: 'the tendency towards absolutism and the drift away from constitutional rule . . . was a matter', Lloyd said, 'about which he could not but be gravely anxious'.[23] On 10 December, he got his posting off to a flying start, and delighted the Wafd, when the King bowed to his pressure, sent Nash'at – who had already done a term as Minister in the Egyptian Legation in Tehran[24] – to be ambassador to Spain and reactivated the constitution. Lloyd's claim that he played 'an indirect part in inducing Ziwar Pasha to restore Parliamentary Government'[25] is justified and perhaps overmodest. Tyrrell wrote to congratulate the new High Commissioner on his victory over Fu'ad:

> I think it is a blessing in disguise that he was so impatient to test your mettle. It is clear to me that he hoped you would be reluctant to engage upon an early struggle with him, and he was banking on having to deal with a trimmer. For all our sakes I am delighted that he has been undeceived.

He added, 'As far as I can judge, there will be little prospect of peace in Egypt until a ministry is created which can hold its own against the King without having to come to terms with Zaghloul.'[26] In fact, after the catastrophe of Stack's assassination, Lloyd noted, 'Zaghlul was exhibiting a discernible tendency towards moderation ... He was anxious ... to remain as far as possible in the background.'[27]

Though extremely cordial personal relations[28] were the concomitant of this early Lloyd success, Chamberlain was quick to caution him against further major interference in Egypt's internal politics and to lay down – in no 1882 spirit – the rules which would govern unavoidable involvement. Tyrrell told him:

> the ultimate object we have in view is to give the Egyptians every chance of managing their own affairs. If they fail and intervention by us becomes inevitable, there are two cardinal points we must observe. One is that British intervention is requested by the native, and the other is that a clear case for such intervention must be made in the House of Commons here.[29]

On 25 February 1926, Chamberlain again hinted at his apprehension about what Lloyd – in the anxiety he already felt to keep Zaghlul from power – might precipitate. He wanted the questions of China – where the previous year there had been disorders in all the Treaty ports and a general strike in Shanghai, with British troops having to be used – and Turkey (over Mosul) settled before 'we find ourselves involved in critical action anywhere else ... Great caution therefore is necessary in the development of our Egyptian crisis'[30] – one which both he and Lloyd envisaged as threatened by the continuing struggle between the King and the politicians. Further restraining attempts followed. On 10 March, Tyrrell told Lloyd, 'your right policy in the existing circumstances at home and abroad is to imitate and copy faithfully the attitude of your close neighbour the sphinx',[31] and on 1 April Chamberlain repeated his theme:

> I think it of great consequence to postpone anything in the nature of a crisis for as long as we can. We have too many difficult questions on our hands just now for me to be anything but most unwilling to face real trouble in Egypt.[32]

With his fingers crossed, on 21 April he reinforced the message: 'I felt it only right and fair to you to put very clearly before you the reasons which make me particularly anxious to postpone a crisis, if crisis there must be.' More widely, he continued that it was his duty to make him aware of 'the larger aspects of British policy, and I am quite satisfied when once I have done so that you will bear my views in mind in framing your own policy and adjust it to them'. Using a Wingate argument which had not convinced the Foreign Office, he added: '*Prima facie* I should have thought that, if Zaghloul holds the power, he would be less dangerous and more amenable to coercion if he also occupied the position of public respons-ibility.'[33] Although Lloyd agreed with the logic of this, he countered that the harm that would ensue to British prestige from the reappointment of Zaghlul – whom Tyrrell characterised to Lloyd at this time as 'so unstable an individual'[34] – must be the deciding factor.[35] The test of their diverging convictions was not long in coming.

On 20 May, a Wafd–Hizb al Ahrar ad Dusturiyyin alliance brought the Wafd victory in parliamentary elections and Ziwar resigned. Chamberlain strongly recommended Lloyd to accept Zaghlul as Prime Minister[36] but it cannot have helped the High Commissioner's attitude to the question that, on 25 May, six of seven of those on trial for Stack's murder – includ-ing the future Prime Minister Ahmad Mahir and Nuqrashy Pasha – were acquitted and only Muhammad Fahmy 'Aly was condemned to death.[37]

Lloyd had the chance for which he had been waiting when he received Zaghlul on 29 May. As the nationalist leader made it clear that the 1922 Declaration was unacceptable and refused to undertake not to raise the subject of the Sudan in Parliament, Lloyd flirted with Chamberlain's feared crisis by taking action which Arthur Henderson, the future Labour Foreign Secretary, was to use against him in 1929. He penned for Cham-berlain's approval a draft letter to Zaghlul and 'in order to prevent a pos-sible repetition of the grave rioting and loss of life of 1921 I suggested the despatch of a battleship to Alexandria'.[38] H.M.S. *Resolute* duly came. Zaghlul's Wafd colleagues, fearing a repeat suspension of the constitution – and doing Lloyd's work for him[39] – persuaded him to stand down on the ostensible grounds of his age and failing health. On 3 June, accordingly, Zaghlul declined the premiership.[40] Lloyd reported, 'He assured me without qualification that he had definitely decided never to take office again in any circumstances: he promised to do all in his power to establish and maintain friendly relations with the British Government.'[41] On the same day, Tyrrell told Lloyd, 'Saad's attitude as displayed in his interview with you last Sunday left the Government no alternative but to refuse him as Prime Minister.'[42] Not unexpectedly, Chamberlain, however, gave only lukewarm endorsement to Lloyd's line[43] and the High Commissioner felt the need to admit to him, 'I always have a fear you think me intemperate.'[44]

On 16 June, Chamberlain – saluting him as 'My dear Lloyd' instead of his usual 'My dear George' – wrote, 'You did for him [Zaghlul] in Cairo what Ramsay MacDonald did for him in London', and to reassure him: 'don't for heaven's sake worry yourself by suspecting that I suspect you of being "intemperate" or rash ... You have our confidence.'[45] Even Selby, in the Foreign Office's Egyptian Department, found praise for him: 'May I congratulate you on the happy issue of the recent crisis, which seems to have resulted in a considerable enhancement of our prestige.'[46]

In the upshot, 'Adly formed a 'largely moderate and anglophile' [*sic*][47] coalition government of three representatives of Hizb al Ahrar and seven

Wafdists. Further boosting the Wafd, when normal parliamentary life resumed on 10 June, Zaghlul became President of the Chamber. Behaving in an unexceptionable manner, he dominated the proceedings.[48] 'Adly and Lloyd agreed that he was being good – as over the question of the Advisers – because he believed that keeping in with the British was the only way to protect the constitution which allowed the Wafd to maintain its majority in parliament.[49] How things had changed was shown when, on 12 December, Lloyd told Chamberlain that he had protested to the King about attacks on Zaghlul by royalist newspapers seeking to persuade him to take a stronger line against the British. Their 'invariable basis' was 'his attempts to be moderate and accommodating in his attitude towards my Government ... That such a campaign should be associated with two newspapers popularly believed to be amenable to His Majesty's wishes was highly regrettable.'[50]

Despite this second Lloyd victory, the home front was disturbed. On 31 July, a letter to Selby from Nevile Henderson – who had got on with Allenby far better than he did with Lloyd – showed that, if superficially relations with Whitehall were normal, all was far from well at the Cairo end. The atmosphere in the Residency – 'not a happy ship'[51] – was dominated by 'the fear of the Lord'. Henderson said of his old school chum:

> I do not see eye to eye on many things with Lloyd. What I find hardest is to do good work and loyal service with a man who is set upon a policy which, though it may promise him kudos for a while ... I regard as contrary to our ultimate advantage. I mean going back if possible on the Milner report and the 1922 declaration; the suspension of the constitution and parliament and the reassumption by ourselves of increased responsibility here involving more and more interference in Egyptian internal affairs.[52]

While his Counsellor was thus engaged, in ignorance, Lloyd wrote to him on 2 August, from a home leave which had begun on 9 July, to say, 'I can't tell you what a difference having you at the other end means to my peace of mind.' He would have been astonished by the references to the constitution which he had just been instrumental in restoring and to his alleged intentions for the Declaration which was his rock.

Henderson was not the only subversive. Grafftey-Smith, in Cairo since the previous year, was also concerned by Lloyd's 'pursuit of a personal policy clashing with British government intentions', as by 'the labyrinthine methods of this pursuit ... for some of us, as for most Egyptians, he was a *Shaitan* ... a disloyal servant, but he was a stimulating master ... we were under constant interrogation'.[53] He observed that Lloyd withheld from London an offer from Zaghlul to receive a British military mission and that he was in general 'inclined to conceal from the Foreign Office developments or trends conflicting with his own personal policy, and this tendency caused alarm in London'. He filled the reporting gap by introducing a weekly return he knew that Lloyd would not read[54] and at times diverged from the High Commissioner's line in his own communications to London.[55] He felt that the High Commissioner's 'virtues were irrelevant to the Egyptian situation' because 'there was no room left for paternalism in Egypt, after 1922'. He was severely critical of the consequences: 'This frustration of his instincts lent some futility to his actions ... there is no more noisily futile an object than a frustrated broody hen.' He found little to approve of in Lloyd, who he said 'liked to impose himself as arbiter of everything, for he had not great sympathy with anyone else'[56] and 'did not like people not to think about him', even if it was God who was preoccupying them.[57]

He recorded of Lloyd that 'his popularity waned within a year. The attitudes of a former Governor of Bombay gave offence. All traffic in side-streets was held up when the High Commissioner drove through Cairo.' Visiting VIPs found the Lloyds' entertainment arrangements discourteous[58] and 'foreign representatives disliked him'. The US Minister, 'furious at the High Commissioner's pomp and circumstance', disputed precedence with him.[59] Selby recalled later that, in the Foreign Office itself, disagreement with Lloyd was already building up: 'It was this very powerful combination [Lindsay, Mervyn Herbert, Jack Murray and himself] at the FO which Lloyd had succeeded in challenging within a year or so of his arrival in Cairo.'[60]

Later in the year, Lloyd further unsettled his relations with Chamberlain and the Foreign Office through his attitude to the question of honours for his staff, when his tone offended the Foreign Secretary and the PUS. Chamberlain wrote:

> Your telegraphic reply to my telegram about Honours was not exactly a pleasant one to receive, my dear George. You do occasionally hold rather severe language to your Secretary of State and speak to him more imperatively than our other representatives abroad are accustomed to do ... if once or twice I have been momentarily upset as I read, I have at once called to my aid Mrs Midshipman Easy and have exclaimed 'Zeal, Sir, all zeal for the Service.'[61]

Reviving the ghost of his correspondence with Reading, on New Year's Day 1927 Lloyd, in a 12-page letter, remarked to Chamberlain, 'It is, I venture to suggest, hard if not impossible for anyone who is not actually handling this problem on the spot fully to realise its peculiar difficulty.'[62]

The controversy over honours was damped down, but another arose in February and March over gun salutes for the High Commissioner. Lloyd, nothing if not concerned for his own dignity and attributing to third parties sentiments which were in fact his own, said to Tyrrell, 'The alter-ation [in salutes] you propose will at once be noticed out here, and will be taken as a reduction in my status ... Egyptians, being Orientals, and attributing perhaps undue importance to such matters, will certainly draw undesirable inferences from the change.'[63]

In the midst of this ill-feeling between Cairo and London, Chamberlain – perhaps hinting that he would rather receive fewer of Lloyd's abrasive letters in future – complained about the High Commissioner's reporting methods, as Graham had about Wingate's. Calling the kettle black,[64] he informed Lloyd that 'private letters are tending to take the place of official despatches which should be the means of conveying to me the picture of the political situation as seen throught the eyes of our representatives abroad'. Incomplete despatch series 'leaves an irreparable gap in the office archives ... I would therefore ask you to regard any private letters which you may have occasion to send me as supplementary to and not in substitution for official despatches.'[65]

Lloyd had been High Commissioner for less than eighteen months, but already the storm clouds were gathering round him. Referring to his dispensation, after a visit to Cairo in March 1927, Hoare, now Minister for Air, told the Viceroy, 'there seemed to me to be a perpetual atmosphere of potential crisis about the regime'.[66]

13 A very serious misapprehension on his part
Diplomatic offensive – Tyrrell

Lloyd is 'apparently quite unable to understand our instructions'.

(Tyrrell)

Lloyd told Henderson that, during his home leave in 1926, he had been instructed by the Cabinet 'to secure an early reduction of the Egyptian army',[1] which – at some 30,000 men and consisting of Egyptian units of the three arms and Sudanese 'shock' troops under elitist British commanders – was always small in size. A decrease would enable the number of matching British troops in Egypt also to be cut, to economic advantage.

In March 1927, 'Adly's government introduced a bill with the opposite intention – to enlarge the army and its reserves, restrict the powers of the Inspector-General and create an air force.[2] Despite the fact that Lloyd, Chamberlain and Tyrrell, who was on a visit to Egypt, did not look with favour on the bill, the Foreign Office said on 11 March that it would accept the Inspector-General part of the plan. Later on in his stay, however, the PUS received a letter from the Foreign Office which advocated an even softer stance on the question[3] and led Lloyd to believe that Whitehall was contemplating 'a settlement with Egypt at the expense of our responsibilities', a retreat from the 1922 Declaration by which he – and he had supposed they – stood. He considered that the letter, which recommended that the aim should be 'some provisional arrangement, pending the final agreement in regard to the four reserved points', could only result in 'a large surrender of our position in Egypt'. He commented, 'It was startling . . . to find that . . . there was set out a series of arguments directed against the line of action which I had proposed, and which had now just been approved by the Secretary of State.' His own position, he claimed, was 'based upon the determination to secure the ultimate friendly agreement upon the reserved points which our policy had always contemplated'. He was 'more convinced than ever' that such an agreement 'could only be secured by our rigid adherence to the whole of the 1922 Declaration, since only by such adherence could we hope to bring Egypt to a frame of mind in which reasonable negotiation would be possible'.[4]

Although the alcoholic[5] Tyrrell turned against Lloyd after his heavy drinking became known in the Residency during his stay,[6] after which he addressed him in a letter *en route* home as 'my beloved George',[7] it was partly thanks to his advocacy that the Cabinet came to agree with Lloyd that there should be no backsliding.[8] As a result, 'Adly – choosing 'a bad ground', according to Lloyd[9] – resigned on 19 April. Chamberlain was not magnanimous in defeat. On 8 May, Lloyd told Tyrrell that he had:

> had a letter from Austen indicating that he still held that I was wrong in regard to the Army but none the less that I should have his support. That was not very cheering just as I was entering upon an anxious and difficult struggle ... I do not think he can really have digested the contents of my telegrams ... if the [Egyptian] cabinet falls as a result of this question he will no doubt blame me ... I am hoping that you may be able to persuade him that I am not so rash as he would appear to think me.

The leader of a team riddled with dissension, he undignifiedly added:

> I have also some reason for thinking that Mervyn [Herbert] and co. will try and cause it to be believed in the [Foreign] Office that the Wafd are really in a most friendly frame of mind and that the policy that I am pursuing is causing us to miss a wonderful opportunity for negotiations. I know that several of the Wafd poured this tale into the ears of Furness[10] and Mervyn.

He was already very much under scrutiny. In a memorandum to the Cabinet, Chamberlain had said that 'the Cairo telegrams convey rather a misleading impression of the historical background, and tend to overestimate the dangers of the present position';[11] he maintained that 'a good many of my colleagues' shared his view. For his part, in a PS to his 8 May letter, Lloyd complained about the unorthodox and untrusting way in which his reports to the Foreign Office were being treated:

> my telegrams have put in a belated appearance, but in a special form with a lengthy covering note by Austen. My despatch amplifying them however has not yet been printed; nor finally has my minute to you, analysing Murray's letter, though the latter appeared in extenso with the telegrams. I cannot but feel uncomfortable at this sort of thing ... I must really speak frankly about this. Not one statement in those telegrams has been specifically controverted or even challenged ... as you may remember, in my minute to you here, I analysed Murray's letter line by line in an honest endeavour to understand exactly what his 'comprehensive scheme' meant. I failed to arrive at a clear conclusion; but I have not a word back in explanation of my minute. When,

finally, I get from Austen the letter referred to above, in the course of which he states he still prefers that 'scheme' I am left feeling, to say the least of it, helpless and in the dark.

He ended by complaining of 'the scant ceremony with which my repeated expositions of my views on the question hitherto have been treated'. Although it was already clear that he was prepared to lose a great deal of face, the humiliations he had already suffered were to be as nothing compared with those which were to follow in the last year of his term of office.

The signs were clear that there was a crisis in the relations of Lloyd and Chamberlain. Lloyd wrote to Tyrrell on 14/15 May about the anxious days he was having as a consequence of knowing that Chamberlain's support for him was half-hearted: 'if you can persuade Austen that this job is not as easy as he thinks I shall be grateful. I am fond of him, as you know, but he does not quite understand, does he?'[12] On 19 May, in Chamberlain's defence, Tyrrell complained about Lloyd's 8 May expression ('rather a cold douche') of 'dissatisfaction with his letter to you on the subject of army reform . . . I am a little disappointed'.[13]

'Adly was followed as Prime Minister on 26 April by Sarwat who, with a cabinet dominated by the Wafd, retabled the bill to enlarge the army. Lloyd reported him as saying on 24 May that, 'from a legal point of view the Egyptian army did not fall under any of our reservations of 1922, and that consequently Egypt had complete liberty in regard to it'. Lloyd considered that this statement made it clear that 'for the moment the extremists had won the day'.[14] He believed it masked an attempt by Zaghlul to politicise the army, which would endanger Parliament/King relations and increase the likelihood of the necessity for British intervention. On 25 May he told Chamberlain that his rejoinder would be to seek enhanced powers for the Inspector-General post, the appointment of a Deputy Inspector-General who would be a Briton, a ban on any enlargement of the army, the funding by Egypt of the costs of frontier defence and administration, and a formal link between the Minister of War and a British–Egyptian Officers' Committee.[15] This largely puerile riposte, he claimed, constituted 'certain demands which would maintain the *status quo* in essentials and guard against future risks'. He proposed that, were the response to them not to be satisfactory:

> we should ask the Egyptian Government definitely and clearly whether they accepted the Declaration of 1922, or not. If they replied in the negative . . . we should procure from the King a suspension of the constitution and the formation of a *Cabinet d'affaires* to which we should present a draft and comprehensive treaty which [shades of Wingate] would settle our relations with Egypt once and for all.[16]

On the same day, he told Chamberlain:

The fact now clearly emerges that Parliamentary Government in its present form is incompatible with the preservation of the reserved points. So long as we allow these to be encroached upon the system functions without serious crises; the moment you have to insist upon a reserved point you arrive at a complete deadlock. A situation where we have to work a declaration which the Egyptians have refused to recognize, still less to accept, is impossible.[17]

He wrote to Sarwat on 29 May. While acquiescing in an increase of the army's rifle strength of more than 1,600 men, he informed him that, in his interpretation of the Declaration, Britain *did* have the right of control over Egypt's armed forces. Next day he submitted his demands to him[18] and asked Sir Roger Keyes, Admiral of the Mediterranean Fleet since May 1925, to forearm him against possible trouble by sending a precautionary warship to Alexandria. Two were despatched from Malta, one to Alexandria, the other to Port Sa'id. On 31 May, Lloyd suggested to the Foreign Office that, if Egypt did not accept his requirements, the 1923 constitution should be withdrawn.[19] On 2 June, Chamberlain approved 'generally' of his plans.[20] When, however, Lloyd saw in the Foreign Office, four years later, a minute of 29 June, he realised that, 'although the Secretary of State had been in agreement with the measures I proposed for dealing with this question, I had been wrong in believing that his advisers took the same view'.[21]

On 3 June, Sarwat accepted Lloyd's demands without admitting their legality. Lloyd considered his reply 'deliberately equivocal'[22] and asked Chamberlain for permission to implement the action agreed. The Secretary of State being now in Geneva, his request reached Tyrrell instead and the PUS on 6 June persuaded Baldwin, the Prime Minister, to put his signature to a telegram to Lloyd, watering his proposals down. A shattering effect on his relations with both the Foreign Office and the Cabinet resulted from what Lloyd saw as a 'radical departure from the agreed plan ... fraught with danger to the success of British policy'.

On 8 June, he telegraphed 'with all the force at my command for a reconsideration' of these 'sudden and unexpected orders to retreat'.[23] He told Baldwin that they were 'a severe blow' and 'a complete reversal' of British policy which would make it seem that he was not trusted by London[24] and would render negotiations pointless.[25] On 10 June, Baldwin replied that Sarwat must be given the chance to accept or reject an agreement. The Foreign Office accordingly backed away from the Lloyd–Chamberlain plan, maintained that Sarwat's reply was 'not wholly unsatisfactory' and included 'useful admissions which are capable of development', and now repeated its offer to allow the abolition of the Inspector-General post. Baldwin, Tyrrell told Lloyd, 'was concerned to be able to show Parliament, if firm action had to be taken, that it was all the fault of the unreasonable Egyptians'.[26] Lloyd, on the other hand, believed that, if the Prime Minister intended 'to call off our demands at this stage and enter into any official negotiation', this 'would immensely strengthen the hands of our extremist opponents'.[27] He was astonished that Baldwin should, in one and the same telegram, have declared that 'the Egyptian Note was unsatisfactory, capable of almost any interpretation' and ordered 'a radical departure from the steps agreed upon so shortly before and after such careful preparation'.[28] On 11 June, he telegraphed again for reconsideration, but on the 13th (the 11th, according to Lloyd)[29] Sarwat confirmed unofficially that he was prepared to accede to Britain's demands. Despite this happy denouement, Lloyd's relations with London were irretrievably soured. He noted that 'official opinion [at home] was shaking its head dolefully even over this' and was of the view that the position reached 'is satisfactory in that possible attacks have been forestalled for the present'. His own contrasting view was that 'we may have lost an opportunity of materially strengthening our position'.[30]

Tyrrell and the Foreign Office seem now to have got the whiphand over the Foreign Secretary, whom the PUS in any case tended to overshadow. On 15 June, he told Chamberlain that Lloyd was 'apparently quite unable to understand our instructions'.[31] With Lloyd due to arrive home on leave the following month, two days later he advised him:

> we shall have to have a heart to heart talk and lay down very clearly for him what the policy of the Government is to be. My impression is that there is a very serious misapprehension on his part as to what we want in Egypt, or rather, as to what we can maintain in Egypt in present conditions.[32]

Since all was temporarily at sixes and sevens, it was perhaps understandable that at the other end Lloyd should momentarily abandon his diehard imperialist stance, admitting to Keyes that 'in my judgement' the 1922 Declaration was 'a pure fraud on our part. To tell a country she is independent while you keep an army of occupation is not only a contradiction in terms but a fraud . . . reserving to yourself all the main attributes of sovereignty'.[33]

At the end of June, King Fu'ad went on a visit to Britain, closely followed by his Prime Minister. Chamberlain received Sarwat on 12 July, affronting both Lloyd and Zaghlul. It is hardly conceivable that Lloyd should not have been present but, although he was home on leave and had asked to be,[34] he was deliberately overlooked. (The Colonial Secretary, Leo Amery,[35] thought that he appeared at this time to be 'still terribly upset over what he considered the readiness of the FO to let him down during the last crisis and not yet recovered from the nervous strain of practically disobeying instructions')[36] Henderson told him that Zaghlul 'is, of course, mad with jealousy and wounded vanity at the reception given to Fuad and Sarwat', which had been 'a great blow to Saad's vanity and amour propre. It has shaken his pet theory that Saad is Egypt and Egypt is Saad.' He believed it highly likely that Zaghlul would 'do something when the travellers return to try and bring it home to them and the public that anything they may have said or done in England [*sic*] or Europe has no weight without his approval'. He had, however, 'no wish to be accused, as after the Adly attempt, of having deliberately and in advance brought about the failure of any negotiations'.[37]

Lamely seeking to excuse himself, Chamberlain said that the purpose of his reception of Sarwat, who 'moved much faster than I had expected',[38] was not to negotiate but 'perhaps prepare the way for conversations between himself and Lord Lloyd when they had both returned to Egypt'.[39] Despite this, in a step which has been interpreted as revenge by Chamberlain and Tyrrell for Lloyd's habit of reporting over their heads to Baldwin,[40] on 13 July Selby and Tyrrell proposed that they should take advantage of Sarwat's visit to discuss a treaty of alliance. Lloyd claimed to have had 'the definite assurance of the Secretary of State that if at any time negotiations should appear to be possible, they would be conducted in Egypt and not in London'.[41] He said of those now in prospect that they were being reopened in a spirit of 'heedless optimism'.[42] On 15 July, a detailed draft had been produced which – with one drawn up by Sarwat which 'could not be accepted by us'[43] – was submitted to Chamberlain three days later; both avoided the question of the Sudan. On the 21st, the Secretary of State placed them before the Cabinet and, with its authorisation, presented them as a Treaty of Alliance to its Egyptian Committee on the 24th.

Lloyd claims to have known little of these developments. Chamberlain, he remarked, 'stated that owing to the pressure of other affairs he had been unable as yet to discuss these drafts in detail with me'. He had never seen them, 'was unaware of their existence, and had not been informed by the Secretary of State that anything was taking place'.[44] It was not until after 28 July, when the Cabinet approved the Foreign Office draft, that the talks were revealed to Lloyd.[45] Henderson had imagined that he was in the picture:

> I take it for granted that any definite negotiations on reserved points in London are out of the question ... Presumably Sir Austen and you will merely discuss the lines on which negotiations, if they are to be undertaken, might proceed in Cairo this next winter. Nor do I suppose that the idea of a Treaty of Alliance in one paragraph will be seriously considered.[46]

He himself perhaps was not aware of much of what was happening until, on 2 August, a Chamberlain telegram informed him that fruitful consultations had taken place with Sarwat but did not mention the drafts or any approval.[47] Only the next day, however, Murray attempted to sell him the story that Sarwat had taken the Foreign Office by surprise in seeking a treaty and 'life was so hectic here and everything was in a state of flux'.[48] On 5 August, Henderson told Lloyd that he had received the text of the Sarwat draft and the Foreign Office counter draft and had sent a memorandum in reply. He now supposed it quite probable that Lloyd 'will be engaged in discussing things with Sarwat in London during the end of that month'.[49] On 10/11 August, Chamberlain's staff were instructed to tell Lloyd that the Foreign Secretary could not see him because he was on leave.

On 23 August Zaghlul died. Henderson described how 'in this land of paradox' he found himself, seconded by Grafftey-Smith,[50] acting as 'one of the chief mourners for England's [*sic*] great opponent in Egypt ... I walked for about a mile along the streets of Cairo behind his coffin ... There were', he concluded, 'three central figures on the Egyptian stage. The Monarch and the Demagogue and the High Commissioner.'[51]

On 30 August, Sarwat left for home. On the same day, Chamberlain, who was continuing to cold-shoulder his High Commissioner in a most unprofessional and inappropriate way, 'implored me to go away and take a holiday and leave him to handle the Sarwat business'. Lloyd 'said no and reminded him of how Cromer had been crushed over Dinshaway[52] during his absence in Scotland and how his repute had never got over the mess that was made in the FO at that time'. Despite this schoolboy exchange, he contrived to 'find the Cabinet in a very good state of mind over Egypt. I think I have still their very solid and practically unanimous support.'[53]

Sarwat returned to London on 8 October, imagining, Henderson supposed, 'that London is his best chance' for the conclusion of a successful negotiation. On 15 September Henderson had sympathised with Lloyd in his difficulties: 'I deeply deplore that they should be added to by the officials of the FO.'[54] Now he regretted 'the atmosphere to which you refer in your letters ... Sarwat will of course discover if you and the Foreign Office are in disagreement and the Cabinet has to be called in to settle the dispute.'[55]

It was only now that Lloyd claimed to have grasped in detail what had been going on: 'the fact that negotiations were well under way was at last disclosed to me on Sarwat Pasha's return [to London] at the end of October' [*sic*]. Finally shown the drafts, at 24 hours' notice he was called on to give his considered opinion of them to Chamberlain. He 'at once predicted that Sarwat would never be able to obtain Egypt's acceptance of the treaty'[56] and made it clear to the Secretary of State that his opinion of the condition of UK–Egyptian relations differed from his. He was nonetheless authorised to express his convictions without inhibition to the Cabinet, before which he was summoned. He gives no account of the occasion, and there is little comment on it otherwise.[57] His view of the likely outcome remained unchanged:

I thought the initiation of these negotiations to have been not only impolitic, and useless, but actually full of harmful possibilities to our interests, and to those of our Egyptian supporters . . . I could . . . entertain little hope that a treaty would be secured.[58]

On 8 November, immediately after his Cabinet interview, Lloyd started back to his post. 'Nothing had finally been decided in regard to the treaty, and I left London with the clear impression that there was no chance of any decision being taken until I was back in Cairo and in communication with His Majesty's Government again.'[59] Sarwat crossed the Channel on the same boat. Although Chamberlain told Selby, 'I have placed my confidence in him. I don't think that he will fail me now',[60] when they reached Paris Sarwat was called away for more urgent talks with Selby there on 9 and 10 November. Lloyd was not brought into them, but on the 10th, in Marseilles, whence he and Sarwat travelled onwards together, he was told of additional changes to the treaty over which he had again not been consulted and received 'an urgent telegram, which informed me that the Cabinet had decided to approve the draft treaty . . . and that I was to arrange for exchange of signatures immediately upon my arrival in Cairo'.[61] Left out of every stage of the negotiations, his advice ignored and his role reduced to that of a postman, he toyed with the idea of resigning, but decided to take no action until he had seen the final text, which reached him in Cairo under cover of a despatch of 24 November.[62]

On 3 December, he communicated the text to Sarwat, who was no doubt already familiar with what it contained. On the 7th, Chamberlain asked Lloyd to tell him that he wanted the treaty signed and published by about the 20th. Sarwat said he needed further discussions with Lloyd on the questions of the future position of British officers in the Egyptian Army, the division of the Nile's waters between Egypt and the Sudan, and the Capitulations. On 16 December he consulted him as to the interpretations to be placed, requesting clarification from the British government, on several of the articles. On the 31st, he said it would be impossible for his parliamentary or cabinet colleagues to accept the draft treaty without the clarifications and modifications requested, and in writing. Chamberlain's reply partly addressed these questions. On 11 January 1928, however, the Foreign Office, uncovering the mailed fist, told Lloyd – whom it suddenly resembled – that, if the treaty did not go through, martial law would be reintroduced and Sarwat would be 'encouraged to dissolve Parliament'.[63] A Murray minute said that 'if we want to get the treaty signed the time has come to take it [the "whip in the cupboard"] out and crack it'.[64]

At this point, Chamberlain, more measured, told Sarwat (it must have pleased his High Commissioner) that 'If Egypt now refuses this settlement, His Majesty's Government will be obliged to insist upon a strict observance of the rights which they reserved to themselves' in the 1922

Declaration.[65] On 1 March, Lloyd received instructions as to action to be taken in the event of a rejection. He was to reiterate to the Egyptian government that Britain 'cannot permit the discharge of any of their responsibilities under the Declaration ... to be endangered'.[66] In the event, on 4 March, the Egyptian cabinet decided not to accept the draft.[67] Sarwat told Lloyd that he and his colleagues had concluded that it, 'by reason both of its basic principles and its actual provisions, is incompatible with the independence and sovereignty of Egypt, and moreover that it legalises occupation of the country by British forces'. Making this statement, he resigned. Despite his opposition to the existence of the draft, Lloyd commented that Sarwat's remarks could not have been 'more remote, both from the truth and from the genuine interests of Egypt'.[68]

He made a show of bewailing the unavailability of the late Leader of the Nation. Zaghlul, he said:

> had been the one person whose support of a treaty with England [*sic*] could have ensured its acceptance. With his death, the possibility of such acceptance was rendered infinitely more remote ... It was ... clear that if any chance had ever existed of accommodation, Zaghlul's death had destroyed it. He had had the power, and upon occasion the will, to restrain the wild men of his left wing. His successor was competely at their mercy ... he was devoid, moreover, of the peculiar gifts of mind and character which had made Zaghlul so powerful a leader.[69]

Henderson agreed. A month before Zaghlul's demise, he had said, 'his own prestige may be less than it was and his followers less united but it is an undeniable fact that no agreement or alliance with England [*sic*] would be accepted by Parliament unless it had Saad's blessing'.[70]

The Foreign Office and Lloyd blamed each other for the failure of the treaty. Tyrrell took the cynical view that for the High Commissioner the wish had been father to the thought: 'that Sarwat was going to prove both slippery and unreliable ... you will recollect', he reminded Chamberlain, 'was the impression of him which Lloyd was very anxious to create when he was over here this summer'.[71] He conveniently ignored the fact that, in August, Henderson too was sceptical that an Egyptian parliament would ratify a treaty and that Egyptians in general and Zaghlul in particular would 'have the moral courage to face facts, and to recognise that it is better to achieve something than to keep a national programme inviolate by achieving nothing';[72] he had remarked in a despatch in October that 'there could be no guarantee that Sarwat Pasha would get any treaty accepted, however far it went'.[73] For his part, Lloyd held to his belief 'that there was no possible prospect of concluding a definite treaty ..., and that the idea was really pushed into Sarwat's mind by permanent officials of the Foreign Office'.[74]

14 Something of a danger in Egypt
Lindsay come full circle

> he does not feel bound, in the ultimate resort, to obey instructions from here.
>
> (Tyrrell)

It is clear that the relations of Lloyd and the Foreign Office headed by Chamberlain were counter-productively bad, with the latter doing his utmost to keep information from a lame duck High Commissioner, negotiating a treaty behind his back and blaming him for its failure. On 1 September 1927, Selby minuted Tyrrell on the Sarwat–Chamberlain negotiations:

> I presume a copy of my record and Sarwat's observations will have to go to the High Commissioner ... He will of course oppose vigorously ... I give him a present of his views on myself. They are as strong as mine are as regards him.

The Foreign Office, he said, was becoming familiar with Lloyd's 'system':

> For instance, we learn ... that the High Commissioner expects another flare up in the autumn when more battleships will be required than those required at Alexandria the other day for 'the final decision'. Very interesting. I hope he will soon tell us about it as well.[1]

On 13 September, Tyrrell informed Chamberlain that Lloyd considered himself 'something between a Secretary of State and an ambassador or Viceroy' instead of the 'common or garden ambassador' he was in fact and that he proposed to speak to Baldwin about him; making an accusation previously levelled at Wilson in Iraq, he maintained that Lloyd was 'aiming at creating for himself an Indian secretariat at Cairo on the model of his Bombay administration. I told him frankly that I could not reconcile that with the policy which he had accepted from you.' Tyrrell believed that 'he does not feel bound, in the ultimate resort, to obey instructions from here'.[2] On 1 October, he passed to Baldwin a Selby minute, critical of Lloyd, which was entitled 'Cromerism in Egypt'.[3]

Chamberlain himself confided to his sister Hilda the 'very big problems confronting me in the near future in Egypt or in connection with Egypt'. There, 'Lord Lloyd does not heartily accept my policy & my principal advisers would wish me to get rid of him, which would make a first class row inside & outside the Cabinet.'[4] Six months after Selby had accused Lloyd of manufacturing crises, Chamberlain wrote a cautionary letter to the High Commissioner on 19 March 1928:

> we have plenty of experience to show that it is not easy to work the declaration of 1922 and that a blunder or an accident may force a crisis where neither party desires one. I should like, therefore, to get a clearer understanding of your policy in such an eventuality.

He expressed the hope:

> in passing but very emphatically that ... you will use no language to anyone to indicate that you expect such a crisis or that the solution to which you look forward is an abrogation of the existing constitution. That may be forced upon us, but if it comes to be thought that you contemplate it as inevitable and even desire it, it will, I think, singularly complicate our position in Egypt ... You cannot, therefore, be too cautious, in this matter.

He pointedly put a series of direct questions to Lloyd which:

> surely ... go to the root of the matter and which you must answer to yourself and to me before we go any further ... now if we find it impossible to work with the present Parliament and the present constitution, what is your alternative? What are the immediate steps which you propose to take when the crisis arises and what are the changes which you would propose to introduce; how would you introduce them and why do you think that they would produce a body more amenable to reason than the present parliamentary majority? You have spoken vaguely once or twice about some sort of chamber of notables, but where are the notables who would have the courage which the present moderates have not, and what reason is there in past history or present circumstances to suppose that you will be able to get along better with such a chamber than with the present parliament?

Finally he asked the British (Welsh) Lloyd, 'Who are the Ministers who would be the instruments of the change which you contemplate and behind whom the Englishmen [*sic*] in the service would work and exert their influence?'[5]

This mortifying interrogation arose in connection with the new Assemblies' Bill, which the Chamber of Deputies had begun to consider at the end of 1927 with a view to relaxing Egypt's political life through freer political association and meetings.[6] In Lloyd's opinion, it was 'a direct incitement to disorder, and a deliberate attempt to discourage officials from doing their duty' which 'would deprive the Police of all right to interfere with or to prevent public meetings, thus securing a fair field for all who were riotously inclined'.[7]

An Nahhas Pasha, who – with the endorsement of Safiyyah Zaghlul – had succeeded the Beloved Leader as head of the Wafd, was asked by the King to form a government on 15 March and inherited the bill, which had been approved by the Senate on 23 January. Lloyd, taking a leaf out of Allenby's book, had discussed with the Secretary of State the possible naval occupation of the Alexandria customs.[8] On 18 and 19 April he was ordered by telegram to warn An Nahhas orally of the dangers he could be courting and to inform him that a written ultimatum would follow if the bill was not abandoned. He delivered the warning on the 29th, requiring him 'to take the necessary steps to prevent the Bill regulating public meetings and demonstrations from becoming law'. He demanded 'a categorical assurance in writing' that it would not be proceeded with and threatened unspecified action if it did not reach him 'before 7 PM on May 2nd'.[9] He asked Keyes to despatch a naval force to Alexandria.

On deadline day, An Nahhas, who strongly attacked the High Commissioner's interference,[10] replied (in Lloyd's words) that Egypt 'could not recognise the right of Great Britain to intervene in Egyptian legislation, nor admit that it was bound by the Declaration of 1922'. He stated, however, that further consideration of the bill would be postponed until the next session of parliament.[11] Not content with this, however, Lloyd recommended that An Nahhas 'should at once be invited to add to his reply a written assurance that the bill would not be proceeded with during his tenure of office'. The British government had, however, gone as far as it intended and did not agree: 'They were satisfied with the Egyptian reply ... They were content to believe that Nahhas Pasha had been sufficiently humiliated.'[12] They insinuated that Lloyd was liable to uncontrolled action: to be satisfied with An Nahhas's response would be 'better calculated than insistence on a more categorical response', one which would 'take on far too closely the character of an unlimited offensive towards ill-defined objectives against opposition of an unknown strength'.[13]

As if the snub were not enough, Lloyd had during the same period also found himself accused of being disloyal to his employers. Now giving significance to the passages in his letter of 19 March about the need for cautious language on Lloyd's part, Chamberlain told him nine days later that an Italian diplomat, Signor Paterno, who had reported him the previous summer:

> says that you showed evident delight at the breaking off of our negotiations, that you told him in confidence that you now believed that it would be possible to obtain from British public opinion the approval of the strong policy which, for a year past, you had been urging upon the British Government, that you thought there should be no further discussion of the four points, and that we should take advantage of any favourable opportunity, such as in your opinion was certain to occur, to dissolve Parliament and proceed to a radical modification of the constitution ... Almost simultaneously ..., a member of my staff reports that he met an American journalist, Mr. Karl von Wiegand, at Geneva

who claimed that he and Lloyd 'discussed the position in Egypt and the Treaty, and in the course of it he told me that he was quite against it: in fact, he said "I am for force both here and in India." ' In conclusion, Chamberlain said:

> I find it impossible to believe that both these men have invented the conversations which they affect to report; yet it is not merely obviously improper that such language should be held by the High Commissioner to foreign representatives, but it is directly contrary to the discretion which I have particularly begged you to observe.

He demanded 'a clear statement' of what Lloyd had said to both informants.[14]

Lloyd replied in an undated letter, apparently of 8 April, completely denying the charges and expressing astonishment 'that on the word of a foreign diplomat and a stray American journalist you are prepared to think it possible conduct on my part'. He complained that, '[A]t the end of six months labour to carry the treaty through ..., I receive from you no word of appreciation of my efforts but what amounts to an accusation of disloyalty.'[15]

On 25 April, Chamberlain gave qualified exoneration, accepting his denial but pointing out that Lloyd's letter 'is largely occupied by just such a criticism of the decisions of the Government and of my own conduct of the London negotiation as was implied in the statements of Paterno and von Wiegand'.[16]

Fu'ad was anxious to remove the Wafd from power, despite its large majority,[17] and to assert his authority over the parliamentarians,[18] action which the British government was prepared to support in part on account of An Nahhas's stance on the Assemblies' bill.[19] On 19 June the King 'effectively hamstrung' Allenby's constitution[20] by summarily sacking his Prime Minister for corruption in connection with a royal family scandal over the landed property of Prince Ahmad Sayf ad Din, who was in exile under restraint at Ticehurst in Kent for an attempt on Fu'ad's life.[21] He replaced An Nahhas by Muhammad Mahmud, the only Hizb al Ahrar ad Dusturiyyin member of the outgoing government, and adjourned Parliament, 'his hated enemy', for a month.[22] Although the new Prime Minister 'steadfastly proclaimed himself, and perfectly sincerely', Lloyd maintained, 'to be a staunch adherent of the Constitution',[23] he considered that, in the High Commissioner's words, 'parliament had degenerated under the influence of the Wafd into an instrument of anarchy and the suppression of political liberty'.[24] On 7 July, he and the King went further. While committed, 'after sorting out the administrative muddle … to restore constitutional rule',[25] they dissolved parliament for three years and gave the death knell to liberal constitutionalism.

With the Wafd replaced by an administration more likely to be co-operative, the British were pleased at this latest successful coup against democracy. Lindsay, the new Foreign Office PUS, rationalised the position to Lloyd, representing it as one in which the Prime Minister was taking the lead, 'trying an interesting and promising experiment'. He deserved to be given a fair chance. Despite appearances, Fu'ad was 'trying to depress the balance against him. I dont see why you should not redress it, if necessary with a bit of a jog'. Since these latest political developments were exactly what Chamberlain had accused Lloyd of planning, at the same time he confessed to a measure of guilt: 'In the abstract this country [Britain] will never be particularly pleased at the suspension of parliaments.'[26] Lloyd himself, who had felt it incongruous at the start of his term that the King should be sole executive, found feeble excuses for the return of a similar arrangement:

> At first sight this might appear to be a state of affairs so unsatisfactory as to demand our intervention. But unfortunately for any idea of intervention, the arguments which the Ministry had used to arraign the Wafd and to justify the dissolution were all of them undeniably and evidently true. The activities of the Wafd had in fact rapidly led to a condition of administrative chaos, in which all useful measures and projects remained suspended … A few years of steady government, undisturbed by sectarian activities, might well serve to re-establish political sanity and poise, and to render possible a return to Parliamentary government, this time of a more moderate and more practical temper.

He would have agreed about the Wafd with Jarvis ('Egypt certainly has done nothing whatsoever to deserve the Wafd; no country in existence has merited such an infliction')[27] and perhaps even with Murray, who said that

Wafdists were 'only reasonable when they are in a funk'.[28] Nonetheless, after six months without a parliament, with some cynicism he admitted to doubts: 'I suppose we shall soon have some pressure . . . for the restoration of Parliament . . . from what quite reasonable people say it does not seem possible to get on for three whole years without some pretence at popular representation.'[29]

Meanwhile, leaving behind the 'thick fog of intrigue, through the darkness of which . . . can almost always be descried the figure of His Egyptian Majesty',[30] Lloyd went on his 1928 home leave, for once in unlikely step with the Foreign Secretary: 'Both Sir Austen Chamberlain and I took the view', he said, 'that a policy of strict non-intervention was the only policy possible in the circumstances.'[31]

The clearing of the Cairo political scene should have diminished the potential for problems for Lloyd. Things, indeed, became a little too quiet for his principals, Lindsay complaining at the end of the year that 'We have heard practically nothing from you for a fortnight or three weeks . . . Have internal politics in Egypt died a sudden death?'[32] Four months later, however, a minuscule cloud appeared in the sky which, though unthreatening enough in itself, was the harbinger of the deluge which was to destroy Lloyd's diplomatic career. The High Commissioner had not long before described Hafiz 'Afify to Lindsay as an intriguer.[33] On 1 May 1929, Chamberlain told him that the former Wafdist, now Egyptian Ambassador in London, had, circumventing Lloyd, sought British sympathy in principle to the idea of British residents paying three taxes – the Ghaffir Tax (obligatory for all residents of Egypt during the First World War to fund the force of village police and night watchmen),[34] the Municipal Tax and the Petrol Tax – and Stamp Duty, and that he proposed to accord it. Lloyd, who suggested to Lindsay that 'they hope that Hafez Afifi may get out of London what he failed to get here',[35] of course had plenty to say. On 6 May, he agreed over the first and the last, urged delay over the second, and said that he would 'like to see a horse-power tax substituted for a petrol tax' because 'a tax based on horse-power would be more favourable to British motor-car industry than a petrol tax'.[36] In general, however, he considered that – in advance of the future of the Capitulations being decided – 'concession would amount in practice to a complete relinquishment of the capitulatory privileges as far as taxation was concerned'.[37] On 9 May, a telegraphic reply was sent by Chamberlain, who – instinctively sharing Cromer's belief that 'the only link between the governors and the governed is to be found in material interests, and amongst those interests by far the most important is the imposition of light fiscal burdens'[38] – said 'I feel it right to agree generally with the request made to me by Hafiz Afifi.'[39]

Lloyd attached no great significance to this apparently innocuous straw until, on 28 May, a despatch from Chamberlain clearly showed him that 'in Whitehall the comments and suggestions offered by the High Commissioner and so solidly supported by all interested or competent opinion were regarded as seriously heretical'. Chamberlain, who had not ceased to consider Lloyd an incorrigible intervener in Egyptian affairs, delivered him a lecture:

> it may be convenient to Your Lordship and is in itself desirable that I should restate briefly the principles upon which His Majesty's Government desire to regulate their policy in Egypt . . . I hold at the present time that, in considering whether in any particular case recourse is to be had to intervention in the internal affairs of Egypt, the criterion to be applied should not be whether the object aimed at is merely desirable, but whether it is necessary in order to safeguard the interests of the Empire . . . I am not convinced that the maintenance of foreign privileges in Egypt, *per se*, is a cause for the defence of which His Majesty's Government is required to exercise pressure on the Egyptian Government . . . nor could I bring my self to believe that British influence could be strengthened or the interests of British subjects permanently served by insistence on the maintenance of an invidious and indefensible exemption from a fair contribution to services of which they share the benefits.[40]

Lloyd, who had a shrewd and well-founded suspicion that treaty negotiations had again opened behind his back, replied to this dressing-down on 7 June with a despatch which, in one opinion, 'was characteristic of his lack of tactical political sense'.[41] He wrote, 'It has always seemed to me . . . a most dangerous course to make further substantial concessions to Egypt, however reasonable in themselves, except as part of a general settlement involving Egypt's acceptance of our minimum requirements.'[42] How far his reaction was disproportionate is clearly shown by his conviction that the petrol tax was a 'substantial concession'. His despatch was summarised by Chamberlain, who said that Lloyd, ' "if he might be permitted a criticism" of my interesting despatch . . . entirely disagreed with me!'[43]

Chamberlain was not the only one feeling the strain of trying to work with Lloyd. Against the background of the imprecision regulating the relations of the High Commissioner in Egypt and the Governor-General of the Sudan, Sir John Maffey in Khartum, successfully complained to the Foreign Office about Lloyd's 'high-handed behaviour' and asked it to tell him that he was going further than he had a right to.[44]

In June 1929, Labour under Ramsay MacDonald returned to power in Britain and Arthur Henderson became Foreign Secretary, enabling Chamberlain to divest himself of the grind of dealing with Lloyd and the strong feeling among Foreign Office staff against a renewal of Lloyd's appointment at the end of its five-year initial period.[45] Henderson, too, 'soon came under vigorous pressure' from Lindsay to remove the High

Commissioner. The PUS told Chamberlain that he had asked Henderson to withdraw Lloyd because his illiberal views were 'so ingrained in his character'.[46] On 19 June, Murray – who not long before had been poised to 'take it out and crack it' – minuted on Lloyd's 7 June despatch:

> We want to avoid having to intervene, Lord Lloyd is on the look out for an excuse for intervention. To him non-intervention or failure to insist on the maintenance of privileges which are difficult to justify and out of harmony with modern developments, spells concession and concession disaster. . .

In a word, Lloyd's search for excuses to intervene and the Foreign Office's disinclination now to do so defined 'the fundamental antithesis between our conception and Lord Lloyd's of what British policy ought to be'.[47]

In line with Lindsay's wishes, a telegram, approved of by MacDonald and with its final touch added by him, was sent to Lloyd on 3 July with the object of provoking him to resign.[48] The High Commissioner told Blanche, his wife, that, if the worst came to the worst, he would at any rate not have been guilty of taking part in the current fashionable 'policy of surrender . . . If I am turned out of office here for refusing to acquiesce in the feeble frittering away of our position here I shall not be ashamed of that.'[49] On 11 July, Henderson told him, 'I should be lacking in frankness did I not warn you that the possibility of your views being harmonised with those of either my predecessor or myself appears to me remote.'[50]

Lloyd departed for his annual leave, arriving on 18 July in London, where the new government had indeed, without telling him, begun with Muhammad Mahmud yet more treaty negotiations. Lindsay had advised Henderson that 'the main point is that Lord Lloyd shall be removed from his post the moment he arrives in England [*sic*]'. Even though Selby, Tyrrell and Chamberlain had had no difficulty in keeping him out of it in 1927, he added, 'If he is given any occasion to intervene in the business which is in progress, I feel that all prospect of success is lost.'[51] Accordingly, on 19 July (as Lloyd's wife recounted), he called at the Lloyds' hotel and took the initiative in an interview:

> which is so amazing that we cannot explain it in any way. RL, . . . who has known us both for years, and who, as far as we know, has no reason whatever to feel any enmity against either of us – allowed himself to be offensive and insulting in the highest degree, treating George *de haut en bas*, telling him that unless he chose to resign he would be fired![52]

Perhaps an element in this was the Wingate case in reverse, Lindsay overreacting because his interlocutor was a parvenu member of the nobility to which he himself belonged.

On 23 July – bitter (though it is hard to see why) that Chamberlain had not spoken up for him – Lloyd resigned and, with his wife, dined at the Egyptian Legation for Muhammad Mahmud. In the House of Commons on the 26th, Henderson, in surprisingly uninhibited terms, spoke of

> the very wide divergence of view . . . between the position taken up by my predecessor in office and Lord Lloyd . . . Could we contemplate a perpetuation of his stream of dissatisfaction, a stream of which it could be said normally it was restless, very frequently it was turbulent, never smooth, and never clear? Could we contemplate going forward with the policy that we hoped eventually to submit to the House with any degree of confidence if this marked determination to misinterpret or ungenerously to apply, that characterised the views of the High Commissioner during the last few years, had to be continued?[53]

While saying that 'I find no fault with the accusation that I was out of sympathy with a "liberal" interpretation of the 1922 Declaration', with some justice Lloyd claimed that these were 'charges more damaging than have ever been publicly brought without examination against a servant of the Crown in any responsible position'.[54] Referring to the three *de facto* rulers of Egypt who preceded him, he added, 'I do not recall . . . that in any of these cases their personal conduct had been subsequently made the subject of a public arraignment.'[55]

It is surprising that, of the four of them, Lloyd was the one who rose furthest in his career and yet plumbed the greatest depths of humiliation on the way. Jarvis, who took a highly favourable view of him, 'the best High Commissioner Egypt has ever seen',[56] believed that Lloyd's 'galvanic activities and very strong Imperial views had proved too drastic altogether for the weak Conservative party in power' and that the difficulties faced by his successors in Egypt from 1929 to 1936 were 'almost entirely due to Mr. Henderson's hasty and misguided action'.[57]

Among post-mortems was one by Chamberlain, who – echoing Curzon's demotion offer to Wingate – told his sister Ida on 1 August, 'I was hoping that a place might be found for him as High Commissioner in East Africa.'[58] Given the way in which he and Lloyd had treated each other, it is difficult to understand the ex-Foreign Secretary's altruism. Two days later, however, writing to his step-brother, he summed Lloyd up: 'a first-class man for a crisis or for an administrative job . . . not one iota of diplomacy in his composition and I could not help sharing the Foreign Office feeling that in present circumstances he was something of a danger in Egypt and created needless difficulties for us'.[59]

Postscript

the July 23 [1952] revolution marks the realisation of the hope held by the people of Egypt since the beginning of modern times: to be ruled by the hands of its own sons and to have itself the final word in its destiny.[1]

(Gamal 'Abd an Nasir)

Following his removal, McMahon quickly nominated himself to be Egypt's representative at the Peace Conference, but Graham noted that 'the idea did not appear to have aroused enthusiasm'.[2] One which must have caused amusement was an Egyptian rumour that McMahon was to succeed Hardinge as Foreign Office PUS. He was not, however, completely ignored by the British government. The Peace Conference found another task for him, appointing him, with Hogarth, as a British representative on the commission of enquiry into the views of the people of Syria about their postwar future, which ended up – without British participation – as the King–Crane Commission.[3]

Wingate[4] received no further government employment. He became instead Chairman of the Tanganyika Concessions and a board member of the Union Minière du Haut Katanga and of the Benguela Railway, travelling regularly to Brussels and Lisbon. He was Chairman of the Egyptian Army dinner, Colonel Commandant of the Royal Artillery, a Vice-President of the Royal African Society and a governor of Gordon College, later Khartum University.

Allenby[5] never forgave Zaghlul and Chamberlain, who had 'not been straightforward with him'.[6] He spent his declining years in such roles as President of the British National Cadet Association, the Veterans' Association – later the Allenby (Services) Club – the Douglas Haig Memorial Homes and the Central Asian Society. He was Colonel of the Life Guards and Gold Stick in Waiting and, as his last appointment, Rector of Edinburgh University. He chaired the committee which erected a bust of Lawrence in St. Paul's.

When McMahon, Wingate and Allenby were ousted, Allenby was too old at 64 to expect further official posts. While McMahon (54) and Wingate (57) could have moved on from Cairo to new appointments – as Wingate, of course, was invited to – Lloyd was far from retirement at 49. There were, however, no more diplomatic posts for him, either. He still had the House of Lords, of course, and when Churchill named him Colonial Secretary in 1940 he became Leader of that House the following year after having to fight for the position. Less than a month later, he died. An essentially self-seeking man who appears to have put his own interests first as Chairman of the British Council (1937–40), the chances seem remote that he would have been able to make his name as Colonial Secretary without 'His vision of his country's imperial destiny', which was 'not compatible with prevailing sentiment',[7] provoking bad relations with his superiors, as it had in both Bombay and Cairo. (Grafftey-Smith, however, considered that now 'The round peg was firmly in the round hole . . . he could shed the insecurity that had diminished his Cairo service. All that immense vitality, energy and missionary faith was perfectly harnessed at last.'[8]

Under McMahon and Wingate, preoccupation with the war – or the belief that the country would quietly await Britain's pleasure – prevented Whitehall from devising a policy for Egypt, a possession the Foreign Office was 'never . . . able to handle . . . with sympathy or tact'.[9] McMahon did not succeed in turning his mind to the question and Wingate failed to persuade his principals that the time had arrived to include nationalists in policy-making. The alternately hot and cold approach of Allenby – who, in one view, discarded the nationalists only to find wanting the moderates who 'he had hoped would govern independent Egypt'[10] – and the hard line of Lloyd resulted by 1929 in an Egypt submissive but devoid of democracy.

Removing Lloyd did not bring about the treaty success Lindsay had hoped for. Mahmud's extensive talks with Arthur Henderson in the summer of 1929 resulted in an agreement in August which would have handed Egypt responsibility for the foreign communities, reduced the number of bases available to Britain's occupying troops, solved the Nile waters' question and allowed the Sudan to retain the status prescribed for it in 1924; British consideration would have been given 'sympathetically' to the return of an Egyptian unit there.[11] The agreement was stillborn, however, because both the Wafd and the British, diverging over the details, decided that a restoration of constitutional life should be a precondition of its implementation[12] and because the British laughably failed to maintain the confidentiality of the deliberations.[13] Mahmud accordingly resigned, on 2 October, and was replaced by 'Adly (now independent), under whose caretaker administration, which lasted until December, the constitution was revalidated. When Mustafa an Nahhas, Prime Minister again from 1 January to 17 June 1930, made another attempt – in talks with Henderson from 31 March to 8 May – to come to terms with Britain, agreement was reached on 13 of the 16 points under discussion, including the withdrawal of British forces to the Canal Zone,[14] before the Sudan once more proved the obstacle to a treaty.

After the Wafd had 'proceeded to pick a quarrel with King Fuad which led them into the wilderness for five years',[15] the womanising tough man of Egyptian politics, Isma'il Sidqy, became the instrument of the third anti-Wafd coup by the monarchy in seven years. In two periods of unpopular strong-arm rule by decree, heading a pro-Palace administration, he replaced the 1923 constitution with one still further enhancing the power of the King, dissolved Parliament, reduced the number of deputies by more than a third[16] and postponed elections; he founded his own Hizb ash Sha'b, the People's Party. He, too, negotiated with Britain, having talks in Geneva with Sir John Simon, Foreign Secretary, in September 1932, in which changes to the Capitulations and Egypt's wish to join the League were his priorities, while Simon stressed Britain's need to retain troops in Egypt and its special concern for the Sudan. Their meetings recorded no progress.

A stroke in September 1933 forced Sidqy to make way first for 'Abd al Fattah Yahya, a puppet of Fu'ad, with members of Hizb ash Sha'b in his team,[17] and then for Tawfiq Nasim. The latter's term of office included a period when the King ruled alone after scrapping Sidqy's constitution and maintained the antidemocratic tone from November 1934 until his resignation on 22 January 1936.

Sir Percy Loraine,[18] Lloyd's successor, gave the British community in Cairo and Sir John Wardlaw-Milne MP 'some grounds for displeasure'[19] and the Foreign Office removed him for allowing King Fu'ad control over his ministers. (On his cross departure for Ankara in 1933 he noted, 'Egypt will thus be gratified with the head on a charger of yet another High Commissioner.')[20] In January 1934, Sir Miles Lampson, who had been Minister in Canton when the Hankow British concession was seized in January 1927[21] and was at Locarno with Chamberlain,[22] took over the Residency and became, with Cromer, the most notorious British ruler of Egypt. Persuaded by the demand of a variegated grouping of parties which had formed themselves into a United Front, and by Britain's resurrection of the demand it had voiced five years before to discuss a treaty with a democratically elected government, the King agreed on 12 December 1935 to bring back the 1923 constitution. He realised that this would open the way to the return to power of a Wafd whose attitude, and however, changed for the better after being in opposition for five years.[23] A caretaker government under his Chief Royal Chamberlain, 'Aly Mahir (30 January to May 1936), resumed negotiations with Britain in talks with Lampson starting on 9 March. Though they broke down over the 'minor point of immigration' into the Sudan,[24] they paved the way for the return of An Nahhas and the Wafd on 10 May.

Fu'ad, highly praised by Symes[25] and 'a better ruler than most of his dynasty and certainly than his son'[26] and successor Faruq, died on 28 April. His demise, and the Italian occupation of Libya and Ethiopia, were the catalysts of progress at last in the relations of Britain and Egypt and led to the immediate resumption of negotiations. They resulted in the Anglo-Egyptian [*sic*] Treaty of 26 August, which – ratified on 19 November – had a life of 20 years and brought Egypt a much larger measure of independence than it had enjoyed since 1882. Progress was made over three of the Reserved Points. The posts of Sirdar and Inspector-General were abolished (enabling Egypt to take long overdue administrative control of its armed forces), as at last were those of the Financial and Judicial Advisers; Britain committed itself to the ending of 'the long scandal of the Capitulations',[27] which were duly terminated by the Montreux Convention of the following year, winning An Nahhas widespread praise. The Treaty left the Sudan problem outstanding[28] but resolved the question of the protection of foreigners and minorities in Egypt. In an emergency, Egypt was to be aided by Britain, which was granted military facilities to guard its lines of communication and permitted to keep 10,000 troops in the Canal Zone in peace time and to retain its monopoly of the Egyptian Army's training and equipment. Both sides pledged themselves to renew their military alliance in 1956.[29] Egypt gained her entrée into the League and a free hand in establishing diplomatic relations; accordingly, the British High Commissioner was retitled Ambassador, suggesting that Britain's representative had no greater status now than his counterparts from other accredited countries. (Grafftey-Smith considered that Lampson should have moved on after the Treaty success and that, because he did not, British–Egyptian relations did not change for the better, as they should have done under the new circumstances.)[30]

Faruq's dismissal of An Nahhas on 30 December 1937 – using as a pretext anti-Wafd demonstrations the King himself had organised[31] – led to a split in the party. An Nahhas expelled An Nuqrashy and Ahmad Mahir from it in late 1937, souring his relations with Safiyyah Zaghlul[32] and bringing to birth a new party, the Sa'adists, named for her husband, in January 1938. As a consequence, the Wafd won only 12 seats in the April elections – as against the Sa'adists' 80 – and Muhammad Mahmud (Hizb al Ahrar ad Dusturiyyin), that 'most talented and capable statesman',[33] came back into power, until he too was ejected in August 1939.

Egypt began the Second World War under a Fascist, Italophile and anti-British Prime Minister, 'Aly Mahir, leading a coalition of independents and Sa'adists. He rapidly incarcerated Egypt's nearly one thousand Germans,[34] but after Italy became a combatant he was exiled to the provinces for failing to take action against its residents in Egypt.[35] He was replaced successively by two independents, Hasan Sabry from 24 June 1940 until he died on his feet in Parliament, and Husayn Sirry (15 November 1940 to 2 February 1942). Sirry took no action against the pro-Axis sympathisers, who were demonstrating and shouting pro-Rommel slogans, and resigned. Fearing the return of Mahir,[36] Britain made a move which would have disturbed Lloyd, must have astonished Wingate and lost the

Wafd much credibility. In his most famous act, Lampson forced King Faruq to empanel a wholly Wafd government under An Nahhas, who 'had already accepted Lampson's instructions to reject anything except a purely Wafdist government'[37] and rode to power on British tanks on 4 February. While the British thus made 'the Egyptian home front ... safe for the Allies ... it is arguable that ... they had destroyed the monarchy, the Wafd and ultimately their own position in Egypt'.[38]

Though Faruq attempted to unseat the new Prime Minister in favour of his own Chief Secretary, Killearn (Lampson's title on his ennoblement in January 1943) was again able to frustrate him and An Nahhas's term lasted until 8 October 1944, when the King was able to dismiss him. (The British no longer needed him since the Axis threat to Egypt had by now disappeared.) Ahmad Mahir, co-leader of the Sa'adists, led the next administration until he was assassinated on 24 February 1945. Elections, which the Wafd boycotted, returned 125 Sa'adists and brought An Nuqrashy, their co-founder, to power with ministers drawn also from Hizb al Ahrar and 'Ubayd's breakaway Al Kutlah al Wafdiyyah al Mustaqillah (the Independent Wafdist Bloc).[39] He declared war on Germany on 26 February 1945 and in December requested new talks with Britain to revise the 1936 Treaty and restore the unity of the Nile Valley, i.e. a Sudan under Egyptian hegemony. Despite his belief that 'Egypt's wartime collaboration with Britain had surely dispelled the British mistrust which had not entirely disappeared in 1936', Britain replied in discouragingly vague terms,[40] provoking demonstrations by student and worker organisations, inspired by communist and opposition groups,[41] 'of unprecedented ferocity and bloodshed'.[42] He resigned when some 20 anti-British demonstrators died[43] in February 1946, when Killearn finally departed.

Though Sidqy returned, heading Independents and Hizb al Ahrar representatives, the rioting continued[44] and was climaxed by the deaths of 28 students in clashes with the police in Alexandria on 4 March. (Overall, more than forty people died and several hundreds were injured.)[45] Negotiations resumed on 9 May in London with Ernest Bevin after Sidqy protested at the plan for the new British Ambassador, Sir Ronald Campbell, to be his opposite number.[46] The draft treaty which resulted, the so-called Sidqy–Bevin Agreement, provided that if accord were reached on the Canal Base it would evacuate its installations elsewhere in the country. Though all British forces were to leave Egypt by September 1949, the 'treaty' debarred any change of status for the Sudan without the consent of the Sudanese and was thus unacceptable to a number of members of the Egyptian delegation. The talks broke down in July and Sidqy resigned in December. (British troops were nonetheless withdrawn from the cities of the Delta and confined to the Canal Zone, but to the number of seven times as many as were provided for in the 1936 Treaty.)[47]

An Nuqrashy came in with a Sa'adist–Hizb al Ahrar administration on 9 December 1946 and took Egypt's case to the Security Council in August

1947. His demand that Britain remove its troops from Egypt and end its rule in the Sudan won the support only of Poland and the USSR[48] and Britain insisted that a settlement would have to be reached on a bilateral basis. On 12 May 1948 An Nuqrashy reluctantly allowed his country to join in the Palestine War,[49] Faruq ordering the departure of the troops without his knowledge.[50] Following his martial law outlawing of Al Ikhwan al Muslimun (the Muslim Brotherhood) in the November, he was assassinated by a member of the organisation in December;[51] on Faruq's instructions, hundreds of students, intellectuals, journalists and political and union leaders were arrested for sedition and the organisations to which they belonged were shut down.

An Nuqrashy was succeded first by Ibrahim 'Abd al Hady, a Sa'adist, and then, on 26 July 1949, by Husayn Sirry, leading a coalition which included the Wafd. In January 1950, An Nahhas returned for the last time. In March, he requested talks with Britain which continued intermittently until October 1951. The British floated a number of new red herrings, including the threat of international Communism and Israel-related matters, and the negotiations – foundering on the rocks of British troop questions and the Sudan – culminated in An Nahhas's 8 October 1951 declaration – following extensive contacts with the USSR[52] – that the Sudan Conventions of 1899 and his own 1936 Treaty were null and void; he announced that Faruq was King of Egypt and the Sudan and harrassed the Canal Zone. These actions provoked three months of serious Egyptian–British clashes around the turn of 1951–1952,[53] climaxing in the killing by British troops of more than 50 police and gendarmes in Isma'iliyyah on 25 January 1952. In response, the mob next day burned down over 750 premises in Cairo, including Shepheard's Hotel and most of the European quarter; at least 30 people died and hundreds were injured. On the 27th, Faruq dismissed An Nahhas's government, which – unconsciously paving the way to the revolution – had declared martial law. He was succeeded by 'Aly Mahir, now of no party, from 1 February to 1 March, then by the independent Nagib Hilaly until 28 June, Sirry (2 to 20 July) and Hilaly again on 22 July. The following day, Gamal 'Abd an Nasir's coup inaugurated a period during which politics were dominated by the military. All the political parties were abolished in January 1953 but 'Aly Mahir was retained as head of an interim civilian council.

Talks with Britain over the Sudan were soon inititated and resulted in an Agreement on 12 February 1953 which provided for Egyptian and British troops to be withdrawn and for the country to become independent, perhaps in union with Egypt, in three years. Separate negotiations began in the April which led to a seven-year Agreement on 19 October 1954. Under this, the Treaty of 1936 was superseded, all British troops were to leave Egypt within 20 months (they had gone by 1 June) and the Canal Base was to be kept in working order lest it be required for British use, under the Eisenhower Plan, in combating aggression from outside against any Arab League member state or Turkey. Right of passage through the Suez Canal in accordance with the Istanbul Convention of 1888 was agreed.

Then arose Egypt's need for arms and a new Aswan Dam. Its frustration by the West led in due course to President 'Abd an Nasir's nationalisation of the Suez Canal Company and the tripartite attack of December 1956. On 1 January 1957, Egypt scrapped the 1954 Agreement, and the Canal and the Canal Base came under sole Egyptian control. Only now had the country attained the total independence from Britain which had been its aim under the British Proconsuls, and their varied responses to which, and to Egyptian nationalism in its various monarchical and parliamentary forms, had brought to a premature end the diplomatic careers of McMahon, Wingate, Allenby and Lloyd.

Appendix 1
Sa'ad Zaghlul (1858–1927)

the landowning and educated official elite of Egyptians ..., between 1907
and 1919, promoted themselves into the governing class of independent
Egypt between 1923 and 1952.[1]

(P.J. Vatikotis)

Sa'ad Zaghlul, a native-born Egyptian and 'a fellah of the fellahin' (a true-
born peasant)[2] came of prosperous middle-class farming stock. He was born
in July 1858 in Ibyanah, a village in the Gharbiyyah province of the Delta of
which his father was the *'umdah* (headman). He went to a local Qur'an
school and then, habitually precocious, on a scholarship in 1873[3] to Al
Azhar, Islam's most famous seat of religious learning, where he became a
pupil and follower of the great reformer, Muhammad 'Abduh,[4] and of
Jamal ad Din al Afghani,[5] the firebrand Islamic activist, one of whose most
intimate disciples he remained throughout the 1870s. His political roots
prospered most, however, not in the religious but in the secularist faction of
'Abduh's Hizb al Ummah, and his nationalist concern was with the Egypt of
both the Pharaohs and the Arabs, the Copts and the Muslims.[6]

Journalist and judge

Zaghlul's first career was that of journalist. In 1880, he became assistant to
'Abduh in the editorship of *Al Waqa'i' al Misriyyah*, the Official Gazette,
and then was appointed first its literary editor and then its editor. In June
of the year following the failure of 'Uraby's movement, which he supported with articles in *Al Waqa'i'*, he was briefly arrested on suspicion of
forming, or belonging to, a clandestine Patriotic Egyptian League or
Vengeance Society which aimed to end the British occupation.[7] After his
release, he worked for almost ten years in the law, that breeding-ground of
nationalism, and in 1892 began 14 years as a judge in the court of appeal.
He was influenced, in addition to 'Abduh, by the ideas of the lawyer
Qasim Amin – a pupil and disciple of 'Abduh who championed the rights
of women in Islam and said that the veil and the harim were post-Qur'an

impositions – and Ahmad Lutfi as Sayyid,[8] who, like himself, believed in reform rather than revolution and in the attainment of self-government and eventual independence through negotiation with Britain.[9] Zaghlul sought to bring both the secular and the religious law up to date and earned a name as an administrator. In 1892 also, he and others joined 'Abduh in founding the Muslim Benevolent Society, which had the object of giving poor Muslim children a modern education in private schools established for the purpose. On the recommendation of the intimate of Layard and Storrs and 'old friend' of Wingate,[10] Princess Nazly Sabry,[11] whose lawyer he was, Zaghlul learned French and studied at the French School of Law in Cairo, gaining a Paris LLB in 1897.

Trainee politician

In 1896, he married Safiyyah, a daughter of Prime Minister Mustafa Pasha Fahmy.[12] In 1902, the couple bought a large villa in Cairo which came to be known as Bayt al Ummah, the House of the Nation. (After Zaghlul's death, it became a museum which recounted Egypt's independence struggle.)[13] Zaghlul made a deliberate move in the direction of politics when he began to frequent the modern Middle East's first political salon, that of Princess Nazly, who in about 1900 took the bold step of admitting to her house a small coterie of male intellectuals.[14] There, during a period when Storrs rated him 'balanced and unspoilt', he 'thundered against his ruler, and supported Lord Cromer with all his strength'.[15]

Cromer's Minister of Education

In 1906, Cromer persuaded Mustafa Fahmy to include his son-in-law in the Cabinet,[16] in which he held the new Education portfolio from 18 November until early 1910. In that capacity, he sought to improve literacy, increasing the number of schools and the use of Arabic instead of English as the medium of instruction; he strenghtened the cadre of Egyptian school inspectors and insisted that they write their reports in Arabic. In 1908, he established a 12-year schooling pattern, with three equal elementary, secondary and higher stages, and brought Al Azhar under firm secular control.[17] His impact on the Ministry, upgraded from the Department of Public Instruction, was one 'from which it has hardly yet recovered', in the enigmatic judgement of Storrs, who added that, while Zaghlul's conscientiousness and honesty were recognised, he was 'a difficult administrator' who often put the interests of individual school pupils before those of their teachers or his Under-Secretary.[18] Humphrey Bowman, who worked in both Department and Ministry from 1903 to 1911, had no doubt who was boss:

> Here was no dummy chief, such as had been commonly appointed to the Council of Ministers in the past, to whom advice offered by

Cromer or by one of his lieutenants was tantamount to a command
... Those of us who worked in the Ministry even in a subordinate position felt aware that an Egyptian personality was at the head of our
little world ... Here, almost for the first time in recent Egyptian
history, was a Minister determined to go his own way[19]

and able to establish his authority over his British Adviser and officials.[20]
Storrs, indeed, claims that he fell out with them, certainly crossing swords
from time to time with Douglas Dunlop,[21] the Education Adviser, who
others maintain[22] 'ran the Ministry like a true martinet'[23] and remained
the 'real power in education'.[24]

In his farewell speech on 7 May 1907, Cromer had eulogised Zaghlul:

I should like to mention the name of one with whom I have only
recently co-operated, but for whom, in that short time, I have learned
to entertain a high regard. Unless I am much mistaken, a career of
great public usefulness lies before the present Minister of Education,
Sa'ad Zaghlul Pasha. He possesses all the qualities necessary to serve
his country. He is honest; he is capable; he has the courage of his convictions; he has been abused by many of the less worthy of his own
countrymen. These are high qualifications. He should go far.[25]

The Khedive

In October 1907, Zaghlul had been among the moderate founders of
Hizb al Ummah, which called for constitutional limits on the monarchy.
He was strongly opposed to the activities and policies of 'Abbas Hilmy,
with whom he never enjoyed cordial relations. Like 'Abduh and As Sayyid,
he considered a diminution of the Khedive's power to be an essential pre-
requisite for reform. He accused him of corruption and supported British
policies which downgraded his status. Until Kitchener removed his right
to do so,[26] 'Abbas Hilmy presided over Cabinet meetings, where he and
Zaghlul clashed in particular over new directions for the Education Ministry. When Zaghlul persuaded the Cabinet to support an idea of 'Abduh's
for the establishment of a Ministry training centre for Islamic Law judges,
the Khedive opposed the measure because Zaghlul had proposed it and
because the centre was not to come under the control of Al Azhar.
Worsted, he announced that he would no longer attend Cabinet meetings
when the Minister of Education was present.

Britain

Before Kitchener, Zaghlul believed in the British connection and – while
criticising their administration when necessary – endeavoured to be
helpful towards the reforms of successive British Agents; in Beaman's

opinion, he was 'the best co-operator, perhaps, that Cromer and Gorst had had'.[27] In 1909 in the Legislative Assembly, of which his ministerial rank had made him an automatic member, he even defended the proposed extension of the Suez Canal Concession which his fellow deputies turned down and he had originally opposed.[28] When, however, he became convinced that the British were happy to see the Khedive diverting Waqf administration money into his own pocket and decided that British policies were in general mistaken, he did not spare Kitchener his criticism. The Consul-General fully reciprocated his disenchantment, Storrs quoting him as saying of Zaghlul, 'He's more trouble than he's worth.'[29]

Minister of Justice and Parliamentarian

Zaghlul was promoted to be Minister of Justice, when he perhaps thought that he should have become Prime Minister, on 23 February 1910. He came into conflict with 'Abbas Hilmy once more, this time over a corruption case which Kitchener considered did him little credit.[30] Now it was his turn to pull out, resigning in March 1912 from the Kitchener-supported government of Muhammad Sa'id[31] to which he and 'Abd al 'Aziz Fahmy had from within led the opposition; Zaghlul's discrediting of the Prime Minister, and the 'baiting of ministers' generally, especially by him, 'reached such a point that they were delighted when the session ended'.[32] (In a characteristically sour view of him as a Minister at this time, Lloyd said, 'His methods were hasty and ill-considered: he showed an unreasonable disregard for routine, and no evidence of a capacity for firm and careful planning. It is more than likely that during this period he began to learn to prefer opposition to office.')[33]

Having used his status as a minister to bring himself before the public,[34] Zaghlul ran for election to the 1913 Legislative Assembly and, without straying towards demagoguery, began to make his name as a 'people's tribune'.[35] He had a 'natural gift of popular eloquence' and the advantage that, as an Azharite, Islamic references in his speeches were respected.[36]

The First World War

Lloyd believed that, if Kitchener had been able to resume his post in Egypt, he would have been able to 'reclaim by careful treatment'[37] the man whom he had alienated. As it was, the outbreak of war brought parliamentary debate to a halt, gagging Zaghlul. Under martial law, he lay low, gathering support.[38] That he had done so to good effect was demonstrated after the war by the way in which, far from attempting to win him back, the British over-reacted to his approach when the leaders of the nationalist movement – quick to realise that much could be made of President Wilson's Fourteen Points – decided on 11 November 1918 that he, Fahmy and 'Aly Pasha Sha'rawy should make their fateful call on Wingate two days later.[39]

Tall, of distinguished appearance, diabetic and fond of cognac, Zaghlul was a fine orator. A committed parliamentarian,[40] he was wily and, although emotional, shrewd. After his first exile, he became domineering, making use of patronage and sometimes of violent mass demonstrations to cow opponents;[41] neither able to share power nor – in the opinion of one observer – to treat his opponents with generosity,[42] he 'seemed to lack the courage of his own convictions' in dealing with them. Grafftey-Smith believed that – deemed inadequate as administrator[43] and statesman[44] – for Zaghlul 'to prefer, in and out of office, the politician's slogan to the statesman's grasp of opportunity, and to fight tooth and nail any rival who looked like accepting less than himself, was a betrayal of his country's hopes'.[45] Zaghlul's personal relations with the British – except with Kitchener and perhaps Allenby – were always friendly, even if, knowing no English, he must have been handicapped in negotiating with them.

Appendix 2
Egyptian personalities

'Adly Pasha Yakan (?–1933)

A great grandson of the sister of Muhammad 'Aly, the first Khedive (1805), he was of Macedonian ancestry and educated in France and Turkey. As Foreign Minister and then Minister of Justice, he was a leading Cabinet member throughout the First World War; afterwards he became Minister of Education (1918) and Interior (1919). Said to have been invited to join Zaghlul's Wafd in 1918,[1] in October 1922 he founded Hizb al Ahrar ad Dusturiyyin but was reconciled with Zaghlul in July 1924.[2] Thin, taciturn, uncharismatic and autocratic, he was 'very well regarded by those who knew him'[3] and even deemed 'noble'.[4] Symes assessed him as 'a conservative in temperament and enterprise alike but with the clear-sightedness and independent judgement of a born aristocrat'.[5] His 'blood was as good as any Khedive's',[6] his presence very impressive. Grafftey-Smith described him: 'He was tall and square-shouldered, of handsome charm, and he had a dignity and courtesy rare outside the circles of arch-dukes and highland lairds ... complete integrity ... great wealth and much wisdom. But a fatal strain of laziness, or lack of ambition, or perhaps an aristocratic distaste for the dustier corners of the arena, frustrated all hopes placed upon him, and condemned the Moderates ... to perpetual insuccess. He was a little too good for the rough and tumble of politics.'[7] '[N]ot a fighter',[8] Allenby considered him 'a broken reed'.[9]

'Afify Pasha, Dr Hafiz (1886–?)

A paediatrician and initially a member of Al Hizb al Watany, he joined the Ummah in 1918[10] and became one of the 14 original Wafd delegates. He resigned from the party in the summer of 1921 but rejoined it after Zaghlul's second period of exile. He soon resigned again when the High Command turned radical[11] and in 1929 became Vice-President of Hizb al Ahrar, whose organ *As Siyasah* he published.[12] He was Minister (1930–34) and Ambassador (1936–38) in the Egyptian Embassy in London. Becoming Governor of Banque Misr, 'he made rather too much money' and became 'scarred for life by experience of an Aswan concentration-camp'.[13] He wrote '*Ala Hamish as Siyasah* (On the Political Fringe – 1938), a 'call for social reform',[14] and was Head of the Royal Cabinet, 1951–52.

Fahmy, 'Abd al 'Aziz (1870–1951)

A student, like As Sayyid, at the Khedivial School of Law (he also studied in France), he became Egypt's leading lawyer and Chairman of its Bar Council. A close friend of As Sayyid and Zaghlul, Wingate's pedestrian view of him was that he was 'much respected by all classes of Egyptian society for his honesty of purpose and outspoken methods'. Grafftey-Smith considered him over-perfectionist: 'He had a look of a stage solicitor, pince-nez'd and pernickety, and his usefulness was diminished by rather doctrinaire attitudes and a petulant impatience with circumstance'.[15]

He joined the Wafd, of which he, with Zaghlul, was the 'brains',[16] but transferred his allegiance to Hizb al Ahrar in 1921. A member of the 1922 Constitutional Committee, he protested at the outcome of its work[17] and rejoined the Wafd after Zaghlul's second exile. Minister of Justice under Ziwar in 1924–25, in September 1925 he was dismissed from office by royal decree on the grounds that he had failed to execute an Al Azhar judgement against Shaykh 'Aly Abd ar Raziq.[18] (This modernist member of the 'ulama' had written a book, *Islam and the Foundations of Authority* which Sultan Fu'ad considered hostile to his ambition to be Caliph of Islam.) Fahmy had succeeded 'Adly as president of Hizb al Ahrar in the autumn and his dismissal led to the resignation of three of his party's ministers including Sidqy and in due course to the fall of Ziwar's government. Fahmy was Head of the Royal Cabinet, 1934–35.[19]

Fahmy, 'Abd ar Rahman

Uncle of 'Aly and Ahmad Mahir, he was dismissed from the Awqaf administration by 'Abbas Hilmy. He became Executive Secretary of the Wafd's Central Committee. During the 1919 events, he arranged for Al Azhar students to keep demonstrations orderly and free from outside infiltration.[20] When Zaghlul went to Paris and they initiated their secret correspondence, Fahmy was at pains to keep news of setbacks there – 'fodder for the traitors' – out of Egypt in order to maintain morale and the flow of contributions to the cause.[21] When the Milner Mission was announced, Allenby blamed him and other Wafd Central Committee members for the disturbances in the country, threatened them with court martial and put Fahmy under surveillance.[22] With 27 others, he was accused by a Wafd member, Muhammad ash Shiri'y, a protégé of Muhammad Sa'id, of being the leader of a second secret Vengeance Society, founded in

February 1920 to challenge martial law. Aiming to overthrow the government, assassinate the Sultan, distribute arms, have the Milner Mission boycotted and – a strange objective for Fahmy – reinstate 'Abbas Hilmy, its members seemed to be 'schoolboy revolutionaries' but their boycott of the Mission was effective[23] and included among its consequences the closing-down of Al Hizb al Mustaqill al Hurr. When Fahmy was arrested on 1 July, Zaghlul – negotiating with Milner in London – protested to Curzon. At the end of his trial in October, despite Russell's doubts about the soundness of the case, seven defendants including Fahmy were sentenced to death, reduced (although Allenby wanted Fahmy executed) to 15 years in prison with hard labour.[24] Zaghlul strongly denied that Fahmy had been the link between the Society and the Wafd but he may have condoned the violence instigated by Fahmy. It died down during the trial but Fahmy was accused of reigniting it from his cell.[25] With the coming of Zaghlul's government, he and the rest of the accused were released,[26] to considerable surprise in his case in view of his 'contribution to the national struggle'.[27]

Muhammad Bey Farid (1868–1919)

'[A]n educated man of considerable means', he funded *Al Liwa'* (The Standard), Hizb al Watan's newspaper[28] and, following the death of Mustafa Kamil, his long-time companion, was unanimously elected chairman of the party in February 1908; it was 'largely through his efforts that the Watani party became more effective'.[29] Sentenced to six months in jail in January 1911 for contributing the foreword to a member's collection of verse which was deemed to be an incitement to murder and to hatred and contempt for the government,[30] he was released on time.[31] In March 1912, however, when he received a year's suspended sentence for sedition (hatred of the government, and in particular for saying that Kitchener, not the Khedive, was the real ruler of the country), he fled to Turkey.[32] Though not an effective leader of Hizb al Watan, his absence weakened the party.[33] Pro-Ottoman, but 'not at Egypt's expense',[34] he attacked 'Abbas Hilmy and Kitchener in Istanbul's Arabic and French newspapers. He went to France and then Switzerland in August 1912 and was never able to return to Egypt. In 1914 he asked for permission to do so but Rushdy, the incoming Prime Minister, said that though he regarded him as loyal he 'was like a faithful dog which had become rabid' and was one of the leaders of Egypt's anarchists.[35] Joined by the deposed Khedive 'Abbas Hilmy, both supporting the Axis,[36] late in the same year Farid issued a *fatwah* against Husayn Kamil when he became Sultan, calling for his assassination for treason against God, Muhammad and the Muslims and for disobeying the Caliph; at about the same time, he promoted a *jihad* against the British.[37]

Holding pompous and often reactionary views, Farid also displayed 'a certain unwillingness to dirty his hands too much'.[38] He died in Berlin after a long illness.

Mustafa Kamil Pasha (1874–1908)

From a middle-class family, 'slender and passionate',[39] with 'enormous liquid eyes and ... undeniably attractive ... to both sexes',[40] he was 'the most charismatic nationalist figure' before Zaghlul,[41] who thought him mad. A powerful orator with a fiery and magnetic personality and the 'ability to sway crowds',[42] he first came to notice, beginning to rival 'Abduh and to influence nationalists, when he led demonstrations against *Al Muqattam* in 1893.[43] He studied law at the Cairo law school and then in Toulouse, graduating in 1894. Until 1896 he in vain tried to drum up support for Egyptian nationalism in France. On his return to Egypt, he established a group, made up of young lawyers and intellectuals, which became Hizb al Watan. Early good relations with Shaykh 'Aly Yusuf, editor of *Al Mu'ayyad*, not lasting, in 1900 he founded *Al Liwa'*, which was widely read and in due course came out in English and French as well as Arabic. Seeking support for Egypt's independence as the envoy of Hizb al Watan,[44] Kamil returned frequently to Europe, principally France, until Fashoda and the conclusion of the Entente Cordiale caused him to turn against France.[45] 'Abbas Hilmy encouraged his endeavours at first, but their relationship ended in the same year, causing Kamil to move away from Egyptian nationalism towards pan-Islam and support for the Ottoman Sultan. Dinshaway having boosted his cause, thanks to Wilfrid Scawen Blunt, the British freelance Arab supporter, he met British Prime Minister Campbell Bannerman in 1906 and was promised 'greater autonomy for the Egyptian government and an increase in political rights and participation'.[46] With Farid, he reformed Hizb al Watan in 1907. The Young Turk Revolution of 1908 made him an Egyptian nationalist once more,[47] but he died of tuberculosis or poisoning[48] in the same year. Fifty thousand mourners followed his coffin[49] and for 40 days black armbands were worn by students, who idolised him.[50]

Dr Ahmad Bey Mahir (1886–1945)

He was a son of a man with sound anti-British credentials. During a visit of inspection by 'Abbas Hilmy to the Egyptian Army at Wady Halfah in January 1894, the 'Frontier Incident' occurred when Mahir Pasha, Under-Secretary of the War Ministry and 'an intriguer well-known for his anti-British proclivities',[51] encouraged the Khedive to indulge in free criticism of British officers and in 'fatal insubordination' against Kitchener, who tried to resign.[52] Mahir was sacked but 'eventually obtained civil employment and worked cordially with the British officials'.[53]

An economics lecturer with a doctorate in law from Montpellier,

Ahmad was active in the formation of the Wafd, particularly its Secret Apparatus.[54] Short and stocky, fleshy and with 'fat chops',[55] he was, although genial, more radical than his brother 'Aly and a member of the Vengeance Society;[56] in 1919–20, he was alleged to have been with an Egyptian police officer when he was killed practising making and throwing bombs.[57] He became Minister of Education in Zaghlul's administration. Tried for the murder of Stack in 1926, he was acquitted in June but remained on the British Black List until the 1940s.[58] (The Residency spoke of the Mahir family being 'tainted' and said of him that, 'Clever and quite unscrupulous, he stands for all that is undisciplined and extremist in Egyptian political life.')[59] He became secretary of the Wafd's parliamentary group in 1927[60] and was in the Egyptian team for An Nahhas's negotiations with the British in 1930 and 1936. Hostile to An Nahhas, and co-leader of the Sa'adists with An Nuqrashy in late 1937, he was Minister of Finance in Muhammad Mahmud's 1938 Hizb al Ahrar government.[61] A member of 'Aly Mahir's administration, and President of the Chamber of Deputies when Hasan Sabry was prime minister (1940), he campaigned for Egypt to join the Allied side in the war so as to be at the eventual peace conference;[62] in the September he resigned with An Nuqrashy over Egypt's failure to declare war[63] on Italy. As Prime Minister in 1944–45, he released all political prisoners, including 'Ubayd and 'Aly Mahir,[64] appointing the former Minister of Finance. Under heavy British pressure,[65] on 24 February 1945 he obtained parliamentary approval for a declaration of war[66] and was assassinated the following day, An Nuqrashy succeeding him. In one view, he was 'An honest and patriotic statesman . . . not politically close to his brother Ali.'[67]

'Aly Mahir Pasha (1883–1960)

Short and stocky, compulsively ambitious ('a small ravenous wolf driven by furnace-heats of ambition')[68] and 'an opportunist whose inclinations for political intriguing and maneuvering [*sic*] were well known',[69] he was in the opinion of Jarvis 'the ablest man in Egypt'.[70] A lawyer, he joined the Wafd after its first internal split in Paris in 1919 and was a member of the delegation which negotiated with Milner. Having reached its Central Committee, he parted from Zaghlul over policy issues in 1921.[71] He was a member of the 1922 Constitutional Commission and a known Palace man.[72] He became Under-Secretary of the Ministry of Education (1924), Vice-President of Hizb al Ittihad (1925) and Minister successively of Education (1925–26), Finance (1928–29) and Education and Justice (1930–32).

In the 1930s he worked with the Shaykh of Al Azhar, Al Ikhwan al Muslimun and Saudi Arabia in drumming up religious opposition to the Wafd.[73] An influential political adviser to King Fu'ad from 1935 who 'ultimately helped the Egyptian monarchy to its downfall',[74] he remained 'a grey eminence in Egyptian politics until 1942 – and later'.[75] Prime Minister, Minister of Interior and Minister for Foreign Affairs from January to June 1936, soon after July 1937 he became Chief of the Royal Cabinet, where 'His influence on young Farouq was wholly unfortunate', steering him 'not only towards an autocratic conception of his relationship to his people but also towards a mistrust of all and every advice coming from the British Embassy' which 'soon became obsessive . . . Maher Pasha was always at hand to place the worst interpretation on any British gesture or remark . . . in his venomous persuasions'.[76] In 1942 dismissed on Lampson's demand, Britain suspected him of being pro-Axis and, an Italophile, of passing military secrets[77] to Italy;[78] in the same year the Wafd government put him under house arrest. He was released by Ahmad Mahir's 1944–45 administration. He was Prime Minister again in 1946 and from February to March 1952. Until he was dismissed in September 1952 for planning to raise the amount of land an individual could hold to 500 feddans,[79] he was the first premier (and Minister of War, Marine and Foreign Affairs) of the revolutionary period. A member of the 1953 Constitutional Commission, he was the only pre-Revolution politician to remain a public figure, until 1954, after it.[80]

Muhammad Mahmud Pasha (1877–1941)

Son of an Upper Egyptian aristocrat from Asyut (a very wealthy, highly respected and influential landowner who had helped found Hizb al Ummah),[81] Mahmud took a good degree at Balliol and then was specially selected for a post in the administration by the Interior Adviser;[82] he became successively Governor of the Fayyum, the Suez Canal District and Buhayrah Province. On suspicion of treating peasants with brutality and of intriguing with the Sanusiyyah, he was removed from the last of these posts – unfairly in the view of many British.[83] In the summer of 1921, he became 'the first to split openly' with Zaghlul, than whom he was 'more pragmatically wise'.[84] He joined other moderate nationalists in founding Hizb al Ahrar,[85] of which he became Vice-President in 1922. He rejoined the Wafd after Zaghlul's second exile and became one of the two Vice-Presidents of the unofficial parliament of November 1925. He was Minister of Communications in the 'Adly government of 1926, when Lloyd rated him as 'one of the most interesting figures in Modern Egypt' and described him as 'a man of great ability and strong ambitions, with a history of intense extremism behind him – there was no telling in which direction he might steer his future course'.[86] He was Minister of Finance in the April 1927 government of Sarwat, who much disliked him,[87] and in An Nahhas's March 1928 administration, from which he resigned on 17 June, two days before the Prince Sayf ad Din scandal struck the Wafd government. In 1929 he was elected president of Hizb al Ahrar; he led the party, co-operating with the Wafd, in opposing the 1930–33 Sidqy government. He was Prime Minister from December 1937 to August 1939.

Though shocked by being turned out of a train compartment by a disrespectful British subaltern soon after his return from Balliol,[88] he resembled the British 'in every respect except that he did not wear a bowler hat, disliked marmalade and did not sing in his bath'.[89] A friend of the Rodds,[90] he was most amiable (although sharp-tempered, sensitive and a bit paranoid),[91] much respected and absolutely honest. He 'lacked all demagogic appeal'.[92]

Mustafa an Nahhas (1879–1965)

Of a merchant family not blessed by wealth, he became a lawyer and a noted judge in Tantah. Initially a member of Al Hizb al Watany,[93] he had become a member of Hizb al Ummah by 1918.[94] He was Minister of Communications in Zaghlul's government. Succeeding Zaghlul as leader of the Wafd, he followed 'Ubayd's lead.[95] In 1926, when he was elected Vice-President of the Chamber of Deputies,[96] Lloyd said that he 'had always stood for a policy of uncompromising hostility to Great Britain and the British connexion' and 'had still not learnt the lesson that hostility to Britain was incompatible with Egyptian progress';[97] as President or Speaker in 1927–28, in an interview with Lloyd about the Sarwat treaty, he 'confined himself to asserting with a damnable iteration that it was quite useless to discuss this or any other issue which did not provide for the complete evacuation of Egyptian territory by the British Army'.[98] Prime Minister in 1928, in the view of Lloyd he was 'not fit for the responsibilities he was now undertaking: whatever his intentions he had neither the capacity nor the experience to ensure that they would be carried out'.[99] His government fell in part because of press allegations of corrupt Wafd–Palace financial dealings,[100] perhaps over the allocation of contracts for public works[101] and certainly in connection with the Prince Sayf ad Din affair, in connection with which he earned an enormous fee of £E130,000. The incoming Mahmud government referred him and two alleged co-conspirators to a Council of Discipline, but he was acquitted.[102]

Under him, in 1935 the Wafd founded the Fascist Al Qumsan az Zarqa' (the Blue Shirts) and other youth organisations. Until it was banned in 1938, its role was to 'mobilise party followers and the masses, as well as to intimidate and terrorise the opposition', particularly Al Qumsan al Khudhra' (Green Shirts) of the Misr al Fatat youth organisation.[103] An Nahhas suffered a split in the party which led to the creation of the Sa'adists in late 1937 and the defection of Makram 'Ubayd, his Minister of Finance, during his next term as Prime Minister (and Minister of Foreign Affairs) from February 1942 to October 1944.[104] The charges 'Ubayd levelled against An Nahhas echoed those that brought down his 1928 administration.[105]

An Nahhas was a major contributor to the creation of the Arab League on 7 October 1944. The Wafd, like all other parties, was abolished in

January 1953, and An Nahhas and his beautiful wife Zaynab al Wakil were tried by a Revolutionary Tribunal for conspiracy and corruption in the September; he was not sentenced and she was fined.

An effective, down-to-earth speaker[106] and demagogue[107] with a trademark of 'unflinching nationalism',[108] he was 'of the same populist mould' as Zaghlul[109] but had none of Zaghlul's 'hypnotic control over the deputies'.[110] The 'most shrewd of all Egyptian politicians',[111] he was called the 'beloved of the nation; sole leader'[112] and known, although he died rich, for his 'solicitude for poor people'.[113] Tall and balding, he had 'two floating eyes, and one never knew where he was focusing'.[114] He was both nervy and 'complacent and happy-go-lucky'.[115] In the time of Lloyd's successor, he was remembered as 'telling jokes in his execrable French and talking enthusiastically and wildly on every subject that Loraine introduced'.[116]

Mahmud Fahmy an Nuqrashy Pasha (1888–1948)

A relative of Safiyyah Zaghlul, he was an engineer who had obtained his higher education in Nottingham. Extreme, he was referred to as 'the Murderer' by the foreign community[117] and regarded by the British Foreign Office as a dangerous agitator.[118] In 1919, a former student of his claimed that An Nuqrashy had provided him with bomb-making materials and practical instruction[119] and encouraged him to throw a bomb at Muhammad Sa'id, whom An Nuqrashy regarded as a traitor, in September 1919. An Nuqrashy was a member of the Vengeance Society[120] and the Secret Apparatus of the Wafd in the early 1920s.

As Under Secretary of the Ministry of Interior under Zaghlul, he was tried for the murder of Stack in 1926. Minister of Communications (over British objections)[121] in An Nahhas's 1929 administration, and Minister of Communications and Transport in his 1936 government, he became 'noted for his political acumen'.[122] After quarrelling with An Nahhas (over the award of public works' contracts and power-sharing) and 'Ubayd,[123] he was expelled from the Wafd in September 1937. In January 1938, as founder and joint leader with Ahmad Mahir of the Sa'adists, he became Minister of Interior in Mahmud's government.[124] He was a member of the 1939–40 administrations of 'Aly Mahir and Hasan Sabry and resigned over Egypt's failure to declare war on Italy.[125] Foreign Minister in Ahmad Mahir's 1944–45 government, he became sole leader of the Sa'adists in 1945.[126]

Husayn Rushdy Topuzade (1863–1928)

'Small and birdlike in appearance, Rushdy was descended from an Albanian officer who accompanied Mohammed Aly to Egypt';[127] Storrs noted that, of his last name, 'as I had the pleasure of informing him, the exact

English rendering is "Son of a gun" '.[128] A Sorbonne-trained judge, 'timid'[129] and with bristling white hair, a moustache and pince-nez,[130] he was Minister of Public Works and Awqaf before becoming Minister of Justice (1908–10) under Butrus Ghaly; when he asked the latter's assassin why he had shot him, he replied, 'Because he selected people like you to be cabinet ministers.'[131] As Minister of Foreign Affairs (1910–12), he was highly co-operative with Britain over arrangements at the start of the war which made Egypt '*de facto*, if not *de jure*, a belligerent'.[132] He was Minister of Justice from 1912 to 1914. As Prime Minister and Minister of Interior (1914–19), he protested neither against the banishment of the Khedive (who appointed him regent) nor the imposition of the Protectorate.[133] 'Abbas Hilmy held him responsible for his exile[134] even though Rushdy kept assuring him that – provided that he shuffled his entourage – his absence would be only temporary and tried to effect his return.[135] Rushdy became Minister of Education in 1919.

An inaugural Vice-Chairman of Hizb al Ahrar,[136] he served in the 1921 'Adly government as Deputy Prime Minister and was appointed a member of the new Egyptian Parliament by King Fu'ad in 1924.[137] He remained President of the Senate until his death.

Muhammad Sa'id (1863–1928)

Sa'id was a lawyer, at first a favourite of 'Abbas Hilmy and Minister of Interior under Butrus Ghaly (1908–10). As Prime Minister (1910–14), under violent attack in the Legislative Assembly and elsewhere from his enemy Zaghlul, he was the first to understand that, with the death of Gorst, relations between the Palace and the British Agency had changed: 'the more he felt the Khedive's trust in him ebb, the more he threw himself into the arms of . . . Kitchener, so that he ended by asking the British Agent for his protection against the Khedive'. Kitchener, who came to think (as he told Grey) that Sa'id had 'a constitutional disability' to maintain 'an open and straightforward course of action in his dealings with colleagues, helpmates, and subordinates' and favoured 'somewhat tortuous methods', was in the end unable to protect him from a Khedive of whom he was very afraid despite his co-operativeness.[138]

To counter the appeal of Zaghlul, Sa'id participated in a counter-Wafd formed by Prince 'Umar Tusun in November 1918, forcing the Sultan to give support to the former. '[A] thick-skinned Turkish Pasha of the old school',[139] Sa'id chaired the Cabinet during the 1919 Revolution;[140] it was 'common knowledge that his intrigues were behind' the Vengeance Society trial.[141] After it, he operated as a liaison between the Palace and the Wafd. In Zaghlul's government, the public referred to him as 'the jack in the box' who 'was kept in a corner'. Whenever Machiavellian handling of a question was required, 'Zaghlul took the box out of its corner, opened it, let Sa'id out, listened to what he had to say, returned him to his box, slapped on the lid and returned the box to its corner.'[142] Sa'id became first Hizb al Ahrar Minister of Agriculture and then manager of Prince Sayf ad Din's estate – only to be dismissed by the King so that he could 'take the pickings himself'.[143]

Chirol regarded him as 'a very skilled operator in his day'[144] but noted 'his inveterate habit of hunting with the hounds and running with the hare'.[145] Lloyd called him 'a man without any ideals to guide him, having every ruse at his command, and no scruples about employing any one of them'; he was 'a disruptive force in the Cabinet, given over to tortuous intrigue, and tactless in the Assembly'.[146]

Huda Sha'rawy (1879–1947)

Noted female activist and feminist, she was from the upper class, daughter of one of Egypt's wealthiest land owners and intimately connected with royalty. At the age of 13 she married one of Wingate's 13 November guests, her guardian 'Aly Sha'rawy. Her husband was some 30 years her senior and she lived apart from him from 1893 to 1900. She inaugurated public lectures for women before helping to found the Intellectual Association of Egyptian Women in 1914. She took part in the 1919 anti-British demonstrations, marshalling women protestors; during the Milner Mission's visit, she organised demonstrations by women opposed to the continuation of the Protectorate. In 1920, she was founding President of the Wafdist Women's Central Committee (inaugurated in the Cathedral of St Mark), which organised an anti-British boycott in 1922 and campaigned for reforms in social welfare and family legislation affecting women and women workers.[147] In 1923 she formed a Union of Egyptian Women and became founder-President of the Egyptian Feminist Union, which was able to sponsor a law to set a minimum marriage age and opened the first secondary school for girls;[148] returning to Cairo from a meeting in Rome in that year, she struck an important blow for Egyptian womanhood by removing her veil at the railway station. A radical nationalist[149] and very anti-British, in May 1924 she turned on Zaghlul for accepting part of Allenby's ultimatum. In 1938, she chaired the first Arab Women's Congress, discussing Palestine, and in 1944 became a Vice-President of the International Alliance of Women and founder-President of the Arab Feminist Union.[150]

Isma'il Sidqy Pasha (1875–1950)

Son of an extremely wealthy father who was Governor of Cairo, Sidqy took a law degree and studied in France. Regarded by the British as an extreme member of Hizb al Watan,[151] he was appointed Minister of Agriculture in 1913 but resigned two years later 'in consequence of a deplorable domestic scandal'[152] which 'created much stir at the time'.[153] It involved the future Prime Minister Yahya Ibrahim's daughter 'and a *dahabiyya* on the Nile'.[154] Sidqy's amours were 'the staple of Cairo gossip'.[155]

At the Paris Peace Conference he split with Zaghlul[156] and after leaving France was dismissed from the Wafd by those remaining there.[157] He joined Hizb al Ahrar in 1921. He was Minister of Finance in 'Adly's March 1921 government and a member of the Prime Minister's delegation to London in the same year. He joined Ziwar's December 1924 government, becoming Minister of Interior, displaying 'a marked degree of strength and ability'[158] and showing that 'there was no more able or determined political fighter in Egypt'.[159] He took a leading part in the campaign against Zaghlul. Referring to him in 1925, Nevile Henderson told Lloyd, 'He is at heart as nationalist as Saad and I am sure he has no real love for us . . . He is unscrupulous and dangerous. But he is far and away the most intelligent man in the Government . . . He is the strong man, as well as the brain, in it . . .' He soon added, 'Of all Egyptians I have met he is by far the most intelligent and dangerous'[160] and 'One must suspect every act of Sidky's.'[161] In 1925, Sidqy chaired the Electoral Law Commission[162] and in 1926 queried the budgetary provision for the Financial and Judicial Advisers.[163]

A man with 'acknowledged financial capacities',[164] during a crisis in the economy in 1931, Loraine said of him, 'with his considerable financial acumen . . . I certainly shudder to think what the economic situation might have been in the hands of a Makram ['Ubayd]'.[165] At the end of his period of unpopular autocratic rule, he joined the National Front which sought the reinstatement of the constitution and had a severe stroke.[166] He was a member of the team which negotiated the 1936 Treaty, Minister of Finance in the 1938 Mahmud government and Prime Minister again from February to December 1946, resigning on account of ill-health.

Grafftey-Smith described him as 'a lone wolf of great intelligence. He was always worth watching and he always needed watching. He played Egyptian politics with ruthless amusement, as a game he must win. If his opponents needed a bad image, he would arrange for the necessary number of bomb-outrages to blame them for.'[167] Lloyd described him as 'That able but incalculable statesman.'[168] He was 'the nearest thing to an objectively minded Egyptian that Loraine had met'.[169] He told the Foreign Secretary in 1932, 'we could not find among Egyptian statesmen a better or more reasonable collaborator than him'.[170]

William Makram 'Ubayd (1889–1961)

A man of 'extraordinary intelligence, wit, eloquence, energy, and organizational and administrative abilities',[171] 'Ubayd was a 'suavely polished'[172] Copt from a middle-sized land-owning family. He attended Asyut American School, obtained a New College, Oxford, law degree and was a student at Lyon. He had 'a lively, generous, and vigorous intellect (and) interest in ideas'.[173] Familiarly known as Al Mujahid al Kabir [the Great Struggler] and Ibn Sa'ad [Son of Sa'ad (Zaghlul)],[174] he was a close friend of the founder of the Wafd who referred to him as 'my adopted son'.[175] Completely uncorrupt and a brilliant orator,[176] he spoke perfect English but was 'implacably anti-British';[177] the Foreign Office deemed him a dangerous agitator and Allenby said he had a 'proclivity for throwing bombs'.[178] His religion was subject to frequent attack.

Associated with the Wafd from the beginning, and its 'master ideologist and rhetorician',[179] he was one of its representatives at talks with the British in 1921, 1929 and 1930. After Zaghlul's death, from 1927 to 1942 he was General Secretary and second-in-command of the Wafd under An Nahhas, whose old friend, right-hand man and intellectual superior he was.[180] He was Minister of Communications in 1928 and of Finance in 1929. Criticised by the Residency's 1930 Egypt Annual Report for spending far too much time 'making speeches from the top of the staircase to schoolboy delegations and other nobodies ... while callers on the serious affairs of State waited in an over-crowded ante-room',[181] in the 1931 economic crisis Sir Percy Loraine was relieved that this 'truly populist leader'[182] was not at his country's financial helm.[183] Minister of Finance in the 1936 government, 'an ex-idol of the students ... he was ... manhandled by a gang of Azharites and his car overturned ... in front of Abdin Palace'.[184] A strong supporter of An Nahhas during leadership challenges, he was Minister of Finance in the 1942 Wafd government.

'Ubayd severed his links with An Nahhas after the Lampson affair and registered strong disapproval of the favouritism the Prime Minister extended to his wife and her numerous relatives.[185] In February 1942, his anti-Wafd *Al Kitab al Aswad* [Black Book] exposed in detail the corruption of An Nahhas and the Wafd leadership.[186] Expulsion from the Chamber,[187] the administration (May 1942)[188] and the Party (July 1942) followed. In reaction, 'Ubayd founded Al Kutlah al Wafdiyyah al Mustaqillah in the same year but was expelled from Parliament in 1943.[189] A sequel to *Al Kitab al Aswad* came out in 1944 and 'Ubayd was arrested by An Nahhas on 19 May. He was rehabilitated by Ahmad Mahir in the same year and served as Minister of Finance from 1944 to 1945, as he did in An Nuqrashy's 1945 Cabinet. He was a member of the Preparatory Committee which formulated the final pact of the Arab League.[190]

Colonel Ahmad 'Uraby 'Al Misry' (1840–1911)

Of fairly humble rural origins,[191] 'Uraby was involved in the first nationalist party, Al Hizb al Watany, and took part in drafting its first manifesto. In a minor army revolt in mid-January 1881, he and two other officers presented a petition to Rifqy Paşa, the Minister of War, a Turk, in which they complained about his policy of favouring Turco-Circassians, and discriminating against native Egyptians, in matters of army pay and promotion.[192]

Demanding that he be replaced by an Egyptian and that 'a true Egyptian' should rule the country, 'Uraby was arrested.

He was retrieved by his regiment the following month, Rifqy was dismissed and the Turkish poet Mustafa Samy al Barudy became Minister of War and President of the Council[193] in a government headed by Sharif Pasha (1881–82). 'Uraby was appointed Deputy War Minister. After his action had secured improved conditions in the army and an important share for it in government decision-making,[194] in February 1882 'Uraby became Minister of War himself; the following month, 'long overdue promotions for … Egyptian officers were announced'. In the spring, a move by 'Uraby against about fifty officers plotting against the nationalist government failed when the Khedive (Tawfia) refused to sign a deportation order. This was 'his decisive confrontation with the Khedive, and ultimately with the British'. After a Franco-British ultimatum in May and the resignation of the Barudy ministry, 'Uraby took control of the government.[195] Instability – leading to rioting in Alexandria on 11 June which brought death and injury to several hundred people – led to British action on behalf of the Khedive. A naval bombardment by ships of Sir Beauchamp Seymour in Alexandria harbour on 11 July, the burning of the city and an occupation by British marines prepared the way for a British landing under Sir Garnet Wolseley in August and the extinguishing of 'Uraby's movement at Tall al Kabir and Isma'iliyyah. 'Uraby was arrested and tried for sedition and, despite Blunt's support,[196] exiled to Ceylon until 1901.

The 'Egypt for the Egyptians' movement of the 'unsophisticated though cunning' 'Uraby, 'a simple soldier with ambitions beyond his capabilities',[197] was disastrous for Egypt, but President 'Abd an Nasir looked back to him as his precursor in the Egyptian awakening.

Ahmad Ziwar Pasha (1864–1945)

A French-educated lawyer of Circassian origin and 'immense bulk',[198] Ziwar was Governor of Alexandria (1913), Minister in the Egyptian Embassy in Rome, Minister of Awqaf (1917), President of the Senate (1918–24), Minister of Education (1919) and Minister of Communications under Wahbah, Nasim (1920) and 'Adly (1921 until January 1924). As Prime Minister and Foreign Minister (1924–26) he was 'eclipsed as a leader within his own government' by Sidqy and fatally weakened by the resignation of 'Abd al 'Aziz Fahmy. He was Minister of the Interior from 1925 to 1926 and Chief of the Royal Cabinet from 1934 to 1935.[199]

In Lloyd's view, 'Ziwar Pasha possessed the happy exuberance of spirit which does not stop to count costs, and feels itself fully equal to difficulties not fully understood';[200] Nevile Henderson rated him 'certainly the most honest and loyal Egyptian I have met'.[201] Jesuit-educated, he was 'alleged to have died a Catholic. He had total moral courage, much humour, and was basically very lazy indeed.'[202]

Appendix 3
British personalities

Gertrude Bell (1868–1926)

Author of such famous books as *Persian Pictures*, *The Desert and the Sown* and *Amurath to Amurath*, she travelled widely in the Near East before the First World War – notably to Hayil in Najd, the seat of the Rashidy rivals of Ibn Sa'ud – and, shortly after it began, was recruited into the Arab Bureau, which she joined in Cairo. She was soon sent to Iraq, first to Basrah and finally to Baghdad, where she became Oriental Secretary to Sir Percy Cox in the British Legation. Incautious remarks during the Iraqi uprising in 1920 lost her the political influence which had enabled her to contribute much to the birth of the new state of Iraq. Emotionally, she never recovered from falling in love with 'Dick' Doughty-Wiley, a married man who was killed at Gallipoli with the Royal Welch Fusiliers, and she died of an overdose of medication. Vansittart said of her, 'There may have been more remarkable women, but I never met one.'[1]

Sir Austen Chamberlain (1863–1937)

Conservative and Unionist Chancellor of the Exchequer (1903–05 and 1919–21), he backed down so that Bonar Law could become leader of the Conservative Party in 1911. He resigned as Secretary of State for India (1915–17) after being censured by the Mesopotamia Commission. Minister without Portfolio in the War Cabinet (April 1918) and Lord Privy Seal and Leader of the Commons when Bonar Law fell ill (March 1921), he succeeded him as Leader of the Conservative Party (1921–22). He became Foreign Secretary (1924–29) – his negotiation of the Locarno Treaty (October 1925) gained him the Nobel Peace Prize – and First Lord of the Admiralty (1931). Unlike his stepbrother, Neville, he was quick to warn of the danger posed by Hitler. In his correspondence, he was in the habit of referring to Baldwin as 'his landlady, Mrs. Watson' or 'the sphinx'.[2]

Brigadier-General Sir Gilbert Falkingham Clayton (1875–1929)

With the Royal Artillery, Clayton fought the Nile campaign under Kitchener (1895–58). After joining the Egyptian Army in 1898, he mixed military and (increasingly) political appointments, as Inspector, Wau (1902–03), Deputy Assistant Adjutant-General, Cairo (1903–08), Private Secretary to Wingate in Khartum (1908–13), Sudan Agent and Egyptian Army Director of Intelligence, Cairo (1913), Colonel and British Army Director of Military Intelligence, Cairo (1914–16), Brigadier-General and Chief Political Officer, Hijaz Operations with the Egyptian Expeditionary Force invading Palestine (1916–17), Military Governor, Palestine (1917–19), Adviser, Egyptian Ministry of Interior (1 September 1919 to 1922), Chief Secretary and Acting High Commissioner, Palestine (1922–25), Special Envoy to Ibn Sa'ud (1925, 1927 and 1928) and responsible for the Bahrah and Haddah Agreements (1925) and the Treaty of Jeddah (1927) and Special Envoy to the Imam of the Yemen (1926). As High Commissioner and C-in-C, Baghdad (1929), he died in harness. He advocated the annexation of Egypt in 1917 and was in favour of it being granted its political freedom in 1921.[3]

Symes called him the 'wisest and kindest of colleagues',[4] Vansittart one of the 'experts who outclassed me . . . one of the many who never got their due',[5] one of the 'quiet capable unremembered men'.[6] He was much more than that and had an influence over the development of the post-Ottoman Middle East which has been sadly underrated and was cruelly abbreviated by his early death.

Evelyn Baring, first (1892) Earl of Cromer (1841–1917)

Baring was Private Secretary to his cousin Lord Northbrook, Viceroy of India, in 1872 (he was himself known as the 'Vice-Viceroy'),[7] British Commissioner on the Egyptian Caisse de la Dette Publique (1877) when it 'extended its control to the Khedive's personal finances and estates',[8] Controller-General of Egyptian Revenues (1879–80), Finance Member of the Council for India (1880–83), Civil Controller with the British army of occupation in Egypt (1883) and Agent and Consul-General in Cairo (1883–1907). Referred to as The Lord, '[e]ven Kitchener quailed as he approached his door'.[9] Ill-health prevented him from chairing the Mesopotamia Commission.

Boyle said of Cromer, 'He is a fine man; in all these years I have never heard him say a word, do an act, or . . . think a thought which was in the least degree small, personal, or unworthy of a great mind.'[10]

Sir Eldon Gorst (1861–1911)

Gorst succeeded Milner as Under-Secretary of the Egyptian Finance Department in 1892. He was promoted to be Financial Adviser

(1898–1904) on the sudden resignation of Edwin Palmer who, in his opinion, was of 'very inferior capacity' and liable to 'Dubious financial arrangements'.[11] He administered the Veiled Protectorate for Cromer. Foreign Office AUS in London from 1904–07, he was a lover of the 'drunken and promiscuous mother'[12] of Sykes, whose brother-in-law he became. He succeeded The Lord as Agent and Consul-General in Cairo (1907–10). Boyle thought that in that post, heralding the cancer which killed him, he 'seemed to have entirely lost ... the immense power to work which had formerly distinguished him'.[13] He 'revived, on an even more lavish scale, the viceregal style of entertaining of Cromer's earlier years'. Although, on the other hand, he 'drove his own motor-car bareheaded through the streets of Cairo and made use of his Arabic to talk to passers-by ... he lacked the stature and inner self-confidence to shrug off the charge that he was undignified'.[14]

Boyle, whose political role he brought to an end, rated him 'before all things, clever'[15] and told his mother that he was 'quick, knows his mind at once'.[16] Vansittart said that he had 'the most powerful brain that I have encountered in the public service or in politics' but that he was 'too clever by half' and held 'an infectiously low opinion of ordinary intelligence'.[17]

Sir Ronald William Graham (1870–1949)

Elder son of Sir Henry Graham and Edith Elizabeth, daughter of the future first Earl of Cranbrook, Graham's first Foreign Service post was Tehran (1897). In 1899 he transferred to St. Petersburg (Hardinge and Lindsay were there) and then to Cairo (1907) before being seconded as Adviser to the Egyptian Ministry of Interior (1910). He was appointed by Maxwell to act for him with the Egyptian administrative authorities, with the rank of chief staff officer, until the safety of the Canal was assured (1914). He was pro-Zionist from 1921 to 1933, he was Ambassador in Rome, enjoying – with his 'exceptional ability' – 'extremely cordial terms' with Austen Chamberlain.[18] He was a British Government director of the Suez Canal Company from 1939 to 1945.

Charles, Baron Hardinge of Penshurst (1858–1944)

Hardinge was with the Foreign Service in Istanbul (1881–84 and 1889–90), Tehran (First Secretary, 1896–98) and St. Petersburg (1898–1903), where he was a Counsellor promoted by Salisbury over 17 more senior aspirants to the post. He became AUS, then PUS, at the Foreign Office (1906–10), Viceroy of India (1910–16, made Baron) and PUS again (1916–19) under Curzon. He and Curzon detested each other on account of the partition of Bengal. They were 'connected by a broad old speaking-tube, and when George blew down Charlie blew up ... thunder was often in the air'.[19] The Mesopotamia Commission report of 1917 left him 'smarting from his tarnished reputation'.[20] An 'expert intriguer'[21] and anti-Crowe, he vainly tried to stop him succeding him as PUS. His last post was as Ambassador, Paris (1920–22).

Treated by Grey 'more as an equal than a subordinate',[22] his star waned when Balfour became Foreign Secretary. 'As [Robert] Cecil's influence increased, so Hardinge's declined, and relations between the two men deteriorated until they were barely on speaking terms.'[23] At the Paris Peace Conference, where Hardinge gave a 'lack-lustre performance' and was outshone by Crowe, Cecil complained about his incompetence.[24] Hardinge hated Lloyd George and had hinted – in connection with air raids – that the Prime Minister was a coward. Now, Lloyd George, who did not much like him, 'deliberately humiliated' him, replacing him as head of the British secretariat by Hankey.[25] Hardinge – 'exceedingly bitter',[26] and scornful of his political masters – had to leave Paris early to avoid a breakdown;[27] Vansittart said, 'Neglected Hardinge turned nasty in his ivory tower . . . and pouted.'[28]

Sir Nevile Meyrick Henderson (1882–1942)

Grafftey-Smith noted of Henderson that 'white heat was generated by any opposition, however courteously phrased. He had . . . a savagely violent temper . . . I was ordered out of the room at least once a week.'[29] After Cairo, Henderson moved on to be Minister in Paris and Belgrade and, in 1935, Ambassador to Argentina. In Jugoslavia, whence he unsuccessfully courted Curzon's elder daughter Irene,[30] Vansittart said that he 'made such a hit with the dictator by his skill in shooting that he was ultimately picked for Berlin. All know the consequences.'[31] Foreign Secretary Hoare recalled that Henderson was 'the man whom the Foreign Office had recommended to me in 1935 as the coming young diplomat in the Foreign Service . . ., very alert, sensitive and agreeable, . . . emotional and expansive'.[32] He became 'Britain's disastrous ambassador'[33] to Germany. (Selby was his counterpart in Vienna.) Henderson 'singularly failed' to understand the threat from Nazism and, 'so far from warning the Nazis, was constantly making excuses for them'.[34] Eden considered his appointment of Henderson 'an international misfortune'; the 'most fancied alternatives', he said, 'were Sir Miles Lampson and Sir Percy Loraine, and I deeply regret that I did not choose either of them'.[35] Henderson 'conceived of himself as endowed with a mission to come to terms with the Nazis, and there were few actions on their part, however monstrous, for which he was not prepared to find some measure of justification. When the Nazis were engineering the destruction of the Czechoslovak State his despatches revealed an almost malicious resentment that the Czechs should betray even the briefest hesitation in hastening the moment of their own enslavement.'[36] Hoare (now Viscount Templewood) said, 'As in the case of the Austrians, so in the case of the Czechs, he was undoubtedly convinced that, if international peace was to be maintained, their small countries must accept virtual absorption in the Reich.'[37] The despatches of the Consul-General in Munich, Donald St. Clair Gainer, 'provided the Foreign Office with priceless ammunition against the smooth assurances flowing from Nevile Henderson in his Berlin Embassy'.[38] Hoare believed that 'his sensitive nerves had been stretched almost to breaking point by Ribbentrop's provocations . . . He was obviously very intelligent. What he lacked was a very necessary measure of British phlegm.'[39]

Sir Ronald Charles Lindsay (1877–1945)

Fifth son of Lord Lindsay, later Earl of Crawford and Earl of Balcarres, he was with the Foreign Service in St Petersburg, Tehran, Washington and Paris (1899–1908) until seconded as Under-Secretary of the Egyptian Ministry of Finance (1913–19). Despite the prediction of Hardinge, an old friend, at the beginning of September 1917 that, on his Cairo resignation he would 'find that it will be very difficult to obtain employment on his return to this country, except in a comparatively subordinate position in this Office',[40] within two years he had become an AUS at the Foreign Office, in charge of the Near East (1921–22); there Kedourie deemed him 'utterly a defeatist in Egyptian affairs'.[41] Later, he was Ambassador to Turkey (1922, where his 'tact and ability' brought about Turkish acceptance of the loss of Mosul),[42] Germany (1926) and the USA (1930–39) and Foreign Office PUS (1928), succeeding Tyrrell. In this last post, his treatment of Lloyd was not unique: his words and tone in handling King Fu'ad during a visit to Britain in 1929 so infuriated that monarch that he curtailed his stay and returned home.[43]

In Tehran, when Cecil Spring Rice, his superior, married the daughter of Sir Frank Lascelles, Bell's step-uncle who was Ambassador in Berlin, he sent to the German press a photograph of Lindsay, who had a 'magnificent physique and distinguished bearing',[44] which was duly published.

Gen. Sir John Grenfell 'Conky' Maxwell (1859–1929)

Originally in the Royal Highlanders, which later became the Black Watch, he was at Tall al Kabir and in the Sudan campaigns of both 1884–89 and 1898. From 1885, he was ADC to the Sirdar, Sir Francis Grenfell. He was unofficial Governor of Nubia in 1897 and, after the overthrow of the Mahdist state at Karary, he commanded, and was Governor, at Omdurman. In February 1900 he was removed by Wingate and transferred to South Africa[45] to take part in the Boer War. From 1902 to 1904 and 1907 to 1908 he was chief staff officer to the Duke of Connaught, Acting C-in-C in Ireland, and from 1908 to November 1912 GOC of British troops in Egypt. After a short spell as Head of the British Military Mission at French HQ on the Western Front with the rank of

Lieut.-General, he replaced General Byng from September 1914 to 1916 as GOC of all troops in Egypt. After repelling the Sanusiyyah in January 1916, he became in addition commander in the Hijaz campaign. He was known for his 'patriarchal militarism' in Egypt[46] and 'respected and popular wherever he served', especially there. After leaving Cairo, he was appointed C-in-C in Ireland where, during the Sinn Fein rebellion, 'as far as anyone could claim success, he had succeeded'.[47] He was, however, dismissed by Asquith for ordering the Kilmainham executions after the Easter Rising. He became a General in 1919. On retirement, 'he was a disappointed man'. He had 'a vivid imagination' and 'combined great shrewdness and forcefulness of character with a phenomenal absent-mindedness in respect of his personal possessions'.[48]

Gen. Sir Archibald James Murray (1860–1945)

At Cheltenham like Maxwell, who was nine months older, he was commissioned into the Royal Inniskilling Fusiliers and served with distinction in the Boer War. He led the BEF to France at the start of the First World War; Haig thought him in awe of Sir John French, the C-in-C, who would in any case – although he had selected him – not listen to him. He collapsed on 26 August 1914, 'the critical day of Le Cateau', early in the retreat from Mons. Liddell Hart thought him a product of 'a system which brought officers to high position at an age when their energy was declining, and their susceptibility to the strain of war increasing'.[49]

He became CIGS with the rank of Lieutenant-General in January 1915. Although a 'Westerner', believing that Europe, not the East, was the place to conquer Germany, he was transferred to Egypt in January 1916 to be GOC of the troops there and commander in the Hijaz campaign. Himself 'respected but not liked',[50] he distrusted McMahon and Clayton, regarding the latter as the voice of Wingate. After driving the Ottomans out of Sinai in 1916 with his Egyptian Expeditionary Force, in March (the month in which Maude captured Baghdad) and April 1917 he failed (little supported by the War Office) to break throught them at the first battle of Gazah. At the second, which he fought against his own better judgement, his attempt on Gazah was successful but, 'owing to a misunderstanding on the part of a subordinate and absence of water for the horses, the troops were withdrawn'.[51] Lloyd George said of this, 'The attack of Dobell and Chetwode on Gaza had been the most perfect sample exhibited on either side in any theatre during this Great War of that combination of muddle-headedness, misunderstanding and sheer funk which converts an assured victory into a humiliating defeat. Gaza was "virtually captured" when the order came to withdraw ... The defences of Gaza when Chetwode attacked were merely skeleton entrenchments and its garrison was heavily outnumbered by our Army in men and artillery.'[52] At a Cabinet meeting, the Prime Minister accused

Murray of 'creeping where he ought to have rushed' and advocated his replacement by Birdwood or Bridges; Curzon defended him and Smuts declined to succeed him.[53]

Allenby, who replaced him on 29 June 1917, refused to move until he had received the two extra divisions his predecessor had in vain asked for. Murray, whose 'supersession was not justified' in the DNB view, left Egypt 'to the regret of no member of the force'[54] to be GOC Aldershot. He was promoted General in August 1919.

Sir Ronald Storrs (1881–1955)

He took a First in Oriental Studies at Cambridge (studying under the great Professor E. G. Browne, like Sykes) and joined the Egyptian Ministry of Finance in 1904. Under Gorst, he succeeded Boyle as Oriental Secretary in 1909 and retained the position under Kitchener and McMahon. He was very close to both Gorst and Kitchener,[55] and extremely popular in many Egyptian circles; as Kitchener's 'self-appointed' *objets d'art* acquisition agent, his 'very forceful endeavours' were 'embarrassing, and sometimes impoverishing'.[56] He was instrumental in making the running in the Husayn–McMahon correspondence initiated by Kitchener. Political Officer in May 1917 representing the Egyptian Expeditionary Force in Iraq, he set out in the June on a journey to see Ibn Sa'ud which ended in catastrophic failure. An anti-Zionist, he became Military, then Civil, Governor of Jerusalem and Judaea (January 1918–26), acting Chief Secretary in Palestine for the High Commissioner, Sir Herbert Samuel, and in Jerusalem repeatedly proposed to Irene Curzon until she was convinced that he was a 'bounder'.[57] He became Governor successively of Cyprus (1926–32) and – a completely inappropriate post – Northern Rhodesia (1932–34); in the burning of his residence in Nicosia, he claimed that sixty to eighty letters from T. E. Lawrence were lost.[58]

Vansittart, who was a colleague in Cairo, found him cosmopolitan, brilliant, 'a hearty companion, bursting with good-will to enter any prank whereby we sought to enliven a staid community, including a carefully rehearsed fight at an Agency garden party'.[59] He was 'No paragon, no puritan, he found little favour at headquarters, partly because he was an interloper, partly because he talked brilliantly on all arts and most people'; he had 'taste as unfailing as his pertinacity'.[60] Lawrence described him as 'the most brilliant Englishman [*sic*] in the Near East',[61] Bell called him 'a Father of Tongues'. He was a womaniser,[62] a 'sybarite'[63] and 'perhaps bisexual'.[64] Fuad Bey, Deputy Saudi Foreign Minister, considered him 'more oriental than the Orientals'.[65] His *Orientations* are the most accessible of memoirs.

Sir Mark Sykes (1879–1919)

Widely travelled in the Middle East in his youth and early manhood, he became Unionist MP for Central Hull in 1911. He worked for General Sir Charles Calwell, DG of Military Operations, in March 1915; in May 1916 he became Middle East Affairs' liaison officer for the Committee of Imperial Defence. Like Amery, he joined Hankey's War Cabinet Secretariat as a Political Secretary and, at the end of 1917, transferred to the Foreign Office as Acting Adviser on Arabian and Palestinian Affairs; he was distrusted by Hardinge and Graham but approved of by Cecil.

Norman Bentwich, the Attorney-General for Palestine, correctly called him an 'amateur and aristocrat', like Balfour.[66] He is known only for the extraordinary and disastrous Sykes–Picot Agreement (May–August 1916), into which he was considered to have been tricked by his French collaborator even though its provisions seemed to mirror his own keenness to bring back the map of the Crusades' period. He quickly turned against his own creation and died, discredited, at the Paris Peace Conference. He had had astonishing influence even though his views on the Middle East were a farrago of prejudice and whim. George Antonius, author of the influential *The Arab Awakening*, said: 'He knew a good deal about the Arabs at first hand, but his knowledge was as remarkable for its gaps as for its range, and his judgments alternated between perspicacity and incomprehension, as though his mental vision were patterned like a chess-board in which the white squares stood for insight and the black for the obscurities and the uncertainties of knowledge acquired in haste.'[67]

William George, Baron Tyrrell of Avon (1866–1947)

For many years Grey's private secretary, he had great influence over a Foreign Secretary who acknowledged 'the great value of Tyrrell's public service' and said that his 'power of understanding the point of view of foreigners has been of the greatest value in making the British position more intelligible and more acceptable to them'.[68] He had a 'dramatic downfall' in 1915[69] but became Foreign Office AUS in October 1918. At the Paris Peace Conference, Vansittart wrote, 'Crowe supplied the industry and Tyrrell the flair, which means that you guess what you ought to know.'[70] He succeeded Crowe as PUS in 1921; he had a 'well-recognised and efficient relationship' with Chamberlain and, at the Foreign Office, was the *alter ego* of Baldwin, 'his old friend'. Vansittart, his successor, 'though abler in many ways, was no substitute' for him.[71] He became Ambassador in Paris in 1928 and a Baron the following year.

Vansittart described him as 'little brown Willie Tyrrell, a puckish and mundane Catholic with no zest for ground-work but strong on the wings of flair and forecast'.[72] He had a 'clear schoolboy signature'[73] but his writing was illegible and his grammar imperfect; he was a careless proof-reader,[74] 'disliked writing' and 'shunned the drudgery of office drafts'.

Robert Gilbert, Baron Vansittart (1881–1957)

He had diplomatic postings to Tehran (1907) and Cairo (1909). He became Foreign Office Assistant Secretary, Private Secretary to Foreign Secretary Curzon (1920–24), Assistant Under-Secretary and PPS to Prime Ministers Baldwin and MacDonald (1928–29) and PUS of the Foreign Office (1930). He 'had long discerned the German menace'[75] but, 'although almost invariably right in his predictions, was given to violent over-statement which deprived his warnings of the greater part of their force'; he 'used an unfortunate style in his minutes to the Cabinet, violent, facetious, fizzing with bad epigrams, and they were read with growing boredom and indifference by Neville Chamberlain and Halifax, a tragic failure which could be blamed almost as much on Vansittart's own temperament and methods as on those who ignored his warnings'.[76] Chamberlain's 'persistent rejection of Vansittart's strongly anti-Nazi opinions' led Loraine's mother-in-law to comment, 'What is disquieting at home is the intrigue going on against Chamberlain in which Vansittart is a moving spirit.'[77] Because of his involvement in the Hoare–Laval Pact fiasco and his hostility to Germany, he was kicked upstairs to occupy the new post of Foreign Office Chief Diplomatic Adviser (1938–41). There he 'found himself trapped in a gilded cage, and ceased to exert any effective influence on foreign affairs'.[78] He wrote *The Mist Procession*, erudite posthumous memoirs.

Appendix 4
Egyptian political parties, in order of founding

Al Hizb al Watany (The National Party, 1879)

This was the first significant nationalist organisation, partly inspired and established by Al Afghany. Members were 'Uraby, some of his officers and Muslim, Christian and Jewish civilians. Al Barudy was the brains of the party, whose programme was drafted by Blunt and 'Abduh.[1] The party was refounded by Mustafa Kamil as Hizb al Watan.

Hizb al Ummah (Party of the Nation, September 1907)

Encouraged by Cromer, who referred to its members as the 'Girondists of Egypt',[2] 'Abduh inspired As Sayyid and others to found the party;[3] Zaghlul was a supporter, if not officially a member.[4] Hizb al Ummah reflected the rift between Kamil and 'Abbas Hilmy over the Khedive's role; *Al Garidah* was its mouthpiece. Moderate, secular and hostile to Pan-Islam, it stood for the attainment of independence through co-operation with Britain and British-introduced reforms and for parliamentary government. Many of its members, who tended to be from the middle class, joined the Wafd in 1918 or Hizb al Ahrar ad Dusturiyyin later.[5]

Hizb al Watan (The Party of the Homeland, 22 October 1907)

A Society for the Revival of the Nation, made up of a group of young lawyers and intellectuals,[6] was founded by 'Abbas Hilmy and a number of Europeans and nationalist Egyptians in 1895.[7] It was with the encouragement of the Khedive, who wanted a counterweight to Hizb al Ummah,[8] that Mustafa Kamil (and Muhammad Farid and Lutfy as Sayyid) amalgamated it and Al Hizb al Watany as Hizb al Watan. Standing for national renewal, the unity of the Nile Valley,[9] Pan-Islam and loyalty to the Ottoman Sultan, it was extremely nationalist and anti-British; it had its own paper, *Al Liwa'*.[10] Following Kamil's death, under Farid it had lost much of its influence by the end of the Gorst period and, with An Nahhas's defection to the Wafd, was not a major force after 1922.[11] It provided Hizb al Ummah with some of its leaders.

Hizb al Islah ad Dustury (The Party of Constitutional Reform, December 1907)

Shaykh 'Aly Yusuf founded the party – characterised by 'Pan-Islamic pro-Ottoman sentimentalism'[12] – to support the Palace in its opposition to Hizb al Watan and Hizb al Ummah. He died in 1913 and his *Al Mu'ayyad*, which first appeared in 1889, was eclipsed by *Al Liwa'*.[13] The party, also referred to as Hizb al Islah 'ala'l Mabadi' ad Dusturiyyah (The Party of Reform on the Basis of Constitutional Principles), advocated increased Egyptian involvement in government but had no popular policies or platform.[14]

Hizb al Wafd (The Delegation Party, 1918)

Farid's absence in exile and divisions within Hizb al Watan ushered the Wafd into existence. Not organised as a parliamentary party (as distinct from a delegation) until 26 April 1924,[15] it won every free Egyptian general election thereafter but never completed a term of government. In due course it renounced its secret wing, Al Gihaz as Sirry (The Secret Apparatus), of which Al Maglis al A'la li'l Ightiyalat (The High Council of Assassinations) – also known as Gam'iyyat al Intiqam (The Vengeance Society) – was part.[16]

Al Hizb al Mustaqill al Hurr (The Free Independent Party, 1919)

This grouping of prominent and wealthy people previously unconnected with politics (its President was 'Urfy Pasha) was bullied into leaving the campaign for Egypt's freedom and independence to the Wafd.[17]

Hizb al Ahrar ad Dusturiyyin (The Free Constitutionalists' Party, 29 October 1922)

Formally organised out of Gam'iyyat Misr al Mustaqillah (The Independent Egypt Society),[18] and drawing most of its membership from the Wafd and from surviving Legislative Assembly delegates,[19] its beginnings went back to the rift between 'Adly and Zaghlul over the leadership of the 1921–22 negotiations with Britain. At that time, 'Adly – with 'Afify,[20] Fahmy, Muhammad Husayn Haykal,[21] Mahmud, Makabaty, As Sayyid and Sidqy,[22] – founded it to underpin his delegation to London with 'a base for those moderate nationalists who opposed the Wafd'. The party's ideologue was As Sayyid and its weekly newspaper was '*As Siyasah al 'Usbu'iyyah* [The Political Weekly, 1922–51], which was subsidised by the Ar Raziq family and Mahmud.[23] Fahmy replaced 'Adly as leader in the autumn of 1925 and Mahmud headed its two governments in 1928 and 1937. The party aimed to secure independence via low-key negotiations with Britain. It stood for constitutional government and the strengthening of Egypt's national identity.[24] 'In many respects ... [it] strongly resembled the old

Umma party, also an extremely conservative and moderate nationalist grouping', hostile to Pan-Islam.[25]

Hizb al Ittihad (The Union Party)

Founded by King Fu'ad in December 1924, the organisation declined after 1936 and eventually merged with Hizb ash Sha'b in 1938. Taha Husayn, the leading writer and future Minister of Education, was appointed editor of its mouthpiece, *Al Ittihad*, in 1925.[26]

Hizb ash Sha'b (The People's Party, November 1930)[27]

Founded by Sidqy as a counterweight to Hizb al Ittihad, it was dominated by landowners and the urban middle class. Eighty-three of its deputies won elections in May/June 1931 but the party, although absorbing Hizb al Ittihad in 1938, declined after 1936 before finally expiring in 1942.

The Sa'adists (1932)

This was a short-lived Wafdist splinter group founded by Hamid al Basil which had 'no significant political impact'.[28]

The Sa'adist Party or Sa'ad Wafd (December 1937)

A grouping of dissident and anti-Nahhas Wafdists founded by An Nuqrashy and led by him and Ahmad Mahir, it stood for constitutionalism, democracy and civil liberties.[29] It claimed to embody Zaghlul's principles but soon took Faruq's side against the Wafd, leading anti-Wafd coalition governments in 1944 and 1949.[30] Its mouthpiece was *Al Asas*, The Foundation.

Young Egypt (Misr al Fatat) (late 1938)

A Fascist paramilitarist party founded by Ahmad Husayn, a lawyer, it sought for Egypt the leadership of Islam and an Egyptian–Sudanese empire. It changed its name, which was also that of its organ, to the Nationalist Islamic Party in March 1940, and to the Socialist Democratic party in October, 1949.[31]

Al Kutlah al Wafdiyyah al Mustaqillah (The Independent Wafdist League, 1942)

Founded by Makram 'Ubayd after he split from An Nahhas but ceased to exist after his rehabilitation two years later.

Egyptian Front Movement (1946)

A 'platform for political moderates', it was founded in 1946 by 'Aly Mahir.

Notes

Preface

1 Lloyd, Lord, *Egypt since Cromer* (London: Macmillan, Vol. II, 1934), pp. 308–9.

Introduction

1 Jarvis, Major C. S., *Desert and Delta* (London: John Murray, 1947), p. 14.
2 Mansfield, Peter, *The British in Egypt* (London: Weidenfeld and Nicolson, 1971), pp. 48–9.
3 Hardinge, Lord, *Old Diplomacy* (London: John Murray, 1947), p. 125.
4 Cromer, The Earl of, *Abbas II* (London: Macmillan, 1915), pp. xii and xiv.
5 Vansittart, Lord, *The Mist Procession* (London: Hutchinson, 1958), pp. 95 and 373.
6 In 1892, Kitchener of Khartum (1856–1916) succeeded Sir Francis Grenfell as Sirdar of the Egyptian Army and General Gordon as Governor-General of the Sudan. He avenged the death of Gordon at Omdurman in 1898 and then became successively Commander-in-Chief in South Africa (1900) and India (1902–11), in the latter post engineering the resignation of Curzon as Viceroy.
7 Cromer, *Abbas II*, p. xv,
8 Beaman, A. A. H., *The Dethronement of the Khedive* (London: George Allen & Unwin, 1929), p. 115.

1 Let everything slide

1 Mansfield, Peter, *The British in Egypt* (London: Weidenfeld and Nicolson, 1971), p. 180.
2 Cromer, The Earl of, *Abbas II* (London: Macmillan, 1915), p. xviii.
3 Ibid., p. xvii.
4 King, Joan Wucher, *Historical Dictionary of Egypt* (Metuchen, NJ: Scarecrow Press, 1984), p. 17.
5 Milne Cheetham (1869–1938) was First Secretary then Counsellor in Cairo (1911–19). He became Counsellor in Paris (1920) to a reluctant Hardinge, who had personally requested Ronald Lindsay for the post. 'The selection proved a failure. Lady Cheetham was very different, very pretty and very capable. As Curzon surmised when Cheetham was appointed, she "would adorn and enliven our circle". She did so.' [Hardinge, Lord, *Old Diplomacy* (London: John Murray, 1947), p. 252] Frank Balfour called her 'the miscreant' (SAD 173/7/5–6: 3 June 1919, to Capt. Ulrich Alexander, Wingate's aide-de-camp), and Grafftey-Smith (*Bright Levant*, London: John Murray, 1970, p. 20) gives a graphic account of her Slav character and paper handling methods.

6   Lloyd, Lord, *Egypt since Cromer* (London: Macmillan, Vol. I 1933), p. 181.
7   Symes, Sir Stewart, *Tour of Duty* (London: Collins, 1946), p. 23.
8   Ibid., p. 25.
9   Cromer, *Abbas II*, p. xvii.
10 Sir Ignatius Valentine Chirol (1852–1929) was deputy head, then head, of the foreign department of *The Times* from 1896. Author of *The Middle Eastern Question* (1903) and *The Egyptian Problem* (1920), he was a close friend of Bell, a 'great authority' [Petrie, Sir Charles, *The Life and Letters of The Right Hon. Sir Austen Chamberlain* (London: Cassell, Vol. 2 1940), p. 333] and a 'really outstanding journalist' (Vansittart, Lord, *The Mist Procession* (London: Hutchinson, 1958), p. 114).
11 Chirol, Sir Valentine, *The Egyptian Problem* (London: Macmillan, 1920), p. 252.
12 Daly, M. W. (ed.), *The Cambridge History of Egypt*, Vol. II (Cambridge University Press, 1998), p. 247.
13 Cromer, *Abbas II*, p. xvi.
14 Muhammad Mazlum Pasha was Minister of Finance in 1921. Described by Harry Boyle as the second most able nationalist politician but 'a less than half-hearted ally of Zaghloul' [Boyle, Clara, *Boyle of Cairo* (Kendal: Titus Wilson, 1965), p. 230], he held the Presidency of the Chamber in Zaghlul's government.
15 ZW. Badrawi, Malak, *Isma'il Sidqi (1875–1950): Pragmatism and Vision in Twentieth Century Egypt* (London: Curzon, 1996), p. 6, says that he was Speaker.
16 Mansfield, *British*, p. 257.
17 Kedourie, Elie, 'Sa'ad Zaghlul and the British' (*Middle Eastern Affairs*, number 2. (St Antony's papers number 11), Chatto and Windus, 1961, p. 142.
18 King, *Historical Dictionary*, pp. 400–1 and 494–5.
19 FO 371/2352/157478: 25 October 1915 minute for Parliamentary Question, in Vatikiotis, P. J., *The History of Egypt* (London: Weidenfeld and Nicolson, 1985), p. 250.
20 Symes, *Tour*, p. 26.
21 Cromer, *Abbas II*, p. xiii.
22 Bowman, Humphrey E., *Middle Eastern Window* (London: Longmans, 1942), p. 151.
23 Kedourie, Elie, *The Chatham House Version and other Middle-Eastern Studies* (London: Weidenfeld and Nicolson, 1970), p. 101.
24 Terry, Janice J., *The Wafd, 1919–1952* (London: Third World Centre, 1982), p. 12.
25 Wingate, Bt., Sir Ronald, *Wingate of the Sudan* (London: John Murray, 1955), p. 201.
26 Badrawi, Malak, *Political Violence in Egypt, 1910–1924* (Richmond: Curzon, 2000), p. 118.
27 Husayn, Sharif of Mecca, was detained in Istanbul by the Ottoman authorities until appointed Amir (later King) of the Hijaz in 1908. He made a vain attempt to become Caliph of Islam after Atatürk's abolition of the Istanbul-based Caliphate in 1924 and was driven out of Mecca by Ibn Sa'ud in the same year.
28 Named for Sir Mortimer Durand (1850–1924), Foreign Secretary to the Government of India (1885–94) and Ambassador to Persia, Spain and the USA.
29 *DNB*.
30 Keown-Boyd, Henry, *The Lion and the Sphinx. The Rise and Fall of the British in Egypt, 1882–1956* (Spennymoor, Co. Durham: The Memoir Club, 2002), p. 75.
31 *DNB*.
32 Mejcher, Helmut, *Imperial Quest for Oil: Iraq 1910–1928* (London: Ithaca Press, 1976), p. 56.
33 Terry, *Wafd*, p. 9; Wingate, *Wingate*, pp. 204–9.

34 SAD 201/4/5: Wingate to Sir W. Robertson, 3 August 1916.

35 FO 371/2352/181179.

36 4 March 1919, by Major Earl Winterton.

37 See Cooper, Duff, *Old Men Forget* (London: Rupert Hart-Davis, 1953), p. 111.

38 Vansittart, *Mist*, pp. 84–5.

39 James Haines (1868–1932) worked in Cairo in the Ministry of Education (1897) before becoming successively Inspector of Finance (1900), Controller of Direct Taxes (1907) and Under-Secretary of State, Ministry of Agriculture (1913).

40 Sir Lee Oliver Fitzmaurice Stack (1865–1924) joined the Egyptian Army from the Border Regiment (1899) and became Private Secretary to Wingate (1904), Sudan Agent and DMI, Cairo (1908), and Civil Secretary, Sudan Government (1914).

41 The duties of the Sudan Agent were to keep the Residency and the Egyptian Government informed about the Sudan and the Governor-General of the Sudan about Egypt, to promote the Sudan in Egypt and to be the Sudan Consul in Cairo (Keown-Boyd, *Lion*, p. 45).

42 SAD 159/3/54: Wingate to Clayton, 23 March 1916.

43 HP 25, 1916, Vol. IV, p. H 7.

44 Private, 28 April 1915, in Warburg, Gabriel, 'The governor-general of the Sudan and his relations with the British consuls-general in Egypt, 1899–1916', *Asian and African Studies* V (1969), p. 128.

45 Lawrence, T. E., *Seven Pillars of Wisdom* (London: Cape, 1935), p. 61.

46 David George Hogarth (1862–1927), Director of the Ashmolean Museum, Oxford (1908–27), planned the Arab Bureau with Capt. W Reginald ('Blinker') Hall, Director of Naval Security, and himself directed it under Clayton's supervision. A delegate to Versailles, he was chosen as a British representative (with McMahon) on the King–Crane Commission and became President of the Royal Geographical Society in 1925.

47 SAD 137/6/85: 29 June 1916.

48 SAD 470/6/3: Cyril Wilson to Clayton, 5 January 1917.

49 Its foundation proposed by Sir Mark Sykes to the Cabinet on 23 December 1915 as an Islamic Bureau, the Arab Bureau was finally set up on the initiative of the Secretary of State for India as a branch of the Department of Military Intelligence. Based in Cairo, it came under the Foreign Office and was funded by the War Office. Mainly because of the opposition of the India Office, which like the Viceroy would not co-operate with it, it was given no policy role. Its aims were to co-ordinate the Near East policies of the Foreign Office, the India Office, the Admiralty, the War Office and the Government of India and to keep them informed of 'the general tendencies of German and Turkish policy'. A large number of people of different walks of life staffed it from time to time, most notably Lawrence, Bell and Leonard Woolley, the archaeologist. Arnold Wilson said of it, 'The Arab Bureau died unregretted . . . having helped to induce HMG to adopt a policy which brought disaster to the people of Syria, disillusion to the Arabs of Palestine, and ruin to the Hijaz' (February 1920. Review of Lawrence, T. E., *Revolt in the Desert*, London: The Folio Society, 1986, in *Central Asian Journal* 1927, Vol. XIV, Part III, p. 232). A modern authority comments, '[J]unior officers in the Bureau's service were able to wander freely around the Middle East with inexhaustible supplies of money, in defiance of generals and in open contempt of official policies and campaign strategies.' It 'could not have survived without the most powerful of patrons' (Winstone, H. V. F., *Gertrude Bell*, London: Constable, 1993, p. 187).

50 October 1916. Lawrence, *Seven Pillars*, p. 109.

51 Symes, *Tour*, p. 26.

52 Col. C. E. Wilson (1873–1938) was Governor successively of the Sennar, Khartum and Red Sea provinces of the Sudan (?–1916). On his secondment from Suwakin to Jiddah he both represented Wingate and liaised with Sharif Husayn (July 1916 to December 1919). '[O]ne of the most underrated figures of the Arab uprising ... he was an admirable spokesman for British policy in the endless, and often futile, arguments raised by King Hussein. He was a courtierly, politically-minded soldier, and in him and his like the Sudan Government in its early days had recruited the salt of the earth' (Grafftey-Smith, *Bright Levant*, p. 145). His presumably pro-Sharif Husayn views were criticised by Sir Percy Cox as 'extremist'. [Graves, Philip, *The Life of Sir Percy Cox*. (London: Hutchinson & Co., 1941), p. 245].

53 Boyle, *Boyle*, p. 157.

54 Brunyate (1867–1943) joined the Egyptian service (1898), became counsellor to the Khedive/Sultan (1903–16), Legal Adviser to the Residency (1915–16) and Judicial Adviser (1916–19). He was Vice-Chancellor, University of Hong Kong from 1921 to 1924.

55 Grafftey-Smith, *Bright Levant*, p. 29.

56 Symes, *Tour*, p. 26.

57 Lloyd, *Egypt* (1933), p. 277

58 Repington, Lt.-Col. C. à Court, *The First World War, 1914–1918: Personal Experiences Of* (Aldershot: Grey Revivals, 1991), p. 101.

59 Col. E. S. Herbert was Wingate's unofficial military representative in the Egyptian War Ministry. Wingate described him as a 'capable officer, who understood things Egyptian and knew the ex-Khedive [Husayn Kamil] and his Ministers well'; he 'acquired the confidence of both the ex-Khedive, the present Sultan and the British and Native administrations'.

60 SAD 136/1/68: 10 January 1916.

61 SAD 136/1/101: 17 January 1916.

62 SAD 136/1/92: Clayton to Wingate, 14 January 1916.

63 King, *Historical Dictionary*, p. 427

64 The Sanusiyyah was a Sufy order, founded in the mid-nineteenth century, which gave Libya the monarchy overthrown by Col. Qadhdhafy. Headed by Sayyid Ahmad as Sanusy (?–1933), it was in conflict with France (in Chad) from 1901. It allied with the Central Powers at the beginning of the First World War and, aided by German submarines and strengthened by Turkish officers, occupied Egypt's Sallum Oasis from November 1915 to March 1916, before joining the Allies and enabling the British to capture Ja'far al Askary, the future Prime Minister of Iraq. Atatürk toyed with the idea of offering Sayyid Ahmad the Caliphate (Kedourie, *Chatham House*, pp. 189–90).

65 SAD 159/3/46–7: 20 March 1916.

66 Bowman, *Window*, pp. 156–7.

67 SAD 236/5/28: 13 September 1916.

68 SAD 136/1/87–9: 13 January 1916.

69 Harry Boyle in 1936, in Boyle, *Boyle*, p. 155.

70 Rose, Kenneth, *The Later Cecils* (London: Weidenfeld and Nicolson, 1975), pp. 207–8.

71 Grafftey-Smith, *Bright Levant*, p. 29.

72 Sir Paul Harvey (1869–1948) was (Assistant) Private Secretary to the Marquess of Lansdowne, War Secretary (1895–1900), and Egyptian Financial Adviser (1907–12 and 1919–20). Later, he edited the *Oxford Companions to English Literature* (1932) and *Classical Literature* (1937).

73 Keown-Boyd, *Lion*, p. 76.

74 SAD 160/3/80: Col. Herbert to Wingate, 14 September 1916.

75 Morris, James, *Pax Britannica* (London: The Folio Society, 1992), Vol. 2, p. 146.

76 Morris, *Pax*, Vol. 3, p. 15.
77 Cecil describes a meeting of the Council of Ministers in a chapter of his amusing *The Leisure of an Egyptian Official*, the one Empire classic (Morris, *Pax*, Vol. 3, p. 304) and better written than his minutes.
78 Rose, *Later Cecils*, p. 222.
79 Wingate, *Wingate*, p. 207.
80 SAD 135/4/13: October 1915.
81 The Turf Club in Cairo enrolled British members only. It occupied the original Agency building and was burned down on Black Saturday 1952. It still flourishes on a different site and is still not open to Egyptians. [Saad ad Din, Mursi, and Cromer, John, *Under Egypt's Spell* (London: Bellew, 1991), p. 167; Sattin, Anthony, *Lifting the Veil: British Society in Egypt, 1768–1956* (London: Dent, 1988), p. 189].
82 SAD 160/3/79–80: 14 September 1916.
83 HP 25, 1916, Vol. IV, p. H 65: Graham to Hardinge, 9 September 1916.
84 Terry, *Wafd*, p. 54.
85 Daly, M. W., *The Sirdar: Sir Reginald Wingate and the British Empire in the Middle East* (Philadelphia: American Philosophical Society, 1997), p. 259; Terry, *Wafd*, p. 14.
86 SAD 469/10/66: 9 September 1915.
87 NOPCE, in Kedourie, 'Sa'ad Zaghlul', p. 145.
88 SAD 135/4/13: to Wingate, 9 October 1915.
89 Mansfield, *British*, p. 221.
90 *DNB*.
91 SAD 163/2/36–7: Private letter, 14 February 1917.
92 HP 25, 1916, Vol. IV, p. H 46: 9 September 1916.
93 SAD 201/7/123: 14 September 1916.
94 Rose, *Later Cecils*, p. 224.
95 SAD 236/5/40–1.
96 Sir Vincent Corbett followed Gorst as Financial Adviser (1904–07) and was succeeded by Harvey. On his resignation, Boyle, spelling him with only one concluding 't', said that he was 'a great loss' (Boyle, *Boyle*, p. 162).
97 Storrs, Ronald, *Orientations* (London: Nicholson & Watson, 1943), pp. 45 and 66.
98 SAD 163/1/102: Private and Personal letter, 31 January 1917.

2 Treated in a disgusting way

1 SAD 194/1/52: Wingate to Col. Herbert, 7 January 1915.
2 SAD 194/1/72 and 469/8/12: 9 January 1915.
3 SAD 469/8/11.
4 SAD 191/1/31 and 469/8/9: 6 January 1915.
5 SAD 469/8/59: to Clayton, 20 March 1915.
6 Terry, Janice J., *The Wafd, 1919–1952* (London: Third World Centre, 1982), p. 14.
7 Daly, M. W., *The Sirdar: Sir Reginald Wingate and the British Empire in the Middle East* (Philadelphia: American Philosophical Society, 1997), p. 206.
8 SAD 469/10/2: 21 August 1915.
9 SAD 469/10/48: 3 September 1915.
10 Lawrence, T. E., *Seven Pillars of Wisdom* (London: Cape, 1935), p. 62.
11 The Sirdar was responsible to the Egyptian Minister of War and the Khedive and communicated direct with the War Office in London.
12 Toynbee, A. J., *Survey of International Affairs, 1925*, Vol. I, Part III (Oxford University Press, 1927), p. 239.

13 Warburg, Gabriel, 'The governor-general of the Sudan and his relations with the British consuls-general in Egypt, 1899–1916', *Asian and African Studies* V (1969), p. 100. See SAD 108/16 (Wingate to Stack, 6 May 1913) and SAD 470/3/64–5 (Wingate to Clayton, 13 September 1916) on Cromer *vis-à-vis* Kitchener).

14 SAD 276/4/93–4: 27 April 1906. See also Symes, Sir Stewart, *Tour of Duty* (London: Collins, 1946), pp. 12–13.

15 Wingate, Sir Ronald, Bt., *Wingate of the Sudan* (London: John Murray, 1955), p. 263.

16 M. W. Daly, Historical introduction to the Wingate Papers, pp. i and iv.

17 Grafftey-Smith, Laurence, *Bright Levant* (London: John Murray, 1970), p. 19.

18 Warburg, 'Governor-general', p. 103.

19 SAD 134/3/1–6: Very Private, 3 March 1915.

20 Lieshout, R. H. 'Keeping Better Educated Moslems Busy'. Sir Reginald Wingate and the origins of the Husayn–McMahon Correspondence', *Historical Journal*, 27, 2 (1984), p. 456n.

21 SAD 134/3/1–6: Very Private, 3 March 1915.

22 SAD 469/10/20–1: 21 August 1915.

23 SAD 135/3/38: 18 September 1915.

24 SAD 135/4/37: PRIVATE, probably October 1915.

25 Jarvis, Major C. S., *Desert and Delta* (London: John Murray, 1947), pp. 187–9.

26 SAD 201/1/85: VERY PRIVATE, 8 July 1916, from Erkowit.

27 SAD 201/1/65: Very PRIVATE, 5 July 1916, from Erkowit.

28 SAD 201/1/49–50: 5 July 1916.

29 SAD 201/1/85: to Parker, 8 July 1916.

30 Warburg, 'Governor-general', pp. 128 and 131.

31 SAD 138/5/23–4 and 201/1/123: 9 July 1916.

32 SAD 138/5/24.

33 SAD 201/2/11: 11 July 1916 from Alexandria.

34 SAD 201/4/4: 3 August 1916.

35 SAD 201/7/123: 14 September 1916.

36 SAD 160/3/106: 17 September 1916.

37 Westrate, Bruce, *The Arab Bureau: British Policy in the Middle East, 1916–20* (Philadelphia: Penn State University Press, University Park, Pennsylvania 1992), p. 33.

38 SAD 139/6/23.

39 SAD 469/10/26: to Clayton, 21 August 1915.

40 SAD 143/5/1: 1 November 1916, from Cairo.

41 SAD 160/5/24: 6 November 1916.

42 SAD 143/5/12: 10 November 1916.

43 Details in Wingate, *Wingate*, p. 172.

44 Jarvis, *Desert*, p. 93.

45 HP 25, 1916, Vol. IV, p. H 47: 9 September 1916.

46 Wingate, *Wingate*, p. 204.

47 Terry, *Wafd*, p. 15.

48 SAD 160/3/135: McMahon to Cecil, 19 September 1916.

49 Letter to Robert Cecil, 15 February 1915, in Rose, Kenneth, *The Later Cecils* (London: Weidenfeld and Nicolson, 1975), p. 221.

50 Storrs, Ronald, *Orientations* (London: Nicholson & Watson, 1943), p. 192.

51 Lawrence, T. E., *Revolt in the Desert* (London: The Folio Society, 1986), p. 2, Collins, Robert O. (ed.), *An Arabian Diary, Sir Gilbert Falkingham Clayton* (Berkeley and Los Angeles: University of California Press, 1969), p. 62.

52 Lawrence, *Seven Pillars*, p. 59.

53 Ibid., p. 62.

54 From Cairo to her mother, 6 December 1915.

55 To her mother, 25 December 1915.

56 *DNB.*

57 FO 371/2352/181179: Telegram 258, 23 December 1915.

58 Ibid., 30 November 1915.

59 Francois-Marie-Denis Georges-Picot (1871–?) had been French Consul-General in Beirut (January 1914) and Cairo (November 1914) and a First Secretary in London (August 1915). 'Tall and pompous, conservative and devout', concerned 'equally for his own dignity and that of France' [Macmillan, Margaret, *Peacemakers. The Paris Conference of 1919 and Its Attempt to end War* (London: John Murray, 2001), p. 394]. McMahon called him 'a notorious fanatic on the Syria question' [Jeremy Wilson, *Lawrence of Arabia, the Authorised Biography of T. E. Lawrence* (London: Heinemann, 1989), p. 233]. Jack Murray maintained that in his Agreement with Sykes he 'did no more than make a very good bargain for his country' (GLLD 13/7: letter to Lloyd, 1 November 1926).

60 Westrate, *Arab Bureau*, p. 34.

61 Terry, *Wafd*, p. 13.

62 Westrate, *Arab Bureau*, p. 33.

63 P. 43.

64 Birkenhead, Lord, *Rudyard Kipling* (London: Weidenfeld & Nicolson, 1978), p. 62.

65 Daly, *Sirdar*, p. 242.

66 P. 121.

67 Winstone, H. V. F., *Gertrude Bell* (London: Constable, 1993), p. 188: 6 July 1916.

68 Winstone, H. V. F., *The Illicit Adventure* (London: Jonathan Cape, 1982), pp. 251–2.

69 Adelson, Roger, *Mark Sykes, Portrait of an Amateur* (London: Cape, 1975), p. 210.

70 Westrate, *Arab Bureau*, p. 58.

71 HP 25, 1916, Vol. IV, pp. H 46–7: 9 September 1916.

72 Daly, *Sirdar*, p. 246.

73 SAD 143/5/50: Admiral Wemyss MS letter to Wingate, 19 November 1916. Grafftey-Smith, *Bright Levant*, p. 22, says that the dismissal came via a Reuter telegram.

74 SAD 237/3/6: Note, 4 November 1919.

75 SAD 160/5/19: 6 November 1916.

76 10 November 1916, in Terry, *Wafd*, p. 18.

77 SAD 160/5/31: telegram, 8 November 1916.

78 Storrs, *Orientations*, p. 181, f. n.

79 Ibid., p. 203.

80 SAD 160/5/20: 6 November 1916.

81 Winstone, *Illicit Adventure*, p. 263.

82 15 December 1916, from Basrah.

83 19 January 1917, to her mother.

84 'Boyle of Cairo' (1863–1937) had arrived there in July 1885. Cromer's Oriental Secretary for 23 years, known as Enoch because he 'walked with the Lord' (Mansfield, *British*, p. 238) was a fine linguist endowed with a prodigious memory. Mansfield maintains that 'His brilliant gifts as a linguist were not supported by political judgement', (ibid., p. 64) but Vansittart (*Mist*, p. 85) said, 'I had never seen anything like him ... the outstanding figure of these parts.' In 1909 he left Egypt, to great local sorrow (Boyle, *Boyle*, pp. 176–80) following Gorst's abandonment of Cromerite policies (ibid., p. 164) and went on from Cairo to be, incongruously, Consul-General in Berlin.

85 Boyle, *Boyle*, p. 238.

86 Grafftey-Smith, *Bright Levant*, p. 23.
87 Corp, Edward T, 'The Problem of Promotion in the Career of Sir Eyre Crowe, 1905–20', *Australian Journal of Politics and History*, 28, 2 (1982), p. 243.
88 SAD 164/6/44: 17 May 1917, Private and Confidential.
89 SAD 160/5/26: 6 November 1916.
90 Daly, *Sirdar*, p. 246; Terry, *Wafd*, p. 18.
91 SAD 160/6/59: 8 December 1916.
92 Edward, 6th Earl Winterton (1883–1962), was briefly attached to the Arab Bureau and spent five weeks in August and September 1918 on Hijaz Railway demolition operations with Lawrence. He became Under-Secretary of State for India (1922–29), Air Minister (1938–39) and Father of the House, where he sat for 47 continuous years. Like his friend Amery, he was a non-appeaser [Birkenhead, Lord, *Halifax, the Life of Lord Halifax* (London: Hamish Hamilton, 1965), p. 400]. He was successfully deputed to use a visit to Shillinglee, his home, by Faysal to persuade the ex-King of Syria (1918–20), dethroned by the French, to accept that of Iraq (1921–33) [Brodrick, Alan Houghton, *Near to Greatness, a Life of Earl Winterton* (London: Hutchinson, 1965), pp. 19, 185].
93 Sir Henry Craik, Bt. (1846–1927) visited Egypt and Syria in 1907. He was Principal of Queen's College, Harley Street (where Bell had crammed for Oxford) from 1911 to 1914 and became the oldest member of the House of Commons. He was an author, e.g. on Swift.

3 All this rush of war work (Wingate of the Sudan)

1 SAD 470/7/1: to Clayton, 15 July 1917.
2 Field Marshal Baron Grenfell of Kilvey (1841–1925) was Sirdar from 1886 to 1892, Commandant of the British garrison in Egypt (1897–98) and Governor of Malta (1899–1903).
3 SAD 160/5/52: Wingate to Cromer, 12 November 1916.
4 Khalid b. al Walid was the flawed 'Sword of Islam', to whose credit stand the religion's first international conquests in the seventh century AD and an historic march from Iraq to Syria.
5 The Mahdiyyah was the revolt by the Mahdy, Muhammad Ahmad (1840–85), against Egyptian rule in the Sudan which culminated in the death of Gordon in 1885 and Kitchener's 1898 reconquest.
6 Gen. (Hon.) Baron Rudolf Karl Slatin (1857–1932), an Austrian, was Gordon's General Governor of Darfur (1878), a prisoner of the Mahdy (1884), a slave of the Khalifah (released 1890), Assistant to Wingate and Egyptian Army Assistant DMI (1895) and Inspector-General of the Sudan, 1900–14.
7 Sir James Rennell Rodd (1858–1941), Chief Secretary to the Cairo Residency and Cromer's deputy from 1894 to 1902, served later in Zanzibar and became Ambassador to Italy in 1908. 'Dapper, and immaculately dressed' [Boyle, Clara, *Boyle of Cairo* (Kendal: Titus Wilson, 1965), p. 86], he was 'a wonderful host and raconteur' and had been a Newdigate Poetry Prizewinner at Oxford. (A sample of his verse is in Ibid., p. 29.) Loraine, who served under him, reckoned him a 'daring and gifted personality' [Daly, M. W., *The Sirdar: Sir Reginald Wingate and the British Empire in the Middle East* (Philadelphia: American Philosophical Society, 1997), p. 219].
8 Details in Wingate, Bt., Sir Ronald, *Wingate of the Sudan* (London: John Murray, 1955), pp. 108–12 and Beachey, Ray, *The Warrior Mullah* (London: Bellew, 1991), pp. 22–9.
9 Daly, *Sirdar*, pp. 109 and 116; Wingate, *Wingate*, p. 141.
10 Boyle, *Boyle*, p. 105, where there are further details. See Symes, Sir Stewart,

Tour of Duty (London: Collins, 1946), p. 12, for the tasks faced by Wingate in the Sudan.

11 C. A. Armbruster, the Arabic and Amharic specialist, was a member of the Sudan Political Service from 1900 to 1926 and Consul in NW Ethiopia from 1912 to 1919.

12 Full details are in Beachey, *Warrior*, pp. 79–84.

13 Wingate, *Wingate*, p. 161.

14 Bowman, Humphrey E., *Middle Eastern Window* (London: Longmans, 1942), p. 126.

15 Lloyd, Lord, *Egypt since Cromer* (London: Macmillan, Vol. I 1933), p. 328.

16 Symes, *Tour*, p. 14.

17 Warburg, Gabriel, 'The governor-general of the Sudan and his relations with the British consuls-general in Egypt, 1899–1916', *Asian and African Studies* V (1969), p. 110: Cromer to Wingate, 2 July 1905.

18 SAD 177/2/41–2: paraphrase of telegram of 11 October 1916.

19 SAD 177/2/28: 3 June 1919.

20 Wingate, *Wingate*, p. 156.

21 Keown-Boyd, Henry, *The Lion and the Sphinx. The Rise and Fall of the British in Egypt, 1882–1956* (Spennymoor, Co. Durham: The Memoir Club, 2002), p. 79.

22 SAD 469/10/19: Wingate to Sir Ian Hamilton, 11 August 1915 [Grafftey-Smith, Laurence, *Bright Levant* (London: John Murray, 1970), p. 24, confirms].

23 Chirol, Sir Valentine, *The Egyptian Problem* (London: Macmillan, 1920), p. 277.

24 Grafftey-Smith, *Bright Levant*, p. 24.

25 Terry, Janice J., *The Wafd, 1919–1952* (London: Third World Centre, 1982), p. 19: W. D. Kenny, the Sultan's British aide-de-camp, to Wingate, 4 December 1916.

26 Terry, *Wafd*, p. 21: to Nina Cust, 18 January 1917.

27 SAD 160/5/20–22: Clayton to Wingate, 6 November 1916.

28 SAD 160/5/23: to Wingate, 6 November 1916.

29 Letter of 15 December from Basrah.

30 SAD 163/1/14–15: 3 January 1917.

31 SAD 163/1/79: Wingate to Lady Cromer, 30 January 1917, on Cromer's death.

32 SAD 164/2/76: 'Observation on Future British Policy with regard to Egypt', 2 March 1917.

33 SAD 160/5/17: 6 November 1916.

34 SAD 163/2/7: Grenfell to Wingate, 7 February 1917.

35 SAD 143/5/25: 14 November 1916.

36 SAD 470/5/6: 22 November 1916.

37 SAD 160/5/33: to Wingate, 9 November 1916.

38 Chirol, *Egyptian Problem*, p. 121.

39 SAD 166/2/14: Private, 3 November 1917.

40 SAD 470/5/8: 18 December 1916.

41 Grafftey-Smith, *Bright Levant*, p. 25.

42 SAD 470/6/25: to Clayton, 22 March 1917.

43 Lt.-Col. Sir George Stewart Symes (1882–1962) was ADC and, later, Private Secretary, to Wingate in Khartum (1915). He became GSO attached to Wingate's staff in Egypt and, after Wingate's fall, Governor of the Palestine North District (1920–25). He succeeded Clayton as Chief Secretary to the Government of Palestine (1925–28) and was Resident, Aden (1928–33), and Governor-General of the Sudan (1934–40).

44 Sir Alexander William Keown-Boyd (1884–1954), a member of the Sudan Political Service from 1907, was Private Secretary to Wingate (1917–19) and Oriental Secretary, Cairo (1919–22). According to Frank Balfour, 'the worst correspondent in the universe' (SAD 173/7/5–6: 3 June 1919 to Capt.

Alexander), Grafftey-Smith (*Bright Levant*, p. 50) rated him 'a first-class Oriental Secretary ... indefatigable, imperturbable, affable and commonsensical,
winning the respect of all Egyptians and the affection of most'; Boyle thought
him 'most admirable and able';. (Boyle, *Boyle*, p. 213: May 1921).

45 SAD 160/5/43.
46 SAD 143/5/45: to Col. Jackson, 9 November 1916.
47 Westrate, Bruce, *The Arab Bureau: British Policy in the Middle East, 1916–20.*
    (Philadelphia: Penn State University Press, 1992), p. 61.
48 SAD 470/6/27: to Clayton, 22 April 1917.
49 Storrs, Ronald, *Orientations* (London: Nicholson & Watson, 1943), p. 203.
50 Hocking, Charles, *Dictionary of Disasters at Sea during the age of Steam, 1824–1962,*
    Vol. 1 (London: Lloyd's Register).
51 SAD 160/5/56–7: 13 November 1916.
52 Bowman, *Window*, p. 132.
53 SAD 160/5/28: telegram, 7 November 1916.
54 SAD 143/5/21: 12 November 1916.
55 SAD 160/5/52: 12 November 1916.
56 SAD 143/5/30: 14 November 1916.
57 SAD 160/5/55: to Col. W. H. Drake (Yattenden, Berks.), 12 November 1916.
58 Lawrence, T. E., *Seven Pillars of Wisdom* (London: Cape, 1935), p. 324.
59 Wingate, *Wingate*, pp. 174, 198, 213 and 221–2.
60 SAD 160/5/58–9: 13 November 1916.
61 SAD 160/5/12.
62 SAD 160/5/99: Wingate to Grey, 23 November 1916.
63 Kedourie, Elie, 'Sa'ad Zaghlul and the British', St Antony's papers number 11,
    Middle Eastern Affairs, number 2 (1961), p. 145.
64 SAD 163/1/87/9: Private and Personal letter, 21 January 1917.
65 SAD 163/1/99: Personal and Secret letter, 31 January 1917.
66 SAD 135/4/7: 9 October 1915.
67 SAD 164/5/19–20: 3 May 1917.
68 Sir William Garstin was Under-Secretary of State, Egyptian Ministry of Public
    Works. He had a major role in the construction (December 1902) and raising
    (December 1912) of the first Aswan Dam. From 1899 to 1904, he made a com-
    prehensive reconnaissance of the Upper Nile basin, from Lake Victoria to
    Khartum, based on a plan for the White Nile to benefit Egypt, the Blue the
    Sudan. His report was 'the basis of Nile development during the next twenty
    years' [Mansfield, Peter, *The British in Egypt* (London: Weidenfeld and Nicol-
    son, 1971), p. 119]; one of the projects outlined in it was the irrigation of the
    Sudanese Gazirah with gravitation water to be obtained by constructing a
    barrage across the Blue Nile near Sannar. Garstin lost his wife through a celeb-
    rated elopement with Col. Repington (Boyle, *Boyle*, p. 143) the 'able but
    unscrupulous intriguer' who forfeited his military career thereby [Dilks, David,
    Curzon in India: Vol. 2 *Frustration* (London: Rupert Hart-Davis, 1970), p. 114].
69 SAD 164/5/25: 3 May 1917.
70 SAD 164/6/83: Private letter, 20 May 1917.
71 Daly, *Sirdar*, p. 239.
72 SAD 164/6/83: Private letter, 20 May 1917.
73 Lloyd, Lord, *Egypt since Cromer* London: Macmillan, Vol. II 1934), pp. 232–3.
74 See Stack to Clayton, 22 February 1917 (SAD 470/6/15).

4 Fullest confidence in you

1 Senior Tory aide quoting Harold Macmillan, *Sunday Telegraph*, 6 December
   1998.

2 SAD 166/2/42: Private, to Wingate, 8 November 1917.
3 SAD 162/4/1–4, paras. 5 and 6.
4 Rose, Kenneth, *The Later Cecils* (London: Weidenfeld and Nicolson, 1975), p. 198.
5 Morris, James, *Pax Britannica* (London: The Folio Society, 1992), Vol. 3, p. 19.
6 P. 224.
7 Wingate, Bt., Sir Ronald, *Wingate of the Sudan* (London: John Murray, 1955), p. 208.
8 Daly, M. W., *The Sirdar: Sir Reginald Wingate and the British Empire in the Middle East* (Philadelphia: American Philosophical Society, 1997), p. 258.
9 Of 22 February 1917 (SAD 163/2/13).
10 25 December 1915 and 1 January 1916.
11 Maxwell was one example, Sir Herbert W. Jackson Pasha another. The one-time 'much respected' CO of the 11th Sudanese battalion [Keown-Boyd, Henry, *The Lion and the Sphinx. The Rise and Fall of the British in Egypt, 1882–1956* (Spennymoor, Co. Durham: The Memoir Club, 2002), p. 46], he commanded with 'firm but tactful diplomacy' (ibid., p. 43) at Fashoda after Marchand had been worsted. Shortly afterwards, when Governor at Berber, an Egyptian Army mutiny in Omdurman in December 1899 was brought to a peaceful conclusion (details, ibid., p. 46), 'largely due to Colonel Jackson's judgement, and to the influence which he possesses over the black troops' [Cromer, 14 January 1901 to Queen Victoria, who died before it could reach her, in Boyle, Clara, *Boyle of Cairo* (Kendal: Titus Wilson, 1965), p. 104]. He later frequently acted as Governor-General for Wingate.
12 28 July 1917, to his eldest brother, in Rose, *Elder Cecils*, p. 225; Daly, *Sirdar*, p. 259.
13 5 November 1917, to his wife, in Rose, *Elder Cecils*, p. 225.
14 Terry, Janice J., *The Wafd, 1919–1952* (London: Third World Centre, 1982), p. 56.
15 Sir William Goodenough Hayter (1869–1924) was a civil judge in the Sudan, Assistant Legal Adviser, Egypt (1904), and Counsellor to the Khedive (1913). His attitudes were 'a shining example' to the other advisers [Grafftey-Smith, Laurence, *Bright Levant* (London: John Murray, 1970), p. 29].
16 SAD 163/1/20/1: to Wingate, 3 January 1917.
17 SAD 163/1/87–9: Private and Personal letter, 21 January 1917.
18 SAD 163/1/57–9: Cecil to Wingate.
19 SAD 163/1/98/9.
20 SAD 163/1/103–5.
21 SAD 163/2/13.
22 SAD 163/2/37: Hardinge Private letter to Wingate, 14 February 1917.
23 SAD 470/6/15.
24 SAD 163/2/72–6.
25 SAD 469/10/39: 25 August 1915.
26 SAD 163/2/72–6: Wingate Private 24 March 1917 letter to Hardinge.
27 SAD 177/1/51/2 19 April 1917: NOPCE Appx. C, pp. 6–7.
28 SAD 236/7/65.
29 SAD 164/6/26–7: Private and Personal letter, 16 May 1917.
30 SAD 165/1/299.
31 SAD 164/3/29–30: 21 March 1917.
32 SAD 164/6/39–43.
33 SAD 164/6/30–5: Cecil to Wingate, 16 May 1917.
34 SAD 164/1/187.
35 Terry, *Wafd*, pp. 60–1.

36 Lord Robert Cecil (1864–1958) was the third Salisbury son. MP for Hitchin (1911–23), Under-Secretary of State for Foreign Affairs (1915–18), Minister of Blockade in the Cabinet (1916–18), (uniquely) Assistant Secretary of State for Foreign Affairs, in charge of the Middle East (1918–19), and Lord Privy Seal (1922–23). He resigned in 1927 over disarmament, of which movement he was 'the Savonarola' [Templewood, Viscount, *Nine Troubled Years* (London: Collins, 1954), p. 114] and won the Nobel Peace Prize (1937). At the State Opening of Parliament in 1924, Duff Cooper observed 'saintly Bob Cecil ... looking incredibly wicked and scheming, like the evil counsellor in the fairy tale, or the bad uncle of a mediaeval king' [Cooper, Duff, *Old Men Forget* (London: Rupert Hart-Davis, 1953), p. 138]. Haig noted that he 'does not waste much money on his clothes. He is long and thin, stoops somewhat' [Cooper, Duff, *Haig*, Vol. 1 (London: Faber and Faber, 1935), p. 28].
37 SAD 236/6/6.
38 Rose, *Later Cecils*, p. 225.
39 SAD 162/4/1–4.
40 Daly, *Sirdar*, p. 263.
41 SAD 164/5/31.
42 SAD 236/7/65–6: letter, 7 September 1917.
43 SAD 166/1/27: to Wingate, 4 October 1917.
44 Terry, *Wafd*, p. 66.
45 SAD 166/2/49–50.
46 HP 1917, Vol. VII, p. 224 and SAD 166/2/138: 30 November.
47 Alfred, 1st Viscount Milner (1854–1925) was Director-General of Accounts and Under-Secretary of the Egyptian Ministry of Finance under Baring in 1889–92; in the latter year he wrote his *England in Egypt* [*sic*]. As High Commissioner in South Africa (1897–1905), he was 'the dynamic proconsul' and 'coldly brilliant exponent of Empire' with 'incomparable organizational talents' [Adams, R. J. Q., *Bonar Law* (London: John Murray, 1999), pp. 74, 116 and 146]. He was a key member of Lloyd George's War Cabinet (1916), Secretary of State for War (April 1918), Haig's strongest supporter, and Colonial Secretary (1919–21), when Baldwin thought that he had outstayed 'his utility and welcome' [Middlemass, Keith, and Barnes, John, *Baldwin* (London: Weidenfeld and Nicolson, 1969), p. 930].
48 SAD 166/1/66–7: to Wingate, 12 October 1917.
49 Storrs, Ronald, *Orientations* (London: Nicholson & Watson, 1943), p. 261.
50 Gilbert, Martin. *Churchill, A Life* (London: Heinemann, 1991), p. 428. See the recommendations of the Prime Minister's Interdepartmental Committee of 31 January 1921, which led to the Department's formation, in Hurewitz, J. C., *Diplomacy in the Near and Middle East* (New York: Van Nostrand for Princeton University Press, 1956), pp. 231–40.
51 SAD 166/1/137: Wingate to Hardinge, 20 October 1917.
52 Keown-Boyd, *Lion*, p. 80.
53 SAD 166/1/136–8.
54 SAD 166/2/74.
55 SAD 166/2/77.
56 SAD 166/2/84: 17 November 1917.
57 FO 371/2928/221521: telegram to Foreign Office, 20 November 1917.
58 To Wingate (SAD 166/3/43).
59 Roberts, Andrew, *Salisbury, Victorian Titan* (London: Weidenfeld and Nicolson, 1999), pp. 710, 748, 762 and 764.
60 Rose, *Later Cecils*, p. 224.
61 16 May 1917 (SAD 164/6/26–7).
62 On 14 March 1920 (Terry, *Wafd*, p. 55).

63 Lloyd, Lord, *Egypt since Cromer* (London: Macmillan, Vol. I 1933), p. 281.
64 SAD 164/2/64: 14 March telegram to Foreign Office.
65 30 June (HP 1918, Vol. III, p. 142).
66 Chirol, Sir Valentine, *The Egyptian Problem* (London: Macmillan, 1920), pp. 145–6.
67 Badrawi, Malak, *Isma'il Sidqi (1875–1950): Pragmatism and Vision in Twentieth Century Egypt* (London: Curzon, 1996), p. 12.
68 Mansfield, P., *The British in Egypt* (London: Weidenfeld and Nicolson, 1971), p. 219; Grafftey-Smith, *Bright Levant*, p. 63.
69 SAD 164/6/26–7: Wingate Private and Personal letter to Hardinge, 16 May 1917.
70 HP, 1918, Vol. III, p. 147 (17 May 1918).
71 To Wingate (SAD 166/3/43).
72 Grafftey-Smith, *Bright Levant*, p. 63.
73 SAD 162/1/25: letter, 11 March 1919.
74 Terry, *Wafd*, pp. 54–5.
75 Lloyd, *Egypt* (1933), p. 281.
76 Chirol, *Egyptian Problem*, p. 218.
77 9 January 1915 (SAD 194/1/72 and 469/8/12).
78 SAD 163/3/106–7: private and personal letter, 31 January 1917.
79 Terry, *Wafd*, p. 69.

5 Not perhaps a very clever man

1 20 July 1916 (Terry, Janice J., *The Wafd, 1919–1952* (London: Third World Centre, 1982), p. 15.
2 Ibid., p. 15.
3 14 September 1915 (SAD 469/10/65).
4 9 July 1916 (SAD 138/5/23–4 and 201/1/123). Also 9 and 11 July to Pearson (SAD 201/1/85 and SAD 201/2/11).
5 SAD 470/6/9: Wilson to Clayton, 16 January 1917.
6 Wilson to Clayton, 20 March 1917 (Collins, Robert O. (ed.), *An Arabian Diary, Sir Gilbert Falkingham Clayton* (Berkeley and Los Angeles: University of California Press, 1969), p. 68.
7 Hill, Richard, *Slatin Pasha* (Oxford University Press, 1965), p. 46.
8 Grafftey-Smith, Laurence, *Bright Levant* (London: John Murray, 1970), p. 31.
9 Vansittart, Lord, *The Mist Procession* (London: Hutchinson, 1958), p. 91.
10 12 October 1916 (Wingate, Bt., Sir Ronald, *Wingate of the Sudan* (London: John Murray, 1955), p. 201.
11 Bell letter, 2 July 1924, from Baghdad to her father, paraphrasing Cromer.
12 SAD 166/2/51: private letter to Wingate, 9 November 1917.
13 SAD 166/2/125: Private and Personal letter to Hardinge, 29 November 1917.
14 SAD 164/6/44: private and confidential letter to Wingate, 17 May 1917.
15 Edwin Montagu (1879–1924), Liberal politician, was Private Secretary to Asquith as Chancellor of the Exchequer and Prime Minister; he married his chief's mistress, Venetia Stanley, in 1915. He became Parliamentary Under-Secretary of State for India (1910–14), Minister of Munitions (1916) and Secretary of State for India (1917–22), vainly pointing the Subcontinent in the direction of 'responsible self-government' in the Montagu–Chelmsford reforms (1919). His resignation in March 1922 followed his anti-Dyer stance over Amritsar, was clinched on a technicality by Lloyd George and had 'Curzon and Montagu both on the verge of tears (literally)' [Austen Chamberlain in Petrie, Sir Charles, *The Life and Letters of The Right Hon. Sir Austen Chamberlain* (London: Cassell, Vol. 2 1940), p. 182]. A Jew, with Curzon he insisted that the

Balfour Declaration should speak of the establishment in Palestine of 'a national home' (rather than a state) for the Jewish people and that its second paragraph ['it being clearly understood'] should be added [Lord, John, *'Duty, Honour, Empire': the life and times of Col. Richard Meinertzhagen* (London: Hutchinson, 1971), p. 359n]. With Grey, he established a bird sanctuary in Norfolk.

16 4 November 1917 (Terry, *Wafd*, p. 64).
17 Symes, Sir Stewart, *Tour of Duty* (London: Collins,1946), pp. 28 and 50.
18 Bowman (1879–1965) was Inspector, Sudan Education Department (1911–13), Director of Egyptian Students in Britain (1913–14) and Director of Education, Iraq (1918–20) and Palestine (1920–36). He was the British escort for Prince (later King) Faysal of Saudi Arabia's visit to Britain in 1919.
19 Bowman, Humphrey E., *Middle Eastern Window* (London: Longmans, 1942), p. 130.
20 Wingate, *Wingate*, p. 78.
21 Warburg, Gabriel, 'The Sudan, Egypt and Britain, 1899–1916', *Middle Eastern Studies* 6, 2 (1970), p. 103n.
22 Vansittart, *Mist*, p. 433.
23 Graham, 20 July 1916 (Terry, *Wafd*, p. 15).
24 3 January 1917 (SAD 163/1/19).
25 22 November 1916 (SAD 470/5/6).
26 11 January 1917 (SAD 163/1/45).
27 Daly, M. W., *The Sirdar: Sir Reginald Wingate and the British Empire in the Middle East* (Philadelphia: American Philosophical Society, 1997), p. 250.
28 General Sir Leslie Rundle (1856–1934) was nicknamed Sir Leisurely Trundle. In the Egyptian Army from 1883, he enjoyed a lasting friendship with Kitchener and was his chief of staff on the Dongola Campaign and at Karary. Governor of Malta (1909–16) and Kitchener's first choice of commander for Gallipoli [Cooper, Duff, *Old Men Forget* (London: Rupert Hart-Davis, 1953), p. 56], he was 'broken as suddenly as was Wingate' (Wingate, *Wingate*, p. 257).
29 19 May 1917 (SAD 164/6/63).
30 27 December 1917 (HP 1917, Vol. VII, p. 307).
31 17 April 1917 (SAD 164/4/84).
32 Letter, 14 November 1918 (SAD 177/1/18–25).
33 23 November 1916 (SAD 160/5/99).
34 28 December 1918 (SAD 171/6/69).
35 Hill, *Slatin*, p. 187.
36 Daly, *Sirdar*, pp. 38, 54, 65 and 73–4.
37 27 March 1915 (SAD 469/8/65).
38 21 August 1915 (SAD 469/10/36).
39 17 March 1916 (SAD 159/3/36).
40 SAD 163/2/60: Wingate Private and Personal letter to Graham, 22 February 1917.
41 Daly, *Sirdar*, pp. 36–7.
42 Boyle, Clara, *Boyle of Cairo* (Kendal: Titus Wilson, 1965), pp. 113–14.
43 Hill, *Slatin*, p. 35.
44 Daly, *Sirdar*, p. 171.
45 To Grey, 19 April 1907 (FO 633/13/2, in Daly, *Sirdar*, p. 147).
46 1 December 1908 (FO 141/416).
47 To Clayton, 28 June 1917 (SAD 470/6/41).
48 SAD 470/6/17: Stack Private MS letter to Clayton, 22 February 1917.
49 16 February 1917 (SAD 470/6/14).
50 22 March 1917 (SAD 470/6/25).
51 7 May 1917 (SAD 164/5/63).
52 Daly, *Sirdar*, p. 261.

53 17 May 1917 (SAD 164/6/54).
54 Daly, *Sirdar*, p. 261.
55 FO telegram, 20 April 1918 (FO 371/3201/66140).
56 FO 371/2928/179037: Wingate private letter to Graham, 18 August 1917.
57 SAD 165/2/228: Lindsay to Wingate, 26 August 1917.
58 29 November 1917 (SAD 166/2/124).
59 *The Sunday Times*, 11 January 1998.
60 SAD 146/10/24: Hardinge telegram to Wingate, 22 November 1917.
61 HP, 1918, Vol. III, p. 154.
62 'Aly was the eldest son of Sharif Husayn and succeeded his father as King of the Hijaz (1924–25). Contact with Kitchener in Cairo, initiated by 'Abd Allah, the second son, led to the mounting of the Arab Revolt with British support. Earmarked at one time for Iraq, he became ruler of Transjordan, later Jordan (Amir 1921, King 1946) and was assassinated in Al 'Aqsa Mosque in Jerusalem in 1953. He was the grandfather of the late King Husayn.
63 Lawrence, T. E., *Seven Pillars of Wisdom* (London: Cape, 1935), pp. 507 and 533.
64 Private letter to Grey, 22 June 1908 (FO 800/47, in Warburg, Gabriel, 'The governor-general of the Sudan and his relations with the British consuls-general in Egypt, 1899–1916', *Asian and African Studies* V (1969), p. 121.
65 Lloyd, Lord, *Egypt since Cromer* (London: Macmillan, Vol. I 1933), pp. 232–3.
66 Ibid., pp. 289–90.
67 Chirol, Sir Valentine, *The Egyptian Problem* (London: Macmillan, 1920), p. 148.
68 Ibid., p. 121.
69 SAD 236/5/44: letter to Graham, 9 October 1916.
70 Keown-Boyd, Henry, *The Lion and the Sphinx. The Rise and Fall of the British in Egypt, 1882–1956* (Spennymoor, Co. Durham: The Memoir Club, 2002), p. 80.
71 Note of 31 January 1917 (Terry, *Wafd*, p. 20).
72 8 November 1918 (SAD 150/6/3).
73 SAD 150/6/28: Wingate telegram to Foreign Office, 9 November 1918.
74 SAD 150/6/51: Foreign Office telegram, 11 November 1918.
75 SAD 150/6/69: Wingate telegram to Hardinge, 12 November 1918.
76 Moosa, Sulaiman, 'T. E. Lawrence and his Arab Contemporaries', *Arabian Studies* 7 (1985), pp. 15–16; and SAD 150/6/70.

6 There seems some faulty staff work here

1 Wingate, Bt., Sir Ronald, *Wingate of the Sudan* (London: John Murray, 1955), p. 220.
2 Daly, M. W., *The Sirdar: Sir Reginald Wingate and the British Empire in the Middle East* (Philadelphia: American Philosophical Society, 1997), pp. 265–6.
3 SAD 164/5/28.
4 Terry, Janice J., *The Wafd, 1919–1952* (London: Third World Centre, 1982), p. 48.
5 Daly, *Sirdar*, pp. 265–6.
6 Keown-Boyd, Henry, *The Lion and the Sphinx. The Rise and Fall of the British in Egypt, 1882–1956* (Spennymoor, Co. Durham: The Memoir Club, 2002), p. 136.
7 Symes, Sir Stewart, *Tour of Duty* (London: Collins, 1946), p. 28.
8 Petrie, Sir Charles, *The Life and Letters of The Right Hon. Sir Austen Chamberlain* (London: Cassell, Vol. 1 1940), p. 341.
9 Chirol, Sir Valentine, *The Egyptian Problem* (London: Macmillan, 1920), p. 277. Austen Chamberlain thought Ahmad Fu'ad (1868–1936) 'sly, scheming, corrupt and autocratic' [Boyle, Clara, *Boyle of Cairo* (Kendal: Titus Wilson, 1965), p. 232] but Jarvis rated him 'possibly the wisest and most far-seeing of

the many rulers who followed Mohammed Ali' [Jarvis, Major C. S., *Desert and Delta* (London: John Murray, 1947), p. 11].

10 King, Joan Wucher, *Historical Dictionary of Egypt* (Metuchen, NJ: Scarecrow Press, 1984), p. 299.
11 To Graham, 3 November 1917 (SAD 166/2/14–15).
12 On 4 November 1917 (Terry, *Wafd*, p. 47).
13 Lloyd, Lord, *Egypt since Cromer* (London: Macmillan, Vol. I 1933), p. 273.
14 Grafftey-Smith, Laurence, *Bright Levant* (London: John Murray, 1970), p. 28.
15 Letter from Baghdad to her father, 23 July 1924.
16 SAD 166/2/116–20.
17 Terry, *Wafd*, pp. 47–8.
18 FO 371/2928/233706.
19 Wingate, *Wingate*, p. 235.
20 SAD 166/3/90–3.
21 Chirol, *Egyptian Problems*, p. 116.
22 Cromer, The Earl of, *Abbas II* (London: Macmillan, 1915), pp. 23–4.
23 SAD 166/3/133.
24 SAD 166/3/152: Terry, *Wafd*, p. 49.
25 NOPCE (SAD 177/1/15).
26 Badrawi, Malak, *Isma'il Sidqi (1875–1950): Pragmatism and Vision in Twentieth Century Egypt* (London: Curzon, 1996), p. 12.
27 FO 141/629 and 371/3199.
28 FO 371/3199.
29 SAD 169/3/171–2.
30 Daly, *Sirdar*, p. 276.
31 FO 371/3199.
32 NOPCE (SAD 177/1/3); Wingate, *Wingate*, p. 233.
33 Wingate, *Wingate*, p. 228.
34 NOPCE (SAD 177/2/3).
35 Lloyd noted that, but for the war, Egypt would not have been declared a Protectorate and therefore was entitled to a place at the Peace Conference and to consideration in the light of the principles of President Wilson (Lloyd, *Egypt* (1933), p. 292).
36 Wingate to Graham, 6 November 1918 (SAD 170/3/58–9).
37 Wingate, *Wingate*, p. 228.
38 Details are in Grafftey-Smith, *Bright Levant*, p. 18.
39 Daly, *Sirdar*, p. 279.
40 Wingate, *Wingate*, p. 232.
41 Private and personal letter, 31 January 1917 (SAD 163/1/100).
42 Letter to Hardinge, 14 November 1918 (SAD 177/1/19).
43 Wingate, *Wingate*, p. 229.
44 Terry, *Wafd*, p. 78.
45 Symes, *Tour*, p. 35.
46 Wingate, *Wingate*, p. 232.
47 Terry, *Wafd*, p. 73.
48 Daly, *Sirdar*, p. 280.
49 'Abd an Nasir, Gamal, *Falsafat ath Thawrah* (Cairo: Ad Dar al Qawmiyyah li't Tiba'ah wa'n Nashr, n.d.), p. 11n.
50 'Aly Pasha Sha'rawy was an aristocratic landowner, prominent in the Legislative Assembly. He became subsidiser and treasurer of the Wafd. After Zaghlul's deportation, he deputised for him and organised the Party's activities during the 1919 revolution. He fell out with his leader and resigned from the Wafd in summer 1921, replacing Zaghlul as 'president of the committee

of independence' and supporting 'Adly. Some 30 years older than his wife, Huda, he died in 1922 [Shaarawi, Huda (tr. Margot Badran), *Harem Years: the memoirs of an Egyptian feminist* (Cairo: American University of Cairo, 1998), pp. 112, 122].

51 Version in NOPCE (SAD 177/1/22, p. 5).
52 Final paragraph, NOPCE, Appendix A (SAD 177/1/27–35).
53 Chirol, *Egyptian Problem*, p. 190.
54 Wingate was prone to pieces of homespun wisdom. He said that, in dismissing Sharif Husayn's aspirations to be Caliph after the anticipated Ottoman overthrow, he had nonetheless told Husayn Kamil that 'nothing succeeds like success' (SAD 174/4: to Hardinge, 17 April 1917).
55 Terry, *Wafd*, p. 12.
56 Daly, *Sirdar*, p. 274.
57 NOPCE, Appendix A, pp. 1–8: 14 November 1918 letter to Hardinge (SAD 177/1/18–25).
58 Vansittart, Lord, *The Mist Procession* (London: Hutchinson, 1958), p. 213.
59 Terry, *Wafd*, p. 80.
60 Since September, Graham had been responsible for Egypt only, and under the supervision of Sir Eyre Crowe, who – on the initiative of Robert Cecil – had in August replaced him as supervising Assistant Under-Secretary of the Middle East Department.
61 SAD 165/2/51.
62 SAD 177/2/3–4: 13 November 1918, received on 14 November.
63 Wingate, *Wingate*, p. 233.
64 Ibid., p. 234.
65 NOPCE, Appendix B, p. 6 (SAD 177/1/41).
66 Symes, *Tour*, p. 35.
67 Of Sir Thomas Wentworth Russell Pasha (1879–1954), the newspaper *Akhir Sa'ah* said: 'Commandant of Police in the capital, guardian of law and order in the country – and then some!' [(Quoted by Jarvis, *Desert*, p. 83. See Mansfield, P., *The British in Egypt* (London: Weidenfeld and Nicolson, 1971), p. 266, for further biographical details of Russell)]. Lampson, on the other hand, described him as 'a bundle of nerves and ... a first-class advertiser' and 'one of our major post treaty problems' (Keown-Boyd, *Lion*, pp. 109–11, where there is much further criticism, e.g. of his 'limited intelligence').
68 Russell Pasha, Sir Thomas, *Egyptian Service, 1902–1946* (London: John Murray, 1949), p. 190.
69 Kedourie, Elie, *The Chatham House Version and other Middle-Eastern Studies* (London: Weidenfeld and Nicolson, 1970), pp. 97–8.
70 SAD 237/10/26.
71 Kedourie, *Chatham House*, pp.108–9. Cf. Balfour's 2 December telegram, Graham's 22 January 1919 note to Hardinge and Curzon's 26 February telegram to Cheetham.
72 Graham two years earlier had anticipated that, after the war, London would receive visits from the Sultan and 'better class Egyptians' (SAD 237/10/28 and NOPCE, p. 6 (SAD 177/1/7).
73 2 March 1917: 'Observations on future British Policy with Regard to Egypt' (SAD 164/2/79).
74 Cooper, Duff, *Old Men Forget* (London: Rupert Hart-Davis, 1953), p. 100.
75 Chirol, *Egyptian Problem*, p. 143.
76 Terry, *Wafd*, p. 90.
77 FO 371/221.
78 Wavell, Field-Marshal Viscount, *Allenby, Soldier and Statesman* (London: Harrap, 1944), p. 331.

79 Kedourie, *Chatham House*, p. 109.
80 NOPCE, Appendix C, p. 7 (SAD 177/1/52).
81 Ibid., p. 8 (SAD 177/1/53).
82 Crowe (1864–1925), a Foreign Office Cecil protégé and unorthodox dresser [Waterfield, Gordon, *Professional Diplomat, Sir Percy Loraine* (London: John Murray, 1973), p. 10] was hated by Lloyd George and Hardinge, the latter 'because he had some middle-class and German connections': his mother and wife were German and his uncle was chief of staff of the German Admiralty (Corp, Edward T., 'The Problem of Promotion in the Career of Sir Eyre Crowe, 1905–20', *Australian Journal of Politics and History*, 28, 2 (1982), pp. 237, 241–2). Vansittart (*Mist*, p. 45) rated him 'the greatest public servant of his age'. Foreign Office PUS (November 1920 to mid-1925), he got into hot water with MacDonald over the Zinoviev Letter which was such an important issue in the General Election of 1924 [See Rose, Kenneth, *King George V* (London: Phoenix, 2000), pp. 326–7, for details]. On his premature death, Baldwin said, 'we have lost the ablest servant of the Crown' (*DNB*).
83 Daly, *Sirdar*, p. 284n; Kedourie, *Chatham House*, p. 109.
84 Telegram to Wingate, 1 January 1919 (SAD 237/10/14).
85 Lloyd, *Egypt* (1933), pp. 287–8.
86 Kedourie, *Chatham House*, p. 109.
87 SAD 237/10/64.
88 SAD 162/1/5.
89 NOPCE, Appendix D, p. 7 (SAD 177/1/62).
90 Ibid., Appendix D, p. 7 (SAD 177/1/60).
91 Ibid, p. 8 (SAD 177/1/9).
92 Terry, *Wafd*, pp. 202–3.
93 NOPCE, p. 9 (SAD 177/1/10).
94 Lloyd, *Egypt* (1933), p. 290.
95 SAD 237/10/114.
96 Kedourie, *Chatham House*, p. 110; Terry, *Wafd*, p. 93; Daly, *Sirdar*, p. 287.
97 King, *Historical Dictionary*, p. 539.
98 SAD 132/1.
99 SAD 162/1/5.
100 Para. 9, SAD 162/4/1–4.
101 Bell diary, 29 September 1919.
102 SAD 177/2/7–8.

7 I can do no more than thank you

1 To Milner, 14 October 1919 (SAD 177/2/34).
2 Main Swete Osmond Walrond (1870–1927) was companion and tutor to Sultan Husayn Kamil's only son, Prince Kamal ad Din, from 1892–94, and worked in the Egyptian Ministry of Finance (1894–97), the Arab Bureau (1917–18) and the Secret Intelligence Service in Egypt. He was Adviser in a private capacity to the Milner Mission (1919–21). Boyle called him both 'a sort of agent for Saad Zaghloul' [26 April 1921, in Boyle, Clara, *Boyle of Cairo* (Kendal: Titus Wilson, 1965), p. 208] and 'a strong supporter of Adly' (24 May 1921, in ibid., p. 217).
3 Monroe, Elizabeth, *Britain's Moment in the Middle East, 1914–56* (London: Chatto and Windus, 1963), pp. 56–7.
4 Hardinge, Lord, *Old Diplomacy* (London: John Murray, 1947), p. 233.
5 HP, 1919, Vol. II, p. 40.
6 Terry, Janice J., *The Wafd, 1919–1952* (London: Third World Centre, 1982), p. 95.

7 Bell diary, 30 September 1919.
8 Seth, Ronald, *Russell Pasha* (London: William Kimber, 1966), p. 138.
9 Terry, *Wafd*, p. 100.
10 Minute of 8 February 1919 (FO 371/3711).
11 Vatikiotis, P. J., *The History of Egypt* (London: Weidenfeld and Nicolson, 1985), p. 261
12 NOPCE, p. 10 (SAD 177/1/11).
13 Wingate, Bt., Sir Ronald, *Wingate of the Sudan* (London: John Murray, 1955), p. 239.
14 Daly, M. W., *The Sirdar: Sir Reginald Wingate and the British Empire in the Middle East* (Philadelphia: American Philosophical Society, 1997), p. 289.
15 NOPCE, Appendix C, p. 1 (SAD 177/1/46).
16 Ibid., pp. 10–11 (SAD 177/1/11–12).
17 Ibid., Appendix C, pp. 4–5 (SAD 177/1/49–50).
18 Hardinge, *Old Diplomacy*, p. 233.
19 Kedourie, Elie, *The Chatham House Version and other Middle-Eastern Studies* (London: Weidenfeld and Nicolson, 1970), p. 100.
20 Lieut.-Col. F. C. C. Balfour (1884–1965) was in the Sudan service from 1906 until the First World War, when he fought in Mesopotamia. He was Military Governor of Baghdad (1919–20), Military Secretary to the Governor of Madras (1924–26) and (Deputy) Governor of two Sudanese provinces from 1926–30.
21 3 June 1919, to Capt. Alexander (SAD 173/7/5–6).
22 Kedourie, *Chatham House*, p. 100; Goldschmidt, Arthur, *Historical Dictionary of Egypt* (Metuchen, New Jersey: Scarecrow Press, 199?), p. 239.
23 Lloyd, Lord, *Egypt since Cromer* (London: Macmillan, Vol. I 1933), p. 301.
24 Kedourie, *Chatham House*, p. 102.
25 Russell Pasha, Sir Thomas, *Egyptian Service, 1902–1946* (London: John Murray, 1949), p. 192.
26 Al Basil was to become a Vice-President of the Wafd before leaving the Party for six months in summer 1921, after being sentenced to death (with six other Wafdists) for demanding the release of Zaghlul and his colleagues. The term was commuted to seven years in prison but he was released by May 1923 while remaining on a Foreign Office 'blacklist of dangerous suspects' (Terry, *Wafd*, p. 215). Finally removed from it, he was turned back at Dover by an immigration official who was not *au courant* [Grafftey-Smith, Laurence, *Bright Levant* (London: John Murray, 1970), p. 129]. He founded the Sa'adist Party in 1932.
27 Grafftey-Smith, *Bright Levant*, p. 129.
28 SAD 237/3/10.
29 See Chirol, Sir Valentine, *The Egyptian Problem* (London: Macmillan, 1920), p. 149, for an account of how it was done.
30 NOPCE, p. 12 (SAD 177/1/13).
31 Badrawi, Malak, *Political Violence in Egypt, 1910–1924* (Richmond: Curzon, 2000), p. 231.
32 Keown-Boyd, Henry, *The Lion and the Sphinx. The Rise and Fall of the British in Egypt, 1882–1956* (Spennymoor, Co. Durham: The Memoir Club, 2002), p. 89.
33 Hughes, Matthew, *Allenby and British Strategy in the Middle East, 1917–1919* (London: Frank Cass, 1999), p. 17.
34 Grafftey-Smith, *Bright Levant*, p. 56.
35 Bell diary, 29 September 1919.
36 Grafftey-Smith, *Bright Levant*, p. 57; Boyle, 224.
37 Boyle memorandum, Boyle, *Boyle*, p. 224.
38 Macbride, Barrie Sinclair, *Farouk of Egypt* (London: Robert Hale, 1967), p. 38.
39 ZW.

40 Ahmad, Jamal Muhammad, *The Intellectual Origins of Arab Nationalism* (Oxford University Press, 1960), pp. 116–17.
41 Shaarawi, Huda (tr. Margot Badran), *Harem Years: the memoirs of an Egyptian feminist* (Cairo: American University of Cairo, 1998), p. 119.
42 Grafftey-Smith, *Bright Levant*, p. 63.
43 Keown-Boyd, *Lion*, p. 86.
44 Grafftey-Smith, *Bright Levant*, p. 63.
45 Kedourie, *Chatham House*, p. 105.
46 Details in Keown-Boyd, *Lion*, p. 86–7.
47 Bell diary, 30 September 1919.
48 'Rough Notes by Sir R. Wingate on the Situation in Egypt', 21 March 1919 (SAD 162/1/41).
49 HP, 1919, Vol. 1, p. 140.
50 Shaarawi, *Harem*, p. 120.
51 After her husband's second exile, Safiyyah Zaghlul formed a Women's Committee of the Wafd. Known as Umm Misr [the Mother of Egypt], she had wished to unveil with Huda Sha'rawy in 1923 but the party thought this inappropriate. She was to be influential in selecting An Nahhas as her husband's successor but, related to An Nuqrashy, split with him when the latter was expelled from the Wafd.
52 Shaarawi, *Harem*, p. 119.
53 Kedourie, *Chatham House*, p. 106.
54 Letter, 16 March 1919, from ?Jimmy Watson (SAD 237/3/18).
55 Kedourie, *Chatham House*, p.106.
56 Appendix D, last item (SAD 177/1/65).
57 Kedourie, Elie, 'Sa'ad Zaghlul and the British' (St Antony's papers number 11, *Middle Eastern Affairs*, number 2, 1961), p. 152.
58 Wingate, *Wingate*, p. 242.
59 SAD 237/3/27.
60 SAD 237/3/54.
61 On 19 October 1919 (SAD 177/2/54).
62 Kedourie, *Chatham House*, p. 109.
63 Telegram in ibid., p. 111.
64 SAD 162/1/40–1 and 177/2/16–17.
65 There had been a case in 1810 when the East India Company and the Foreign Office had rival ambassadors, Sir John Malcolm and Sir Harford Jones, on Persian soil at the same time.
66 SAD 177/2/11–12 and 237/3/79–80.
67 See Carman, Barry, and McPherson, John, *The Man who Loved Egypt: Bimbashi McPherson* (London: Ariel Books/BBC, 1985) for the most graphic account
68 Terry, *Wafd*, p. 98.
69 Carman and McPherson, *Man who Loved*, p. 205. King, Joan Wucher, *Historical Dictionary of Egypt* (Metuchen, NJ: Scarecrow Press, 1984), p. 528, claims that 40 Britons and at least several hundred Egyptians died.
70 SAD 162/1/44.
71 SAD 162/1/59.
72 NOPCE, p. 13 (SAD 177/1/14). Wingate does not give a precise date for this but his son (in Wingate, *Wingate*, p. 243) suggests that it was at the time of Zaghlul's release.
73 Telegram in Daly, *Sirdar*, p. 294.
74 HP, 1919, Vol. 1, p. 52.
75 Daly, *Sirdar*, p. 294.
76 Kedourie, *Chatham House*, p. 115.
77 Wingate letter, 27 November 1927, to his cousin Dan (SAD 115/13/27).

78 Terry, *Wafd*, p. 111. See Wingate, *Wingate*, p. 243, for further details.
79 'Memorandum on Unrest in Egypt', 9 April 1919, in Lloyd, *Egypt* (1933), pp. 300, 301 and 307–9.
80 NOPCE, pp. 12–13 (SAD 177/1/13–4).
81 SAD 237/4/39.
82 Corp, Edward T., 'The Problem of Promotion in the Career of Sir Eyre Crowe, 1905–20', *Australian Journal of Politics and History*, 28, 2 (1982), p. 245.
83 SAD 173/7/8–9.
84 Wingate letter to Balfour from Braemar, 30 September 1919, in NOPCE, Appendix D, pp. 7–8 (SAD 177/1/60–1).
85 Wingate, *Wingate*, p. 245.
86 Note of 21 July 1919, enclosed in his letter of 1 October 1919 to Milner (SAD 177/2/37).
87 Letter of 31 March 1921 to Curzon, in NOPCE, Appendix F, p. 2 (SAD 177/1/75).
88 3 June (SAD 173/7/5–6).
89 16 June (SAD 173/7/1046).
90 28 June (SAD 173/7/154)
91 4 February 1920 (SAD 174/2/20 and 176/1/43).
92 13 and 20 September (SAD 162/3/54 and /56).
93 *Private*, 30 September 1919 (SAD 162/3/61).
94 23 October (SAD 162/4/32).
95 Wingate of course was a Scot.
96 26 October 1919 (SAD 162/4/36).
97 Wingate, *Wingate*, p. 254.
98 9 June 1919, in Kedourie, *Chatham House*, p. 112.
99 NOPCE, Appendix D, p. 9 (SAD 177/1/62).
100 Ibid., Appendix D, pp. 1–4 and 8 (SAD 177/1/54–7, 61).
101 SAD 177/2/45.
102 Lloyd, *Egypt* (1933), p. 307.
103 Bowman, Humphrey E., *Middle Eastern Window* (London: Longmans, 1942), p. 132.
104 SAD 177/2/50.
105 SAD 177/2/57.
106 Wingate, Bt., Sir Ronald, *Not in the Limelight* (London: Hutchinson, 1959), p. 28.
107 14 October 1919 (SAD 177/2/34).
108 2 January 1920 (Daly, *Sirdar*, p. 305).
109 14 December 1919 (SAD 162/4/56).
110 Kedourie, *Chatham House*, p. 112.
111 Goldschmidt, *Historical Dictionary*, p. 302.
112 On 21 November 1927 (SAD 115/13/27).
113 22 October 1919 (SAD 175/1/141). Grafftey-Smith gives a contrary view in *Bright Levant*, p. 61.
114 Letter, 2 October 1917, to Mrs. Frances Parker (SAD 146/6/2).
115 Daly, *Sirdar*, pp. 309–10.
116 NOPCE, Appendix F (SAD 177/1/73–8).
117 Wingate letter to Milner, 14 May 1922 (SAD 240/5/64–5).

8 Unequipped personally

1 Wingate letter to Balfour, 30 September 1919, from Braemar, NOPCE, Appendix D, p. 6 (SAD 177/1/59).

2 Wingate, Bt., Sir Ronald, *Wingate of the Sudan* (London: John Murray, 1955), pp. 245–6.
3 SAD 111/1/2, p. 1.
4 30 September 1919: NOPCE, Appendix D, pp. 1–4 and 8 (SAD 177/1/54–7 and /61).
5 Grafftey-Smith, Laurence, *Bright Levant* (London: John Murray, 1970), p. 75.
6 Lloyd, Lord, *Egypt since Cromer* (London: Macmillan, Vol. I 1933), pp. 285–6; Daly, M. W. (ed.), *The Cambridge History of Egypt*, Vol. II (Cambridge University Press, 1998), p. 248.
7 Lloyd, *Egypt* (1933), p. 285.
8 Wingate note, SAD 170/3/3.
9 NOPCE, pp. 5–6 (SAD 177/1/6–7).
10 Private MS letter, 7 May 1917 (SAD 164/5/52).
11 Para. 10, SAD 162/4/1–4.
12 SAD 177/1/52.
13 SAD 177/2/7–8.
14 Wingate, *Wingate*, p. 229.
15 30 September 1919 (SAD 177/1/54–7 and 61).
16 Kedourie, Elie, *The Chatham House Version and other Middle-Eastern Studies* (London: Weidenfeld and Nicolson, 1970), p. 96.
17 SAD 177/1/18–25.
18 SAD 177/1/41.
19 HP 1919, Vol II, p. 40.
20 SAD 163/1/100.
21 SAD 177/1/52.
22 To Cheetham (SAD 177/1/49–50).
23 Kedourie, Elie, 'Sa'ad Zaghlul and the British' (St Antony's papers number 11, *Middle Eastern Affairs*, number 2, 1961), p. 147.
24 Goldschmidt, Arthur, *Historical Dictionary of Egypt* (Metuchen, New Jersey: Scarecrow Press, 199?), p. 301.
25 *DNB*.
26 Kedourie, *Chatham House*, p. 103.
27 30 September 1919, from Braemar: NOPCE, Appendix D, p. 5 (SAD 177/1/58).
28 NOPCE, 'Removal', p. 5 (SAD 177/1/6).
29 MAIN POINTS 7, para. 8 (SAD 162/4/1–4).
30 Private: SAD 164/7/21.
31 Private: SAD 164/3/28–9.
32 Private letter , 24 March 1917 (SAD 163/2/72–6).
33 NOPCE, p. 3 (SAD 177/1/4).
34 SAD 166/3/57.
35 Private, 18 August 1917 (FO 371/2928/179037).
36 HP 1918, Vol. 3, p. 238.
37 NOPCE, p. 3 (SAD 177/1/3–4).
38 Ibid. (SAD 177/1/4).
39 Final paragraph, NOPCE, Appendix A (SAD 177/1/27–35).
40 13 January 1920 (SAD 176/1/28).
41 Kedourie, *Chatham House*, pp. 108–9.
42 Symes, Sir Stewart, *Tour of Duty* (London: Collins, 1946), p. 12.
43 Wingate, *Wingate*, p. 264.
44 Ibid., p. 266.
45 5 August 1917 (SAD 470/7/4).
46 Terry, Janice J., *The Wafd, 1919–1952* (London: Third World Centre, 1982), p. 30.

47 Note of 21 July 1919, enclosed in his letter of 14 October 1919, to Milner (SAD 177/2/36–7).
48 Daly, *Cambridge History*, p. 247.

9 A man of no principles

1 Vansittart, Lord, *The Mist Procession* (London: Hutchinson, 1958), p. 172.
2 Storrs, Ronald, *Orientations* (London: Nicholson & Watson, 1943), p. 291.
3 Kedourie, Elie, *The Chatham House Version and other Middle-Eastern Studies* (London: Weidenfeld and Nicolson, 1970), p. 111.
4 Daly, M. W., *The Sirdar: Sir Reginald Wingate and the British Empire in the Middle East* (Philadelphia: American Philosophical Society, 1997), p. 293; Wavell, Field-Marshal Viscount, *Allenby, Soldier and Statesman* (London: Harrap, 1944), p. 270.
5 Lloyd, Lord, *Egypt since Cromer* (London: Macmillan, Vol. I 1933), p. 302.
6 Bell diary, 2 October 1919.
7 To Wavell, 20 March 1919 (SAD 473/3/4)
8 King, Joan Wucher, *Historical Dictionary of Egypt* (Metuchen, NJ: Scarecrow Press, 1984), p. 528.
9 Cooper, Duff, *Haig*, Vol. 1 (London: Faber and Faber, 1935), pp. 180, 208.
10 Mansfield, Peter, *The British in Egypt* (London: Weidenfeld and Nicolson, 1971), p. 225.
11 Toynbee, A. J., *Survey of International Affairs, 1925* (Oxford University Press, 1927). Vol. I, *The Islamic World since the Peace Settlement*, Part III, p. 191.
12 Wavell, *Allenby*, pp. 270–1.
13 Terry, Janice J., *The Wafd, 1919–1952* (London: Third World Centre, 1982), p. 109.
14 Gardner, Brian, *Allenby* (London: Cassell, 1965), p. 221, quoting an undated issue of the paper; Lloyd, *Egypt* (1933), p. 303. See also Kedourie, *Chatham House*, p. 113.
15 Kedourie, *Chatham House*, p. 114; Mansfield, *British*, p. 228. Sir Reginald A. Stewart Patterson (1878–1930), a 'man of exceptional charm and ability', was 'deservedly popular with Egyptians and ... an able administrator' when in Education and Finance [Bowman, Humphrey E., *Middle Eastern Window* (London: Longmans, 1942), p. 243]. After his 1923–27 term as Financial Adviser, Lloyd said that 'the British officials in this country ..., after the Patterson régime, badly want disciplining and a new broom' (22 July 1927: GLLD 13/15).
16 Wavell, *Allenby*, p. 272; Mansfield, *British*, p. 228.
17 'Rough Notes by Sir R. Wingate on the Situation in Egypt', 21 March 1919 (SAD 177/2/18).
18 Ibid.
19 Lloyd, *Egypt* (1933), p. 303.
20 Symes, Sir Stewart, *Tour of Duty* (London: Collins, 1946), p. 35.
21 SAD 162/1/59.
22 Terry, *Wafd*, p. 110.
23 Mansfield, *British*, p. 229.
24 Cooper, Duff, *Old Men Forget* (London: Rupert Hart-Davis, 1953), p. 101.
25 Wavell, *Allenby*, pp. 271–3.
26 Daly, in Daly, M. W. (ed.), *The Cambridge History of Egypt*, Vol. II (Cambridge University Press, 1998), p. 250.
27 Chirol, Sir Valentine, *The Egyptian Problem* (London: Macmillan, 1920), p. 195.
28 Grafftey-Smith, Laurence, *Bright Levant* (London: John Murray, 1970), p. 72.
29 Bell diary, 2 October 1919.

30 Ibid., 3 October 1919.
31 Ibid., 30 September 1919.
32 Wavell, *Allenby*, p. 278.
33 Lloyd, *Egypt* (1933), p. 341.
34 Grafftey-Smith, *Bright Levant*, p. 66.
35 Lloyd, *Egypt* (1933), pp. 303, 340.
36 Hardinge, Lord, *Old Diplomacy* (London: John Murray, 1947), p. 234.
37 Vansittart, *Mist*, p. 213.
38 Bimbashi Joseph McPherson (1866–1946) was 45 years in Egypt. He was the author of *The Moulids of Egypt*, about the fairs and religious festivals of the Delta, which, in a preface, Laurence Durrell called a 'little classic'. He was a Department of Public Instruction/Ministry of Education teacher and educational administrator in Cairo and Alexandria (1901–14), a Red Cross Officer at Gallipoli, a member of the Camel Transport Corps in the Sinai campaign and Acting Head of the Egyptian Secret Police (1918–24).
39 Letter to his brother, 1 May 1919, in Carman, Barry, and McPherson, John, *The Man who Loved Egypt: Bimbashi McPherson* (London: Ariel Books/BBC, 1985), pp. 205–15.
40 Lloyd, *Egypt* (1933), pp. 305–7 and 351.
41 Sir Sheldon Amos, prominent in the legal establishment, in 1912 was hounded out of his position as a judge in the Native Court of Appeal by British expatriate pressure but later acted as Judicial Adviser.
42 Lloyd, *Egypt* (1933), p. 352.
43 SAD 694/8/12.
44 'Abd al Latif Bey Makabaty, a Legislative Assembly member from a landowning family, left the Wafd to join Hizb al Ahrar ad Dusturiyyin in the summer of 1921 but rejoined it after Zaghlul's second exile. He soon returned to Hizb al Ahrar when more radical members were appointed to the Wafd High Command (Terry, *Wafd*, p. 148).
45 Clayton to Cheetham, 14 April 1919 (SAD 470/9/1).
46 Badrawi, Malak, *Political Violence in Egypt, 1910–1924* (Richmond: Curzon, 2000), p. 170.
47 Ibid., pp. 139 and 165.
48 Terry, *Wafd*, p. 115.
49 Grafftey-Smith, *Bright Levant*, p. 67.
50 Terry, *Wafd*, p. 114.
51 Ibid., p. 203.
52 To the Foreign Office, 19 April 1919 (FO 371/3715).
53 Details in Chirol, *Egyptian Problem*, pp. 196–202.
54 Kedourie, *Chatham House*, p. 117.
55 1 May 1919 letter to his brother, (Carman and McPherson, *Man who Loved*, pp. 205–15).
56 Beaman, A. A. H., *The Dethronement of the Khedive* (London: George Allen & Unwin, 1929), p. 122.
57 Grafftey-Smith, *Bright Levant*, p. 72.
58 Badrawi, *Political Violence*, p. 140.
59 Terry, *Wafd*, p. 112.
60 Bell diary, 30 September 1919.
61 Chirol, *Egyptian Problem*, p. 256.
62 See Badrawi, Malak, *Isma'il Sidqi (1875–1950): Pragmatism and vision in Twentieth Century Egypt* (London: Curzon, 1996), p. 142 for his achievements in office.
63 Badrawi, *Political Violence*, p. 149.
64 Kedourie, *Chatham House*, p. 119.
65 Badrawi, *Political Violence*, p. 146.

66 Lloyd, *Egypt* (1933), pp. 355–6.
67 Bell letter to her father from Baghdad, 7 December 1919.
68 Kedourie, *Chatham House*, pp. 118–19.
69 Carman and McPherson, *Man who Loved*, p. 205.
70 Austen Chamberlain to Tyrrell, 18 October 1925 [(Petrie, Sir Charles, *The Life and Letters of The Right Hon. Sir Austen Chamberlain* (London: Cassell, Vol. 2 1940)], p. 288.
71 Graham letter to Crawford, 10 July 1919 (FO 371/3710/98148).
72 Mansfield, *British*, p. 233.
73 Vansittart, *Mist*, p. 165.
74 Badrawi, *Political Violence*, p. 144.
75 Ibid., p. 146.
76 Lloyd, *Egypt* (1933), p. 343.
77 Terry, *Wafd*, p. 121.
78 Chetwode, who commanded the desert column in Murray's Egyptian Expeditionary Force at Rafah and in both assaults on Gazah and made the plan for Allenby's capture of the latter, told Wavell that when Smuts, accompanied by Amery, came out to the Levant to reinforce Lloyd George's Easterner strategy and give him unwanted advice from 12 to 22 February 1918, he could hardly describe Allenby's attitude to him, 'at any rate at Jerusalem, as "cordial". He was bored to death with his being there' [Hughes, Matthew, *Allenby and British Strategy in the Middle East, 1917–1919* (London: Frank Cass, 1999), p. 68].
79 Bell diary, 2 October 1919.
80 Bell diary, 29 September 1919.
81 Bell letter from Baghdad to her mother, 12 January 1920 [Wallach, Janet, *Desert Queen, the extraordinary life of Gertrude Bell* (London: Weidenfeld and Nicolson, 1986), p. 249].
82 Lloyd, *Egypt* (1934), p. 15; Kedourie, *Chatham House*, p. 134.
83 Details in Ibid., pp. 17ff. and 367.
84 Further details in Terry, *Wafd*, pp. 125–6.
85 Mansfield, *British*, p. 234.
86 Lloyd, *Egypt* (1934), p. 367.
87 FO 371/5109/5311.
88 Kedourie, *Chatham House*, p. 132.
89 Lloyd, *Egypt* (1934), pp. 23–4.
90 Text in FO 371/4979/10237.
91 Terry, *Wafd*, p. 128.
92 Lloyd, *Egypt* (1934), pp. 25–6.
93 Details in FO 371/4979/10237.
94 Mansfield, *British*, p. 236.
95 Kedourie, *Chatham House*, pp. 134–5.
96 14 September (FO 371/4979/11364/6/16).
97 Grafftey-Smith, *Bright Levant*, p. 74.
98 Lloyd, *Egypt* (1934), p. 28; Kedourie, *Chatham House*, p. 140.
99 Shaarawi, Huda (tr. Margot Badran), *Harem Years: the memoirs of an Egyptian feminist* (Cairo: American University of Cairo, 1998), p. 122.
100 Kedourie, *Chatham House*, p. 135.
101 Details in FO 371/4979/10237.
102 Cooper, *Old Men Forget*, p. 102.
103 Isma'il Pasha Sirry, an engineer, was Minister of Public Works in Butrus Ghaly's government and until November 1918, when Chirol (*Egyptian Problem*, p. 120) named him among Egyptian politicians 'of considerable capacity'. Thereafter he became a prominent Cabinet member, as Minister of War (a bomb was thrown at him), until the resignation of Rushdy's first government.

104 Bell diary, 29 September 1919.
105 Letter, 28 December 1920 in Gardner, *Allenby*, p. 232.
106 Details in Lloyd, *Egypt* (1934), pp. 22, 31, 242–3 and 367–94.
107 Terry, *Wafd*, p. 132.
108 Lloyd, *Egypt* (1934), p. 39.
109 Mansfield, *British*, p. 236.
110 Kedourie, *Chatham House*, pp. 138–9.
111 King, *Historical Dictionary*, pp. 18 and 647.
112 Faris Nimr in Bell diary, 2 October 1919.
113 Grafftey-Smith, *Bright Levant*, p. 76.
114 Jarvis, Major C. S., *Desert and Delta* (London: John Murray, 1947), pp. 50–1.
115 Kedourie, *Chatham House*, p. 137.
116 King, *Historical Dictionary*, p. 647.
117 Ibid., p. 18.
118 Badrawi, *Political Violence*, p. 134.
119 Mansfield, *British*, p. 248.
120 Ibid., p. 230.
121 Letter, 29 April 1921, in Gardner, *Allenby*, p. 235.
122 Boyle, Clara, *Boyle of Cairo* (Kendal: Titus Wilson, 1965), pp. 201–38.
123 Ibid., p. 201: letter, 2 March 1921.
124 Ibid., p. 202: letter from Crowe's Private Secretary, 14 March 1921.
125 Lloyd, *Egypt* (1934), pp. 44 and 46.
126 Mansfield, *British*, p. 237.
127 Boyle, *Boyle*, pp. 215 and 218: Boyle to his wife, 20 May 1921.
128 Ibid., pp. 209 and 217.
129 Ibid., p. 217.
130 Ibid., p. 228.
131 Ibid., p. 214: Boyle to his wife, 16 May 1921.
132 Boyle Memorandum, in ibid., p. 223.
133 Boyle Memorandum, in ibid., p. 224.
134 Boyle Memorandum, in ibid., p. 226.
135 Boyle Memorandum, in ibid., p. 235.
136 Boyle Memorandum, in ibid., p. 236.
137 Mansfield, *British*, p. 64.
138 Boyle, *Boyle*, pp. xiv and 218.
139 Ibid., p. 218.
140 Ibid., pp. xiv and 222.
141 Ibid., p. 213; Wavell, *Allenby*, p. 281: letter, 10 May 1921.
142 Boyle, *Boyle*, p. 211: letter, 4 May 1921.
143 Boyle Memorandum, in ibid., pp. 234–5.
144 Ibid., p. 205: Boyle to his wife, 18 April 1921.
145 'Abd al Khaliq Sarwat (1873–1928), a Turco-Egyptian, was prosecutor in the trial of the assassins of Butros Ghaly and a consistent upholder of the rule of law (Badrawi, *Political Violence*, pp. 39 and 45). He was in the Cabinet throughout the First World War as Minister of Justice. Until reconciled late in the day (Grafftey-Smith, *Bright Levant*, pp. 105–6), he was no admirer of Zaghlul. A close friend of 'Adly, he was Minister of Interior in his 1921 administration, in 1922 and in 1927–28. He was Hizb al Ahrar Prime Minister and Foreign Minister in 1922–23, Foreign Minister in 'Adly's 1926 administration and Prime Minister in 1927–28, retiring on account of ill-health. He had been defeated by Zaghlul in his bid to be Speaker of Parliament in 1925. Lloyd (*Egypt* (1934), p. 283) surprisingly characterised him as possessing 'great personal charm, a keen and supple intellect, a high degree of political ability, and a self-mastery which was rare in the councils of Egypt'. Grafftey-Smith (*Bright*

Levant, p. 106) deemed him 'the bravest and one of the best of Egypt's political figures in the decade following the war'.

146 Boyle, *Boyle*, pp. 231 and 232–3.

147 Mansfield, *British*, p. 237.

148 Wavell, *Allenby*, pp. 280–1.

149 Yusuf Sulayman, a Copt, was born in 1862. He was Chief Prosecutor (1890), judge (1906) and Minister first of Agriculture and then Finance (1922–23).

150 King, *Historical Dictionary*, p. 435.

151 See account in Cooper, *Old Men Forget*, pp. 104–6.

152 Gardner, *Allenby*, pp. 235–7.

153 Cooper, *Old Men Forget*, p. 105.

154 Gardner, Allenby, pp. 233–4.

155 Sir John Murray (1883–1937) served in the Egyptian Civil Service (1905), Foreign Office (1919–31), Rome and Mexico City. In connection with the fall of Muhammad Mahmud in 1929, he congratulated Loraine for 'changing horses in mid-stream without wetting your or our feet, accompanied ... by ... throwing our friends to the wolves (we have had heaps of practice at this)' (Terry, *Wafd*, p. 83).

156 Foreign Office minutes of first meeting, 13 July 1921 (SAD 470/12/8).

157 Terry, *Wafd*, pp. 138 and 159.

158 Mansfield, *British*, p. 239.

159 Letter, 17 October 1920, in Gardner, *Allenby*, p. 234.

160 Cooper, *Old Men Forget*, pp. 105–6: diary, 4 and 5 November 1921.

161 Kedourie, Elie, 'Sa'ad Zaghlul and the British' (St Antony's papers number 11, *Middle Eastern Affairs*, number 2, 1961), pp. 157–8.

162 Details in Lloyd, *Egypt* (1934), pp. 51 and 243.

163 Grafftey-Smith, *Bright Levant*, p. 82.

164 Lloyd, *Egypt* (1934), p. 243.

165 Kedourie, *Chatham House*, p. 151.

166 Mansfield, *British*, p. 240n.

167 Keown-Boyd, Henry, *The Lion and the Sphinx. The Rise and Fall of the British in Egypt, 1882–1956* (Spennymoor, Co. Durham: The Memoir Club, 2002), p. 132.

168 Terry, *Wafd*, p. 83.

169 Col. Richard Meinertzhagen (1878–1967) was a bloodthirsty soldier, fanatically anti-Arab and famous for the 'haversack ruse', which aided Allenby in his capture of Gazah, and for his wildlife collections, now regarded with suspicion.

170 Mansfield, *British*, p. 227.

171 Meinertzhagen, Richard, *Middle East Diary, 1917–56* (London: Cresset Press, 1959), pp. 33–4 (24 December 1921).

10 Treated very scurvily

1 Mansfield, Peter, *The British in Egypt* (London: Weidenfeld and Nicolson, 1971), p. 241.

2 Lloyd, Lord, *Egypt since Cromer* (London: Macmillan, Vol. II, 1934), p. 360.

3 Terry, Janice J., *The Wafd, 1919–1952* (London: Third World Centre, 1982), p. 206.

4 Further details in Lloyd, *Egypt* (1934), p. 56.

5 Kedourie, Elie, 'Sa'ad Zaghlul and the British' (St Antony's papers number 11, *Middle Eastern Affairs*, number 2, 1961), pp. 157–8.

6 Details in Badrawi, Malak, *Isma'il Sidqi (1875–1950): Pragmatism and Vision in Twentieth Century Egypt* (London: Curzon, 1996), p. 27.

7 Kedourie, 'Sa'ad Zaghlul', pp. 157–8, and *The Chatham House Version and other Middle-Eastern Studies* (London: Weidenfeld and Nicolson, 1970), p. 163.

8 Gardner, Brian, *Allenby* (London: Cassell, 1965), p. 240: FM Sir Henry Wilson unpublished diary, 25 January 1922.

9 Cooper, Duff, *Old Men Forget* (London: Rupert Hart-Davis, 1953), p. 107.

10 SAD 470/14/7–11.

11 Cooper, *Old Men Forget*, p. 107.

12 (Sir) Ernest Dowson, Acting Financial Adviser, was to spend many years in Iraq before returning to Egypt as Education Adviser in 1932.

13 Lloyd, *Egypt* (1934), p. 57.

14 Sir Walford Selby (1881–1965) was Assistant Private Secretary to Grey (1911–15), First Secretary in the Residency in Cairo (1919–22) and 'the principal negotiator of the 1922 Declaration' [Charmley, John, *Lord Lloyd and the Decline of the British Empire* (London: Weidenfeld and Nicolson, 1987), pp. 132–3]. He succeeded Vansittart as Curzon's press liaison with Lloyd George and became Private Secretary to Chamberlain, whom he accompanied to Locarno. He was Minister at Vienna (1933–37) – where 'he had no patience with Simon nor the methods of the Foreign Office and looked back constantly to the halcyon days of Austen Chamberlain' [Middlemass, Keith, and Barnes, John, *Baldwin* (London: Weidenfeld and Nicolson, 1969), p. 783] – and Ambassador to Portugal (1937–40).

15 Cooper, *Old Men Forget*, p. 107.

16 Ibid., p. 108.

17 Kedourie, *Chatham House*, p. 158.

18 Lloyd, *Egypt* (1934), p. 58 and Cooper, *Old Men Forget*, p. 108. See also Gilmour, David, *Curzon* (London: Papermac, 1995), p. 526 and Wavell, *Allenby*, pp. 296–305.

19 Terry, *Wafd*, p. 143.

20 SAD 470/14/2/3.

21 SAD 470/14/23/4.

22 See Lloyd, *Egypt* (1934), pp. 59–61 and Kedourie, *Chatham House*, p. 157.

23 Cooper, *Old Men Forget*, p. 108.

24 Gardner, *Allenby*, pp. 239–40.

25 Cooper, *Old Men Forget*, p. 108.

26 BA: Bell 2 February letter from Baghdad.

27 Cooper, *Old Men Forget*, p. 108.

28 SAD 470/14/25–53.

29 Cooper, *Old Men Forget*, p. 109.

30 Grafftey-Smith, Laurence, *Bright Levant* (London: John Murray, 1970), p. 83.

31 Gardner, *Allenby*, pp. 240–1: FM Sir Henry Wilson unpublished diary, 11 February 1922.

32 Ibid., p. 242: FM Sir Henry Wilson unpublished diary.

33 Details, Terry, *Wafd*, pp. 144–6.

34 Cooper, *Old Men Forget*, p. 110.

35 Ibid., and Gardner, *Allenby*, p. 243.

36 Mansfield, *British*, p. 252.

37 Details in Monroe, Elizabeth, *Britain's Moment in the Middle East, 1914–56* (London: Chatto and Windus, 1963), p. 69.

38 Kedourie, 'Sa'ad Zaghlul', p. 144.

39 Kedourie, *Chatham House*, p. 157.

40 Mansfield, Peter, *The Ottoman Empire and its Successors* (London: Macmillan, 1973), p. 62.

41 Keown-Boyd, Henry, *The Lion and the Sphinx. The Rise and Fall of the British in Egypt, 1882–1956* (Spennymoor, Co. Durham: The Memoir Club, 2002), p. 91.

42 Lloyd, *Egypt* (1934), pp. 63–4.
43 Toynbee, A. J., *Survey of International Affairs, 1925* (Oxford University Press, 1927), Vol. I, *The Islamic World since the Peace Settlement*, Part III, pp. 195, 197 and 230. The text of the Declaration is on pp. 194–5.
44 Mansfield, *Ottoman Empire*, p. 62.
45 King, Joan Wucher, *Historical Dictionary of Egypt* (Metuchen, NJ: Scarecrow Press, 1984), p. 609.
46 Toynbee, *Survey*, p. 231.
47 Kedourie, *Chatham House*, pp. 165–6.
48 Ibid., p. 165.
49 SAD 470/15/11.
50 King, *Historical Dictionary*, p. 609 and Toynbee, *Survey*, p. 196.
51 Nash'at Pasha's 'talents fitted him for the highest post' (Grafftey-Smith, *Bright Levant*, p. 102). He entered the Palace in 1921, rose to enjoy almost limitless authority and 'made himself a *persona grata* at the Residency, especially with all the Chancery and the Councillor acting in the absences of Allenby. He was naturally in the best position to render small services of every kind, arrange duck shoots, facilitate train journeys' [Beaman, A. A. H., *The Dethronement of the Khedive* (London: George Allen & Unwin, 1929), pp. 135–6]. He seems to have been exiled by the British in 1923 for his part in contemporary Wafd terrorist activities (Kedourie, *Chatham House*, p. 173). In 1924, as Under-Secretary for Awqaf, he promoted the idea of an Egyptian Caliphate (Ibid., p. 186) and arranged anti-Zaghlul and pro-Fu'ad demonstrations by Al Azhar students until Zaghlul, who had tried to have him retired that year [Badrawi, Malak, *Political Violence in Egypt, 1910–1924* (Richmond: Curzon, 2000), pp. 203 and 222], persuaded the King to downgrade him to be Head of his Cabinet (Terry, *Wafd*, p. 166). It was a common belief that, on behalf of the Palace and in order to do Zaghlul down, he had been behind the assassination of Stack (Badrawi, *Political Violence*, pp. 205 and 215. Details in Keown-Boyd, *Lion*, p. 121). After Spain, he was Egyptian ambassador in London.
52 Kedourie, *Chatham House*, p. 171.
53 Muhammad Tawfiq Nasim Pasha (1875–1938), an Anatolian, was a judge. A bomb meant for Stack was thrown at him in June 1920 (Terry, *Wafd*, p. 131). Chief of the Royal Cabinet in April 1922, he was a strong defender of Palace interests and associated with the founding of Hizb al Ittihad. Though not a particularly keen supporter of the nationalists [Badrawi, Malak, *Political Violence in Egypt, 1910–1924* (Richmond: Curzon, 2000), pp. 198 and 222], he was Minister of Finance in Zaghlul's government. He was 'widely and justifiably regarded as a British puppet' when he became Prime Minister again (Mansfield, *British*, p. 261) from November 1934 to January 1936; he reinstated the 1923 Constitution in December 1935.
54 Toynbee, *Survey*, p. 244.
55 Kedourie, *Chatham House*, p. 172.
56 Toynbee, *Survey*, pp. 201 and 202n.
57 FitzHerbert, Margaret, *The Man who was Greenmantle* (London: John Murray, 1983), p. 242.
58 Yahya Ibrahim Pasha (1861–1936) was a 'prominent judge and suspected royal courtier' [Vatikiotis, P. J., *The History of Egypt* (London: Weidenfeld and Nicolson, 1985), p. 276]. He was a member of the wartime Cabinet and became Minister of Justice in Wahbah's government and Minister of Education in 1922–23. After his resignation in January 1924, he became president of Hizb al Ittihad, was Minister of Finance (1925–26) and joined the 1934–35 campaign by Egypt's political parties to restore constitutional government (King, *Historical Dictionary*, pp. 345–6).

59 Toynbee, *Survey*, p. 203.
60 Lloyd, *Egypt* (1934), p. 75.
61 Some details of the draft are given in Kedourie, *Chatham House*, p. 168.
62 See ibid. p. 175 for differences between the consitution in draft and final forms.
63 For details, see Grafftey-Smith, *Bright Levant*, p. 124.
64 Petrie, Sir Charles, *The Life and Letters of The Right Hon. Sir Austen Chamberlain* (London: Cassell, Vol. 2 1940), pp. 336–7; Toynbee, *Survey*, p. 205. Mansfield, Peter, *Nasser's Egypt* (Harmondsworth: Penguin, 1965), p. 27, says that the King could appoint two-fifths of the Senators.
65 Mansfield, *Nasser*, p. 27. Details of the constitution are in Grafftey-Smith, *Bright Levant*, pp. 78–9.
66 Jarvis, Major C. S., *Desert and Delta* (London: John Murray, 1947), p. 74; Lloyd, *Egypt* (1934), p. 184; Charmley, *Lord Lloyd*, p. 135.
67 Mansfield, Peter, *The Ottoman Empire and its Successors* (London: Macmillan, 1973), p. 63.
68 Grafftey-Smith, *Bright Levant*, p. 28.
69 For details, see ibid., p. 124.
70 Lloyd, *Egypt* (1934), p. 77.
71 On the strength of his duck-shooting prowess, Jarvis, the author of a number of funny books on Egypt, was promoted from District Commander of the Khargah, Dakhlah, Bahariyyah and Farafrah Oases in the 1920s to be Sub-Governor of Sinai (Keown-Boyd, *Lion*, p. 55).
72 Jarvis, *Desert*, p. 51.
73 FO 371/220: Allenby letter to ?Ramsay MacDonald, 31 March 1924.
74 Gardner, *Allenby*, pp. 245–6.
75 Toynbee, *Survey*, pp. 206–7.
76 Grafftey-Smith, *Bright Levant*, p. 104.
77 Lloyd, *Egypt* (1934), p. 244.
78 7 April (FO 371/245).
79 7 April (FO 371/254).
80 FO 371/250.
81 16 April: Lloyd *Egypt* (1934), p. 86.
82 FO 371/341; Toynbee, *Survey*, p. 207.
83 12 May (FO 371/358).
84 Toynbee, *Survey*, p. 244.
85 Ibid., p. 245.
86 Ibid., p. 246.
87 FO 371/267.
88 FO 371/267/24424.
89 Waterfield, Gordon, *Professional Diplomat, Sir Percy Loraine* (London: John Murray, 1973), p. 176; Toynbee, *Survey*, p. 207.
90 Toynbee, *Survey*, p. 208.
91 Lloyd, *Egypt* (1934), p. 243.
92 Seth, Ronald, *Russell Pasha* (London: William Kimber, 1966), p. 155; Toynbee, *Survey*, p. 208.
93 MacDonald despatch, 7 October 1924, in Toynbee, *Survey*, p. 214.
94 Ibid., p. 250.
95 Mansfield, *British*, p. 250.
96 Grafftey-Smith, *Bright Levant*, p. 87. Full details of the assassination are in Keown-Boyd, *Lion*, pp. 99–101.
97 Badrawi, *Political Violence*, p. 204.
98 Mansfield, *British*, p. 250.
99 Russell Pasha, Sir Thomas, *Egyptian Service, 1902–1946* (London: John Murray, 1949), p. 220; Seth, *Russell*, p. 158.

100 Toynbee, *Survey*, p. 222.
101 Ibid., pp. 222–4.
102 Wingate, Bt., Sir Ronald, *Wingate of the Sudan* (London: John Murray, 1955), p. 251.
103 Toynbee, *Survey*, p. 197.
104 Petrie, *Life and Letters* (1940), p. 338 and Terry, pp. 170 and 178.
105 Brodrick, Alan Houghton, *Near to Greatness, a Life of Earl Winterton* (London: Hutchinson, 1965), p. 169.
106 Kedourie, *Chatham House*, p. 159.
107 Gardner, *Allenby*, p. 248.
108 Lloyd, *Egypt* (1934), pp. 143–4.
109 Warburg, Gabriel, 'The Sudan, Egypt and Britain, 1899–1916', *Middle Eastern Studies* 6, 2 (1970), p. 174.
110 Toynbee, *Survey*, p. 229.
111 Monroe, *Britain's Moment*, pp. 75–6.
112 Toynbee, *Survey*, p. 251.
113 Ibid., p. 264.
114 Mansfield, *British*, p. 250.
115 Grafftey-Smith, *Bright Levant*, p. 88.
116 Monroe, *Britain's Moment*, pp. 75–6.
117 BA: Bell letter, 23 December 1924, from Baghdad to her father.
118 Jarvis, *Desert*, p. 21.
119 Texts of both communications are in Toynbee, *Survey*, pp. 216–17.
120 Ibid., p. 251.
121 See Terry, *Wafd*, p. 171.
122 Grafftey-Smith, *Bright Levant*, p. 88.
123 Mansfield, *British*, p. 251.
124 FO 371/10044.
125 Petrie, *Life and Letters* (1940), p. 338.
126 Gardner, *Allenby*, p. 291.
127 Toynbee, *Survey*, p. 217.
128 Lloyd, *Egypt* (1934), p. 101.
129 Terry, *Wafd*, p. 172.
130 Shaarawi, Huda (tr. Margot Badran), *Harem Years: the memoirs of an Egyptian feminist* (Cairo: American University of Cairo, 1998), p. 131.
131 Terry, *Wafd*, p. 172 and Gardner, *Allenby*, p. 249.
132 Terry, *Wafd*, p. 172.
133 Toynbee, *Survey*, pp. 217–18.
134 Details in ibid., pp. 220–2.
135 Ibid., pp. 218–19.
136 Selma Botman in Daly, M. W. (ed.), *The Cambridge History of Egypt*, Vol. II (Cambridge University Press, 1998), p. 291; Mansfield, *British*, p. 251; Terry, *Wafd*, pp. 175–6 and Vatikiotis, *History*, p. 281. Details in Lloyd, *Egypt* (1934), p. 103.
137 Toynbee, *Survey*, p. 219n.
138 Ibid., p. 229.
139 Ibid., pp. 225–6.
140 Botman, in Daly, *Cambridge History*, p. 291.
141 Toynbee, *Survey*, p. 225.
142 Ibid., p. 251.
143 The second point of the ultimatum was met with the executions of 23 August 1925, the sixth with the formation in the same year of a British–Egyptian commission to work out a formula for the division of the waters of the Nile between Egypt and the Sudan (Mansfield, *British*, p. 258 and Lloyd, *Egypt*

(1934), p. 288) which reached final agreement in May 1929 (ibid., p. 289) when Egypt's share was fixed at nineteen-twentieths of the Sudan's (King, *Historical Dictionary*, p. 484).

144 Toynbee, *Survey*, p. 265.
145 Ibid., pp. 264–5: 26 January 1925.
146 Amery, L. S., *My Political Life*, II (London: Hutchinson, 1953), p. 305.
147 Wavell, Field-Marshal Viscount, *Allenby, Soldier and Statesman* (London: Harrap, 1944), pp. 345–6.
148 Ibid., pp. 343–4.
149 Carman, Barry, and McPherson, John, *The Man who Loved Egypt: Bimbashi McPherson* (London: Ariel Books/BBC, 1985), p. 248.
150 Gardner, *Allenby*, p. 251.
151 Petrie, *Life and Letters* (1940), pp. 339–40 and Terry, *Wafd*, p. 179.
152 Petrie, *Life and Letters* (1940), p. 340.
153 Gardner, *Allenby*, p. 251.
154 *DNB.*
155 Lloyd, *Egypt* (1934), p. 162 and Mansfield, *British*, p. 254.
156 Gardner, *Allenby*, p. 244.
157 Lloyd, *Egypt* (1934), p. 105.
158 Toynbee, *Survey*, p. 225. Cf. Mansfield, *British*, p. 251, who says that, 'demoralized . . . [it] won barely half the seats'.
159 Toynbee, *Survey*, p. 225. Cf. Mansfield, *British*, p. 251, who calls him President.
160 Grafftey-Smith, *Bright Levant*, p. 99.
161 FO 141/819.
162 Grafftey-Smith, *Bright Levant*, p. 90.
163 BA.
164 Mansfield, *British*, p. 252.
165 Gardner, *Allenby*, p. 244.
166 Ibid., p. 254.
167 Keown-Boyd, *Lion*, p. 82.
168 Mansfield, *British*, p. 227.
169 Ibid., p. 252.
170 Grafftey-Smith, *Bright Levant*, p. 66.
171 Ibid., pp. 90–1.

11 Arch-champion of British firmness

1 Marlowe, John, *Late Victorian, The Life of Sir Arnold Talbot Wilson* (London: Cresset Press, 1967), p. 149.
2 Mansfield, Peter, *The British in Egypt* (London: Weidenfeld and Nicolson, 1971), p. 252.
3 Marlowe, *Late Victorian*, p. 43.
4 According to Wingate, Lloyd spoke no Arabic but, when Sir Percy Cox suggested that he become the Arab Bureau's Basrah correspondent in 1915, 'I said at once that I was not a good enough Arabic scholar' and Bell took the job [Winstone H. V. F., *Gertrude Bell* (London: Constable, 1993), p. 180]. A later report by Jarvis – whose occasional (transliterated) Arabic does not suggest that he was much of a judge – rates Lloyd's as 'not in the same class as Sir Reginald Wingate's but it was quite good enough' [Jarvis, Major C. S., *Desert and Delta* (London: John Murray, 1947), p. 32. See also Westrate, Bruce, *The Arab Bureau: British Policy in the Middle East, 1916–20* (Philadelphia: Penn State University Press, 1992), p. 50.
5 Charmley, John, *Lord Lloyd and the Decline of the British Empire* (London: Weidenfeld and Nicolson, 1987), p. 121.

6 Monroe, Elizabeth, *Britain's Moment in the Middle East, 1914–56* (London: Chatto and Windus, 1963), p. 118.
7 Vansittart, Lord, *The Mist Procession* (London: Hutchinson, 1958), p. 327.
8 Ibid., p. 372.
9 Mansfield, *British*, p. 253.
10 Grafftey-Smith, Laurence, *Bright Levant* (London: John Murray, 1970), p. 51.
11 Vansittart, *Mist*, p. 372.
12 Amery, L. S., *My Political Life*, II (London: Hutchinson, 1953), p. 306.
13 Middlemass, Keith, and Barnes, John, *Baldwin* (London: Weidenfeld and Nicolson, 1969), p. 365.
14 In the House of Commons, 26 July 1929. [Lloyd, Lord, *Egypt since Cromer*, (London: Macmillan, Vol. II 1934), pp. 305–6].
15 Grafftey-Smith, *Bright Levant*, p. 102.
16 Of Sir Laurence Barton Grafftey-Smith (1892–1989), Lloyd said that he 'is almost a brilliant linguist, and has at any rate most of the qualities which would make him a really good Oriental Secretary' (Lloyd to Lindsay *Personal*, 17 March 1929, GLLD 13/7). His postings included Cairo (1925–35), Mosul (1935–37), Baghdad (1937–39), Tirana (1939) and Cairo again (1940–42). He became Minister to Sa'udi Arabia (1945) and High Commissioner to Pakistan (1947–51).
17 Goldschmidt, Arthur, *Historical Dictionary of Egypt* (Metuchen, New Jersey: Scarecrow Press, 199?), p. 172.
18 Charmley, *Lord Lloyd*, p. 11.
19 Aubrey Herbert (1880–1923) was the second son of the 4th Earl of Carnarvon, brother of the archaeological Lord Carnarvon and related to Mervyn Herbert. Pro-Turk and Albanian, he was Honorary Attaché also in Tokyo. Handicapped by very poor eyesight, he became Unionist MP for the Southern (1911–18) and Yeovil (1918–23) Divisions of Somerset.
20 Grafftey-Smith, *Bright Levant*, p. 180.
21 Sir Percy Cox (1864–1937) was Political Resident in the Gulf (1909–13), Government of India Foreign Secretary in succession to McMahon (1914), Chief Political Officer to Indian Army Expeditionary Force 'D' on the invasion of Mesopotamia (1914), Civil Commissioner, Baghdad (1917–18), Acting British Minister to Persia (1918–20) and High Commissioner to Iraq (1920–23).
22 Petrie, Sir Charles, *The Life and Letters of The Right Hon. Sir Austen Chamberlain* (London: Cassell, Vol. 1 1939), pp. 369–77.
23 BA: Bell letter from Cairo to her mother, 1 January 1916.
24 BA: Bell letter from Basrah, 8 May 1916.
25 Maj-Gen. Sir Charles Vere Ferrer Townshend (1861–1924), the foremost British military expert on the subject, had been besieged at Gilgit (1895), in addition to Kut, after which – unlike his troops – he spent the rest of the war luxuriously imprisoned in Turkey. He became Independent Conservative MP for the Wrekin in November 1920.
26 Lieut.-Gen. Sir Frederick Stanley Maude (1864–1917) was Tigris Corps Commander (July 1916), GOC the Army in Mesopotamia (August 1916) and the conqueror of Baghdad in March 1917. He died of cholera there in the November.
27 BA: Bell letter to her parents, 23 July 1916.
28 Storrs, Ronald, *Orientations* (London: Nicholson & Watson, 1943), p. 285.
29 The British co-operated with Brémond's mission from August 1916 [Wingate, Bt., Sir Ronald, *Wingate of the Sudan* (London: John Murray, 1955), p. 192].
30 Charmley, *Lord Lloyd*, p. 60.
31 12 May: Fitzherbert, Margaret, *The Man who was Greenmantle* (London: John Murray, 1983), p. 72.

32 Charmley, *Lord Lloyd*, p. 55.
33 Westrate, *Arab Bureau*, p. 154.
34 Charmley, *Lord Lloyd*, p. 65: Lloyd letter to Clayton, 30 September 1917.
35 Ibid., p. 75.
36 To Chelmsford, in ibid., p. 76.
37 Philby, H. St John B., *Arabian Days* (London: Robert Hale, 1948), pp. 49 and 105.
38 Charmley, 87: 18 July 1919.
39 Ibid., p. 114.

12 Rather severe language

1 BA: Letter from Bell in Baghdad to her father, 24 May 1925 [Bell used the term on several other occasions, e.g. *The Desert and the Sown* (London: Virago, 1985), p. 56].
2 Charmley, John, *Lord Lloyd and the Decline of the British Empire* (London: Weidenfeld and Nicolson, 1987), p. 118.
3 GLLD 13/3
4 Henderson to Lloyd, 21 May 1925 (GLLD 13/14).
5 To Henderson, 3 June 1925 (GLLD 13/14).
6 Henderson to Lloyd, 17 July 1925 (GLLD 13/14).
7 Henderson to Lloyd, 19 June 1925 (GLLD 13/14).
8 Henderson to Lloyd, 5 July 1925 (GLLD 13/14).
9 Henderson to Lloyd, 12 July 1925 (GLLD 13/14).
10 Henderson to Lloyd, 15 August 1925 (GLLD 13/14).
11 Henderson to Lloyd, 19 June 1925 (GLLD 13/14).
12 Henderson to Lloyd, 26 September 1925 (GLLD 13/14).
13 Henderson to Lloyd, 17 July 1925 (GLLD 13/14).
14 Lloyd, Lord, *Egypt since Cromer* (London: Macmillan, Vol. II 1934), p. 114.
15 Grafftey-Smith, Laurence, *Bright Levant* (London: John Murray, 1970), p. 99.
16 Ibid., p. 100.
17 Kedourie, Elie, *The Chatham House Version and other Middle-Eastern Studies* (London: Weidenfeld and Nicolson, 1970), pp. 185–6. Awqaf (sing. Waqf) are religious endowments.
18 Henderson to Lloyd, 15 August 1925 (GLLD 14/14).
19 Grafftey-Smith, *Bright Levant*, p. 100.
20 Beaman, A. A. H., *The Dethronement of the Khedive* (London: George Allen & Unwin, 1929), pp. 135–6.
21 Botman, in Daly M. W. (ed.), *The Cambridge History of Egypt*, Vol. II (Cambridge University Press, 1998), p. 287.
22 Lloyd, *Egypt* (1934), p. 151.
23 Ibid., p. 148.
24 Badrawi, Malak, *Political Violence in Egypt, 1910–1924* (Richmond: Curzon, 2000), p. 216.
25 Lloyd, *Egypt* (1934), p. 326.
26 16 December (GLLD 13/5).
27 Lloyd, *Egypt* (1934), p. 155.
28 See, e.g., an Austen Chamberlain letter of 2 November 1925, in Petrie, Sir Charles, *The Life and Letters of The Right Hon. Sir Austen Chamberlain* (London: Cassell, Vol. 2 1940), pp. 341–2.
29 6 January 1926 (GLLD 13/5).
30 To Lloyd (GLLD 13/3).
31 GLLD 13/5.
32 To Lloyd (GLLD 13/3).
33 Chamberlain to Lloyd (GLLD 13/3).

34 26 May (GLLD 13/5).
35 23 April and 2 May, Charmley, *Lord Lloyd*, p. 122.
36 Telegram, ibid.
37 On 23 August, seven of the eight men who were still accused of involvement in the assassination of Stack and had been sentenced to death, were executed. Their plot, in connection with which over 700 people were arrested, had in fact had no link with the Wafd [Seth, Ronald, *Russell Pasha* (London: William Kimber, 1966), p. 166].
38 Lloyd, *Egypt* (1934), p. 165.
39 Grafftey-Smith, *Bright Levant*, p. 102.
40 Details in Lloyd, *Egypt* (1934), pp. 166–7.
41 Ibid., p. 168.
42 GLLD 13/5.
43 Charmley, *Lord Lloyd*, pp. 124, 131.
44 Letter 6 June (Charmley, ibid., p. 131).
45 Private and Personal letter (GLLD 13/3).
46 Manuscript addition to a letter of 17 June 1926 to Lloyd (GLLD 13/7).
47 Lloyd, *Egypt* (1934), p. 169.
48 See ibid., pp. 177–8.
49 Ibid., pp. 186–7.
50 Ibid., pp. 179–80 and 191; FO 141/819.
51 Grafftey-Smith, *Bright Levant*, p. 104.
52 Charmley, *Lord Lloyd*, p. 132.
53 Grafftey-Smith, *Bright Levant*, p. 109.
54 Ibid., p. 105.
55 Charmley, *Lord Lloyd*, p. 133.
56 Grafftey-Smith, *Bright Levant*, p. 101.
57 Ibid., p. 106.
58 Ibid., p. 108.
59 Ibid., p. 109.
60 Memorandum, 20 October 1948, in Charmley, *Lord Lloyd*, p. 133.
61 GLLD 13/3.
62 GLLD 13/4.
63 20 February (GLLD 13/6).
64 The habit was widespread. At the end of June 1917, Chamberlain himself had been criticised by the Mesopotamia Commission Report 'for saying in "private" telegrams or letters what I ought to have said in public, i.e., formal, official despatches'.
65 25 January (GLLD 13/3).
66 To Lord Irwin, 2 March 1927, in Charmley, *Lord Lloyd*, p. 135.

13 A very serious misapprehension

1 On 26 July (Letter of 2 August, in Charmley, John, *Lord Lloyd and the Decline of the British Empire* (London: Weidenfeld and Nicolson, 1987), p. 133).
2 Charmley, *Lord Lloyd*, pp. 135–6; Lord Lloyd, *Egypt since Cromer* (London: Macmillan, Vol. II 1934), p. 202; and Mansfield, Peter, *The British in Egypt* (London: Weidenfeld and Nicolson, 1971), p. 255.
3 13 April 1927 (Terry, Janice J., *The Wafd, 1919–1952* (London: Third World Centre, 1982), p. 194).
4 Lloyd, *Egypt* (1934), pp. 205–7.
5 Keown-Boyd, Henry, *The Lion and the Sphinx. The Rise and Fall of the British in Egypt, 1882–1956* (Spennymoor, Co. Durham: The Memoir Club, 2002), p. 131.
6 Charmley, *Lord Lloyd*, p. 139.

7 21 April from Rome (GLLD 13/5).

8 Charmley, *Lord Lloyd*, p. 136.

9 Lloyd, *Egypt* (1934), p. 225.

10 Sir Robin Allason Furness (1883–1955). In the Egyptian Service from 1906, he was Oriental Secretary (1923–26) and remained in Egypt until 1950. Grafftey-Smith, his junior, described him as 'a remarkable and gifted man, . . . a major figure in the Residency for many years' until Lloyd did him down [Grafftey-Smith, Laurence, *Bright Levant* (London: John Murray, 1970), pp. 70 and 104].

11 1 April, 1927 (Charmley, *Lord Lloyd*, p. 136).

12 14/15 May (GLLD 13/6).

13 To Lloyd (GLLD 13/5). The Lloyd Papers contain only one more letter, of 27 November, from Lloyd to Tyrrell, who was transferred as Ambassador to France in 1928 and succeeded by Lindsay.

14 Lloyd, *Egypt* (1934), p. 208.

15 Charmley, *Lord Lloyd*, p. 137 and King, Joan Wucher, *Historical Dictionary of Egypt* (Metuchen, NJ: Scarecrow Press, 1984), p. 169.

16 Lloyd, *Egypt* (1934), p. 220.

17 Charmley, *Lord Lloyd*, p. 137.

18 Text in Lloyd, *Egypt* (1934), pp. 400–2.

19 Charmley, *Lord Lloyd*, p. 137.

20 Details in Lloyd, *Egypt* (1934), p. 209.

21 Details in ibid., pp. 219–21.

22 Ibid., p. 213.

23 Ibid., p. 214. For more details of his disagreement with Baldwin, see ibid., pp. 220–1.

24 Charmley, *Lord Lloyd*, p. 138.

25 Terry, *Wafd*, p. 195.

26 Charmley, *Lord Lloyd*, p. 138. Lloyd got his own back on Baldwin in 1931/2 by siding with Churchill against his India policy and in 1938 by attacking him for his alleged 'failure to rearm' [Middlemass, Keith, and Barnes, John, *Baldwin* (London: Weidenfeld and Nicolson, 1969), p.1047].

27 Lloyd, *Egypt*, p. 221.

28 Ibid., p. 215.

29 Ibid., p. 216.

30 Ibid., p. 222.

31 In Charmley, *Lord Lloyd*, p. 139.

32 Tyrrell to Chamberlain, in ibid.

33 19 June (ibid., p. 140).

34 GLLD 13/4: Lloyd letter to Chamberlain, undated but apparently 8 April 1928.

35 Leo Amery (1873–1955), assistant to Chirol at *The Times* in 1899, became – with Sykes – a political secretary to Lloyd George's Cabinet in 1916 and then Parliamentary Under-Secretary to Milner, Colonial Secretary (1919–21), First Lord of the Admiralty (1922), Colonial Secretary (1924–29), Secretary of State for Dominion Affairs (1925–29) and – after saying to Neville Chamberlain, 'In the name of God, go' in the famous Norway Debate of 7 May 1940 – Secretary of State for India under Churchill (1940–45). In the Debate, Keyes, Conservative MP for North Portsmouth since February 1934, 'the loyalest of men' [Cooper, Duff, *Old Men Forget* (London: Rupert Hart-Davis, 1953], p. 278) and 'a famously bad speaker', rose to the occasion to give conclusive support.

36 Diary of Leo Amery, 16 July 1927 (Self, Robert C. (ed.), *The Austen Chamberlain Diary Letters* (Cambridge University Press, 1995), p. 302.

37 9 and 25 July 1927 (GLLD 13/15).

38 Chamberlain to Lloyd, in Petrie, Sir Charles, *The Life and Letters of The Right Hon. Sir Austen Chamberlain* (London: Cassell, Vol. 2 1940), pp. 344–5.

39 Lloyd, *Egypt* (1934), p. 227.
40 Middlemass and Barnes, *Baldwin*, p. 365.
41 Lloyd, *Egypt* (1934), pp. 227–8.
42 Ibid., p. 244.
43 Chamberlain to Lloyd (Petrie, *Life and Letters* (1940), pp. 344–5).
44 Lloyd, *Egypt* (1934), pp. 228–9.
45 Charmley, *Lord Lloyd*, p. 142.
46 Henderson to Lloyd, 25 July 1927 (GLLD 13/15).
47 Lloyd, *Egypt* (1934), p. 230.
48 Charmley, *Lord Lloyd*, p. 142
49 5 August 1927 (GLLD 13/15).
50 Grafftey-Smith, *Bright Levant*, p. 106.
51 To Lloyd, 27 August 1927 (GLLD 13/15).
52 Dinshaway was the incident on 13 June 1906 when the insensitivity of a party of five British officer pigeon-shooters led by Major Pine-Coffin provoked a pitched battle at a village near Tantah which ended with one villager and one officer dead, four villagers injured and harsh sentences imposed. The villagers were made to watch them (one execution, four hangings and several whippings) carried out. (Of other alleged assailants, four were given life or shorter terms of imprisonment.) (King, *Historical Dictionary*, pp. 260–1). Dinshaway (details, Keown-Boyd, *Lion*, pp. 59–64) was claimed to have gained Mustafa Kamil a million followers and perhaps led to the assassination of Butrus Ghaly (1846–1910), who was Minister of Justice at the time and involved in the controversial trial (King, *Historical Dictionary*, pp. 217–18).
53 Lloyd to Henderson, 30 August 1927 (Charmley, *Lord Lloyd*, p. 144).
54 Henderson to Lloyd, 15 September 1927 (GLLD 13/15).
55 Henderson to Lloyd, 8 October 1927 (GLLD 13/15).
56 Mansfield, *British*, p. 257.
57 See, for example, Charmley, *Lord Lloyd*, p. 146.
58 Lloyd, *Egypt* (1934), pp. 233–4.
59 Ibid., pp. 234–5.
60 Letter, 6 November 1927 (Petrie, *Life and Letters* (1940), p. 347).
61 Lloyd, *Egypt* (1934), pp. 235 and 238.
62 Ibid., p. 245. The text is on pp. 259–67 and in Petrie, *Life and Letters* (1940), pp. 347–50.
63 Terry, *Wafd*, p. 214.
64 FO 371/13114.
65 Lloyd *Egypt* (1934), p. 256: Chamberlain to Lloyd, 5 February 1928.
66 Ibid. pp. 266–7.
67 Text in ibid., pp. 259–65.
68 Ibid., pp. 258–9.
69 Ibid., pp. 231 and 269.
70 To Lloyd, 25 July 1927 (GLLD 13/15).
71 12 December 1927 (Charmley, *Lord Lloyd*, p. 148).
72 Lloyd, *Egypt* (1934), p. 229.
73 Lloyd *Egypt* (1934), p. 233: 22 October.
74 Petrie, *Life and Letters* (1940), p. 351.

14 Something of a danger

1 To Chamberlain, 13 September 1927 [Charmley, John, *Lord Lloyd and the Decline of the British Empire* (London: Weidenfeld and Nicolson, 1987), pp. 144–5].
2 Charmley, *Lord Lloyd*, p. 145.

3 Self, Robert C. (ed.), *The Austen Chamberlain Diary Letters* (Cambridge University Press, 1995), p. 302.

4 4–22 October (Charmley, *Lord Lloyd*, p. 147).

5 Self, *Austen Chamberlain*, p. 318.

6 GLLD 13/3.

7 King, Joan Wucher, *Historical Dictionary of Egypt* (Metuchen, NJ: Scarecrow Press, 1984), p. 170.

8 Lloyd, Lord, *Egypt since Cromer* (London: Macmillan, Vol. II 1934), pp. 257 and 268.

9 GLLD 12/21.

10 Lloyd, *Egypt* (1934), pp. 271–2.

11 King, *Historical Dictionary*, p. 170.

12 2 May (Lloyd, *Egypt* (1934), pp. 272–3).

13 Lloyd, *Egypt* (1934), p. 273.

14 GLLD 12/9.

15 GLLD 13/3.

16 To Lloyd (GLLD 13/3).

17 Letter, 23 December 1928 (GLLD 13/7).

18 Kedourie, Elie, *The Chatham House Version and other Middle-Eastern Studies*, (London: Weidenfeld and Nicolson, 1970), p. 198.

19 Lloyd, *Egypt* (1934), p. 274.

20 Grafftey-Smith, Laurence, *Bright Levant* (London: John Murray, 1970), p. 107.

21 In love with his own sister, Princess Shevekiyar, in 1897 Ahmad Sayf ad Din lodged a bullet in the throat of the future King Fu'ad, his former brother-in-law who had divorced her, and bequeathed him an off-putting bark which spasmodically punctuated his speech and from the gangrene underlying which he eventually died. Prince Ahmad was sent to Britain in June 1900 and only escaped 30 years later, joining his sister, and her fifth husband, in Istanbul (Boyle, Clara, *Boyle of Cairo* (Kendal: Titus Wilson, 1965), pp. 39–40; Cromer, The Earl of, *Abbas II* (London: Macmillan, 1915), pp. 74–5. Grafftey-Smith, *Bright Levant*, p. 48, gives the length of his stay in Britain as 20 years).

22 King, *Historical Dictionary*, p. 170.

23 Lloyd, *Egypt* (1934), p. 278.

24 Ibid., p. 276.

25 Waterfield, Gordon, *Professional Diplomat, Sir Percy Loraine* (London: John Murray, 1973), p. 150.

26 To Lloyd in MS, 1 December 1928 (GLLD 13/7).

27 Jarvis, Major C. S., *Desert and Delta* (London: John Murray, 1947), p. 48. See also pp. 52 and 56.

28 Waterfield, *Loraine*, p. 147.

29 Private to Lindsay, 13 January 1929 (GLLD 13/7).

30 Lloyd to Lindsay, 7 April 1929 (GLLD 13/7).

31 Lloyd, *Egypt* (1934), pp. 276–7.

32 Letter, 13 December 1928 (GLLD 13/7).

33 Private letter, 13 January 1929 (GLLD 13/7).

34 Private letter, 21 April 1929 (GLLD 13/7).

35 In Petrie, Sir Charles, *The Life and Letters of The Right Hon. Sir Austen Chamberlain* (London: Cassell, Vol. 2 1940), pp. 359–60.

36 Telegram 173 to Chamberlain (GLLD 12/24).

37 Lloyd, *Egypt* (1934), pp. 298–9.

38 Cromer, *Abbas II*, p. xxii.

39 Lloyd, *Egypt* (1934), p. 293.

40 Details in ibid., pp. 293–6.

41 Charmley, *Lord Lloyd*, p. 157.
42 Mansfield, British, p. 259.
43 FO 371/5031/14060.
44 Waterfield, *Loraine*, pp. 170–3.
45 In Petrie, *Life and Letters* (1940), pp. 359–60.
46 Self, *Austen Chamberlain*, p. 332.
47 Charmley, *Lord Lloyd*, p. 159.
48 Details in ibid., pp. 159–61.
49 Ibid., p. 161.
50 Lloyd, *Egypt* (1934), pp. 306–7.
51 Charmley, *Lord Lloyd*, p. 161.
52 Ibid., p. 163.
53 Lloyd, *Egypt* (1934), pp. 305–6.
54 Ibid., p. 307.
55 Self, *Austen Chamberlain*, p. 340.
56 Jarvis, *Desert*, pp. 25–34.
57 Ibid., p. 31.
58 Charmley, *Lord Lloyd*, p. 168.
59 Wingate to Balfour, 26 September 1917 (FO 371/2928/193705). Details in Terry, *Wafd*, p. 216.

Postscript

1 'Abd an Nasir, Gamal, *Falsafat ath Thawrah* (Cairo: Ad Dar al Qawmiyyah li't Tiba'ah wa'n Nashr, n.d.), p. 10.
2 Letter to Wingate, 7 February 1917 (SAD 163/2/14).
3 25 March 1919 [Antonius, George, *The Arab Awakening* (Beirut: Khayats, n.d.), pp. 287–8; Wavell, Field-Marshal Viscount, *Allenby, Soldier and Statesman* (London: Harrap, 1944), p. 260].
4 Wingate, Bt., Sir Ronald, *Wingate of the Sudan* (London: John Murray, 1955), p. 254.
5 Wavell, *Allenby*, pp. 352–6; Gardner, Brian, *Allenby* (London: Cassell, 1965), pp. 255–63.
6 Wavell, *Allenby*, p. 350.
7 *DNB*.
8 Grafftey-Smith, Laurence, *Bright Levant* (London: John Murray, 1970), pp. 111–12.
9 Wavell, quoted in Keown-Boyd, Henry, *The Lion and the Sphinx. The Rise and Fall of the British in Egypt, 1882–1956* (Spennymoor, Co. Durham: The Memoir Club, 2002), p. 155.
10 Mansfield, Peter, *The British in Egypt* (London: Weidenfeld and Nicolson, 1971), p. 251.
11 Vansittart, Lord, *The Mist Procession* (London: Hutchinson, 1958), p. 383.
12 Vatikiotis, P. J., *The History of Egypt* (London: Weidenfeld and Nicolson, 1985), p. 285.
13 For details, see Waterfield, Gordon, *Professional Diplomat, Sir Percy Loraine* (London: John Murray, 1973), p. 154.
14 Mansfield, *British*, p. 260.
15 Jarvis, Major C. S., *Desert and Delta* (London: John Murray, 1947), p. 35.
16 Waterfield, *Loraine*, p. 187.
17 Vatikiotis, *History*, p. 289.
18 Loraine got on famously with Atatürk and then became Ambassador in Rome, perhaps being made a scapegoat by Churchill when Italy entered the Second World War (Grafftey-Smith, *Bright Levant*, p. 212).

19 Ibid., p. 125.
20 Waterfield, *Loraine*, p. 195.
21 Petrie, Sir Charles, *The Life and Letters of The Right Hon. Sir Austen Chamberlain* (London: Cassell, Vol. 2 1940), p. 364; Middlemass, Keith, and Barnes, John, *Baldwin* (London: Weidenfeld and Nicolson, 1969), p. 728.
22 Petrie, *Life and Letters* (1940), p. 286.
23 Mansfield, *British*, p. 265.
24 Vansittart, *Mist*, p. 407.
25 Symes, Sir Stewart, *Tour of Duty* (London: Collins,1946), p. 28.
26 Keown-Boyd, *Lion*, p. 136.
27 Grafftey-Smith, *Bright Levant*, p. 137.
28 King, Joan Wucher, *Historical Dictionary of Egypt* (Metuchen, NJ: Scarecrow Press, 1984), p. 529.
29 Mansfield, *British*, p. 265, where are details of the treaty.
30 Grafftey-Smith, *Bright Levant*, pp. 138, 232–3.
31 Terry, Janice J., *The Wafd, 1919–1952* (London: Third World Centre, 1982), p. 241.
32 Ibid., pp. 274–5; Vatikiotis, *History*, p. 292.
33 Jarvis, *Desert*, p. 67.
34 Geniesse, Jane Fletcher, *Freya Stark. Passionate Nomad* (London: Chatto & Windus, 1999), p. 246.
35 Mansfield, *British*, p. 272.
36 Grafftey-Smith, *Bright Levant*, p. 233–4.
37 Mansfield, *British*, p. 276.
38 Mansfield, Peter, *The Ottoman Empire and its Successors* (London: Macmillan, 1973), p. 99.
39 Ginat, Rani, 'The Egyptian Left and the roots of neutralism in the pre-Nasserite era', *British Journal of Middle-Eastern Studies* 30, 1 (2003), p. 10
40 Daly, M. W. (ed.), *The Cambridge History of Egypt*, Vol. II (Cambridge University Press, 1998), p. 304.
41 Ginat, 'Egyptian Left', p. 11.
42 26 January 1946 (Vatikiotis, *History*, pp. 358 and 360).
43 King, *Historical Dictionary*, p. 492.
44 See Vatikiotis, *History*, pp. 360–1.
45 Ginat, 'Egyptian Left', p. 11.
46 Mansfield, *British*, p. 285.
47 Mansfield, *Ottoman Empire*, p. 108.
48 Ginat, 'Egyptian Left', pp. 14–15.
49 King, *Historical Dictionary*, p. 492.
50 Kedourie, Elie, *The Chatham House Version and other Middle-Eastern Studies* (London: Weidenfeld and Nicolson, 1970), p. 216.
51 King, *Historical Dictionary*, pp. 492, 539.
52 Ginat, 'Egyptian Left', p. 22.
53 See Vatikiotis, *History*, pp. 368–70.

Appendix 1 Sa'ad Zaghlul (1858–1927)

1 Vatikiotis, P. J., *The History of Egypt* (London: Weidenfeld and Nicolson, 1985), p. 176.
2 Lloyd, Lord, *Egypt since Cromer* (London: Macmillan, Vol. I 1933), p. 50.
3 ZW.
4 Muhammad 'Abduh (1849–1905) collaborated with Al Afghani until he found himself unable to support his political activism. He was an energetic participant in the Legislative Council from 1899 until his death. His championing of

secular Egyptian nationalism, with Egypt a nation-state on the European model, inspired several of the early political parties [Long, Richard, *Tawfiq al Hakim, Playwright of Egypt* (London: Ithaca Press, 1979), p. 5; King, Joan Wucher, *Historical Dictionary of Egypt* (Metuchen, NJ: Scarecrow Press, 1984), pp. 100–1]. He advocated co-operation with the British and believed that Egypt would arrive at independence through their reforms; Cromer approved of him and his group [Kedourie, Elie, *The Chatham House Version and other Middle-Eastern Studies* (London: Weidenfeld and Nicolson, 1970), p. 84].

5 Jamal ad Din al Afghani (1838/9–97) was a Persian who lived in Egypt only from 1872 to 1879. His call for Pan-Islam and the revitalisation of the religion was the chief inspiration for its nationalism and for many of its early protagonists, especially Mustafa Kamil and his Hizb al Watan (King, *Historical Dictionary*, p. 109).

6 Hourani, Albert, *Arabic Thought in the Liberal Age, 1798–1939* (Oxford University Press, 1970), p. 214.

7 Badrawi, Malak, *Political Violence in Egypt, 1910–1924* (Richmond: Curzon, 2000), p. 69.

8 Lutfi as Sayyid (1872–1963) was a government lawyer, and 'the philosopher of Egyptian nationalism' [Grafftey-Smith, Laurence, *Bright Levant* (London: John Murray, 1970), p. 132]. He edited Hizb al Ummah's paper *Al Garidah* from 1907 to 1915 and then, in the latter year, became Director of the National Library. After Zaghlul's second deportation, he broke with him over his attitude to the 1921 'Adly ministry and resigned from the Wafd in 1922, co-founding Hizb al Ahrar ad Dusturiyyin. He helped to establish the Egyptian University in 1908 and was first its Professor of Philosophy and then its Rector (Long, *Tawfiq al Hakim*, pp. 11–12). He was Minister of Education in the governments of Muhammad Mahmud (1928–29 and 1938–39).

9 Vatikiotis, *History*, p. 247.

10 Wingate, Bt., Sir Ronald, *Wingate of the Sudan* (London: John Murray, 1955), p. 131.

11 Princess (later Queen) Nazly Sabry, a niece of Khedive Isma'il and first cousin of Khedive Tawfiq, was witty and 'extraordinarily beautiful in her youth'. A great champagne-drinker, she was married first to Halil Paşa, a Turk who had the reputation of being 'the most passionate and reckless gambler in Europe' [Boyle, Clara, *Boyle of Cairo* (Kendal: Titus Wilson, 1965), p. 41]; her second husband was King Fu'ad. Faruq was her son. An alleged nymphomaniac [Keown-Boyd, Henry, *The Lion and the Sphinx. The Rise and Fall of the British in Egypt, 1882–1956* (Spennymoor, Co. Durham: The Memoir Club, 2002), p. 137], it was rumoured that she also married Ahmad Hasanayn, the explorer who travelled with Rosita Forbes and was King Faruq's Chief Secretary who saved his throne for him on 4 February 1942 (Keown-Boyd, *Lion*, p.141). Boyle considered her 'one of the most brilliant women the Near East had produced' (Boyle, *Boyle*, pp. 41–2).

12 Mustafa Pasha Fahmy (1840–1914) was a Turco/Circassian-Egyptian aristocrat and loyal friend and collaborator of Cromer, who described him as 'a very honest and well-intentioned, but extremely weak, prime minister' [Mansfield, Peter, *The British in Egypt* (London: Weidenfeld and Nicolson, 1971), p.152]; others called him 'Cromer's puppet' for not being sufficiently active in resisting his interventions in government policy and being over-friendly towards him. The 'lukewarm foreign minister in the last Nationalist Government before the occupation' (ibid., p. 90), he was Prime Minister from 1891 to 1893 and 1895 to 1908. When he died, Egyptians said that he should have been buried 'wrapped in the Union Jack'. He was succeeded by the Copt, Butrus Ghaly (1846–1910), who mediated between the Khedive and the 'Uraby nationalists

and was Foreign Minister from 1894 until his assassination in 1910 by a Muslim, after he had supported the proposed extension of the Suez Canal Company's concession to 2008.

13 Goldschmidt, Arthur, *Historical Dictionary of Egypt* (Metuchen, New Jersey: Scarecrow Press, 199?), p. 58.

14 Details in Storrs, Ronald, *Orientations* (London: Nicholson & Watson, 1943), pp. 87ff.

15 Ibid., p. 89; Lloyd, *Egypt* (1933), p. 51.

16 Chirol, Sir Valentine, *The Egyptian Problem* (London: Macmillan, 1920), p. 112.

17 Vatikiotis, *History*, p. 300.

18 Storrs, *Orientations*, pp. 69 and 108.

19 Bowman, Humphrey E., *Middle Eastern Window* (London: Longmans, 1942), p. 75.

20 Hourani, *Arabic Thought*, p. 211.

21 In 1890, Baring gave Douglas Dunlop the job of organising Egypt's education service. In the light of the Consul-General's veto against 'adopting an educational policy so advanced as to necessitate the imposition of burdensome taxation' and his scepticism about the ability of education to bring about the 'transformation of the national character' [Cromer, Lord, *Abbas II* (London: Macmillan, 1915), pp. xxiii–xxiv], this was a difficult task. Dunlop rose to become, first, Secretary-General and then Adviser in the Ministry. He exercised 'harsh discipline and rigid uniformity' (Badrawi, *Political Violence*, p. 27) and was inflexible and insensitive to cross-cultural factors. '[A] man who was far too limited to impose his culture on any one' (Mansfield, *British*, p.149), he initially insisted that British teachers should know no Arabic (ibid., pp. 143 and 145). Bowman (*Window*, p. 48) said that Dunlop 'had laboured selflessly for twenty-five years or more . . . and retired . . . without any public recognition of his long and arduous service', but in general he has had a bad press. 'Although a few intimates claimed to have detected a warm heart in Dunlop, he appeared to most as cold, unimaginative and arrogant . . . imposing an absolute uniformity in curriculum and teaching methods throughout the country' (ibid., p. 143). Grafftey-Smith (*Bright Levant*, p. 29) thought the portly and bearded Dunlop 'Hardly less unpopular' than Brunyate, and Storrs named him as 'one, indeed the chief of the Big Four indirectly responsible for the Egyptian Revolution' (Introduction to Bowman, *Window*, p. xv, where he makes some generous comments about Dunlop).

22 Bowman, *Window*, p. 74; Storrs, *Orientations*, p. 47.

23 Storrs, *Orientations*, p. 108.

24 Ibid. (Introduction to Bowman, *Window*, p. xv).

25 Ibid., p. 47; Bowman, *Window*, p. 74; Carman, Barry, and McPherson, John, *The Man who Loved Egypt: Bimbashi McPherson* (London: Ariel Books/BBC, 1985), p. 74; Goldschmidt, *Historical Dictionary*, p. 99.

26 Mansfield, *British*, p. 195.

27 Beaman, A. A. H., *The Dethronement of the Khedive* (London: George Allen & Unwin, 1929), p. 114.

28 Badrawi, *Political Violence*, p. 43.

29 Storrs, *Orientations*, p. 108.

30 Kedourie, *Chatham House*, p. 85.

31 Lloyd, *Egypt* (1933), p. 102. An alternative version is that he resigned as Minister of Justice in 1913 over the conviction of Muhammad Farid [Toynbee, A. J., *Survey of International Affairs, 1925*. Vol. I, *The Islamic World since the Peace Settlement*, Part III (Oxford University Press, 1927), p. 645].

32 Mansfield, *British*, p. 200.

33 Lloyd, *Egypt* (1933), p. 86.

34 Graham minute to Wingate, 20 December 1917 (FO 371/2928/233706).
35 Chirol, *Egyptian Problem*, p. 274; Kedourie, *Chatham House*, p. 142.
36 Boyle, *Boyle*, p. 229.
37 Lloyd, *Egypt* (1933), p. 181.
38 Mansfield, *British*, p. 221.
39 Terry, Janice J., *The Wafd, 1919–1952* (London: Third World Centre, 1982), p. 46.
40 Ibid., p. 160.
41 Botman in Daly, M. W. (ed.), *The Cambridge History of Egypt*, Vol. II (Cambridge University Press, 1998), p. 293.
42 Grafftey-Smith, *Bright Levant*, p. 76.
43 Keown-Boyd, *Lion*, p. 132.
44 Mansfield, *British*, p. 210.
45 Grafftey-Smith, *Bright Levant*, p. 75.

Appendix 2 Egyptian personalities

1 King, Joan Wucher, *Historical Dictionary of Egypt* (Metuchen, NJ: Scarecrow Press, 1984), p. 106.
2 Terry, Janice J., *The Wafd, 1919–1952* (London: Third World Centre, 1982), p. 164.
3 Badrawi, Malak, *Political Violence in Egypt, 1910–1924* (Richmond: Curzon, 2000), p. 181.
4 Grafftey-Smith, Laurence, *Bright Levant* (London: John Murray, 1970), p. 130.
5 Symes, Sir Stewart, *Tour of Duty* (London: Collins, 1946), p. 27.
6 Grafftey-Smith, *Bright Levant*, p. 27.
7 Ibid., p. 28.
8 Kedourie, Elie, *The Chatham House Version and other Middle-Eastern Studies* (London: Weidenfeld and Nicolson, 1970), p. 170.
9 Ibid., p. 173.
10 Vatikiotis, P. J., *The History of Egypt* (London: Weidenfeld and Nicolson, 1985), p. 262.
11 Terry, *Wafd*, p. 148.
12 Goldschmidt, Arthur, *Historical Dictionary of Egypt* (Metuchen, New Jersey: Scarecrow Press, 199?), p. 81.
13 Grafftey-Smith, *Bright Levant*, p. 131.
14 Daly, M. W. (ed.), *The Cambridge History of Egypt*, Vol. II (Cambridge University Press, 1998), p. 322.
15 Grafftey-Smith, *Bright Levant*, p. 130.
16 Terry, *Wafd*, p. 75.
17 Toynbee, A. J., *Survey of International Affairs, 1925*. Vol. I, *The Islamic World since the Peace Settlement*, Part III (Oxford University Press, 1927), pp. 274–6.
18 5 September 1925 (ibid., p. 227).
19 King, *Historical Dictionary*, pp. 649–50.
20 Badrawi, *Political Violence*, p. 136.
21 Ibid., pp. 139, 142, 165 and 171.
22 Ibid., p. 145.
23 Ibid., pp. 146 and 151.
24 See the account in Grafftey-Smith, *Bright Levant*, p. 81.
25 Badrawi, *Political Violence*, pp. 151–62 and 168.
26 Ibid., p. 197.
27 Ibid., p. 218.
28 King, *Historical Dictionary*, p. 382.
29 Badrawi, *Political Violence*, p. 21.

30 Ibid., pp. 79–80.
31 Ibid., p. 85.
32 Ibid., pp. 85–6.
33 Ibid., p. 138.
34 Ibid., p. 99.
35 Ibid., p. 131.
36 Vatikiotis, *History*, p. 258; King, *Historical Dictionary*, pp. 285 and 480.
37 25 December 1914 (Badrawi, *Political Violence*, p. 117).
38 Ibid., p. 130.
39 Mansfield, Peter, *The British in Egypt* (London: Weidenfeld and Nicolson, 1971), p. 163.
40 Ibid., p. 164.
41 King, *Historical Dictionary*, p. 382.
42 Mansfield, *British*, p. 167.
43 King, *Historical Dictionary*, p. 382.
44 Mansfield, *British*, p. 163.
45 Ibid., p. 66.
46 King, *Historical Dictionary*, p. 383.
47 Long, Richard, *Tawfiq al Hakim, Playwright of Egypt* (London: Ithaca Press, 1979), pp. 4–6.
48 Goldschmidt, *Historical Dictionary*, p. 156.
49 Mansfield, *British*, p. 183.
50 Badrawi, *Political Violence*, pp. 21 and 69.
51 Grafftey-Smith, *Bright Levant*, p. 230.
52 Wingate, Bt., Sir Ronald, *Wingate of the Sudan* (London: John Murray, 1955), pp. 97–8.
53 Cromer, The Earl of, *Abbas II* (London: Macmillan, 1915), p. 50n. The full account of the episode is in pp. 50ff.
54 King, *Historical Dictionary*, p. 411.
55 Grafftey-Smith, *Bright Levant*, p. 230.
56 Kedourie, *Chatham House*, p. 117.
57 Badrawi, *Political Violence*, pp. 210 and 225.
58 Terry, *Wafd*, p. 177.
59 FO 141/493.
60 King, *Historical Dictionary*, p. 411.
61 Terry, *Wafd*, p. 242.
62 Mansfield, *British*, p. 282.
63 King, *Historical Dictionary*, p. 491.
64 Vatikiotis, *History*, p. 354.
65 Terry, *Wafd*, p. 291.
66 Ibid., p. 292.
67 Goldschmidt, *Historical Dictionary*, p. 175.
68 Grafftey-Smith, Bright Levant, pp. 230–1.
69 Terry, *Wafd*, p. 230.
70 Jarvis, Major C. S., *Desert and Delta* (London: John Murray, 1947), p. 66.
71 King, *Historical Dictionary*, p. 412.
72 Vatikiotis, *History*, p. 289.
73 King, *Historical Dictionary*, p. 413.
74 Mansfield, *British*, p. 262.
75 Vatikiotis, *History*, p. 292.
76 Grafftey-Smith, *Bright Levant*, pp. 232–3.
77 Mansfield, Peter, *Nasser's Egypt* (Harmondsworth: Penguin, 1965), p. 36.
78 Ibid., p. 29.
79 Ibid., p. 46.

80 King, *Historical Dictionary*, p. 413.
81 Lloyd, Lord, *Egypt since Cromer* (London: Macmillan, Vol. II 1934), pp. 175–6.
82 Ibid., p. 176.
83 Chirol, Sir Valentine, *The Egyptian Problem* (London: Macmillan, 1920), p. 149; Lloyd, *Egypt* (1933), p. 297.
84 Grafftey-Smith, *Bright Levant*, p. 130.
85 Terry, *Wafd*, pp. 83–4.
86 Lloyd, *Egypt* (1934), pp. 175–6.
87 Ibid., p. 283.
88 Grafftey-Smith, Bright Levant, p. 130.
89 Mansfield, *British*, p. 258n.
90 Waterfield, Gordon, *Professional Diplomat, Sir Percy Loraine* (London: John Murray, 1973), p. 150n.
91 Lloyd, *Egypt* (1934), p. 278.
92 Grafftey-Smith, Bright Levant, p. 130.
93 Terry, *Wafd*, p. 82; King, *Historical Dictionary*, p. 460; Badrawi, *Political Violence*, p. 165.
94 Vatikiotis, *History*, p. 262.
95 Terry, *Wafd*, p. 245.
96 Vatikiotis, *History*, p. 283.
97 Lloyd, *Egypt* (1934), p. 169.
98 Ibid., p. 258.
99 15 March 1928 (ibid., pp. 270–1).
100 King, *Historical Dictionary*, p. 460.
101 Ibid., pp. 460 and 491.
102 Mansfield, *British*, p. 258.
103 Vatikiotis, *History*, p. 292.
104 Details of this administration are in ibid., pp. 349–54.
105 King, *Historical Dictionary*, p. 617.
106 Terry, *Wafd*, p. 278.
107 Grafftey-Smith, *Bright Levant*, p. 129.
108 Goldschmidt, *Historical Dictionary*, p. 200.
109 Mansfield, *British*, p. 264.
110 Ibid., p. 257.
111 Keown-Boyd, Henry, *The Lion and the Sphinx. The Rise and Fall of the British in Egypt, 1882–1956* (Spennymoor, Co. Durham: The Memoir Club, 2002), p. 139.
112 Vatikiotis, *History*, p. 353.
113 Goldschmidt, *Historical Dictionary*, p. 200.
114 Grafftey-Smith, *Bright Levant*, p. 129.
115 Waterfield, *Loraine*, p. 176.
116 17 September 1929 at a Residency dinner (Waterfield, *Loraine*, p. 161).
117 Ibid., p. 174.
118 Terry, *Wafd*, p. 215.
119 Badrawi, *Political Violence*, p. 217.
120 Kedourie, *Chatham House*, p. 117; Badrawi, *Political Violence*, p. 227.
121 King, *Historical Dictionary*, p. 491.
122 Terry, *Wafd*, p. 220.
123 King, *Historical Dictionary*, p. 491.
124 Vatikiotis, *History*, p. 321; King, *Historical Dictionary*, p. 539.
125 King, *Historical Dictionary*, p. 491.
126 Goldschmidt, *Historical Dictionary*, p. 216.
127 Mansfield, *British*, p. 203.
128 Storrs, Ronald, *Orientations* (London: Nicholson & Watson, 1943), p. 89n.
129 Mansfield, *British*, p. 229.

130 Grafftey-Smith, *Bright Levant*, p. 27.
131 Badrawi, *Political Violence*, p. 32.
132 Mansfield, *British*, p. 203.
133 Badrawi, *Political Violence*, p. 118.
134 Ibid., p. 114.
135 Ibid., p. 118.
136 Ibid., p. 181.
137 King, *Historical Dictionary*, p. 539.
138 Badrawi, *Political Violence*, pp. 110–11.
139 Mansfield, *British*, p. 229.
140 Goldschmidt, *Historical Dictionary*, p. 252.
141 Badrawi, *Political Violence*, p. 170.
142 FO 141/786/17329/2.
143 Grafftey-Smith, *Bright Levant*, p. 133.
144 Ibid., p. 132.
145 Chirol, *Egyptian Problem*, p. 205.
146 ZW.
147 King, *Historical Dictionary*, p. 636.
148 Shaarawi, Huda (tr. Margot Badran), *Harem Years: the memoirs of an Egyptian feminist* (Cairo: American University of Cairo, 1998), p. 135.
149 Ibid., p. 131.
150 Ibid., p. 135.
151 Badrawi, *Political Violence*, p. 121.
152 Chirol, *Egyptian Problem*, p. 120.
153 Lloyd, Lord, *Egypt since Cromer* (London: Macmillan, Vol. I 1933), p. 297.
154 Grafftey-Smith, *Bright Levant*, p. 28; Terry, *Wafd*, p. 84.
155 Grafftey-Smith, *Bright Levant*, p. 132.
156 Joel Beinein in Daly, *Cambridge History*, p. 324.
157 Terry, *Wafd*, p. 116.
158 Lloyd, *Egypt* (1934), p. 112.
159 Ibid., p. 110.
160 5 and 25 July 1925 (GLLD 13/14).
161 26 September 1925 (GLLD 13/14).
162 King, *Historical Dictionary*, p. 573.
163 Lloyd, *Egypt* (1934), p. 186.
164 Ibid., p. 280.
165 Waterfield, *Loraine*, p. 191.
166 Mansfield, *British*, p. 261.
167 Grafftey-Smith, *Bright Levant*, p. 132.
168 Lloyd, *Egypt* (1934), p. 186.
169 Waterfield, *Loraine*, p. 191.
170 Loraine in a despatch to Simon, June 1932 (Waterfield, *Loraine*, p. 192).
171 Coury, Ralph M., 'The Arab Nationalism of Makram Ubayd', *Journal of Islamic Studies*, 6, 1 (January 1995), p. 77.
172 Mansfield, *British*, p. 264.
173 Coury, 'Makram Ubayd', p. 83.
174 Ibid., p. 77.
175 Terry, *Wafd*, p. 199.
176 Ibid., pp. 159 and 279.
177 Ibid., p. 167.
178 Ibid., p. 215.
179 Coury, 'Makram Ubayd', p. 87.
180 Terry, *Wafd*, p. 254.
181 Waterfield, *Loraine*, p. 174.

182 Coury, 'Makram Ubayd', p. 77.
183 Waterfield, *Loraine*, p. 190.
184 Jarvis, *Desert*, p. 67.
185 Mansfield, *Nasser's Egypt*, p. 31.
186 King, *Historical Dictionary*, p. 617.
187 Vatikiotis, *History*, pp. 351–2.
188 King, *Historical Dictionary*, p. 617, gives the month as July.
189 Ibid., p. 617.
190 Coury, 'Makram Ubayd', p. 79.
191 Vatikiotis, *History*, p. 154.
192 King, *Historical Dictionary*, pp. 162–3.
193 Ibid., p. 163.
194 Vatikiotis, *History*, p. 145.
195 King, *Historical Dictionary*, p. 163.
196 Ibid., p. 164.
197 Vatikiotis, *History*, p. 160.
198 Grafftey-Smith, *Bright Levant*, p. 99.
199 King, *Historical Dictionary*, pp. 649–50.
200 Lloyd, *Egypt* (1934), p. 109.
201 To Lloyd, 26 June 1925 (GLLD 13/14).
202 Grafftey-Smith, *Bright Levant*, p. 99.

Appendix 3 British personalities

1 Vatikiotis, P. J., *The History of Egypt* (London: Weidenfeld and Nicolson, 1985), p. 204.
2 Middlemass, Keith, and Barnes, John, *Baldwin* (London: Weidenfeld and Nicolson, 1969), p. 355.
3 *DNB.*
4 Symes, Sir Stewart, *Tour of Duty* (London: Collins, 1946), p. 37.
5 Vansittart, Lord, *The Mist Procession* (London: Hutchinson, 1958), p. 204.
6 Ibid., p. 261.
7 Mansfield, Peter, *The British in Egypt* (London: Weidenfeld and Nicolson, 1971), p. 60.
8 King, Joan Wucher, *Historical Dictionary of Egypt* (Metuchen, NJ: Scarecrow Press, 1984), p. 221.
9 Mansfield, *British*, p. 61.
10 To his mother, 8 May 1907 [Boyle, Clara, *Boyle of Cairo* (Kendal: Titus Wilson, 1965), p. 153].
11 Mansfield, *British*, p. 179.
12 Macmillan, Margaret, *Peacemakers. The Paris Conference of 1919 and Its Attempt to end War* (London: John Murray, 2001), p. 394.
13 Details are in Boyle, *Boyle*, p. 158.
14 Mansfield, *British*, p. 184.
15 To Rennell Rodd, 21 April 1907 (Boyle, *Boyle*, p. 150).
16 8 May 1907 (ibid., p, 153).
17 Vansittart, *Mist*, pp. 85–6.
18 Petrie, Sir Charles, *The Life and Letters of The Right Hon. Sir Austen Chamberlain* (London: Cassell, Vol. 2 1940), p. 247.
19 Vansittart, *Mist*, p. 233.
20 Dockrill, M. L. and Steiner, Zara, 'The Foreign Office at the Paris Peace Conference in 1919', *International History Review* 2, 1 (January 1980), p. 57.
21 Corp, Edward T., 'Sir Eyre Crowe and Georges Clemençeau at the Paris Peace Conference, 1919–20', *Diplomacy and Statecraft*, 8, 1 (1997), p. 237.

22 Ibid., p. 239.
23 Ibid., p. 244.
24 Dockrill and Steiner, 'Foreign Office', p. 60.
25 Ibid., p. 58.
26 Hardinge, Lord, *Old Diplomacy* (London: John Murray, 1947), p. 229.
27 Corp, 'Sir Eyre Crowe', p. 246.
28 Vatikiotis, *History*, p. 210.
29 Grafftey-Smith, Laurence, *Bright Levant* (London: John Murray, 1970), p. 100.
30 De Courcy, Anne, *The Viceroy's Daughters* (London: Phoenix, 2001), pp. 216–18, 224–5 and 318.
31 Vansittart, *History*, p. 360. Lord Birkenhead, *Halifax, the Life of Lord Halifax* (London: Hamish Hamilton, 1965), p. 358, however, states that Eden appointed him 'on the strong recommendation of Sir Robert Vansittart and the Foreign Office'.
32 Templewood, Viscount, *Nine Troubled Years* (London: Collins, 1954), p. 299.
33 Mansfield, *British*, p. 252.
34 Memoirs of Sir Anthony Eden, on a 'diplomatic disaster', in John Lucas: 'Our Man in Berlin – friend to the Nazis' (*Daily Telegraph*, 2 September 1999).
35 Eden, Sir Anthony, *Facing the Dictators* (London: Cassell, 1962), p. 504.
36 Birkenhead, *Halifax*, p. 358.
37 Templewood, *Nine Troubled Years*, p. 299.
38 Grafftey-Smith, *Bright Levant*, p. 4.
39 Templewood, *Nine Troubled Years*, p. 299.
40 7 September 1917 (SAD 236/7/66).
41 Kedourie, Elie, *The Chatham House Version and other Middle-Eastern Studies* (London: Weidenfeld and Nicolson, 1970), p. 145.
42 Toynbee, A. J., *Survey of International Affairs, 1925*, Vol. I, *The Islamic World since the Peace Settlement*, Part III (Oxford University Press, 1927), pp. 526–7.
43 Waterfield, Gordon, *Professional Diplomat, Sir Percy Loraine* (London: John Murray, 1973), p. 155.
44 *DNB*.
45 Daly, M. W., *The Sirdar: Sir Reginald Wingate and the British Empire in the Middle East* (Philadelphia: American Philosophical Society, 1997), p. 142.
46 Morris, James, *Pax Britannica* (London: The Folio Society, 1992), Vol. 3, pp. 196 and 198.
47 Bowman, Humphrey E., *Middle Eastern Window* (London: Longmans, 1942), p. 157.
48 Ibid., pp. 156–8.
49 Liddell Hart, B. L., *History of the First World War* (London: Book Club Associates, 1973), pp. 59 and 93.
50 Mansfield, *British*, p. 213.
51 *DNB*.
52 George, Lloyd, *War Memoirs* (London: Odhams, 1938), pp. 1922–3.
53 5 April 1917 [Mejcher, Helmut, *Imperial Quest for Oil: Iraq 1910–1928* (London: Ithaca Press, 1976), pp. 23 and 43n].
54 Hughes, Matthew, *Allenby and British Strategy in the Middle East, 1917–1919* (London: Frank Cass, 1999), p. 14, quoting Meinertzhagen.
55 Mansfield, *British*, p. 193.
56 Grafftey-Smith, *Bright Levant*, p. 23.
57 De Courcy, *Viceroy's Daughters*, p. 78
58 *DNB*; Morris, *Pax Britannica*, Vol. 3, p. 329.
59 Vansittart, *Mist*, pp. 89–90.
60 Ibid., pp. 430–1.
61 Lawrence, T. E., *Seven Pillars of Wisdom* (London: Cape, 1935), p. 57.

62 Private information.
63 Morris, *Pax Britannica*, Vol. 3, p. 326.
64 Asher, Michael, *Lawrence, the Uncrowned King of Arabia* (London: Viking, 1998), p. 126.
65 Bullard, Sir Reader, *The Camels Must Go* (London: Faber, 1961), p. 193.
66 Bentwich, Norman and Helen, *Mandate Memories, 1918–48* (London: Hogarth Press, 1965), p. 13.
67 Antonius, George, *The Arab Awakening* (Beirut: Khayats, n.d.), p. 250.
68 Grey of Fallodon, Viscount, *Twenty-five Years, 1892–1916* (London: Hodder & Stoughton, 1928), Vol 1, p. 27.
69 Corp, 'Sir Eyre Crowe', p. 241.
70 Vansittart, *Mist*, p. 194.
71 Middlemass, *Baldwin*, pp. 720, 820 and 860.
72 Vansittart, *Mist*, p. 45.
73 *DNB*.
74 *DNB*, quoting Sir Lewis Namier, *Avenues of History* (1952).
75 Birkenhead, *Halifax*, p. 376.
76 Ibid., p. 422.
77 Waterfield, *Loraine*, p. 225.
78 Birkenhead, *Halifax*, p. 376.

Appendix 4 Egyptian political parties, in order of founding

1 Long, Richard, *Tawfiq al Hakim, Playwright of Egypt* (London: Ithaca Press, 1979), pp. 2 and 3.
2 Vatikiotis, P. J., *The Modern History of Egypt* (London: Weidenfeld and Nicolson, 1969), p. 220.
3 Long, *Tawfiq al Hakim*, pp. 5, 7. Vatikiotis, *Modern History*, who calls it 'The People's Party' (p. 205), gives the date of its foundation as March/April, 1907.
4 Goldschmidt, Arthur, *Historical Dictionary of Egypt* (Metuchen, New Jersey: Scarecrow Press, 199?), p. 287.
5 King, *Historical Dictionary*, pp. 621–2; Long, *Tawfiq al Hakim*, pp. 2, 5 and 7.
6 Long, *Tawfiq al Hakim*, pp. 2 and 4–5.
7 Goldschmidt, *Historical Dictionary*, p. 20.
8 Vatikiotis, *Modern History*, pp. 212–14, who conflates Watani and Watan.
9 Ibid., p. 218.
10 King, *Historical Dictionary*, p. 479. *Al Liwa*', antagonistic towards *Al Muqattam*, had *Al Akhbar* as a rival mouthpiece (Vatikiotis, *Modern History*, pp. 216, 301
11 Ibid., p. 481.
12 Vatikiotis, *Modern History*, p. 248.
13 Goldschmidt, *Historical Dictionary*, p. 188.
14 King, *Historical Dictionary*, pp. 69 and 240.
15 Toynbee, A. J., *Survey of International Affairs, 1925*. Vol. 1, *The Islamic World Since the Peace Settlement*, Part III (Oxford University Press, 1927), p. 194.
16 Badrawi, Malak, *Political Violence in Egypt, 1910–1924* (Richmond: Curzon, 2000), p. 160.
17 Ibid., p. 151.
18 August 1921, according to Toynbee, *Survey*, p. 194.
19 Goldschmidt, *Historical Dictionary*, p. 81.
20 Terry, Janice J., *The Wafd, 1919–1952*. (London: Third World Centre, 1982), pp. 149–50.
21 Daly, M. W. (ed.), *The Cambridge History of Egypt*, Vol. II (Cambridge University Press, 1998), p. 289.
22 Vatikiotis, P. J., *Modern History*, p. 274.

23 Goldschmidt, *Historical Dictionary*, p. 268.
24 King, *Historical Dictionary*, pp. 402–3.
25 Goldschmidt, *Historical Dictionary*, p. 81.
26 Vatikiotis, *Modern History*, p. 477.
27 Grafftey-Smith, *Bright Levant*, p. 124, calls Hizb ash Sha'b 'The People's Party of Reform'.
28 Daly, *Cambridge History*, p. 282; King, *Historical Dictionary*, p. 539.
29 Daly, *Cambridge History*, p. 289.
30 Goldschmidt, *Historical Dictionary*, p. 251.
31 Ibid., pp. 327–30, 375.

Bibliography

Manuscript collections

Foreign Office files, Public Record Office
Clayton Papers, Sudan Archive, Durham University
Hardinge Papers, University Library, Cambridge
Lloyd Papers, Churchill College, Cambridge
Arnold Wilson Papers, British Library
Wingate Papers, Sudan Archive, Durham University

Contemporary sources

Amery, L. S., *My Political Life*, II (London: Hutchinson, 1953).

Beaman, A. A. H., *The Dethronement of the Khedive* (London: George Allen & Unwin, 1929).

Bowman, Humphrey E., *Middle Eastern Window* (London: Longmans, 1942).

Cecil, Edward, *The Leisure of an Egyptian Official* (Cairo: Parkway Publishing, 1996).

Chirol, Sir Valentine, *The Egyptian Problem* (London: Macmillan, 1920).

Cooper, Duff, *Old Men Forget* (London: Rupert Hart-Davis, 1953).

Fahmy, 'Abd ar Rahman, *Yawmiyyat Misr as Siyasiyyah: Mudhakkirat*, Vol. 1 (Cairo: Markaz Watha'iq wa Ta'rikh Misr al Mu'asir, 1988).

Grafftey-Smith, Laurence, *Bright Levant* (London: John Murray, 1970).

Grey of Fallodon, Viscount, *Twenty-five Years, 1892–1916* (London: Hodder & Stoughton, 1928).

Hardinge, Lord, *Old Diplomacy* (London: John Murray, 1947).

Jarvis, Major C. S., *Desert and Delta* (London: John Murray, 1947).

Lawrence, T. E., *Seven Pillars of Wisdom* (London: Cape, 1935); *Revolt in the Desert* (London: The Folio Society, 1986).

Lloyd, Lord, *Egypt since Cromer* (London: Macmillan, Vol. I 1933, Vol. II 1934).

Meinertzhagen, Richard, *Middle East Diary, 1917–56* (London: Cresset Press, 1959).

Milner, Alfred, *England in Egypt* (London: Edward Arnold, 1894).

Repington, Lt.-Col. C. à Court, *The First World War, 1914–1918: Personal Experiences Of* (Aldershot: Grey Revivals, 1991).

Russell Pasha, Sir Thomas, *Egyptian Service, 1902–1946* (London: John Murray, 1949).

As Sayyid, Lutfy, *Qisat Hayati* (Cairo, 1962).

Shaarawi, Huda (tr. Margot Badran), *Harem Years: the memoirs of an Egyptian feminist* (Cairo: American University of Cairo, 1998).

Storrs, Ronald, *Orientations* (London: Nicholson & Watson, 1943).

Symes, Sir Stewart, *Tour of Duty* (London: Collins, 1946).

Vansittart, Lord, *The Mist Procession* (London: Hutchinson, 1958).

Wilson, Lt.-Col. Sir Arnold T., *Loyalties, Mesopotamia, 1914–1917* (New York: Greenwood Press, 1969).

Zaghlul, Sa'ad, *Mudhakkirat*, Vols 1–6 (Cairo: Markaz Watha'iq wa Ta'rikh Misr al Mu'asir, 1987–93).

Secondary sources

'Abd an Nasir, Gamal, *Falsafat ath Thawrah* (Cairo: Ad Dar al Qawmiyyah li't Tiba'ah wa'n Nashr, n.d.).

Adam, C. F., *The Life of Lord Lloyd* (London: Macmillan, 1948).

Adams, R. J. Q., *Bonar Law* (London: John Murray, 1999).

Adelson, Roger, *Mark Sykes, Portrait of an Amateur* (London: Cape, 1975).

Ahmad, Jamal Muhammad, *The Intellectual Origins of Arab Nationalism* (Oxford University Press, 1960).

Antonius, George, *The Arab Awakening* (Beirut: Khayats, n.d.).

Badrawi, Malak, *Isma'il Sidqi (1875–1950): Pragmatism and vision in Twentieth Century Egypt* (London: Curzon, 1996); *Political Violence in Egypt, 1910–1924* (Richmond: Curzon, 2000).

Beachey, Ray, *The Warrior Mullah* (London: Bellew, 1991).

Bentwich, Norman and Helen, *Mandate Memories, 1918–48)* (London: Hogarth Press, 1965).

Birkenhead, Lord, *Halifax, the Life of Lord Halifax* (London: Hamish Hamilton, 1965); *Rudyard Kipling* (London: Weidenfeld & Nicolson, 1978).

Blythe, Ronald, *The Age of Illusion: England in the Twenties and Thirties, 1919–40* (Harmondsworth: Penguin, 1964).

Botman, Selma, *Egypt from Independence to Revolution, 1919–52* (Syracuse University Press, ?1991).

Boyle, Clara, *Boyle of Cairo* (Kendal: Titus Wilson, 1965).

Brodrick, Alan Houghton, *Near to Greatness, a Life of Earl Winterton* (London: Hutchinson, 1965).

Bullard, Sir Reader, *The Camels Must Go* (London: Faber, 1961).

Butt, Gerald, *The Lion in the Sand* (London: Bloomsbury, 1995).

Carman, Barry, and McPherson, John, *The Man who Loved Egypt: Bimbashi McPherson* (London: Ariel Books/BBC, 1985).

Charmley, John, *Lord Lloyd and the Decline of the British Empire* (London: Weidenfeld and Nicolson, 1987).

Collins, Robert O. (ed.), *An Arabian Diary, Sir Gilbert Falkingham Clayton* (Berkeley and Los Angeles: University of California Press, 1969).

Cooper, Duff, *Haig*, Vol. 1 (London: Faber and Faber, 1935).

Cowper, Col. J. M., *The King's Own: the Story of a Royal Regiment* (Aldershot: Gale & Polden, 1957).

Cromer, The Earl of, *Abbas II* (London: Macmillan, 1915).

Daly, M. W., *The Sirdar: Sir Reginald Wingate and the British Empire in the Middle East*

(Philadelphia: American Philosophical Society, 1997); (ed.), *The Cambridge History of Egypt*, Vol. II (Cambridge University Press, 1998).

Darwin, J., *Britain, Egypt and the Middle East: Imperial Policy in the Aftermath of War, 1918–1922* (London: Macmillan, 1981).

De Courcy, Anne, *The Viceroy's Daughters* (London: Phoenix, 2001).

Dictionary of National Biography.

Fitzherbert, Margaret, *The Man who was Greenmantle* (London: John Murray, 1983).

Gardner, Brian, *Allenby* (London: Cassell, 1965).

Gilbert, Martin, *Churchill, A Life* (London: Heinemann, 1991).

Gilmour, David, *Curzon* (London: Papermac, 1995).

Goldschmidt, Arthur, *Historical Dictionary of Egypt* (Metuchen, New Jersey: Scarecrow Press, 199?).

Goldsmith, Arthur jnr., *The Memoirs and Diaries of Muhammad Farid, an Egyptian Nationalist Leader (1868–1919)* (San Francisco: Mellen University Research Press, 1997).

Graves, Philip, *The Life of Sir Percy Cox* (London: Hutchinson & Co., 1941).

Haim, Sylvia (ed.), *Arab Nationalism, an Anthology* (Berkeley: University of California Press, 1962).

Haythornthwaite, P. J., *The World War One Source Book, Arms and Armaments* (London: Arms and Armour Press, 1999).

Hill, Richard, *Slatin Pasha* (Oxford University Press, 1965).

Holt, P. M., *The Mahdist State in the Sudan* (Oxford University Press, 1970).

Hourani, Albert, *Arabic thought in the Liberal Age, 1798–1939* (Oxford University Press, 1970).

Hughes, Matthew, *Allenby and British Strategy in the Middle East, 1917–1919* (London: Frank Cass, 1999).

Jackson, H. C., *Pastor on the Nile* (London, 1960).

James, Lawrence, *Imperial Warrior, the Life and Times of Field Marshal Viscount Allenby, 1861–1936* (London: Weidenfeld and Nicolson, 1993).

Judd, Denis, *Balfour and the British Empire* (London: Macmillan, 1968).

Kedourie, Elie, *The Chatham House Version and other Middle-Eastern Studies* (London: Weidenfeld and Nicolson, 1970).

Keown-Boyd, Henry, *The Lion and the Sphinx. The Rise and Fall of the British in Egypt, 1882–1956* (Spennymoor, Co. Durham: The Memoir Club, 2002).

King, Joan Wucher, *Historical Dictionary of Egypt* (Metuchen, New Jersey: Scarecrow Press, 1984).

Liddell Hart, B. L., *History of the First World War* (London: Book Club Associates, 1973).

Lockman, J. N., *Meinertzhagen's Diary Ruse. False Entries on T. E. Lawrence* (Grand Rapids, Michigan: Cornerstone, 1995).

Long, Richard, *Tawfiq al Hakim, Playwright of Egypt* (London: Ithaca Press, 1979).

Lord, John, *Duty, Honour, Empire: the life and times of Col. Richard Meinertzhagen* (London: Hutchinson 1971).

Lukitz, Liora, *Iraq: the Search for National Identity* (London: Frank Cass, 1995).

Macbride, Barrie Sinclair, *Farouk of Egypt* (London: Robert Hale, 1967).

Macmillan, Margaret, *Peacemakers. The Paris Conference of 1919 and Its Attempt to end War* (London: John Murray, 2001).

Mansfield, Peter, *Nasser's Egypt* (Harmondsworth: Penguin, 1965); *The British in*

Egypt (London: Weidenfeld and Nicolson, 1971); *The Ottoman Empire and its Successors* (London: Macmillan, 1973).

Marlowe, John, *Late Victorian, The Life of Sir Arnold Talbot Wilson* (London: Cresset Press, 1967).

Mehra, Parshotam, *The McMahon Line and After* (London: Macmillan, 1974).

Mejcher, Helmut, *Imperial Quest for Oil: Iraq 1910–1928* (London: Ithaca Press, 1976).

Middlemass, Keith, and Barnes, John, *Baldwin* (London: Weidenfeld and Nicolson, 1969).

Monroe, Elizabeth, *Britain's Moment in the Middle East, 1914–56* (London: Chatto and Windus, 1963).

Morris, James, *Pax Britannica*, Vols 1, 2 and 3 (London: The Folio Society, 1992).

Petrie, Sir Charles, *The Life and Letters of The Right Hon. Sir Austen Chamberlain* (London: Cassell, Vol. 1 1939, Vol. 2 1940).

Philby, H. St John B., *Arabian Days* (London: Robert Hale, 1948).

Presland, John, *Deedes Bey: a Study of Sir Wyndham Deedes, 1883–1923* (London: Macmillan, 1942).

Roberts, Andrew, *Salisbury, Victorian Titan* (London: Weidenfeld and Nicolson, 1999).

Rodd, James Rennell, *Social and Diplomatic Memories, Third Series, 1902–1919* (London: Edward Arnold, 1925).

Rose, Kenneth, *The Later Cecils* (London: Weidenfeld and Nicolson, 1975); *King George V* (London: Phoenix, 2000).

Saad ad Din, Mursi, and Cromer, John, *Under Egypt's Spell* (London: Bellew, 1991).

Sachar, Howard M., *The Emergence of the Middle East, 1914–24* (London: Allen Lane the Penguin Press, 1970).

Sattin, Anthony, *Lifting the Veil: British Society in Egypt, 1768–1956* (London: Dent, 1988).

Self, Robert C. (ed.), *The Austen Chamberlain Diary Letters* (Cambridge University Press, 1995).

Seth, Ronald, *Russell Pasha* (London: William Kimber, 1966).

Sonbol, Amaira (ed.), *The Last Khedive of Egypt: Memoirs of 'Abbas Hilmi II* (Reading: Ithaca Press, 1991).

Sykes, Christopher, *Crossroads to Israel* (London: Collins, 1965).

Templewood, Viscount, *Nine Troubled Years* (London: Collins, 1954).

Terry, Janice J., *The Wafd, 1919–1952* (London: Third World Centre, 1982).

Tignor, Robert L., *The Egyptian revolution of 1919: new directions in the Egyptian economy. Modernization and British colonial rule in Egypt, 1882–1914* (Princeton University Press, 1966).

Toynbee, A. J., *Survey of International Affairs, 1925*, Vol I, *The Islamic World since the Peace Settlement*, Part III (Oxford University Press, 1927).

Turner, John, *Lloyd George's Secretariat* (Cambridge University Press, 1980).

Vatikiotis, P. J., *The Modern History of Egypt* (London: Weidenfeld and Nicolson, 1985).

Vatikiotis, P. J., *The History of Egypt* (London: Weidenfeld and Nicolson, 1985).

Waterfield, Gordon, *Professional Diplomat, Sir Percy Loraine* (London: John Murray, 1973).

Wavell, Field-Marshal Viscount, *Allenby, Soldier and Statesman* (London: Harrap, 1944).

Westrate, Bruce, *The Arab Bureau: British Policy in the Middle East, 1916–20* (Philadelphia: Penn State University Press, University Park, Pennsylvania, 1992).

Who was Who?

Wingate, Bt., Sir Ronald, *Wingate of the Sudan* (London: John Murray, 1955); *Not in the Limelight* (London: Hutchinson, 1959).

Winstone, H. V. F., *Gertrude Bell* (New York: Quartet, 1978) (London: Constable, revised edition, 1993); *The Illicit Adventure* (London: Jonathan Cape, 1982); *Woolley of Ur* (London: Secker & Warburg, 1990).

Internet sites

Bell Archive: Gertrude Bell letters and diaries

Zaghlul Website: http://www.us.sis.gov.eg/calendar/html/cl 230897.htm and 23086b.htm

Thesis

Terry, Janice J., *Sir Reginald Wingate as high commissioner in Egypt, 1917–1919* (London University PhD, 1968).

Dissertation

Coventry, Donald C., *The Public Career of Sir Frederick [sic] Reginald Wingate, High Commissioner for Egypt, 1917–19*, DAI 1990 51(5) 1730-A DA9027884.

Articles

el-Amin, M.H., 'International communism, the Egyptian Wafd Party and the Sudan', *BRISMES Bulletin* 16, 1 (1989), pp. 27–48.

Bishku, Michael B., 'The British Press and the future of Egypt, 1919–1922', *International History Review* (Canada), 8, 4 (1986), pp. 604–9.

Cobb, Lt.-Col E. H., 'A Frontier Statesman', *The Piffer* (London) V, 6 (May 1963).

Corp, Edward T., 'The Problem of Promotion in the Career of Sir Eyre Crowe, 1905–20', *Australian Journal of Politics and History*, 28, 2 (1982), pp. 236–49; 'Sir Eyre Crowe and Georges Clemençeau at the Paris Peace Conference, 1919–20', *Diplomacy and Statecraft*, 8, 1 (1997), pp. 10–19.

Coury, Ralph M., 'The Arab Nationalism of Makram Ubayd', *Journal of Islamic Studies*, 6, 1 (January 1995), pp. 76–90.

Daly, M. W., 'The Egyptian Army Mutiny at Omdurman, Jan.–Feb. 1900', *BRISMES Bulletin* 8, 1 (1981), pp. 3–12.

Dockrill, M. L. and Steiner, Zara, 'The Foreign Office at the Paris Peace Conference in 1919', *International History Review* 2, 1 (January 1980), pp. 55–86.

Fitzgerald, Edward P., 'France's Middle Eastern Ambitions, the Sykes–Picot Negotiations and the Oilfields of Mosul, 1915–18', *The Journal of Modern History* (Chicago) 66, 4 (1994), pp. 697–725.

Ginat, Rami, 'The Egyptian Left and the Roots of Neutralism in the Pre-Nasserite Era', *British Journal of Middle Eastern Studies* 30, 1 (2003), pp. 5–24.

Goldberg, Ellis, 'Peasants in Revolt – Egypt 1919', *International Journal of Middle Eastern Studies* 24, 2 (1992), pp. 261–80.

Goold, J. Douglas, 'Lord Hardinge as Ambassador to France and the Anglo-French Dilemma over Germany and the Near East, 1920–3', *Historical Journal* 21, 4 (1978), pp. 913–37.

Israel, Gershoni, 'The Egyptian Nationalist Movement: a Self-Portrait, 1904–19', *Asian and African Studies* 27, 3 (1993), pp. 313–41.

Kedourie, Elie, 'Sa'ad Zaghlul and the British', *Middle Eastern Affairs*, number 2 (St Antony's Papers number 11), Chatto and Windus, 1961, pp. 139–60.

Lieshout, R. H., 'Keeping Better Educated Moslems Busy. Sir Reginald Wingate and the origins of the Husayn–McMahon Correspondence', *Historical Journal*, 27, 2 (1984), pp. 453–63.

McCale, Donald M., 'Influence without Power: the last Khedive of Egypt and the Great Powers, 1914–1918', *Middle Eastern Studies* 33, 1 (Jan. 1997), pp. 20–39.

Mehra, Parshotam, 'A Forgotten Chapter in the History of the New Frontier, 1914–36', *Journal of Asian Studies* 31, 2 (1972), pp. 299–308.

Moosa, Sulaiman, 'T. E. Lawrence and his Arab Contemporaries', *Arabian Studies* 7 (1985).

Newell, Jonathan Q. C., 'Learning the Hard Way. Allenby in Egypt and Palestine, 1917–19', *Journal of Strategic Studies* 14, 3 (1991), pp. 363–87.

Omar, Saleh, 'Arab Nationalism, a retrospective evaluation', *Arab Studies Quarterly* 14, 4 (1992), pp. 23–37.

Sharp, Alan J., 'The Foreign Office in Eclipse, 1919–22', *History* 61, 202 (1976), pp. 198–218.

Tauber, Eliezer, 'Rashid Rida's Political Attitudes during World War I', *The Muslim World* 85, 1–2 (January–April 1995), pp. 107–121.

Terry, Janice, 'Official British Reaction to Egyptian Nationalism after World War I', *Al Abhath* (Beirut), 21, 2–4 (1968), pp. 15–29.

Tignor, Robert L., 'Maintaining the empire: Sir John Maxwell and Egypt during World War 1', *Princeton University Chronicle*, 53, 2 (1992), pp. 173–99.

Walker, Dennis, 'Modernities, Particularism and the Crystallization of Pan-Arabism in Egypt in the 1920s', *Islamic Culture* 60, 2 (April 1986), p. 64.

Warburg, Gabriel, 'The governor-general of the Sudan and his relations with the British consuls-general in Egypt, 1899–1916', *Asian and African Studies* V (1969), pp. 97–132; 'Wingate and the Sharifian Revolt, 1915–16', *Hamizrah Hehadash*, 19, 4 (1969), pp. 355–63; 'The Sudan, Egypt and Britain, 1899–1916', *Middle Eastern Studies* 6, 2 (1970), pp. 163–78.

Warman, Roberta M., 'The Erosion of Foreign Office Influence in the making of Foreign Policy, 1916–18', *Historical Journal* 15, 1 (1972), pp. 133–159.

Index